THE EVOLUTION OF LOVE
From Quarks to Culture—
the Rise of Evolutionary Relationships
in Response to the Meta-Crisis

The Evolution of Love: From Quarks to Culture
—the Rise of Evolutionary Relationships
in Response to the Meta-Crisis

For more information, please contact:
World Philosophy and Religion Press
Dandy Lion Publishing Group
4401 Friedrich Lane #302
Austin, TX 78744

contact@worldphilosophyandreligion.org

Cover art by Kohlene Hendrickson (kohlene.com)

ISBN 979-8-9928719-2-0

Printed in the United States

In conjunction with

IP Integral Publishers

To my beloved Dr. Kristina Kincaid

To the holy band of Outrageous Lovers
who are my evolutionary family—
all of us madly committed
to the Evolution of Love
and to each other and to the whole

And to my children:
Rachel Singerman Gur
Eytan Gafni
Yair Gafni
Zion Caplan Gafni

THE EVOLUTION OF LOVE

From Quarks to Culture

The Rise of Evolutionary Relationships
in Response to the Meta-Crisis

Dr. Marc Gafni

with Dr. Zachary Stein and
Dr. Elena Maslova-Levin

In conjunction with

IP Integral Publishers

CONTENTS

FOREWORD

by Aubrey Marcus

There comes a certain point in time where ideas no longer serve the collective culture and are in desperate need of evolution and transformation. Our understanding of relationships is in that position right now. Like tectonic plates that are stuck under tension, the inspired concepts contained within this volume, *The Evolution of Love from Quarks to Culture: The Rise of Evolutionary Relationships in Response to the Meta-Crisis*, will assuredly change your world and quite possibly the world itself in ways that are beyond our capacity to imagine. The first step, of course, begins with the transformation of your own most intimate relationships.

I have experienced this firsthand in the relationship with my partnership dynamic. The elucidation of the three types of relating—role mate, soul mate, and whole mate—clarified the areas of my marriage that were no longer serving us and the world at large. It pointed the way forward to a different way of loving, not because it was simply a new cultural construct but because it contained a deeper truth about relationships that was true all the way up and down the Cosmic Order.

I have taught the models contained within this paradigm-shifting book in my community, Fit for Service, and seen similarly powerful effects. By placing attention on each of the three "contexts for relating," each quality of relationship had the opportunity to reach the full wonder and fruition of its unique potential.

Before answering the heavy question "Should I stay with my partner or should I leave?" the first step is to analyze the relationship from these different perspectives. Only from this place can the question be effectively explored.

The strength of any community is built upon the strength of each dyad. The aphorism that a chain is only as strong as its weakest link indeed contains important truth. To solidify and immeasurably deepen the strength of each individual relationship is not only the remedy for loneliness, although it is surely that. And that alone is more than enough. But it is a solution to what Dr. Gafni calls the *"global intimacy disorder."*

The macro is a model of the micro. How you relate to a friend or a partner participates in the same pattern through which national super-powers relate to each other in this increasingly multipolar world. ***It is not hyperbole to imagine that this book might not only help your marriage, it might save the world.***

It has been with great delight and a voracious appetite that I have consumed the teachings of Dr. Marc Gafni and colleagues whose world philosophy they call CosmoErotic Humanism. Gafni holds the distinguished position in my heart as my lineage master in the original wisdom of Solomon and later CosmoErotic Humanism lineage.

But Gafni is also my beloved brother and inspired evolutionary partner in changing our world. A world in desperate need of what Dr. Gafni calls a "new world religion, rooted in a universal grammar of value—telling a Story of Value—as a context for our diversity."

And there is no better Story of Value than the one proposed by the Center for World Philosophy and Religion, founded by Marc Gafni in partnership with Ken Wilber, Sally Kempton, and Zachary Stein, which is where our book publishing imprint gets its moniker.

Our first title, *First Principles and First Values*, written by Gafni together with Stein and Wilber under the pseudonym David J. Temple, is the tip of the spear in articulating the road from "Crisis to Crossing." This work is already beginning to catalyze the emergence of a New Human and New Humanity in response to the meta-crisis of our time, which threatens our very humanity.

This book, *The Evolution of Love: From Quarks to Culture—the Rise of Evolutionary Relationships in Response to the Meta-Crisis*, and its sister volume, *Whole Mate: The Future of Relationships*, place attention on a crucial aspect of that new story. Keep your eye out for new titles releasing regularly from World Philosophy and Religion Press, and check out the Aubrey Marcus Podcast for more conversations surrounding this groundbreaking work.

NOTES ON PROCESS AND AUTHORSHIP

by Marc Gafni

I was greatly delighted to be the first writer of the core distinctions in this book and its companion volume. They are sourced in my own interior process, as well as in my readings of the lineage of Solomon, coupled with decades of study in the world philosophies and religions, as well as in new ways of reading the hidden implied ontologies and phenomenologies in the classical sciences, often with my dear friend Ken Wilber's Integral Theory as the invisible scaffolding, which clarifies the framework in which all insights are offered.

I am honored to have had Dr. Zachary Stein and Dr. Elena Maslova-Levin as key interlocutors in this volume. I am engaged with Zak as both an initiate and lineage holder in the wisdom of Solomon lineage, and as my partner in the articulation of CosmoErotic Humanism, co-president of Center for World Philosophy and Religion,[1] and dearest beloved brother. The volume has been prepared on multiple levels *with* Elena, ranging from scientific content to artistic editing, literary architecture, and more. We are just beginning our whole mate journey, and I very much look forward to deepening our partnership in key future volumes in the Great Library.

The Center for World Philosophy and Religion, the think tank where Barbara Marx Hubbard served as board chair, was the precious and wondrous context for our co-creation. I cofounded the think tank with Ken Wilber, Sally Kempton, and Zak Stein. All four of us have remained active in leadership since the inception of the think tank.

---

1 Formerly the Center for Integral Wisdom (see also chapter 13).

Sally, sadly, passed in the summer of 2023. Among key board chairs and leaders across the years were Lori Galperin, Kate Maloney, John P. Mackey, Barbra Marx Hubbard, Shareef Malnik, Gabrielle Anwar, Adam Bellow, Carrie Kish, and Daniel Schmachtenberger. The board chair who took the reins after Barbara is also the visionary publisher of World Philosophy and Religion Press, the inestimable Aubrey Marcus. The Center and Barbara's own think tank, the Foundation for Conscious Evolution, are now part of a larger holding organization called the Office for the Future, chaired by Stephanie Valcke and cochaired by Wouter Torfs and Mathi Gijbels.

The Center is the context for the emergence of what we are calling *the Great Library of CosmoErotic Humanism in response to the meta-crisis*. The emergence of the Great Library is the great mission and dream of the think tank. The volume you hold in your hands is one part of the fulfillment of that dream.

CosmoErotic Humanism includes Unique Self theory, the Amorous Cosmos, the Tenets of Intimacy, and multiple other vectors, including a vision of Conscious Evolution somewhat different than the earlier version of Conscious Evolution that my beloved whole mate Barbara Marx Hubbard had been advocating. In whole mate teaching, I formulated the core set of distinctions around the whole mate level of consciousness, which resonated quite beautifully with Barbara's distinctions around what we both called *evolutionary relationships*.

This book would have been impossible without all the people who have been involved in its development. Dr. Clint Fuhs formed the raw material into a book with his trademark depth, precision, and brilliance. The baton was passed to the inestimable Kerstin Zohar Tuschik, a senior editor, researcher, and longtime partner in the Great Library project, who took it an equally significant third step on multiple levels. Kerstin is a dear friend, as well as being an initiate in the wisdom of Solomon lineage. Kerstin's works included but were not limited to key scientific work in Part Two.

And finally, all of this then landed with the artist intellectual Dr. Elena Maslova-Levin, who approached the book as an artistic canvas, first masterfully embracing the entire manuscript and then significantly impacting the aesthetics of structure and argument and insight on so many levels.

Dr. Marc Gafni
March 2019 (Portland, OR)—February 2025 (Saint Johnsbury, VT)

INTRODUCTION

Postmodernity argues that Reality is merely a story, that no story is better or worse than any other story, and that stories are but social constructs, fictions, or figments of our imagination.[2] Postmodernity is deconstructing not only the ontology (that is, reality) of Story but also the ontology of Value.[3]

These deconstructions of Story and Value are true but partial. It is true that there is a plentitude of stories we tell about Reality, and that Story is the underlying unit that constitutes Reality. But it is not true that Story is mere fiction. There is an abundance of stories not because there is no real Value or Meaning but rather because there is an abundance of Value and Meaning.

Story is the structure of the Real. Story itself is the source code—not only of culture and consciousness but of all Reality all the way down and all the way up the evolutionary chain.[4] That's why to evolve the

---

2 For example, Yuval N. Harari explicitly embraces this postmodern view of story through his writing on history. See, for example, Harari's Sapiens: A Brief History of Humankind (2015), chapter 2, and Homo Deus: A Brief History of Tomorrow (2017), chapter 7, where he explicitly writes that all stories are but social constructs, fictions, and figments of our imagination and that no story is intrinsically better than any other story. A second important source that, like Harari, is reflective of the leading-edge embrace of postmodern deconstruction into the fabric of society is Irvin Yalom's classic Existential Psychotherapy (1980), where he understands story in precisely this manner.

3 Both Harari and Yalom embrace the deconstruction of value as well.

4 As a First Principle and First Value of Reality, Story runs all the way up and all the way down the evolutionary chain. There are four core elements that define all stories—whether at the level of matter, life, or the depth of the self-reflective human mind: (1) Events are not merely random but inherently connected in their unfolding. (2) The story has telos or direction—what we have called plotlines. (3) The plotlines are driven by inherent value and the desire for more value. (4) There is some degree of freedom in the story. See David J. Temple's First Principles and First Values: Forty-Two Propositions on CosmoErotic Humanism, the Meta-Crisis,

Story is to evolve the source code. Emergent from the recognition of the ontology of Story is the recognition that we live in inescapable narrative frameworks—Stories of Value—which define the nature and quality of our personal and collective human lives.

Stories are not merely randomly contrived conjectures. They are attempts to gather information about the nature of Reality and translate it into a coherent Story of Value.

Not all stories are equal. There is a hierarchy of stories. In other words, there are better and worse stories.

- A better story takes a deeper account of more meaning or information, exterior and interior, and weaves them together in the most elegant, good, true, and beautiful fashion.

- A better story is aligned with more and wider Fields of Value, even as it integrates more contradictions into greater wholes.

- A better story weaves a narrative thread that articulates the most coherent and compelling framework, which embraces, honors, and uplifts the greatest possible number of people.

- A better story must be not only an eternal story, aligned with eternal structures of value, but also an evolving story, aligned with the evolution of value, the evolution of love, the evolution of the Good, the True, and the Beautiful.

A better story is an eternal and evolving story. We cannot trust stories that claim to be only eternal stories, or that claim to be ever-evolving stories with no ground in Eternity—in the Real, independent of the changing mores of time. The more deeply we investigate Cosmos, both in its exterior and interior faces, deploying the interior and exterior sciences, the better, truer, and more beautiful story we can tell.[5]

and the World to Come (2024).

5 You may have noticed some unconventional deployments of capitalization. For

A story with flawed, incomplete, or distorted plotlines can bring us—and indeed has brought us—to the brink of existential risk, the potential end of humanity as we know it. To respond to this meta-crisis, we need to evolve the story, which is to evolve the source code of culture itself.

Decades of research and study have led us to the conclusion that only a New Story of Value can avert unimaginable suffering and change the vector of history toward ever-deepening expressions of the Good, the True, and the Beautiful. As perceptive historians point out, history changes when a compelling New Story emerges, a story that changes the vector of cultural evolution. Indeed, it is only a New Story that has the capacity to change the course of history. Technology matters. But the story we tell about technology matters as well. Exponential technology matters. But the story we tell about exponential technology matters exponentially more.

If we fail to articulate a New Story of Value, the results will be excruciating for billions of human beings and for the entire life system—as well as for the trillions of lives that will remain unborn.

All of the past depends on us to fulfill its dreams.

All of the present depends on us to live.

All of the future depends on us to be born.

The overall purpose of this book and its companion volume, *Whole Mate: The Future of Relationships,* is to provide a first articulation of this New Story of Value in the domain of relationship. In the first volume, we explored in depth the evolution of human relationships from *role mate* to *soul mate* to *whole mate*, the correlated evolution of identity from separate self to Unique Self and Evolutionary Unique Self, and the social implications of this ongoing transformation of humanity—Planetary Awakening in Love through Unique Self Symphony. In this volume, we put this transformation in a broader and deeper context to show that

---

instance, we use capitalization to distinguish between a reductionist cosmos and a living Cosmos, or between the degraded sense of fuck and the Eros quality of Fuck. We are also referring, for example, to all of Reality, God, Goddess, the Intimate Universe, the Amorous Cosmos, et cetera. This mode of capitalizing is intended both as an expression of the author's emphasis and as an invocation of intrinsic Qualities of Eternal and Infinite Value into otherwise ordinary or degraded terms.

this leap in evolution is both urgently needed by Reality itself and is rooted in its core structure. This is but a part of a large cultural project, akin to the global genome project but focusing not on human genetics but on the cultural memes that animate and define Reality. We call this project *the Great Library*. Its purpose is to initiate a new Renaissance, which would integrate the leading edges of human wisdom from the traditional (premodern) period, the modern era, and the postmodern moment into a New Story of Value, which evolves the source code of culture and consciousness. At the core of this New Story of Value are a new Universe Story and a new narrative of identity, which we have called *CosmoErotic Humanism* and *Homo amor*.

In Part One, we locate the emergence of whole mate relationships within the large context of the meta-crisis. We show that the meta-crisis and the personal crisis of relationship share the same root and structure and thus have the same potential resolution—the emergence of whole mate and *Homo amor* (Essay One). Particularly, we focus on the meaning of *whole* in the context of *whole mate* (Essay Two), which has two key dimensions. The first is the *prior wholeness* that the whole mate brings to the relationship. In this sense, the large whole that we are talking about *lives within us* and is prior to relationship. We also locate the experience of whole mate—wholeness desiring more wholeness—in the ontology of the Wholeness of the Infinite, as understood by the interior sciences. Just as the Infinite Intimate[6] is Whole and yet desires more wholeness and hence enters relationship, so, too, the human being, an incarnation of the Infinite Intimate, needs to be whole prior to relationship even as he/she seeks ever-deeper wholeness in relationship. So, in the second sense, the whole in whole mate is about relationship to the large whole that *we live within*. In Essay Three, we locate the emergence of whole mate and *Homo amor* in an even broader context of the narrative thread of Cosmos as the Fourth Big Bang (after the emergence of matter, life, and the human mind).

In Part Two, *Reality Is Relationship*, we offer first contemplations on

---

6 We are deploying the Infinite Intimate as a new name of the Divine in CosmoErotic Humanism, which reflects the highest integration of the leading edges of the exterior and interior sciences.

relationship as the core structure of Reality, which revolve around the physical and biological sciences. We show that the notion of evolution of relationship in response to crisis is not just a flight of fancy: It is rooted in the newly emerging scientific understanding of Reality. This knowing births in us the urgency to transform our own relationships, as well as the profound trust and hope that we are supported by Reality in this great evolutionary undertaking. We realize that the Cosmos is partial to our hope.

Hope is a memory of the future.

Hope is a memory of our future relationships.

Hope is the future of relationships.

Hope is the evolution of love.

—

PART ONE

THE EMERGENCE OF *HOMO AMOR* IN RESPONSE TO THE META-CRISIS

—

ESSAY ONE

A NEW STORY OF VALUE IN RESPONSE TO THE META-CRISIS

1. What Is the Meta-Crisis?

Let us start with a simple image: the Death Star in the cinematic classic of the late twentieth and early twenty-first century, *Star Wars*. The Death Star is a battleship armed so intensely that it poses an existential risk. It has the destructive capacity not just to attack and damage but to destroy a planet.

Existential risk is a risk to our very existence. There are two forms of existential risk: the potential death of humanity (the Death Star has the capacity to destroy a planet) and the death of our humanity (the Death Star has the capacity to exert totalitarian control over a planet). The genealogy of the existential risk on our planet is, of course, very different from the precise plotline of *Star Wars*.[7] But that does not matter.

---

7 The Death Star depicts an Orwellian totalitarianism of the kind that is enacted today in China, for example. There is, however, a more ostensibly covert totalitarianism, of the kind that is now gradually disclosing its nature in open societies, which seeks to enclose the world in a planetary stack, designed and monitored for maximum control. We call it TechnoFeudalism.

The Death Star emerges in culture as a foreshadowing of both forms of existential risk.

1.1. The Death Star as a Symbol for a Culture of Death

From the deeper perspective of cultural myth and prophetic symbol, the Death Star is not one weapon. It is *a culture*. It is a systemic culture of death that leads to intense suffering for the majority of human beings in the present, catastrophic risk in the immediate future, and impending existential risk in the near or intermediate future.

According to the most hardheaded analysis from multiple vectors of leading-edge policy and social analysis,[8] we are now confronted by the Death Star in a myriad of distressing disguises. That is quite evident to anyone who has the willingness and capacity to do genuine sensemaking, which begins by reading the serious background material available beneath the headlines.[9]

In the cinematic version, there is a realization that the only way to take out the Death Star is with a direct hit: a direct hit that gets through all the defenses, all the structural obstacles, and explodes culture into a new possibility. This book explores one dimension of how we can score that direct hit.

In a word, the direct hit is a New Story of Value. It is only a New Story of Value that truly changes the course of history. The Story of Value is an interior technology of culture. It is the space from which everything is generated. A New Story of Value itself is generated by new insights into the nature of Self and Reality. These new insights often come from interior practice and contemplation, which generate the evolution of

---

8 See, for example, The Precipice: Existential Risk and the Future of Humanity, by Toby Ord (2020).

9 See The End of the World Is Just the Beginning: Mapping the Collapse of Globalization, by Peter Zeihan (2022). Zeihan advises energy corporations, financial institutions, business associations, agricultural interests, universities, and the US military. See also Principles for Dealing with the Changing World Order: Why Nations Succeed and Fail, by Ray Dalio (2021).

consciousness. However, they can also be provoked by new exterior technologies, from the plough to the printing press to the internal combustion engine to the personal computer to social media to machine intelligence–driven data sciences.

This book and its sister volume[10] are about one dimension of that New Story of Value, the emergence of a new structure of relationship. It is filled with hope, for hope is a memory of the future, and the future is called into existence by a New Story of Value.

Before we turn to the direct hit, however, we need to understand the Death Star more deeply. When we are talking about the Death Star, the culture of death, we are talking about the meta-crisis, or the second shock of existence.[11] The second shock of existence, of course, implies the *first* shock of existence, with which we will begin.

1.2. The First Shock of Existence

The first shock of existence is the realization of mortality of human beings—our realization that we will die—which dawns in human consciousness at the beginning of history. We are not talking about the biological fact of death but about the existential realization of death.

The existential fear or dread of death begins in the prehistoric period,

---

10 Whole Mate: The Future of Relationships, by Marc Gafni and Barbara Marx Hubbard (2025).

11 A colleague, Mauk Pieper, an excellent thinker in his own right, attended my seminars themed around Your Unique Self in response to collective existential crises in Holland between 2009 and 2013. He published a book, Humanity's Second Shock and Your Unique Self (2014), for which I gladly wrote an afterword. He understood well the basic premise of our work, the Unique Self Theory, an emergent new theory of identity as an accurate response to the first great question of CosmoErotic Humanism: Who Am I? (See Your Unique Self: The Radical Path to Personal Enlightenment, by Marc Gafni [2012], and the special issue on Unique Self of the Journal of Integral Theory and Practice 6:1 [2011]). The Unique Self Theory as part of a larger Story of Value is crucial if we are to respond to the meta-crisis of the twenty-first century and beyond. Pieper coined the term second shock of existence to capture the notion of existential risk, which we happily acknowledge. The term shock of existence seems to have been coined by philosopher Robert F. Creegan in his book The Shock of Existence: A Philosophy of Freedom (1954).

either during the hunter-gatherer era[12] or when we began to have surplus food. In the second reading, it had to do with having time on our hands. We started to think about our lives. We were much less worried than the hunter-gatherers about the mammoth or lion who could kill us this afternoon—the natural fear of biological death that the human shares with the animal world. But when that fear became less immediate, the fear of death did not disappear. Rather, we began to think about death not in terms of warding off an immediate threat but in terms of what we might call the existential fear of death. We thought, *Oh my God, I'm going to die.*

The ego structure, which we developed after we emerged from humanity's early sense of being almost coextensive with nature, became afraid. The ego sought to arrogate to itself its intuition of immortality, which in reality belonged to Spirit or Essence. The ego desired its own immortality and was therefore shocked by the reality of its impending death. I realize that my personality, family, social status, farming community—with my relatively stable home, identity, and existence—are ephemeral. I am going to die. This existential fear of death is the first shock of existence.

Tastes of the Fear of Death

There are many flavors to the existential fear of death, but four interrelated elements are central:

- There is a fear of **nothingness**. There is a fear that death may be oblivion. If death is oblivion, then I will lose not only myself but the precious connections to all that I hold dear and love.

- There is a fear of **the pain of the body**. The body will betray me, and that betrayal will be painful.

---

12 According to some historians, the existential fear of death was already present in hunter-gatherer societies. David Graeber has correctly problematized the linear unfolding of hunter-gatherer to farming communities on several key accounts, showing conclusively that larger organized gatherings with sophisticated religions appeared in the hunter-gatherer era. See The Dawn of Everything: A New History of Humanity, by Graeber and David Wengrow (2021).

- There is the fear of **accountability**. Life itself is filled with injustice. Death is the door to justice in most great traditions. We know in our bodies that Reality should be fair. We know that there is a vast difference between a life lived as Hitler and one lived as Mother Teresa. In death, the promissory note of fairness is potentially paid. It is that promissory note that in many ways makes life bearable. And yet it creates a fear of death, not only for Hitler but for every ordinary human being who has committed offense against their own conception of intrinsic and eternal value. In life, these offenses can at least sometimes remain hidden. In death, all is revealed. That was Woody Allen's point in his epic movie *Crimes and Misdemeanors*. The good character in the movie—a rabbi—dies of cancer. His brother, by contrast, murders his mistress so his wife will not find out and leave him, and he gets away with it. Allen's point is clear: The notion that Reality holds one accountable in the course of a lifetime is not true. Death is often the first moment of accountability.

- But there is a deeper fear of death. It is the fear of accountability in an entirely different fashion. It is the fear of **not counting**. The fear of death is the fear of insignificance, the fear of living a life that does not matter. This is the fear of being a side effect in your own life, or—closely related—the fear of living a life that is not your own. It is the fear that you did not live the life that was yours to live. Your ladder was perched against the wrong wall, so all of your climbing was in vain.

The fear of death of this fourth form is to die when your death is not held in a larger story of existence. If you have no compelling Universe Story, no narrative of identity, no narrative of community, desire, Eros, and ethos that meaningfully weave your life into the larger narrative fabric of Cosmos, then the fear of death will destroy you. But if you are able to access the inner knowing that your story—your love story—is chapter and verse in the Universe: A Love Story, then the natural fear of death is relocated to a larger context, and death, upon deeper investigation, reveals its true nature as a night between two days.

Although the interior sciences disclose that death is a portal between two days, and there is vast empirical,[13] philosophical,[14] and anthro-on-tological evidence for the continuity of consciousness, yet death is also, for our own direct surface experience, a stark end. All the stories, all the plotlines, and all the threads of living end at that moment. What happens beyond is a different conversation. Even though mounds of evidence indicate that there is a continuity of consciousness, yet we have an actual experience of ending. We have an *experience* of death, and this experi-ence—if encountered without reflection and transformation—engenders fear. The encounter with death, and the experience it may evoke, is not a bug but a feature of Reality.

Our first-person surface experience is that death ends this life. It is not the totality of our experience if we go deeper inside, but it is obviously intended to be the central, potent, and painful dimension of every human life. Indeed, as Ernest Becker potently reminded us, we deny death at our peril. Paradoxically, this ending, the experience of our finality or mortality, is what presses us into life. From the implicit demand of the first shock of existence, human beings were activated into creative emergence, and what emerged was all of human culture in its interior and exterior dimensions.

The First Shock of Existence Activated Our Inner Gnosis

The first shock of existence pressed the human being into disclosing meaning. The Eye of Consciousness was pressed into service.[15] The result

---

13 Evidence gathered by the most serious researchers beginning with Henry and Eleanor Sidgwick at Cambridge University and William James at Harvard University and continuing, in highly rigorous forms, for the last 150 years, as recapitulated by David Ray Griffin in multiple volumes. See also, for example, Real Magic: Unlocking Your Natural Psychic Abilities to Create Everyday Miracles, by Dean Radin (2018), The Conscious Universe: The Scientific Truth of Psychic Phenomena, by Dean Radin (2009), and the earlier classic by Frederic William Henry Myers, Human Personality and Its Survival of Bodily Death (1907).

14 This requires a cogent analysis of materialism and dualism, and the introduction of a far more cogent third possibility, which we have called pan-interiority (see Sections I.1–I.3 in part two).

15 On the Eye of Consciousness, see Section I.6 in part two.

was the great religions, the result was great art, the result was great music, the result was law and the cornerstones of civilization.[16]

The fear of death generated a depth of vision and understanding of human nature that invited human beings into a larger story, where they could, at least in potential, participate in immortality. The fear of death focused our attention inside. When we went inside, we accessed the deepest wellsprings of the interior face of Cosmos. The fear of death generated some of the great beauties and critical movements of value— including ethics, Spirit, and religion (the word *religion* comes from Latin *religare*, "to reconnect, to realign with the nature of Reality"). The fear of death entering Reality generated a blossoming of Spirit—a story of value, a story about what it means to be a human being in the Cosmos. In the premodern period, this story of value was almost always called religion.

The old religions transcended the fear of death by realizing the immortal Infinite Nature of the human Essence, or Value, which transcends the limitations of finitude. However, locked in their ethnocentric prisms, they hopelessly entwined their genuine realization of the Infinite with dogmatic baggage, which now blocks our access to this realization. The realization of immortality was linked not to the alignment with a universal structure of value but to dogmatic obedience, and every religion, locked in a win/lose metric with all the others, saw only its dogmatic coin as earning Eternity.

Of course, many of us have left the old religions behind. The intuition of immortality was priceless, but the ticket price demanded by each religion was too high. Every religion claimed, in one form or the other, that Eternity, or immortality, was available only to its adherents and only in exchange for various forms of submission, which ranged from doctrinal to psychological, theological, political, and economic. We are children of Voltaire, who led the liberation from the corruptions of religion's many shadows with the battle cry *Remember the cruelties*. Those cruelties were

---

16 Of course, many of these great revelations were mediated through distorting prisms resulting in the horrific pain inflicted by the ethnocentric bias of virtually all of the great traditions. But underneath their public ethnocentric teachings were also teachings of profound depth and realization revolving around the nature of meaning, justice, goodness, ethos, relationship, and joy.

often bound up with the ethnocentric prisms of all the premodern religions, which mediated between human beings and the Infinite.

But we threw out the baby with the bathwater. We rejected the ways of obedience and submission demanded by the religions along with their essential intuition, which remains powerfully resonant and true: the realization of the first shock of existence, the overwhelming existential fear of death, and the need to respond to it.

To transcend the fear of death beyond the old religions, we need to make our life a triumph. It is only a well-lived life that does not fear death, but a life well lived is no longer reducible to obedience to the dictates of a local god who is alienated from Cosmos and denies human dignity and capacity. Instead, a life well lived is a life aligned with the eternal yet evolving Values of Cosmos. It is not only about *alignment* with these Values but also about the *incarnation*. In incarnating the eternal yet evolving Values that transcend death, we most naturally transcend death ourselves—for we ourselves *are* these death-transcending Values.

Postmodernity, however, has moved to savagely deconstruct all previous narratives of the well-lived life as a life rooted in the personal incarnation of Values aligned with Cosmos. Indeed, postmodernity claimed that the very idea of a well-lived life, a life of intrinsic value, was itself a social construction of reality, not backed by the Universe.

1.3. The Second Shock of Existence

The first shock of existence is the realization of the death of the human being. The second shock of existence is the realization of the potential death of humanity.

Having gone through all the stages of history—of matter, life, and mind, in all of their stages of evolutionary unfolding—we have now come to this moment of dire existential risk. The gap between our exterior technologies—from atomic bombs to social media to weaponized drones to artificial intelligence—and our failure to develop genuine shared interior technologies of value has created extraction models and exponential growth curves, rivalrous conflicts based on win/lose metrics, and complicated, incoherent world systems. All of these together threaten the very existence of humanity.

When the coronavirus crisis hit in 2020, a catastrophic risk scenario exploded on the public stage. We had been warning about that possibility for many years already, but most people pretty much thought that the systems were too big to fail; they would just keep on going, one way or another. Many of us wrote that the combination of the win/lose metrics and the complicated systems optimized for efficiency instead of resiliency was vulnerable to a thousand different forms of so-called black swans. Our core infrastructure had become inherently fragile, and the realization of catastrophic risk scenarios was just a matter of time.[17] All of this began to be visible to a limited extent in the financial meltdown of 2008, but it became unmistakably recognizable with the eruption of the long-awaited and long-predicted coronavirus crisis.

Of course, this catastrophic risk was actually a dress rehearsal for the existential risk—or the second shock of existence, the potential death of humanity.

The coronavirus had evoked both the first and the second shock of existence. The fear of death, which presses into the life of every human being, was now unavoidable—we couldn't split it off—but the crisis also had the fragrance of the second shock of existence.[18] The catastrophic risk, which was now manifest in many forms as global risk, where all of a sudden everybody was interconnected, raised the specter of a looming existential risk—through climate change; destabilization of ecosystems; rogue weapons; exponentialized destructive technologies; runaway machine learning and AI; methane gas under the tundra; peak oil and peak phosphorus; resource depletion based on extraction models, which feed exponential growth curves based on fractional-reserve banking; the Bretton Woods economic structures, fragile, complicated, spread-out systems that are radically vulnerable to myriad forms of attack. This is

---

17 Although the corona threat itself was of course relatively "minor" in terms of the destabilizing power of catastrophic risk, it indicated how potentially fragile the systems are.

18 COVID-19 itself was self-evidently not an existential risk. But it pointed to the fragility of the interlocking world systems and exploded the myth that the world system was too big to fail.

only a partial list of possible causes for existential risk. These causes are real, and yet we have split them off from our awareness. But then, seemingly out of nowhere, the potential catastrophic risk of the coronavirus brought existential risk into our hearts and into our living rooms. The fear of death was suddenly radically present. The skull grinned at the banquet again—in the form of both the first and second shock of existence.

Catastrophic and existential risk emerges from the gap between our exponentially expanding exterior technologies and our stalled or even regressive interior technologies. This gap has created the tragedies of the commons[19] and multipolar traps,[20] in which everyone has to keep producing to the nth degree. We created weaponized exponential threats to our very existence because we were afraid that if we were not going to do it, the other parties would, and they would hide it from us and then dominate us.

There are two major generator functions of the existential risk:

- **Rivalrous conflict governed by zero-sum win/lose metrics.** This is the success story that dominates the cultural landscape of modernity, the interior North Star that guides virtually every person and group of people. Success, within the context of this story, is almost always defined by objective, measurable, exterior indicators in relation to economic growth, levels of consumption, resources, and power. This success story generates extraction

---

19 The tragedy of the commons is an economic theory that was first conceptualized in 1833 by British writer William Forster Lloyd. The term refers to a situation in which individuals who have access to a public resource (i.e., a common) deplete the resource by acting in their own interest.

20 A multipolar trap (in game theory, also known as destructive defection) is a group situation where individual incentives produce a suboptimal outcome for all participants. When individual actors obtain a benefit (an advantage over the other actors in the system) from taking action that is detrimental to the group as a whole (i.e., a defect), the other actors are then faced with the choice to either defect themselves or slide into irrelevance. If all actors assume that the other actors are rational and self-interested, this kind of defection will propagate through the system until everyone is contributing to the harm of the group—and is losing their initial advantage. In fact, the situation of each individual is probably worse than before.

models and exponential growth curves at the core of the economic system, driven by artificially manufactured desires and needs, delivered into culture by ever-more precise forms of microtargeting individuals and groups through the ever-more immersive environment of the worldwide web.

- **Fragile and complicated (rather than *complex*) systems.**
Extraction models and exponential growth curves, animated by win/lose metrics, generate highly vulnerable, fragile world systems that are subject to myriad forms of collapse. In systems theory, fragile systems are often called *complicated* systems. Both terms describe systems in which different parts are acting independently—each within their own success story—and are disassociated from each other. As a result, each part pulls in its own direction, unaware of the effect of their pulling on the rest of the system, resulting in systemwide breakdown and ultimate collapse. Fragile local systems are made exponentially more fragile on a global level by our inability to meet global challenges with only local social, legal, political, economic, and ethical infrastructures.

1.4. The Unique Terror of Death in the Time of the Meta-Crisis

In our moment of meta-crisis, we are caught without a Story of Value. Modernity and postmodernity threw out the great traditions of premodernity, which became identified with their great shadows. That was, at least for a time, understandable, but the result has been a collapse of Story, and particularly the collapse of a Story of Value rooted in First Principles and First Values. We are at a time between worlds, a time between stories. The crucial gifts of the transcultural perennial truths shared by virtually all the great traditions have been lost.

One of those shared truths was the understanding that it is not over when it's over—that what we call *death* is indeed a portal into a deeper Reality of consciousness. The great traditions were able to locate the truth of the continuity of consciousness as a shared human truth. This was a core part of the shared gnosis of humanity, and when modernity and postmodernity discarded this gnosis, nothing was left in its place.

Without a larger Story rooted in genuine gnosis to hold us, the fear of death turned into a terror that needed to be avoided at all costs. This has created two distinct movements in our culture. The first is an obsession with busyness, entertainment, and diversion, to avoid facing this terror. It is easy to hijack our attention, because we do not want to place our attention on the ultimate dread, the fear of death. We allow the tech plex[21] in myriad forms to steal our attention. This is one form of pseudo-eros—the covering up of the emptiness with imitation erotics that dull the terror of mortality. The second is to make death the enemy. The frantic obsession with life extension and even immortality—what has been called the War on Death—is a direct expression of this terror.

Because we have ripped death from its mooring in a larger ocean of sense and meaning, we are left, in this moment of meta-crisis, only with its terror and not with its essential gifts. For it is only in confronting death that we find our own deepest integrity. To paraphrase William James: *It is only death that makes life a genuine option.*[22] Or, as Rilke wrote, "Death is our friend precisely because it brings us into absolute and passionate presence with all that is here, that is natural, that is love."[23] Without death,

---

21 By tech plex we mean the technological infrastructure of society, which includes the entire planetary stack (Benjamin Bratton's term), as well as the daily immersive environment constituted by social media and the internet of things. The tech plex is unique in that it has facilitated a new world in which technology is no longer a tool, but an immersive environment. We live inside of that plex. It moves all the way up and all the way down the planetary stack. The tech plex is constituted by infrastructure, social structure, and superstructure. Clearly, there is infrastructure, in terms of the actual physical structures of the tech plex. There is social structure, in relationship to the laws (and the absence of laws) that govern the tech plex. And third, there is superstructure: The technology actually codifies particular values and ignores, bypasses, or rejects other values. In other words, the tech plex is not value-neutral; the tech plex implies a set of worldviews or superstructures.

22 See the essay "The Will to Believe" by William James, first published in The New World, Volume 5 (1896), 327-347.

23 Rainer Maria Rilke, Anita Barrows, and Joanna Macy (2009). A Year with Rilke: Daily Readings from the Best of Rainer Maria Rilke.

life all too easily devolves into *The Picture of Dorian Gray*, Oscar Wilde's classic where the protagonist does not age. But without the process of aging, decadence sets in. We have lost connection to death's blessings, so we are left only with her ugly terror.

None of this suggests that our moral passion at this moment of meta-crisis dares to be invested in anything other than the transformation of self and culture necessary to avert dystopia and manifest Reality as it truly desires to be: a love story. This is a moment when we must rage against death and do battle with all the Promethean force of human dignity. It is in that sense that the prophetic mystic cries out in Isaiah 25:8, *Let death be swallowed forever*. But when the battle is not set in the dialectical context of a larger Story of death, then we are left only with the fear that devolves into terror when denuded of narrative. The prophet speaks against death, even as he tastes the eternity that lives beneath the flow of time.

All of this is the particular contemporary expression of the first shock of existence—the fear of death rearing its head—mediated through this postmodern moment, a time between stories, where the sacred heroic battle against death, which requires all of our moral, economic, and political passion, remains untampered by a larger narrative of meaning. The result is that the inner knowing, activated in prehistoric times by the first shock of existence, is missing, and this induces a worldwide terror.

1.5. The Second Shock of Existence Activates Our Inner Gnosis

Just as the first shock of existence created a first wave of value realization—a new level of Spirit, a new level of meaning in the world—because it pressed us into our own interior realization, now the second shock of existence needs to press us into ever-deeper gnosis, where we begin to articulate a universal grammar of value as a context for our diversity.

The second shock of existence must press us into new gnosis, and at the core of new gnosis is a new grammar of value—evolving yet eternal value—with which we are aligned and which we incarnate. Such a new grammar of value would engage both the terror of death and the terror of a life devoid of intrinsic meaning backed by the Cosmos.

The new gnosis is the articulation of a new set of First Principles and First Values, eternal yet evolving, embedded in a New Story of Value. The First Principles and First Values are the plotlines of the Universe: A Love Story. The shared grammar of value is the only possible context for a global civilization that wouldn't self-terminate.

This is the deeper sensemaking that seeks to emerge from the second shock of existence.

At this moment, it is not enough to be activists to heal the direct crises—be they medical crises, environmental crises, AI threats, or wars. We need to reenvision our infrastructures and our social structures. But we dare not waste the meta-crisis, or it will be the last crisis we are privileged to navigate. We must allow this moment to spur us and invite the second shock of existence into our hearts—not in a way that paralyzes us, but in a way that inspires new levels of insight and realization—precisely the insights and realizations that will be necessary to prevent the second shock of existence from ever actualizing.

1.6. A Time between Worlds, a Time between Stories

We stand in this moment poised between utopia and dystopia. We are at a time between worlds and a time between stories. We need a New Story of Value, eternal yet evolving, rooted in First Principles and First Values, which would become a universal grammar of value as a context for our diversity.

This is exactly what the Renaissance was—it was a time between worlds and a time between stories. In the Renaissance, we were challenged by the Black Death, a pandemic that swept Europe. The Black Death destroyed between a third to half of the population of Europe and a huge part of Asia. People died horribly, brutally, in the streets. They had no idea how to meet this challenge. In response to the Black Death, da Vinci, Ficino, and their cohorts understood that they had to tell a New Story of Value—and that story was the story of modernity.

Did they get the story right? They got part of it right, and this birthed, to use Jürgen Habermas's phrase, "the dignity of modernity," the new way of information-gathering and universal human rights. But the story of modernity also, at least to some extent,

- disqualified interiors,

- deconstructed the source of value,

- downgraded the dignity and Eros of human nature and identity,

- undermined the moral coherence of human communion,

- and disenchanted the Universe from the rivers of the sacred that nourished its core.

This gradually generated the disasters of modernity and has led us to this point where our very future is at risk.

Modernity lost the basis for the Good, the True, and the Beautiful.

This basis used to be Divine Revelation (*God told us*), but that Divine Revelation was owned by religion, and every religion had overreached and overclaimed. The revelation was often mediated through cultural categories and wasn't fully accurate, so modernity threw out revelation but was unable to establish a new basis for value. Value was just *assumed* to be real; as it says in the founding document of the American revolution, the Declaration of Independence, "we hold these truths to be self-evident"—that is, we don't really have a basis for value, but we just take it as a given. In other words, modernity took out a loan of social capital from the traditional world, but the source of value has never been worked out, and then, gradually, value began to collapse.

The Universe Story began to collapse.

The belief that the Good, the True, and the Beautiful are real began to collapse.

The belief that Love is real began to collapse.

As Bertrand Russell said,

I cannot see how to refute the arguments for the subjectivity of ethical values, but I find myself incapable of believing that all that is wrong with wanton cruelty is that I don't like it.[24]

What do you do if you grew up in a world in which Value is not real—a world without a source of value, without a Universe Story, without a story of human identity, without a story of desire, without a narrative of power?

In the words of W. B. Yeats, "the centre cannot hold."[25]

Or, in the words of T. S. Eliot, we become "the hollow men" and "the stuffed men"; "shape without form . . . gesture without motion."[26]

We have a collapse at the very center of society because we no longer have Eros. We no longer have a Reality in which Value is real—and so there is this lingering sense of emptiness. This complete collapse at the very center is the source of existential risk.

But we are not hopeless. On the contrary, we are filled with great hope. Hope is a memory of the future. This memory of the future is the direct hit that takes down the Death Star—the culture of death.

2. The Meta-Crisis Is a Crisis of Intimacy

2.1. The Root Cause of the Meta-Crisis

To recapitulate: The second shock of existence is the realization of the potential death of humanity. It is the second shock of existence that

---

24 Charles Pigden, ed., Russell on Ethics (1999), 310–11.

25 William Butler Yeats in his poem "The Second Coming": "Turning and turning in the widening gyre / The falcon cannot hear the falconer; / Things fall apart; the centre cannot hold."

26 T. S. Eliot, "The Hollow Men."

is the Death Star moment of our species. What is our direct hit move in response to the Death Star? How do we respond to the imminent existential risk?

The direct hit must be—as it has always been in history—the emergence of a new stage of evolution.

Crisis is an evolutionary driver. Every crisis is, at its core, a crisis of intimacy. The direct hit, therefore, is to evolve intimacy itself. Intimacy is always rooted in a Shared Story of Value. A crisis of intimacy, at its core, is a crisis of value. To evolve intimacy is therefore to evolve a New Story of Value. A new—emergent—Shared Story of Value generates a new—emergent—global intimacy.

The generator functions of the meta-crisis—rivalrous conflict governed by win/lose metrics and the fragile systems they engender—are the direct results of the failure to develop more adequate interior technologies, sufficiently compelling to displace rivalrous conflict governed by win/lose metrics as the motivational architecture for the human lifeworld. This failure has led to the conditions for the essential implosion of our social and ecological systems, which are already on the brink of collapse.

But there is a deeper root cause for existential and catastrophic risk that lurks underneath these generator functions, and we cannot take the Death Star down without discerning and addressing it. **The deeper root cause of the meta-crisis is a global intimacy disorder.**

This ostensibly surprising statement can be understood in a few simple steps:

- All of the catastrophic and existential risk challenges we face are *global* challenges—from climate change to artificial intelligence, to pandemics, to systems collapse, to the exponential arms races of weaponized technologies.

- All of these factors are driven by the tragedies of the commons, multipolar traps, and races to the bottom[27]—all of which are

---

27 The Oxford English Dictionary defines a race to the bottom as a situation characterized by a progressive lowering or deterioration of standards, especially (in business contexts) as a result of the pressure of competition.

expressions of the rivalrous conflict meta-architecture, and all of which generate fragile systems subject to multiple forms of gradual or sudden collapse.

- Every global challenge self-evidently requires a global solution.

- Global solutions can only be implemented with global coordination.

- Global coordination is impossible without global coherence.

- Global coherence is only possible if there is resonance between the parts—global resonance.

- Global resonance is only possible if we have global intimacy.

- Global intimacy—just like intimacy in a couple—is only possible when there is a shared story—not just a shared *history*, but a shared *story*—guiding us into the future. It is only a shared global story that can generate a new emergent quality of intimacy—global intimacy.

A shared story must be a Shared Story of Value. A Shared Story of Value is rooted in shared ordinating values, or what we have called *Evolving First Values and First Principles*. Intimacy requires a shared grammar of value as a matrix for a shared Story of Value.

Without a shared grammar of value, there is no global intimacy, and therefore no global coherence, and no global coordination in response to catastrophic and existential risk, and the latter means—put simply—there will quite literally be no future.

The global intimacy disorder is rooted in the failure to experience ourselves in a Field of shared intrinsic Value, in a shared Story of Value rooted in First Principles and First Values. This failure itself derives from the deconstruction of value that has been one of the defining characteristics of modernity and postmodernity.[28]

2.2. Global Intimacy Disorder as Alienation from Wholeness

A story weaves separate fragments into a larger whole. The fragments, however, are not ontologically separate; they are unique expressions of the larger whole, inherently allured to other parts. The unique parts—animated by the currency of attraction that is the inherent nature of their uniqueness—are always seeking each other, feeling allured to each other, to birth the emergence of ever-greater wholeness. These unique parts that make up a larger story may be subatomic particles, atoms, molecules, macromolecules, cells—all the way up the evolutionary chain to human beings and ideas, through all the levels of matter, life, and the further depths of the self-reflective human mind. The deeper and wider the ground of the whole, the better the story.

It is our alienation from wholeness—at a moment when wholeness is necessary for our survival—that is the root cause of the meta-crisis.

When we speak of *wholeness*, we include at least two primary dimensions:

- The interior wholeness of Self, which is one ground of our identity.

- Our relationship to the larger Whole of Reality in all of its dimensions—exterior and interior—from the biosphere to the larger Field of Consciousness, which is a second ground of our identity.

---

28 The modern and postmodern period are characterized by two paradoxical vectors, the evolution of value and the deconstruction of value. Both modernity and postmodernity are characterized by both movements—think, for example, of universal human rights and the rise of the feminine in modernity, and the reaching out to embrace and honor and protect marginalized communities in postmodernity. The evolution of value in both eras, however, was funded by social capital borrowed from premodernity—the traditional period. That social capital was the core common-sense sacred axiom that Value is Real. That loan was then deconstructed in postmodernity—which deconstructed the very Reality of Value itself as being anything more than a contrived social construct, a fiction, or a figment of our imagination.

These dimensions are inseparable. It is only the interior wholeness of our wider Self that turns to embrace the larger Whole.[29]

Relationship and wholeness are intimately inter-included. New structures of relationship emerge from deeper levels of wholeness and generate ever-greater wholeness. The response to the alienation from wholeness—the deepest root of the meta-crisis—can be nothing other than the rise of a new form of relationship, which we call *whole mate relationship*. One of the key qualities of the whole mate relationship is a more profoundly evolved relationship to the larger Whole. Indeed, whole mate relationship is demarcated by two primary dimensions of wholeness. They are—not surprisingly—precisely the two dimensions we noted above: the interior wholeness of Self and our relationship to the larger Whole of Reality in all of its dimensions.

In other words, the rise of whole mate relationships is an essential dimension of the response to the meta-crisis. This is the inherent logic of Cosmos, once we understand the following discernments, to which we have already alluded above and will return repeatedly throughout this book:

Reality is relationship.

Reality is evolution.

Reality is the evolution of relationship.

All relationships emerge from crisis.

All crisis is a crisis of relationship.

The crisis of relationship is solved by the emergence of a higher level of relationship.

Wholeness is another word for relationship; it means right relationship between parts that synergize as a larger whole. The evolution of relationship is thus the evolution of our relationship to the larger Whole, both as it lives in us and as we live in it. This is the essence of the new evolutionary emergence of whole mate relationship.

---

29 We explore these topics in more depth in Essay Two.

2.3. What Is Intimacy?

All dimensions of our alienation are expressions of one core dynamic—a core alienation from the Whole. *Eros, intimacy, value,* and *wholeness* are words pointing to the same ontology.

Reality is the movement of Eros toward ever-deeper contact and greater wholeness—the progressive deepening of intimacies—ever-deeper and wider shared identities defined by mutuality of recognition, feeling, value, and purpose, which themselves generate the ever-deeper and more evolved values.

Intimacy depends on the capacity of parts to generate a shared identity while retaining their otherness, or distinct identity, at the very same time. This requires multiple mutualities, including recognition, feeling (or pathos), value, and purpose. The parts must recognize and feel each other, even as they share value and purpose, but all of this must lead to intimate union and not pathological fusion, where the distinct identity of the parts disappears. (Think subatomic particles that successfully become an atom or two persons who successfully become a couple.)

This understanding of intimacy is formalized in the following intimacy equation:[30]

Intimacy = Shared Identity × [Relative] Otherness ×
Mutuality (Recognition + Feeling + Value + Purpose)

---

30 Our equations of interiors are not to be understood in quantitative terms. They are not technically equations in the mathematical sense. They are not intended to be used to quantify an amount of a particular value. This is not possible, because value is ultimately not quantifiable. It is a basic question, whether the qualities of the interiors (value/consciousness) are measurable, the way material realities are measurable. We don't think they are. For example, asking someone to put a number on how much they love you compared to how much they love their dog is absurd. While there are identifiable differences of intensity, there is no common metric that allows us to put a verifiable number on amounts of love (nor should there be!). We are, of course, aware that, normally, a mathematical equation works with numerical values—even if it would be just 0 and 1, with 0 meaning that quality is not present and 1 meaning it is present. Even though that is something we are able to say even for subjective qualities, at least for ourselves—and for ourselves, we may also be able to say that maybe a quality is only about halfway present—we are not using these equations in that way.

With this in mind, let's return to the two major generator functions for existential risk, whose root cause we have identified above as a global intimacy disorder:

- Our modern success story is rivalrous conflict governed by win/ lose metrics, which violates all the terms of the intimacy equation. There is no shared identity and no mutuality of recognition, feeling, value, or purpose. Instead of *relative* otherness, there is *alienated* otherness.

- Such a story generates complicated, fragile systems with no allurement or intimacy between the parts, systems that optimize for efficiency (as an expression of win/lose metric) and not for resiliency and life.

The global intimacy disorder is rooted, as we have shown above, in the deconstruction of intrinsic value itself. Human value does not participate in any sense in the intrinsic Value of the Real, for the Real is dogmatically declared to have no intrinsic value. Thus, there is no shared identity—no intimacy—between the interior of the human being and Reality. There is no common participation in a Field of shared intrinsic Value. Instead of intimacy with Value, we are alienated from Value—and only intrinsic value can arouse political, moral, and social will.

The root cause of the generator functions of existential risk might also be called a breakdown of Eros, for it is Value itself and the value of desiring ever-deeper value that are the nature of Eros itself.[31] When value is deconstructed, the center doesn't hold.

Coupled with the intimacy equation is the scientifically grounded realization that reality is the progressive deepening of intimacies[32]—or, said slightly differently:

---

31 See the next section for our definition of Eros.

32 This realization is grounded in both the exterior and interior sciences. We unpack it in depth in First Principles and First Values.

- Reality is evolution.

- Evolution is the evolution of intimacy.

The evolution of intimacy requires—personally and collectively—a deeper, more accurate discernment of the nature of our Universe, ourselves, and our beloveds. In other words, the evolution of intimacy requires the best possible, the most accurate, and therefore the most compelling emergent responses to the three great inquiries of CosmoErotic Humanism, to which we will turn in Section 3 below.

This new discernment generates a New Global Story of Value. The New Global Story of Value generates an emergent global intimacy—healing the global intimacy disorder. The New Global Story of Value is the direct hit that takes down the Death Star and replaces it with the hope that invokes the memory of our best future.

Global intimacy facilitates global coherence, which facilitates global coordination, which activates the possibility of our creative and effectively coordinated global responses to the global meta-crisis, in its entirety and its specific expressions.

2.4. From a Crisis of Eros to a Culture of Eros

Eros is life. Eros is a First Principle and First Value of Reality itself. Eros is Value. Value is Eros. It is for that reason that we coined a new term, *ErosValue*—for there is no ultimate split between them.

The failure of Eros destroys life. Our lack of Eros is poised to destroy the world. That is what we referred to earlier as existential risk, or the second shock of existence.

We define Eros through the following interior science equation:

Eros = Radical Aliveness × Desiring (Growing + Seeking) × Deeper Contact × Greater Wholeness × Self-Actualization/ Self-Transcendence (Creation [Destruction])

But for now, let's describe Eros simply, outside of the formal equation:

Eros is the experience of radical aliveness moving toward—seeking—desiring—ever-deeper contact and ever-greater wholeness.

Eros is a core Value of Reality. It is the movement toward ever-deeper contact and ever-greater wholeness. Another way to express this core movement of Cosmos is the progression toward ever-deeper intimacy—ever wider and deeper shared identities, characterized by mutuality of recognition, pathos (feeling), value, and purpose. In other words, the Eros equation and the intimacy equation are two articulations of the same mathematics of interiors. Eros and intimacy—and the movement toward their progressive deepening—are two of the First Principles and First Values of Reality, the core plotlines in the Story of the ever-evolving Value that is Reality itself.[33]

Eros is the core fabric of Reality's *being* and the motivational architecture of Reality's *becoming*. Eros is what animates the evolutionary impulse itself, from the very inception of Cosmos all the way to our very selves, as we awaken to the realization that the evolutionary impulse throbs uniquely in every single one of us. The realization of human awakening and transformation that lies at the core of the interior sciences is the invitation—or even the demand, the plea, the tender and fierce command—of a madly loving Cosmos animated by Infinities of Power and Infinities of Intimacy. The demand is *to awaken*—to awaken to our true nature as unique incarnations of Eros and ethos that are needed and desperately desired by All-That-Is. Or, said slightly differently:

Reality is Eros.

Which could also be formulated as:

God is Eros.

The failure of Eros destroys life. The collapse of Eros is the hidden

---

33 For a deeper exploration of this theme, see chapter III in part two.

root cause for the collapse of ethics, both personally and collectively.

We live in a moment of a worldwide and personal collapse of Eros. Our lack of Eros is poised to destroy the world. It is only a culture of Eros—rooted in the New Story of Value—that has the capacity to respond to this meta-crisis.

3. Planetary Awakening in Love through Unique Self Symphonies

3.1. The First and Second Shock of Existence Merge in the Meta-Crisis: Birthing *Homo amor*

The postmodern deconstruction of value, story, and self induces the unique terror of death at this moment in time. We have rejected the old stories of value given to us by the old religions; their ethnocentric cruelty blocked our access to their deeper realizations, and the first shock of existence, the terror at the realization of our individual death as human beings, has returned to the center of our existence.

As a result, the second shock of existence comes together with the first shock of existence. We cannot face what Robert J. Lifton called the apocalypse of our being, so we turn our attention to every manner of pseudo-eros—for culture has denied us access to Eros. It has deconstructed Eros and claimed that *She* is, in the language of Yuval Harari, one popular purveyor of the postmodern consensus, a fiction, a figment of our imagination, and a mere social construct.

It is from the depth of this very crisis—this terror of both the first shock and second shock of existence—that we have begun to articulate a New Story of Value. The New Story of Value, CosmoErotic Humanism, is a post-postmodern story that integrates the leading-edge validated insights of the premodern, modern, and postmodern wisdom streams. At the very core of this deeper vision is the emergence of the New Human and the New Humanity, the evolutionary progression from *Homo sapiens* to *Homo amor*, in alignment with the inherent plotlines or vectors of evolution. This is not a fanciful conjecture. The realization of *Homo amor* as a necessary new level of human evolution is the result of decades of work. It integrates the leading-edge, validated insights of the exterior and interior sciences from the premodern, modern, and postmodern periods woven together in a New Universe Story, and a new understanding of identity as Unique Self.

Homo amor is the New Story of Value in person, the incarnation of the New Story, rooted in the New Universe Story and the new narrative of identity for both Me and We, I and Us, that is articulated in CosmoErotic Humanism. Downloading *Homo amor* into the source code of culture is the direct hit that takes down the Death Star, the culture of death. As we will see, *Homo amor* responds both to the second shock of existence—the realization of the potential death of humanity—and to the first shock of existence—the realization of the inevitable death experience of every human being.

The encounter with death presses us into new gnosis, and what emerges is a momentous evolutionary leap in what it means to be human. Central to *Homo amor* is an emergent value theory, the reclamation of value in a post-postmodern context, coupled with Unique Self Theory and its vision of the four selves.

3.2. The Three Great Inquiries of CosmoErotic Humanism

How does a world spiraling toward ten billion people, all engaged in various forms of rivalrous conflict governed by win/lose metrics, avoid collapse and self-termination? A key can be found through a careful study of complexity theory, in part rooted in Alan Turing's epic essay "The Chemical Basis of Morphogenesis."[34] One of its core inquiries is:

---

34 Alan Turing, "The Chemical Basis of Morphogenesis." Philosophical Transactions of the Royal Society of London. Series B, Biological Sciences 237, no. 641 (1952): 37–72.

What generates coherent complex systems that do not break down? An important dimension of the response given by complexity theory is that simple first rules, iterated exponentially, generate vast, coherent, complex systems.

When I was first reading the complexity theory literature many years ago, I realized that this is true not only about exteriors but also about interiors. Just as simple first rules generate coherent complex exteriors, so, too, do simple First Principles and First Values embedded in a simple Story of Value generate the hypercomplex world of consciousness and interiors.

In the world of interiors, therefore, we have looked for the most basic elements of our Story of Value as expressed in responses to the three most simple questions:

- Who?

- Where?

- What?

These are three great inquiries that form the motivational architecture of CosmoErotic Humanism. An inquiry is not merely a question. It is a question upon which virtually all future choices depend—a question about the essential nature of Reality itself.

It is worth pointing out here that the *why* question is off the table. It almost always gets mired down in dogma, abstract philosophy, and *theo-logic*, none of which is grounded in any direct sense of knowing. If we engage the *where*, *who*, and *what* questions, the *why* resolves itself in a self-evident way.

The essential *who* question is: *Who am I?*

This is the great question of identity: Who am I? What is my true nature?

The question might also be expressed as: *Who are you?*

The *Who are you?* question may be directed toward a fellow human being but also toward other living beings, or even Infinity itself. When directed toward Infinity, the question of *Who are you?* is really: Is there a *who* in Infinity facing me with whom I might commune?

In the plural, a subset of the fundamental *Who am I?* question emerges, which is dependent on, but not at all redundant with, the first question. This is the question of *Who are we?*—the *Who am I?* question of the collective.

These are the great questions of identity. An identity crisis, or a breakdown in identity, which leads to collective or personal insanity, stems from our incapacity to adequately answer these questions.

The second question is the *where* question: *Where am I?*

This is a question of the Universe Story: Where do I live? What is the nature of this Reality in which I breathe and upon which and within which I operate?

In a sense, this question precedes the first one: The nature of the Universe determines the nature of the individual. Our response to the *where* question directly informs our answer to the *who* question. But from the perspective of the interior sciences, the vector of in-formation is somewhat different, for the interior sciences point out that the mysteries live within us. Thus, from the perspective of the interior sciences, it is not only the *where* that directs us to the *who*, but it is also the *who* that directs us to the *where*.

The third question is: *What is there for me to do?*

That question is but another way of stating a deeper question: *What do I want?*

Or, said slightly differently: *What do I desire?*

This is an action question. Of course, it may be expressed in multiple forms. For example, we might express it as: What do I need? Or, more broadly: What do I truly desire? What is my deepest heart's desire?

Or, more broadly still: What does evolution, or Reality, or God, need from me—desire from me—in the very next moment? For at the deepest level of realization, we gain direct access to the truth that our deepest heart's desire is the desire of evolution itself. Evolution is desire, and evolutionary desire lives intimately, personally, uniquely in us as the deepest heart's desire (but we are ahead of ourselves).

We might move from the *I* to the *We* and ask:

- What is there for us to do?

- What do we truly desire?

- What is our deepest heart's desire?

These questions imply a distinction between our surface desire and our depth desire, necessitating a process of deepening, an invitation, and even a demand to engage in the clarification of desire.

Another way to ask the same question might also be, in the *where* form: Where are we going? Or: Where is it all going?

There are no answers to these questions, at least no answers that would make the question disappear and the mystery abate. We humans are always dancing between certainty and uncertainty. Gnosis and revelation—certainty and uncertainty—clarity and mystery—are themselves First Principles and First Values of Cosmos.

But there are potent and poignant *responses* to these questions. Responses are orienting certainties that locate us in the Cosmos and guide our dance amid the uncertainties. They are not answers but the intrinsic Values of Cosmos that is awake, alive—and therefore accessible—in us.

3.3. The Realization of Unique Self

Who are you? We are not talking about your separate self or ego self, but you as an irreducibly unique expression of the larger Field of Value.

You are an irreducibly unique expression of the LoveIntelligence, LoveBeauty, and LoveDesire, of the initiating and animating Eros and energy of All-That-Is that lives uniquely in you, as you, and through you that never was, is, or will be ever again in anyone other than you. The central realization crystallizing in this evolutionary moment is that each of us is *a Unique Self*, with a unique perspective and quality of Self, and a unique capacity for action.[35]

---

35 The concepts of Unique Self, Evolutionary Unique Self, and Unique Self Symphony are discussed in depth in Whole Mate.

This is not simply our talents as separate monadic units. According to the best of the interior and exterior sciences, we are each not fundamentally apart but rather part of the larger Whole of existence—but we are *distinct* parts. Each of us is a unique emergent of the entire system. We are unique configurations of the larger Field of Eros, Value, Life, and Consciousness. Therefore, we each have a unique incarnation of value to live and to give that is needed by the Whole. That is our core identity.

In the deepest sense, the fear of dying is the fear of not having lived your Unique Self—the life that was yours to live. It is the fear of dying and not having made the contribution that your very cells know is yours to make. The way to transcend the fear of death is therefore clear: to live your story—your Unique Self—to the fullest, giving your unique gift, writing your poem, singing your song, and being the unique configuration of intimacy and desire that Reality intended in its incarnation as you.

Your unique value is not a psychological construct, not the details of your social status, bodily form, or personality. Rather, it is your unique *essence*—a unique incarnation of Value that participates in the Field of eternal yet evolving Value. Your unique value is irreducible and irreplaceable. It is the source of your eternal dignity, which, by its very nature, transcends death.

Unique Self is your personal realization of your fully connected uniqueness.

Your entire biological matrix is unique, from your molecular and cellular structure to your immune system, but these unique aspects do not stop at the biology of your Unique Self. To awaken to your Unique Self is to know that you occupy a particular place in the space-time continuum. You are an irreducibly unique emergent value of the whole thing. But you don't exist without the atmosphere, the plants that produce it, the hydrological cycles that water the plants, or the gravity driving the thermonuclear fusions that fuel our planet. You do not exist independently of everything or everyone else.

In many ways, you are also the same as everyone and everything. You are inter-included and inter-connected—*inter-being*—with everything and everyone, even as you are irreducibly unique—a unique value in Cosmos, a new ontic identity. You are singularly unique and therefore irreplaceable and irreducibly valuable. Your unique expression and experience of consciousness and agency are emergent properties of All-That-Is, uniquely configured in relationship as you. Although you are a novel property of Eros, you are not reducible to your constituent parts or the laws that govern them at lower levels. You are a new ontological emergent that both generates newness, including new value, and is governed by new sets of laws.

Once you realize that you are an irreducibly unique expression of the LoveIntelligence of Cosmos, you realize that there is a corner of the world that lacks Love and can only be transformed by you. Evolution took 13.7 billion years of synchronicity to produce the unique expression of you. You are the personal face of the evolutionary impulse. You are not irrelevant.

Emergence theory[36] reminds us that evolution moves from unconscious to conscious when you awaken as evolution in person. In our interconnected world of quantum entanglement, we begin to understand that your next evolutionary act sends ripples throughout Reality that literally affect everything.

These are among the revelations newly pressed into our knowing by the contemplation of death, both in the original, first shock of existence and in the new, second shock of existence with which we are now confronted.

3.4. Your Unique Gift Is Your Outrageous Act of Love

As a Unique Self, you have an irreducibly unique perspective and qualities of Eros, intimacy, desire, and power, which come together to activate your unique capacity to live your unique life and give your unique gift. Your unique gift is your unique quality of being in the world—interacting, interfacing, interactivating with Reality—your *inter-being* with Reality.

It is also your unique quality of *becoming*—your unique gift is the unique gift that you have to give to Reality. Through your unique gift, you are uniquely empowered to address a unique need in your unique circle of intimacy and influence, which can be addressed by you alone,

---

36 See Phillip Clayton and Paul Davies, eds., The Re-Emergence of Emergence: The Emergentist Hypothesis from Science to Religion (2006).

in the special way that you are able to address it. When you address that unique need in your unique circle of intimacy and influence, you are responding to Reality. That is your unique response-ability.

To address that need is your calling and obligation. This obligation is not imposed from without but is the expression of your unique configuration of LoveIntelligence, LoveDesire, LoveValue, and LoveBeauty. Indeed, in the original Semitic languages, love and obligation share the same root word. In other words, your unique gift, an expression of your Unique Self, is the unique expression of your LoveIntelligence, LoveDesire, and LoveBeauty, which can be manifested and gifted into Reality only by you.

You recognize the unique need that is yours to address because it arouses your deepest heart's desire. Giving your unique gift to address that need is the unique joy and responsibility of your life. Even more: It is your own deepest need, your deepest heart's desire. In giving your unique gift, you awaken as the leading edge of evolution and incarnate a unique quality of Evolutionary Love. You become the personal face of Conscious Evolution.

Your Unique Self is your unique configuration of being and becoming. Your unique configuration of being includes the full spectrum of your qualities of presence and interiority. Your unique configuration of becoming includes your unique transformation, which is evolution itself continuing its own process of transformation in you, as you, and through you. In the depth of your Unique Self Realization, it becomes clear that your unique need is your transformation—which is the transformation of the whole—that can be uniquely accomplished only by you.

Every person is a unique configuration of the Eros of the Cosmos. One word for the Eros of Cosmos—deployed by CosmoErotic Humanism in evolving the great lineage traditions—is Outrageous Love. The Eros of Cosmos—Outrageous Love—configures uniquely in you, as you, and through you and capacitates your unique gift into Reality, which is desperately needed by All-That-Is. Your unique gift is your Outrageous Act of Love.

You are welcome in Reality. You cannot feel welcome if you do not realize that you are always, ever, already in relationship. To be in relationship is to be needed. The deeper and wider the relationship, the deeper and wider is Reality's need for you, the more you are welcome—at home in Reality.

You are needed by All-That-Is. You have irreducibly unique gifts, which are the very engine of evolution. Need drives evolution. You are the unique expression of evolution's need. The great refrain of the Story of Value was expressed by the great Spanish interior scientist of the Renaissance, Meir Ibn Gabbai, paraphrased by us as *Reality needs your service.*[37]

Imagine you have been invited for dinner. Great pains were made to find the food that you love, the decor that pleases you, and the guests that interest you. You arrive at the time designated on this generous invitation in your honor. You receive with grace all the effort poured into welcoming you, making you feel at home. But in the back of your mind, you wait for it to be over, when you can really get home, let down your hair, and spread your heart, mind, and body out into the spacious fullness of yourself. You are welcome here, you appreciate the effort made on your behalf, but you do not quite feel at home.

Now, imagine that you are sitting next to the host of the dinner—and lo and behold, he or she must take an emergency call. The phone is brought to the table, and by their expression, you realize that some very serious situation has developed. They get off the phone and turn to you with these words:

> Thank God you are here. This is what just happened. I know
> your work and your unique gifts. You are the only one in the
> world that has the capacity to address this most serious and
> world-shattering challenge with which we have just been

---

37 Arthur Green, in his essay "God's Need for Man: A Unitive Approach to the Writings of Abraham Joshua Heschel" (2015), writes: "In his summary of kabbalistic teaching 'Avodat ha-Kodesh,' Rabbi Meir Ibn Gabbai, who lived in the Ottoman Empire in the early sixteenth century, offers a great synthesis of Jewish mystical wisdom in the generation immediately preceding that of Moshe Cordovero and Yizhak Luria, who were to make such great additions and changes to that tradition. The key theme of the work, repeated frequently throughout, is ha-'avodah tsorekh gavoha (lit.: 'service is a need on high'), that worship, including the life of the mitzvot, fulfills a divine need."

confronted.

The host tells you of the challenge, and you realize that she is right, you are uniquely gifted to address this huge challenge, which—without you—might have wrought great destruction. In that second, for the first time, you feel fully needed and therefore fully welcomed, fully at home, fully intimate with your hosts and all of the assembled.

But you are not merely needed by the dinner host. You are needed by Reality itself.

The realization of Unique Self is the realization that you are uniquely needed by All-That-Is. That is the ontological disclosure that springs from the very fact of your uniqueness. It is only the experience of being in such a relationship—of being uniquely needed—that allows you to feel fully intimate, welcome, and at home in Reality.

3.5. Unique Self Symphony

Unique Self Symphony is the answer to the question of *Who are we?* We are playing our unique instruments in the Unique Self Symphony. When you are acting for the sake of the larger Whole—which is your deepest heart's desire, the evolutionary impulse lived as you—you are living your Unique Self and giving your unique gift.

- When we give our unique gifts in a way that is omni-considerate, omni-responsible, and omni-loving—for the sake of the Whole . . .

- When we intend our unique gifts as an expression a larger evolutionary purpose and Evolutionary Love . . .

- When we are allured to other Unique Selves, each giving their unique gifts for the sake of the Whole . . .

. . . then a new emergent discloses itself—a new structure of Evolutionary Intimacy—a Unique Self Symphony. That's what it means to play your unique instrument in the Unique Self Symphony.

Homo amor—the New Human and the New Humanity, incarnate as the Unique Self Symphony—is not a top-down, command-and-control structure. It is the human beings self-organizing—self-actualizing—to their highest, deepest, most wondrous and beautiful self, which is their Evolutionary Unique Self—their Unique Self in an evolutionary context.

Unique Self Symphony is the new emergent of Evolutionary Intimacy, which is the natural product of the self-organizing Universe and the self-actualizing Cosmos. Unique Self Symphonies, as a very specific kind of superorganism, endowed with collective intelligence, will only emerge when all of us have a shared sense of the inviolability and value of each individual's Unique Self, of each person as a unique expression of the larger Field of Consciousness and Desire—an individuation beyond ego, the personal beyond the impersonal.

It is only such a narrative of realized identity that constitutes the evolution and health of any group. When a group comes together in such a way that no one's Unique Self is diminished but all are leveraged, there emerges a Unique Self Symphony. This requires all the members to hold the group in mind, to be omni-considerate of the whole, to envision their part in the self-organizing and self-orchestrating social reality, in which they consent to participate.[38]

To participate in a self-conscious Unique Self Symphony is the feeling of being ethically integrated into a larger totality without being absorbed by it. The felt integrity of one's Unique Self is the core of an evolutionary

---

38 In my own anecdotal experience, I have found that, if there is a strong enough center of gravity in a community that has realized Unique Self identity, it creates a vortex that draws in and positively shapes even those who have not experienced such realization. This requires further research, both quantitative and qualitative. On the qualitative side, depth of uniqueness and the capacity to generate Unique Self Symphonies are an essential next step in evolving democratic forms of self-governance. This line of thinking is very much in tune with the design principles for CPR (common-pool resource)—organizational governance structures outlined by Elinor Ostrom (summarized by David Sloan Wilson in his essay "The Tragedy of the Commons: How Elinor Ostrom Solved One of Life's Greatest Dilemmas" (2016). Yet not all forms of deliberative democracy are created equal. See We the People: Consenting to a Deeper Democracy, by John Buck and Sharon Villines (2007), and Between Facts and Norms: Contributions to a Discourse Theory of Law and Democracy, by Jürgen Habermas (1996).

phenomenology of moral consciousness. To fit into the evolutionary puzzle, or story, the shape must be unique.

When a once open society closes through force—violence or the move to a totalitarian system—it will ultimately be undone, unseated—not because it is physically unsustainable but because it is unbearable for human identity formation and moral development.[39] Every human being must feel that their uniqueness is recognized, felt, and needed by the larger group. Without accounting for the dignity of irreducible uniqueness, all superorganic communities will ultimately break down.

Without an elaborate language of moral consciousness, a language of strong evaluation (as Charles Taylor would put it[40]), all talk about the superorganisms of tomorrow will fall short of catalyzing them. The emerging insights from mainstream evolutionary sciences need to be enlivened with the insights of the alternative narrative, where interiors—consciousness and value—implicated in the next steps of human evolution have been the focal point of concerted scholarly efforts for over a century.

3.6. The Evolution of Intimacy: Evolutionary Intimacy

At every stage of evolution, there is a crisis. It is always a crisis of intimacy, and the response is always a new configuration of intimacy—a new configuration of relationship—that invokes ever-more wholeness. The Universe self-organizes to greater and greater levels of intimacy because evolution itself is the progressive deepening of intimacies.

The new configuration of intimacy that responds to the meta-crisis—a

---

39 Human systems are different from other biological systems in the sense that they can have identity crises (of self-understanding and conscience) as well as systemic crises (of resources and reproductive capacities). The book Legitimation Crisis, by Jürgen Habermas (1988), makes this point, suggesting the limits of views of social evolution that focus on systems, objectives, resources, and economies while neglecting the fact that meaning-making systems are equally important in sustaining the continuity of society and life.

40 See Sources of the Self: The Making of the Modern Identity, by Charles Taylor (1989).

new level of Evolutionary Intimacy in this generation—is Unique Self Symphony. The strange attractor toward this actualization is Unique Self. We are uniquely individuated expressions of the evolutionary Field of Eros—of the LoveIntelligence, LoveDesire, and LoveBeauty that is the fabric of Cosmos. Uniqueness is a core First Principle and First Value of Cosmos calling every human being to their Unique Self—and to play their unique instrument in the Unique Self Symphony. In other words, uniqueness is, at the human level, like the pheromones that self-organize an ant colony, or the inherent intelligence of bees that calls each bee to their vocation. We know scientifically that beehives are wildly organized, allured, and uniquely emergent in myriad wonderful expressions of intelligence. But ants and bees are not human beings.

So how does that work on the human level? What calls human beings to their vocation? Human beings, at this stage of history, are, for the first time, expressions of Conscious Evolution. So, what drives us? What guides us? What is our North Star? What is our compass of joy?

Our uniqueness itself. Our Unique Self calls us to our true nature and true vocation of consciousness and desire as an expression of the larger Field of Desire and Consciousness. Your Unique Self is the unique set of allurements that call you forward to express your unique gift.

Your Unique Self is your unique configuration of desire—but not surface desire or pseudo-desire, not the lowest common denominator of desire manipulated for the sake of profit and control. We are talking about your deepest heart's desire, your clarified desire, which capacitates your unique gift and invites you to play—even demands that you play—your instrument in the Unique Self Symphony. Sometimes we play together. Sometimes ten of us, or twenty of us, or thirty, or a whole division, or a whole people, are playing different notes on the same Unique Self instrument. That Unique Self instrument gives a unique gift to society.

So, I, human being, who am I?

I am a Unique Self. I have an instrument to play in the Unique Self Symphony, and I am needed by All-That-Is. That is the realization of Unique Self. This implies personhood, which means there is a personal relationship. Reality intended me—that's what uniqueness tells me. Uniqueness tells me:

- I am unique; I am not generic.

- I am irreducibly unique.

- Reality intended me. Reality chose me. Reality recognizes me. Reality loves and adores me. Reality desires me. Reality needs me. Reality needs my own growth and my own transformation.

Reality is evolution. Evolution is a series of transformations animated by the inherent LoveIntelligence and LoveDesire and LoveBeauty of Cosmos. Transformation is Reality's inherent purpose and goal.

At the human level, transformation is the transformation of identity. It is my transformation from separate self to *True Self* (I am part of the Field), to *Unique Self* (a unique expression of the Field), to *Evolutionary Unique Self* that feels the evolutionary impulse pulsing in him, pulsing in her. These distinctions can be visualized as a puzzle and its distinct pieces: The separate self is a puzzle piece without a puzzle, True Self is the puzzle without the pieces, Unique Self is the puzzle piece that completes—and is needed and held by—the puzzle, and Evolutionary Unique Self not only completes but evolves the whole puzzle.

In Evolutionary Unique Self, that evolutionary impulse has a personal face, and that personal face is my Unique Self playing the music of my Unique Self instrument. That is how I join the Unique Self Symphony made up of Evolutionary Unique Selves acting as unique expressions of the LoveIntelligence, LoveBeauty, and LoveDesire—joining together across space and time—to participate in the evolution of consciousness.

The Unique Self Symphony is the only authentic and potent response we have to existential risk: a new narrative of identity. Unique Self and Unique Self Symphony are not just transformations of personal identity but transformations of the narrative of identity itself.

Who am I? I am a Unique Self, I participate personally in the LoveIntelligence of Cosmos, and we join in Unique Self Symphonies all over the world—as expressions of a bottom-up, grassroots, self-organizing Universe—self-organizing to ever-higher, deeper, and wider expressions of the Good, the True, and the Beautiful.

That is quite a different vision than the attention-hijacking, low-est-common-denominator vision of the rapidly proliferating global technocracy. Indeed, it is this vision that must animate the tech environments in all their noble and also distressing disguises.

The response to existential risk is a Planetary Awakening in Love through Unique Self Symphonies.

3.7. The Crossing: From *Homo sapiens* to *Homo amor*

To recapitulate briefly:

1. The meta-crisis is rooted in our alienation from wholeness, and this alienation can only be healed by a new shared Story of Value.

2. At the core of this New Story of Value is a new Universe Story and a new narrative of identity, CosmoErotic Humanism and *Homo amor*.

3. At the core of the New Universe Story and our narrative of identity—the story of *I* and the story of *We*—is a new story of relationship.

We look at the future of relationship as a key plotline in the New Story. Relationship and wholeness are intimately inter-included: New structures of relationship emerge from deeper levels of wholeness and generate ever-greater wholeness. In other words, the essence of the meta-crisis is a breakdown of Eros, which is expressed as our fundamental alienation from the whole, the larger whole of which we are a part and the deeper whole in which we rest that is our core. The healing of the meta-crisis is in the emergence of a new level of relationship to the whole. This is what we describe in these two volumes as the rise of whole mate relationship. Whole mate relationship is a key characteristic of *Homo amor*.

We call stepping into the lived identity of *Homo amor*, the New

Human, and New Humanity *the Crossing.*

In the great lineages, there is a turn of phrase: *our side* and *God's side.* In the Crossing, we cross to the other side. We no longer see ourselves only as separate-self humans, lost in the grasping of the lonely and traumatized ego. We cross over. We begin to see Reality with God's eyes. We not only *love* but we are *lived as Love,* and to be a lover is to see with God's eyes. We are not merely separate parts seeking our own good. We become omni-considerate for the sake of the Whole.

In other words, the response to the questions of *Who am I?* and *Who are we?* must include the Whole. Indeed, once we are individually omni-considerate for the sake of the Whole, then our relationships are naturally omni-considerate for the sake of the Whole. This is what happens in whole mate relationships, which we described in depth in volume one, *Whole Mate: The Future of Relationships.* This is precisely the movement—the crossing—from *Homo sapiens* to *Homo amor.* In the language of one lineage—and every lineage has their own unique, intimate language that alludes to the crossing—we reenact, in an evolutionary context, the story of Abraham, the Hebrew. The word *Hebrew* means the one who crosses over to the other side.

The experience of the crossing is the awakening to the Fourth Big Bang,[41] in which I experience the Field of LoveIntelligence, LoveBeauty, and LoveDesire holding me in every moment. At the same time, I experience all the Field in me—irreducibly and uniquely in me—and I realize, "I matter. I impact Reality. For Real. I am not an extra on the set, but I am fundamentally and poignantly needed by All-That-Is."

This is, in some very deep sense, precisely the ancient teaching of *Hineni.* When the Divine Voice calls Abraham, he responds with this one word, "*Hineni*"—"Here I am."

There are, of course, two ways to interpret that response. The first is an expression of utter obedience and submission: *Here I am, thy will be done.* But the other way, which appears in the hidden texts of nondual humanism, is that it's not that I am completely obliterating my selfness to become an empty vessel for the Divine. Rather, I am so in my selfness,

---

41 For more on the Fourth Big Bang, see Essay Three.

my depth, my uniqueness that my radical subjectivity merges with the Divine. My unique individuated configuration of matter is alive with Divinity. I ultimately matter. And when I say "*Hineni*," "Here I am," I realize that I am found.

4. Conclusion

Crisis is an evolutionary driver, and every crisis is at its core a crisis of intimacy.[42]

We have identified the global intimacy disorder as the root cause of the existential risk, but the underlying ultimate failure of intimacy is the deconstruction of value itself. This means that human value does not participate in any sense of intrinsic Value of the Real. It is not about *values* but about the *Field of Value* that underlies all individual values. When the human being, moved by myriad cultural, historical, and psychological confusions, claims to have stepped out of the Field of Value, then intimacy itself is deconstructed. The deconstruction of value is the deconstruction of intimacy.

In the absence of a shared Story of Value, a story that's an expression of Reality's Eros, a story rooted in pseudo-eros takes center stage, becoming the generator for existential risk.

Our modern pseudo-eros story is a rivalrous conflict, governed by win/lose metrics. Such a story catalyzes the second generator function of existential risk: complicated, fragile systems with no allurement or intimacy between the parts. It is in that sense we have argued that the success story is the first generator function for existential risk.

The failure of intimacy is precisely the impotent experience that there is no shared identity between the interiors of the human being and Reality. There is no shared identity in the sense of any common

---

42 We discuss this idea in more detail in part two of this book, in particular in Section V.3.

participation in a Field of shared intrinsic Value. But only a shared Story of Value can arouse the global will required to engage catastrophic and existential risk. It is only global political, moral, and social will—erotic will—that can generate the most good, true, and beautiful world we have always known is possible.

All civilizations have fallen because the stories that they lived in were, in some sense, based on rivalrous conflict governed by win/lose metrics. Every civilization was weakened by interior polarization caused by the lack of a shared Story of Value. We now have a global civilization, but we haven't created a Shared Story of Value. We haven't solved the generator functions that caused all civilizations to fall. Our global civilization has exponential technologies and extraction models depleting the Earth of resources that it took billions of years to create, which is going to lead to a civilizational collapse.

Existential risk is a risk to our very existence.

The choice is clear: Love or die.

It is that simple. Eros is no longer a luxury. It is an absolute necessity for the survival of the individual and of the planet.

In the last half of the twentieth century, modern psychology has documented an age-old truth: A fully nourished baby who is not held in loving arms will die. So too our world, personally and globally, even with all the resources of intelligence and technology at our disposal, will die without being held in Love—in the embrace of Eros.

We must embrace a personal path of Love and a global politics of Love—not the ordinary love, a mere human sentiment, but Eros, or what we sometimes call *Outrageous Love*, the heart of existence itself. We live in a world of outrageous pain. The only response to outrageous pain is Outrageous Love.

To love means to participate in the evolution of love, which is the evolution of the human Story of Value. It means to evolve, to activate a new cultural enlightenment, rooted in a new narrative of identity, a new narrative of value, a new narrative of intimate communion, a new narrative of desire, a new narrative of power. All of this will birth new narratives of economics and politics.

The evolution of love is the telling of a New Story. It must be told as a Love Story, for in fact that is the deepest truth of Reality, rooted in the best exterior and interior sciences that we have at this moment in time:

- Reality is not merely a fact. Reality is a story.

- Reality is not an ordinary story. Reality is a love story.

- Reality is not an ordinary love story. Reality is an Outrageous Love Story.

A New Story doesn't mean a made-up story. It means doing the hard work of integrating the validated insights of the traditional world, the modern world, and the postmodern world. This is the intention at the heart of CosmoErotic Humanism.

Together with other emergent strands, CosmoErotic Humanism needs to become the ground of a world religion as a context for our diversity. We need religion, even as we need science, to articulate a shared global grammar of value. A New Story means that we come to the Story from a new interior wholeness—with a new relationship to the larger Whole.

ESSAY TWO

THE EMERGENCE OF WHOLE MATES IN THE BREAKDOWN OF ROLE MATE AND SOUL MATE RELATIONSHIPS

1. Crisis of Intimacy Is an Evolutionary Driver

Reality is relationship—all the way up and down the evolutionary chain. This is the core scientific structure of Reality, whether we are talking about the subatomic level, the atomic and molecular level, or the cellular and multicellular level—from plants, to animals, to mammals, to human beings (*scientific* in this sentence refers both to the exterior sciences, which govern the laws of exteriors, and the interior sciences, which govern the laws of interiors). Therefore, science is the science of relationships.[43]

Reality is not an eternal fact but an evolving story. That is one of the single biggest insights of science, with implications that change everything about everything.

---

43 See part two for a detailed unpacking of this sentence.

Yet this does not mean that evolution is inevitable. It does not mean that evolution is linear. It does not mean that evolution cannot stall. Neither does it mean that the higher levels of evolutionary development and potency do not birth new pathologies. Indeed, new potency in evolution always breeds new promise and new peril. For example, life is more evolved than matter. Therefore, life has a level of consciousness that matter does not have, but with consciousness comes cancer: In the world of matter, there is no cancer, and in the world of life, there is cancer. Rocks do not have cancer, but horses do. The more complex and the more interconnected a phenomenon, the deeper the pathology—and the deeper the potential and promise.

We live in the Anthropocene—the age in which human action, more than ever before, directly participates in shaping the evolutionary trajectory of Reality toward its greatest promise. This is what we call *Conscious Evolution*:

- We awaken to the evolutionary story.

- We become aware of the entire spiral of evolution—from matter to life to mind.

- Moreover, we realize our capacity to evolve to a deeper incarnation of our humanity, where the human being realizes our participation in the Field of Value itself and begins to take genuine ecstatic responsibility for the evolution of culture and consciousness. In other words, we realize that we are the actors in the story, the storytellers, and the writers of the next chapters in the story.

All of this is part of the great promise—the realization of Conscious Evolution, the realization that we are Conscious Evolution in person.

But with this great promise of the evolution of consciousness comes the potentially most tragic peril. The peril comes from the evolution of exterior technologies, while the evolution of interior technologies—for example, the realizations of Conscious Evolution—remain but an unrealized potential, an unfulfilled promise. In this scenario—the one we live in right now—the exterior technologies generate, together with their own promise, great peril. The peril is that we generate a system that is inherently fragile—subject to every manner of systems breakdown.

But even more insidiously, we create a system in which we experience ourselves outside the Field of Eros and Value. In other words, we experience ourselves outside of the Tao (an ancient term that points to the Field of Eros and intrinsic Value) because we assert that there is no intrinsic value and therefore no inherent Eros of Reality, and therefore no such Field exists. The result is that pseudo-eros and pseudo-value drive the system, which moves us toward destruction. The generator functions of existential risk—rivalrous conflict governed by win/lose metrics and the fragile systems it generates—are expressions of pseudo-eros, the pseudo-eros of the modern success story.[44]

There are no longer any negative actors needed. No Hitler, no Stalin, no Pol Pot, and no Mao are necessary to generate existential risk. Rather, the system itself moves toward its own destruction.

As a result, we are poised between utopia and dystopia. Which way we go will almost entirely depend on the story we tell ourselves about ourselves—who we are, where we are, and what is ours to do. At the core of the story is the story of relationship—not the story of a particular relationship, but the story of relationship itself. At this juncture in history, the future depends on human action. The most important human action is telling the right story—the best possible story—based on integration of the most accurate and validated information about who we are, where we are, and what is ours to do. How we tell those stories will sculpt the nature of our relationships.

The right story of relationship—iterated again and again, exponentially, through the billions of relationships on the planet—moves Reality to ever-deeper and higher levels of possibility—through higher and deeper levels of relationship. From atom to amoeba to plant to animal to mammal to human to more evolved human, Reality moves toward more complex exteriors coupled with ever-deeper interiors (consciousness), ever-deeper possibility, and ever-deeper forms and depths of relationship.

---

44 See Essay One, Sections 1–2.

There is a holy trinity to Reality's plotline, which can be concisely but accurately recapitulated in three short sentences:

1. The core of Reality is relationship.

2. The core of Reality is evolution.

3. The core of Reality is the evolution of relationship.

In other words, the story of evolution is the progressive deepening of intimacies. Each new level of evolution is caused by a new configuration of intimacy: between atomic particles, between cells, between organs, all the way up the evolutionary chain to human beings and then to groups of human beings.

Reality is the evolution of intimacy—ever-deeper levels of shared identity (within the context of otherness) characterized by mutualities of recognition, feeling, value, and purpose. Another word for intimacy is wholeness. Eros is the drive of Reality toward ever-deeper contact and ever-greater wholeness. In other words, Eros is the drive for more intimacy. Deepening this realization, we might accurately say that **evolution is driven by two forces, Eros and crisis.**[45]

Crisis is an evolutionary driver. For example, the major evolutionary leap from prokaryotes to eukaryotes was caused by a crisis: The new eukaryotes were able to breathe oxygen instead of being killed by it (unlike the early prokaryotes). Eukaryotes emerged from the capacity of two prokaryotes to merge and form a larger union, which was a monumental leap in relationship.[46] This ultimately led to the emergence of multicellular organisms, and later human beings. In other words, in the broadest sweep, the movement of evolution from single-celled to

---

45 See Section V in Part Two for an unpacking of this statement.

46 While there is great agreement among biologists that eukaryotes first arose as the result of a merger of two prokaryotic cells—one of which appears to have been a member of a subgroup of Archaea, whereas the other appears to have been related to Alphaproteobacteria—it is not yet clear how exactly this merger happened. See, for example, "The Merger That Made Us," by Buzz Baum and David A. Baum (2020).

multicellular life—a monumental leap in relationship—was driven by a series of crises.[47] The same happens on the human level: Crisis in relationship leads to the next stage of evolution.

Any crisis is, at its core, a crisis of relationship. Said only slightly differently, any crisis, at its core, is a crisis of intimacy. No crisis can be solved at the level of consciousness at which it was created. A level of consciousness is characterized by a particular story of relationship. A crisis in relationship is resolved by the birth of a higher level of relationship—which requires a higher level of consciousness. This is true about personal crises, local collective crises, and the global meta-crisis.

The crisis in relationship is rooted in an alienation from Wholeness. Alienation means the collapse (or rupture) of a relationship. The alienation is from the larger Whole in which we participate on the exterior level (biosphere and physiosphere, planet, planetary culture, galaxy, and wider). The alienation is no less from the interior Whole in which we participate—the Field of Consciousness, Value, and Wholeness. This Field has been called by many names, including the Tao. It has also been called the Shekhinah, or simply the Divine or consciousness. Human participation in the Field has been called True Self; more accurately, *human realization* of participation in the Field has been called the realization of True Self. In CosmoErotic Humanism, we call the Field *the Infinite Intimate* or *the Infinity of Intimacy*; human participation in the Field has four names, each emerging from the previous one: True Self; Unique

---

47 As we will see later in Section V.3, there was more than one crisis involved, each followed by a huge evolution of relationship: (1) The oxygen crisis was followed by a prokaryote learning to become intimate with oxygen and learning to thrive again by breathing it. (2) The oxygen-breathing prokaryotes invaded larger prokaryotes—another crisis in relationship—until the two cells became so intimate that they needed each other. The invading cell became the mitochondria of the invaded cell, generating the first (proto) eukaryote. (3) A similar process happened a couple of times. Each time, the new eukaryote became a bit more complex and gained many functions (like sexual reproduction, motility, DNA repair, and, in some eukaryotes, which are the ancestors of our plants, the ability to do photosynthesis through their chloroplasts) until, after many relationship crises and evolutions of relationship, a eukaryote emerged like the ones we know today. (4) And finally, two or more cells came together and became so intimate with each other that they became one organism—the first multicellular organism.

Self; Evolutionary Unique Self; Unique Self Symphony.[48]

The realization of human participation in the Field—what we might also call participation in the Whole—is deepened at each of these four levels. Each of these four levels corresponds to a deepening in relationship to the Whole. We call the new level of relationship that emerges from this new relationship to the Whole *evolutionary relationships*, or *whole mate relationships*. The crisis in intimacy is resolved by the birth of a higher level of intimacy, *Evolutionary Intimacy*. Said only slightly differently: Crisis births the next stage in the evolution of relationships, which is the evolution of intimacy, which is the evolution of love.

The nature of the Intimate Universe is that the personal and the political, social, cultural, and economical are always intimately related. In other words, **the personal crisis and the meta-crisis share one root cause and therefore one root solution**. The response to one crisis—the personal crisis of relationship—always provides the solution to the larger context and its crisis—the meta-crisis.

We are in the midst of a crisis in relationship. The meta-crisis is rooted in the alienated relationship from the Whole, as we described in Essay One. The personal crisis in relationship means that the old forms of relationship, while important, valid, and compelling in many ways, are no longer sufficient: They no longer bring us depths of joy and satisfaction, they do not respond to our core personal needs, and they don't respond to the core needs of the larger whole—the world situation in which we live.

---

48 See Essay One, Section 3; for a more in-depth conversation, see Whole Mate, chapters 7, 8, and 11.

2. The Emergence of Soul Mate from the Crisis of Role Mate

The ongoing revolution in relationships, like all great revolutions, is catalyzed by our interior consciousness meeting exterior changes in technology and the marketplace. As always, money and economics play a big part in this story. A major premise of the old relationship deal was that mutual dependency and imposed social roles were necessary for survival (we call this old relationship style *role mates*):

- Men were breadwinners. Men guided and directed. Men were protectors and providers.

- Women were homemakers. Women mused and inspired. Women were nurturers and caregivers.

- Men operated in the public sphere and women in the private sphere.

There was an invisible but inherent social coercion for men and women to fall into the classical role mate positions that defined the old relationship deal.

Now, man as sole or even primary breadwinner is no longer a given. It is nearly impossible to overstate the significance of this momentous shift. It changes the very structure of society and is every bit as dramatic as the Industrial Revolution. As it did then, this change is evoking a complete reenvisioning of both identity and relationship. If women become the primary breadwinners, what happens to the old relationship deal, where the Eros of exchange between men and women was based on the male breadwinner and the female homemaker? From this perspective, a crucial question emerges for the feminine: *Why do I need a man?* Whatever the answer is, the very fact that it *is* a question is radically new. It was never a question at the role mate stage. Moreover, men do not necessarily need to have a wife and children to be socially acceptable. The relation to both marriage and children has changed dramatically.[49]

It is not just economic conditions that are driving the emergence of the new relationship deal. A huge driver is that women are discovering new answers to the question of identity. They are responding very differently to the questions of *Who am I?* and *Who do I want to be and become?* than they did just a short time ago. In the past half-century, the shift in women's consciousness has expanded their sense of choice. As women—especially women of the upper middle and professional classes—were liberated from the role of homemaker, many discovered that they could either choose the traditional roles or pursue professional and public success. They could also choose, as many have, to integrate their efforts in the public and private sphere. This increase in options—raising children, bringing in money, or doing some combination of both—encourages women to wake up from socially imposed roles and choose for themselves what it means to be a woman. Put differently, women hunger for a way to access the full power of their Mars qualities without losing the depth of their Venus qualities.[50]

Changes are equally dramatic for men. Until now, societies survived based on men's ability to play very specific roles: provider, protector, and leader. Playing those roles successfully meant they were "real men." Their success earned them society's respect and women's love. Failure to play those roles meant a failed life, dishonor, and shame. Society imposed such roles in order to survive: To survive wars, revolutions, movements, and rapid change, we needed boys and men not to question their duty to give their lives for their families and their countries. We needed them to buy

---

49 This crisis is described in depth in Whole Mate especially in chapter 4.

50 We are borrowing John Gray's terms Mars and Venus—see his book Men Are from Mars, Women Are from Venus: A Practical Guide for Improving Communication and Getting What You Want in Your Relationships (1993)—to refer to different polarities (whether we call them Mars/Venus, lines/circles, yang/yin, or masculine/feminine), whether these live in a man and a woman, two women, two men, or between nonbinary people. In the old relationship deal, these were clear: Venus referred to women, Mars to men. In the new relationship deal, we go beyond Venus and Mars.

into the belief that being a good protector, provider, and leader would make them heroes and bring them glory, love, and respect.

But at this point the moral goodness and rightness of both men's and women's classic roles have been irreversibly challenged. Moreover, as women moved into the workplace and their old networks of feminine support were consequently dismantled, they turned to the communion of the couple for intimacy and communication. Ironically, in doing what he needed to do to be a provider and protector, a man was often unavailable for intimacy. Success as an attorney means learning to argue; being intimate as a husband or dad means listening like the sky. Being a great warrior means developing a killer reflex; being an available husband and dad means developing a love reflex. As a result, women often felt that their deep need for intimacy was not being satisfied.

For a long time, that did not matter. Passion and intimacy were not part of the old relationship deal. But as women found their voice, independence, and power, they also related in a whole new way to their need for intimacy and passion with their partners. Men have generally awakened to the realization that being the sole breadwinner did not train them for intimacy. Men have realized that the very skills they needed for traditional success were often antithetical to intimacy, and that success training was all too often divorce training. Men's jobs took them away from the home so they could support the home. The home they supported often became the home they were thrown out of for failing to be good husbands.

While the men thought that being a good husband meant providing, newly conscious women found their voice and asked men to provide something else—a greater depth of intimacy and communication. In other words, they needed a new level of relationship, *soul mate*. When men could not meet women's needs, women felt unfulfilled, and they often left the relationship.

Moreover, the erotic bonding between men, which is natural to men and took place, for example, in armies and in the religious and premodern world, was displaced by the success story of the modern world, which set up all men against all men, in what Hobbes called a state of war. Men needed therefore to turn for intimacy to their partners in love instead of to their brothers in arms. Many men have recognized their partner's unfulfilled needs and their own. They are now reaching for increased depths of intimacy and communion. They are seeking to access and deploy a far greater range of their Venus qualities than ever before.

3. The Personal Crisis and the Meta-Crisis: A New Relationship to the Whole

From the personal crisis in relationships, we turn back to the meta-crisis. The meta-crisis is an evolutionary crisis of the first order. We are facing catastrophic and existential risk.

As we articulated in Essay One, the response to the meta-crisis will not be sufficient if it only comes from new forms of politics, economics, or technology. Neither the social structure (politics and economics) nor the infrastructure (technologies) is sufficient to address the meta-crisis. We require new forms of identity, which in turn birth new forms of relationship—new forms of intimate communion. We need a new superstructure, a new shared set of evolving First Principles and First Values rooted in a shared Story of Value. It is only First Principles and First Values embedded in a shared Story of Value that can generate a new form of relationship to the Whole.

Let's deepen our understanding. We have articulated the realization, rooted in the interior and exterior sciences, that crisis is an evolutionary driver, and that any crisis is a crisis of intimacy. Therefore, it must be responded to through a new level of intimacy or relationship. With this in mind, the careful diagnostic of the meta-crisis that we articulated above begins to become almost self-evident.

As shown in Essay One, the root cause underlying the core generators of existential and catastrophic risk is a global intimacy disorder. In other words, like every crisis, the meta-crisis is a crisis of intimacy—a crisis in relationship. It is a crisis in our relationship with each other and with ourselves, that is, in relationship to the larger whole and to the original wholeness in ourselves. Therefore, like every crisis, it must be healed at a new level of consciousness, which means a new level of intimacy, which means a new structure or form of relationship.

Intimacy is always rooted in a shared Story of Value. Therefore, the global intimacy disorder can be transformed by the emergence of a New Story of Value. In the twin crises of this moment—the personal crisis of intimacy and global intimacy disorder—we see the elegance of the Intimate Universe and its invitation. The two crises are inextricably entwined, and a resolution of the personal crisis of intimacy is necessary for the resolution of the meta-crisis of intimacy. Said slightly differently, the resolution of the personal alienation from wholeness and the resolution of our meta collective global alienation from our own wholeness and the larger Whole are inextricably entwined.

Why?

At the core of the global intimacy disorder is a narrow vision of human identity. The human being self-conceives as a *separate self*, disconnected, alienated, and disassociated from the larger Whole. Thus, the individual participates with full power only in their local lives, which is inevitably some form of rivalrous conflict governed by zero-sum win/lose metrics, one of the primary generator functions of existential risk. The win/lose metrics, iterated exponentially throughout the systems, generate the fragile world order and, ultimately, the meta-crisis.

In other words, the win/lose metrics are rooted in a narrow view of both self and *We*—inaccurate answers to the three great questions of CosmoErotic Humanism: Who am I? Who are We? Where are We? What is there to do?

Inaccurate answers to these questions, answers not rooted in First Values and First Principles, are the root causes of the global intimacy disorder. Accurate responses to these questions, rooted in First Values and First Principles, inform our vision of relationship. Clearly then, an evolution of relationship is both urgently necessary and desired.

We need relationships in which couples don't just look to fulfill each other's core survival needs or emotional needs (as critical, beautiful, desirable, and necessary as those both are). We need a new form of relationship in which both parties are looking at a shared horizon:

- Both parties are omni-considerate for the sake of the Whole.

- Both parties are erotically connected to the larger Whole.

- Both parties are intimate with the larger Whole; that is, they share identity with the larger Whole, recognize and feel the larger Whole, and share its value and purpose. Moreover, they also feel recognized, felt, valued, and participatory in—*needed for*—the purpose of the Whole.

These qualities characterize the emergence of *whole mate relationship*—an evolutionary relationship. The whole mate relationship emerges not just from the pseudo-eros of superficial or unclarified need—which often expresses itself as a codependent pathological need—but also from the deeper, sacred need, which is the ontology of wholeness itself. Deep in the interior sciences is the realization that wholeness desires ever-more wholeness. As such, the whole mate comes to the relationship with a dimension of prior wholeness—ground and depth—even as he/she yearns for ever-greater wholeness. Such a relationship generates an entirely new form of erotic relationship to the Whole and an entirely new depth of erotic relationship between the beloveds at the same time.

The whole mate relationship begins to engender a worldwide Unique Self Symphony, in which human beings are omni-considerate for the sake of the Whole and understand their relationships in the larger context of the Whole. Unique Self and Unique We are emergent from and in service to the larger Whole. This new form of relationship, iterated exponentially through the world system, changes the system.

Relationship is the fundamental structure of Reality. Evolving the way relationships are enacted—by changing the story of relationship within which the partners live—up-levels the entire system. The system changes from a *complicated* system, fragile and subject to breakdown, to a *complex* system with allurement between the parts, who experience themselves as part of the larger Whole. Evolving the story of relationship both evolves and transforms the world story, even as it evolves and transforms the personal love story between the beloveds. The evolution of relationship is therefore the evolution of love.

To recapitulate: The new level of intimacy emerges in direct response to the crisis of intimacy. This crisis is twofold: It is both the personal crisis and the meta-crisis—the global intimacy disorder. Both are crises of relationship and intimacy, and both move toward resolution through the emergence of a new level of intimacy: Evolutionary Intimacy and evolutionary relationship (whole mate relationship).

It is the nature of the Intimate Universe that the resolution of one crisis also addresses the meta-crisis. The emergence of whole mate relationship, iterated through the world system, births a new level of relationship and a new structure of intimacy. This changes the system itself, resolving a key dimension of the meta-crisis, which, at its core, is rooted in an alienation from the Whole, expressed as rivalrous conflict governed by zero-sum win/lose dynamics, iterated structurally all through the world system. Thus, the twofold crisis of intimacy can and must be resolved in the same way that evolution always resolves crisis: through the emergence of a new order of intimacy and of relationship.

4. The Emergence of Whole Mate in the Breakdown of Soul Mate

The ultimate experience in a soul mate relationship is looking deeply into each other's eyes. After all, they say, the eyes are windows to the soul. So, what could be more appropriate for soul mates than to locate themselves in the deep wells of being—in the eyes of the other? Each feels held, received, and witnessed. This is what we call (borrowing our friend

John Gray's term) a Venus-Mars relationship in one of its most beautiful and potent expressions. By Venus-Mars relationship we mean the classic relationship between two people with different polarities, whether we call it Mars/Venus, lines/circles, yang/yin, or masculine/feminine.[51]

This works particularly well in the first station of love—falling in love or infatuation[52]—but soul mate relationships do not end when the first joy of falling in love gives way. But at some point, when your primary focus is looking deeply into each other's eyes, your eyes start to hurt. At some point, the joy of being becomes insufficient, and you search for a deeper vision of why you are together. That is when the transition to evolutionary or whole mate relationships potentially takes place.

Our use of the term *whole*—besides the fact that it rhymes with role and soul—is gradually made clear in this work. Whole mate is whole in multiple ways. But at its core, a whole mate is whole in one of two primary ways:

- First, a whole mate is one who enters relationship from the space of *a prior wholeness*.

- Second, a whole mate is living in *relationship to the larger Whole*. Both partners, both whole mates, serve a vision that is larger than themselves.

---

51 Whether these live in a man and a woman, two women, two men, or between nonbinary people.

52 I proposed the category of stations for Integral Theory in a series of conversations with Ken Wilber and Clint Fuhs, in order to describe the three stations of love, which was a central category in the 2011 event convened by Ken and me together with Diane Hamilton and Sally Kempton, entitled The Future of Love. The three stations of love are referred to in Hebrew wisdom lineage source as submission, separation, and sweetness. These stations are also implicitly referred to in more classical psychological terms as identification, disidentification, and integration. In the three stations, as applied to love, they appear as follows: The first station is falling in love, or ecstatic infatuation. The second station is when the falling-in-love euphoria fades and the power struggle begins. And the third station is when the power struggles recede and the couple falls in love more deeply, after integrating the new depth of wisdom and love that is gained through stations one and two. See https://www.marcgafni.com/main-teachings/divine-eros/a-teaching-on-the-three-stations-of-love.

Let us first focus on the latter sense of whole, which appears as the relationship evolves—including but transcending soul mate—into whole mate relationship.

In a whole mate or evolutionary relationship, you begin not by looking deeply into each other's eyes but by looking at a shared horizon. An evolutionary relationship is sourced in a shared vision. There is a dream of fulfillment that you can both see. You first look deeply at a shared horizon, and from that place, you then turn to look deeply into each other's eyes.

I recently read an interview with a music icon, Rolling Stones lead singer Mick Jagger. Whether or not you like their music, one fact about the Stones is startling. At the time of the interview, the relationship between the core members of the band had lasted fifty years. The band survived all kinds of relationship challenges that took other music groups out. When Jagger was asked how they did it, he said something like "The Stones were always larger than us. Holding the vision of the Stones kept us together." While the image is imperfect, it begins to get at the nature of an evolutionary relationship.

Every level or stage[53] of relationship has its own core values:

1. The core values of role mate relationships are to survive and thrive, not only as individuals but as family. To thrive is usually defined in conventional terms—material success and obedience to the norms and codes imposed by society.

---

53 We often refer to the levels or stages of relationship: stage one, role mate; stage two, soul mate; stage three, whole mate. These are not, however, developmental levels of individuals. We could see them as evolutionary stages of relationship that, once they have emerged in evolution and if both partners have reached a certain minimum level of consciousness that is required for that stage of relationship, can (potentially) also show up in the relationships of individual partners. So, although these are not classical developmental levels, where the next level can only emerge once the previous level has been sufficiently lived through, there is an actual evolution involved, which is in part a cultural evolution but also involves an evolution of the personal relationship (that transcends and includes the former stages).

2. The most important core value of soul mate relationships is personal fulfillment. Personal fulfillment may or may not involve children. But the intention of the relationship is to serve the couple and those near and dear to them. The core value of a role mate relationship is not physical prosperity but the prosperity of the relationship itself.

3. A whole mate or evolutionary relationship includes the best of role mate and soul mate, but it goes one momentous step farther. The core values of an evolutionary relationship are beyond the relationship itself. The relationship serves those core values.

At the level of relationship consciousness expressed as soul mate,[54] we generally understand having a good relationship as the sign of a good life: The goal of a good life is a good relationship. At the level of whole mate or evolutionary relationship consciousness, we are also able to reverse the equation: The goal of a good relationship is a good life. The relationship is the vehicle that serves the larger goal of living a good life—but the good life is not only for the couple but for *all* of life. Relationship is in devotion to a larger vision and purpose. In other words, we reach for whole mate when personal fulfillment is no longer personally fulfilling. We reach for whole mate when we awaken to the powerful realization that we are personally fulfilled when we are fulfilling missions, values, and visions beyond ourselves.

---

54 We are referring here to the minimum level of consciousness that is required for any person to enter a soul mate relationship. In that sense, we sometimes refer to level one, two, and three of consciousness, or alternatively to role mate, soul mate, and whole mate consciousness, when referring to the levels of consciousness required for role mate, soul mate, and whole mate relationships.

5. Value in Role Mate, Soul Mate, and Whole Mate Relationships

In role mate relationships, the centrality of shared value has always been taken as a given. For role mates to function, they need to share both an implicitly theoretical vision of value and a pragmatic practice of value.

This is self-evidently true for beloveds who are parents. It is almost impossible to raise children without a shared ground of value. But parenting needs to be the model and not the exception. In our own lives, we can somehow manage to ignore the fact that we are living in relation to value, and that the nature of that relationship changes every single dimension of our lives.

The proscription against intermarriage, whether of soft social nature or of more serious, legal, or tribal nature, generally had something to do with the desire of the community to perpetuate both its particular vision of value and its accurate view of value as the foundation stone of relationship. Granted, of course, some of these proscriptions in society were related to an ethnocentric sense of racial superiority. That dimension of these proscriptions needs to be roundly rejected—as it has been by liberal societies the world over. But this rejection should not blind us to the essential wisdom of the great traditions: Relationship is bound up with value. In the emergence of soul mate relationships, the classic proscription of relationships to other communities of ethnicity and value was swept away. Indeed, they were regarded as regressive, and, as we noted, in part—but only in part—for good reason.

But beyond the rejection of ethnocentric proscriptions, the level of soul mate consciousness is making a more essential proclamation. Love is said to conquer all—*including value*. And for that reason, for soul mates, value was simply not part of the relationship's conversation. Many more times than once, I have met with couples in counseling and asked what drew them together. Italian food and dancing or their equivalents came up far more often than a shared framework of value. But it is not that value was entirely rejected in soul mate relationship. Rather, love was taken to be the primary value, at whose altar all other values were required to kneel.

It is not, however, that the soul mate level of consciousness necessarily opposes value. Rather, soul mate consciousness took one of two attitudes to value. In some cases, value was assumed, in the form of *the common-sense sacred axioms of value*. These implicit axioms emerged because a strain of modernity borrowed the *reality* of value from premodernity, even as it rejected premodernity's sources of value. The underlying cultural basis of this strain of thought is:

> Value just *is*. We don't know its source, and we don't really
> care. You don't need to think about it a lot. Take it as a
> self-evident given, and get on with your life.

However, other strains of soul mate consciousness are more caught up in various forms of existentialism or early postmodernism, which followed the primary thread of modernity that deconstructed value altogether. But in both approaches, value was written out of the essential terms of the soul mate equation.

This became one of the primary reasons that soul mate relationships failed. Once the experience of looking deeply into the eyes of the beloved is no longer sufficiently compelling, the beloveds need to turn to a shared ground and vision of value. When that is no longer available, the relationship loses its allure, for part of the ground of allurement between beloveds is value itself.

The nature of value at the level of whole mate relationship integrates and evolves the nature of value at both the role mate and soul mate levels of relationship. Love remains central for whole mate, but the nature of that love is understood differently from what it is at the soul mate level of relationship. Love is understood not as a social construct or human contrivance but as the very nature of Reality itself. This is what we have described as *Evolutionary Love*, or *Outrageous Love*. This love is intrinsic to Cosmos; it is the heart of existence itself. Evolutionary Love, also called Eros, is the primary value of Cosmos, from which all other values flow. Personal love is experienced as a unique expression of the larger Field of Eros—Evolutionary Love that animates all of Reality.

At the level of whole mate relationship, value comes back online as being central to the relationship. When we say that whole mates need to look at a shared horizon and only then turn and look deeply in each other's eyes, we are talking in large part about a shared horizon of value. It is the allurement of value that is central in the very serious play of Eros—intimacy and joy that bind whole mates. Of course, the nature of value often changes from role mate to whole mate. For role mate, the context is often local to the individual, whether local means cultural, economic, political, or religious. For whole mate, value is always the intrinsic value of the Whole, as it applies to their lives and their intentions for the sake of the Whole.

6. Eros and Value

One of the qualities of value is that it arouses will. The word *will* in the original Hebrew, *ratzon*, is an Eros word. It is drawn, among other sources, from the *Song of Songs*, an erotic expression of Reality that declares that "its insides are lined with love"—in other words, Reality itself is Eros.[55] At the outset of the *Song of Songs*, the lover says to her beloved, "Draw me after you, and I will run toward you."[56] The term for "run toward you"—in Hebrew, *rutza*—shares its etymological root and meaning with the Hebrew word *ratzon*, which translates as "will." In other words, draw me after you; I will surrender my lower will to you and allow myself to be

---

55 The Song of Songs is understood by Akiba, the central figure in the transition from the Jerusalem Temple to the oral law, in one text as participating in the ontology of the Holy of Holies of the Jerusalem Temple, and in another text as being a sufficient basis to guide the moral world if the Torah had never been given.

56 Song of Songs, 1:2–4.

taken over by the deeper will of Reality—Eros moving through me—that arouses me to you and overwhelms all separation and boundary.

In the deeper presentations of soul mate relationship, this Eros was understood—intuitively, if not explicitly—to be the ground of Value itself, hence the appropriate devotion at its altar. For soul mates this centrality of Eros as Value sweeps away all other values. At the level of whole mate consciousness, however, there is a deeper clarification at work that understands that Eros as Value does not sweep away the Field of Value but is rather *the ground* of Value. Eros, at this clarified level of consciousness, does not oppose ethics; rather, a clarified Eros is the source and ground of all ethics.

In this sense, we often talk of Eros and ethics in terms of three levels.

- Level one is the level of Eros that precedes the depth of work in ethos and distinction, Eros prior to ethos.

- This is followed by level two, which is the great work of ethos and distinction.

- This is then, theoretically, followed by level three, which is Eros that includes and transcends ethos.

Like all models of unfolding, these stages are not necessarily linear but can appear in multiple ways in our lives.

In CosmoErotic Humanism, we distinguish the level-one Eros from the level-three Eros that includes all of ethos, even as it both forms the ground of ethos and is shaped by it. Indeed, in the *Song of Songs*, as it is read in the interior sciences of Hebrew wisdom, Eros is understood as Value itself. In other words, Eros is ontologically understood to be identical with ethos. There is no ultimate split between Value and Eros at all. This is part of the general sense of the interior sciences of Hebrew wisdom that, from the ultimate perspective, will and Eros are identical. Will is the interiority of Cosmos that desires Value; or, said differently, will is the appetite of Cosmos itself for value. This is captured in the root word *ratzon*, which stands for both *will*, which includes moral will, and

Eros, erotic will.

Value, both in its fulfillment and its violation, literally arouses our will. When we see value violated, we are aroused to action. Our desire to fulfill value arouses us to action. When we step out of the Field of Value, our will to action—be it political, moral, or economic—goes limp. We become impotent. This relationship between value and will is one of the core clarifications of the interior sciences of CosmoErotic Humanism, intimately linked to its vision of a shared ground of Value—a Field of Value—that underlies polarizing clashes around specific dogmatic applications of specific values.

Reality itself is Eros, which means that Reality is Value. That is the essential realization of the Solomon lineage, exemplified in many texts, including the *Song of Songs*. It is in this sense that whole mate consciousness includes and transcends soul mate consciousness. Whole mates recognize, as do soul mates, the utter centrality of Eros. But for soul mates, Eros becomes the only value. Sometimes that means the soul mate consciousness replaces the Field of Value with the romantic story, even though it is a social construction. But in other writings and expressions, the soul mate consciousness may have killed all the other goddesses but still offers devotion to Aphrodite—the value of Eros. In other words, the Field of Value has been deconstructed, and only the value of Eros still allures us.

Soul mate relationship breaks down because it makes a false split between the value of Eros and the Eros of Value. The value of Eros is embraced, but the Eros of Value is rejected.

7. The Third Side: Relationship in Service to the Whole

For many if not most people, relationships are a soul mate proposition, with the goal of personal fulfillment. That's why, soon after the first station of falling in love ends, the power-struggle station begins. Much of relationship advice is about the art of negotiation and dealmaking: How can I make a deal to get as much as I can? Since people are basically good, they want the deal to be fair. Since people are basically kind, they want their partner to feel good. Since people are fundamentally loving, they enjoy giving to their partner. Nonetheless, the power struggle goes on. Dealmaking still remains the core staple of most soul mate relationships.

At the whole mate level, the conflict is transcended because it is no longer just about the two sides. A third side is introduced:[57] the shared larger context and purpose of the relationship. Both parties are committed to the third side, as much or even more than they are to each other. The third side forms a triangle. We have moved from a dyad to a triad. Triangles are known to be exceptionally stable. Instead of there being a constant win/lose or compromise dynamic, there is something much more potent. The third side is the attractor that draws the couple into the future. It has a pull dimension rather than a push dimension.

Usually, a relationship is pushed from behind by the past. This includes the personal histories and wounding of each party as well as the personal history as a couple. This push factor all too often pushes the relationship off a cliff. Evolutionary relationships are pulled forward by a memory of the future rather than being weighed down by memories of the past. The third side of a whole mate relationship can be anything from shared values, shared life purposes, or shared visions. It cannot just be harmony in your relationship. Even if it begins with harmony in your relationship, it must then evolve to harmony itself. You might begin with the value of love in your relationship but then up-level to the value of love itself. Your love becomes service and devotion to love itself.

The second you begin to be in service and devotion to a value beyond the relationship, you have begun to make the transition from soul mate to whole mate relationship. This is the change that begins to change everything. This is the beginning of what it means to participate, through your consciousness, in the larger evolution of consciousness. This is what it means to participate, through your love, in the evolution of love. Love

---

57 We borrow the term "third side" from our colleague Bill Ury.

THE EVOLUTION OF LOVE

itself evolves by your evolving your love.

Reality is relationships, and relationships are in service to Reality. To be in an evolutionary relationship, you must be able to admit something very big, but when you admit that, everything else opens: You admit that there is something in life that is larger than you, to which you are in service.

Paradoxically, that is the beginning of truly being alive. We only start to be truly alive when we identify and align with a value that is larger than just our own life. But this value cannot be a value imposed by a government or by society. It is a value or a vision or a purpose that we are freely choosing. Evolutionary relationships allow us to pursue the goals that give meaning to our lives. A relationship that does not contribute significantly to the realization of life goals beyond the relationship eventually stagnates and dissolves, even if the couple stays together.

As whole mates, we realize that we are not separate and set apart behind the wall of our relationship. Rather, we are an inextricable part of the larger Whole. In that precise sense, we are whole mates. From that place of connection to the larger Whole, we offer up our own transformation for the sake of the transformation of the Whole.

We commit to our love not only to fulfill ourselves but to strengthen Love. We participate in our own evolution for the sake of the evolution of love. It is through this larger shared intention and commitment that we begin to step out of our fragmented selves. We begin to feel and taste a connection to the larger Wholeness, in which we are full participants. In this, we become whole mates, partners in evolutionary relationship.

When you choose an evolutionary partner, there is a thrill and sensual attraction that runs much hotter than hormones and infatuation. You are attracted to your evolutionary partner because you can fulfill your most precious life dreams and purpose with them and through them in a way that you could not by yourself. What you are saying to your whole mate partner is: I can be *Me* better than I could ever be by myself through *Us* being *We* because together We see. That is the shared horizon that births evolutionary partnership. That is shared values and vision.

In an evolutionary relationship, you want to love and appreciate not just each other's good qualities or cuddly body (both of which are lovely). Rather, in an evolutionary relationship, you have a shared aesthetic of the

Good, the True, and the Beautiful that creates shared purpose. That is the third side to which both sides are committed. A shared evolutionary vision with your partner causes you to evolve and grow together, rather than devolve and grow apart.

If we were to create some new language around this, we might say: Whole mate evolutionary relationship is an emergent that sustains Eros because it is sourced in shared telos.

Eros is radical aliveness with purpose. Telos is purpose that is radically alive. Telos and Eros together create *Teleros*. Evolutionary relationships are telerotic partnerships. Whole mates live in a potency of polarity and attraction, which can last a lifetime.

Whole mates are not necessarily focused on *joining genes*. Whole mates are focused on *joining genius*, so that each beloved and their Unique Self, and their shared Unique We, can go the whole way in this lifetime in service of the Whole—emergent from the deeper whole within and in service to the larger whole of physical, social, and political reality.

This is not better than role mate relationship or merged role mate/soul mate relationships, whose primary context is often in service of family—birthing children, raising children, and transmitting values to the next generation (which is a noble and wondrous expression of role mate or role mate/soul mate at its best). It is a different context for relating, with different core values animating the relationship. For example, in the classical role mate relationship, the focus is on the birthing, raising, and educating of the children so that the children not only survive but thrive. In whole mate relationship, where there are sometimes no children, the focus is on birthing one's own highest realization of wholeness in service to the larger Whole.

These different forms of relationship often show up in different people. There are couples of all sorts, in romance, family, business, friendship, study, activism, and in myriad other contexts, that are primarily role mate, primarily soul mate, or primarily whole mate. These forms show up not only in different people but also in the same people at different stages in their relationship lives.

It is entirely possible—and wonderful—for a couple to begin as role mates, deepen into a role mate/soul mate relationship, and then, as the children grow up, deepen ever more into a whole mate relationship. Alternatively, at key points in their relationship, one couple may be embodying all three relational forms at the same time.

8. The Evolution of Wholeness from Role Mate to Soul Mate

At every stage—role mate, soul mate, and whole mate—*to be whole* means something different. In other words, what it means to be whole *evolves*. That is what we mean by the evolution of love and the evolution of consciousness: Our very conception of wholeness evolves and transforms.

At level one, role mate relationship, it is impossible to be whole by yourself. A man or woman can only access wholeness through each other. To continue to deploy the terms of our dear friend John Gray, Mars and Venus need to come together to create a constellation of wholeness.

This is true because masculine and feminine characteristics are understood as being very different from each other. Men are masculine and women are feminine. To have a complete whole of masculine and feminine, a man and woman need to join in union. This is expressed as sexual union and as role mate partnership. Men took on what were considered the more masculine roles of provider, protector, and breadwinner, while women took on the more feminine roles of nurturer, caretaker, and homemaker.

This creates a natural dependency between men and women. This dependency was considered the objective natural order of the Universe. Men are from Mars, women are from Venus, and that is the law of nature. No one ever asks at level one, Why do I need a man? Of course a woman needs a man. Of course a man needs a woman. The question of *why* does not even occur. Men and women are role mates. The natural wholeness of masculine and feminine, which creates a good life, comes from each gender playing their unique role and joining forces as role mates. Sexual polarity is a direct expression of the natural polarity of life. Just like in electromagnetic attraction, which is love at the unconscious level of particles, opposites attract each other. It is from the differential of roles that yearning, desire, and sexual polarity emerge. It is polarity that births passion and potency in a great role mate relationship.

At level two, soul mate relationship, the meaning and experience of wholeness begin to shift. For many at the soul mate level, the core Mars/Venus distinction remains in place, but there is a recognition that there is some Venus in men and some Mars in women. Being able to create some kind of internal balance between your Venus and Mars qualities, where you have access to both sides, is seen as great progress. This is the first intimation of a higher wholeness in yourself that is not accessible at the role mate level.

Men are still primarily rooted in classic Mars qualities, and women are still rooted in classic Venus qualities. However, the rigidity of roles begins to soften and expand. There is a clear shift from precise and predetermined roles to more fluidity of functions. Men begin to access some of their Venus qualities. Women begin to access some of their Mars qualities.

The distinction between the male brain and the female brain, as documented in extensive literature, is still valid.[58] There is still a core Mars

---

58 It is worth reading the excellent essay by David Linden, "Sexual Self," in Unique: The New Science of Human Individuality (2020), pp. 91–130, where he carefully reviews the literature on the classical distinctions between the male and female brain, the attempt to qualify those distinctions, the partial validity of those qualifications, and the affirmation of the core distinction. There is, of course, zero question that there are a multiple anatomical and molecular distinctions between men and women, even as there is zero doubt that these cannot and should not be used as distinctions that create any form of unjust differences between men and women in any dimension of human life. The literature also makes it quite clear that large swaths of men can express in ways more classically associated with the feminine and that large swaths of women can express in ways more classically associated as masculine. At the soul mate level, men and women work to balance those qualities. At the whole mate level, we no longer deploy the language of masculine and feminine. Rather, we borrow two terms from Luria, lines and circles, that refer to

matrix for men and a Venus matrix for women, but a new balance begins to appear. Each gender begins to do some significant cross-training. What leading edges of research have called *an intersex brain* begins to emerge.

The slogan for level two is balance and freedom. The essential split between Venus and Mars is challenged. There is a leveling of differences between men and women, with both sides accessing some balance of all the qualities. There is no longer a definitely strong sense of either masculine or feminine that identifies a person in an almost coercive fashion. People are human, and to be whole is to have achieved a balance between your masculine and feminine qualities. At the soul mate level, the question of *why I need a man* might well emerge:

- If I do not need a man to be a protector and provider because I can access those qualities in myself, then what good is a man?

- And if I do not need a woman for childbearing or sexuality, then why do I need a woman?

The answer, of course, is that there are many reasons that men and women need each other besides the classic role mate expectations.

For example, you might need a man to evoke your feminine. A man invites you to be a woman in a way that your own self-invitation does not arouse. You might need a man because the intimate, erotic experience of meeting a flesh-and-blood, breathing man is very different than accessing your inner masculine and balancing it with your feminine. You need a man to adore you in a way that your self-love can only approximate.

You might need a woman because the intimate, erotic experience of meeting a flesh-and-blood, breathing woman is very different than accessing your inner feminine and balancing it with your masculine. You

---

qualities of Cosmos, from the moments of the Big Bang, that, in many cultures, much later in evolutionary history, engendered as masculine and feminine. At the whole mate level, a synergy—not merely a balance—takes place between the classical line expressions (engendered masculine) and the classical circle expressions (engendered feminine), in which a new quality of what we have called Unique Gender emerges.

need a woman to hold you and mirror back to you that you are a good child of the Universe in a way that your inner feminine cannot easily do. You need a woman to nurture you in a way that your own self-care cannot begin to achieve. You need a woman to appreciate your goodness in a way that only she can. Obviously, these qualities can also be experienced in same-sex relationships.

At the level of soul mate relationship, however, the survival dependency, and therefore absolute necessity of a role mate partner to thrive, is rejected. Women do not want to depend on a man, and men do not want to depend on a woman, at least not in the old role mate manner of things. While the dependency does not disappear, it is at least softened and attenuated.

Women access their own masculine and become financially independent. Both men and women become more sexually independent. The combination of changing ethical codes, which embrace premarital sex and the birth control pill, allows for sex in many more contexts than only your married role mate. Choice replaces dependency.

Each side wants to feel at least somewhat whole by themselves. Each side wants to feel like they were able to choose their partner as their soul mate and not be forced by the invisible pressure of survival and social obligation to marry or partner with the appropriate role mate.

At the same time, in soul mate relationships, there is often a loss of passion because there is a loss of polarity. Both sides try and fulfill the categorical imperative of this level, which is choice and balance. Both sides access both their masculine and their feminine, and both sides choose each other for the sake of personal fulfillment. Man and woman (and other sexes) do not choose each other merely in order to complete each other in terms of survival and thriving through playing their respective roles. That is precisely the move from role mate to soul mate.

At level two, both man and woman are whole in and of themselves in the sense that they do not need each other in order to survive, but they can only achieve a level of fulfillment and joy together. However, man and woman want each other, so they freely choose each other. Dependency disappears. Need disappears. Balance, choice, and want for fulfillment rule:

Wholeness rests in me, at least psychologically. I do not need you to survive, and I am beginning to balance between my own natural masculine and feminine qualities. There is often a lot of confusion over whom to choose, but there is a new freedom. I do not need to choose you in order to survive.

This is very different from level one, role mate, where there is no wholeness at all by yourself. Balance is only possible in a couple. Need comes from necessity. Necessity, not choice, guides your selection of a partner. There is no real freedom, but there is a lot of clarity about whom to choose. You choose the best role mate.

It is not that there is no great love at the soul mate level. There is. But as we will show later, based on empirical information, soul mate love—purely by itself—without any role mate dimension at all—lacks a sufficiently compelling narrative to sustain the relationship. There comes a point when the relationship needs to move from looking deeply into each other's eyes to some vision of a shared horizon.

9. On the Meaning of "Whole" in Whole Mate Relationships

In a whole mate relationship, what it means to be whole evolves dramatically. Pretty much everything changes. An entirely new level of wholeness emerges in two primary ways, deeply entwined and even interdependent:

The relationship of our identity, intimacy, and service to the larger Whole. This is the first meaning of *whole* in "whole mate relationship."

The primary or original wholeness that each partner brings
into the relationship. This is the second meaning of *whole* in
"whole mate relationship."

There are at least three distinct ways that the whole in whole mates
refers to the original wholeness that the beloveds bring to the relationship:

- their realization of Self,

- their realization of the precise nature of their personal incarnation
  of the larger Field of Eros,

- and their unique personification of gender (which we refer to as
  Unique Gender).

In this section, we briefly describe each of these dimensions.

9.1. Whole Mates in Erotic Relationship to the Whole

Whole mates must devote a core dimension of their relationship to
something beyond themselves. Whole mates must say to each other:

We are doing our work of healing and holding each other not
just for each other, but for the sake of the larger Whole. We
love each other, not only for each other, but also for the sake
of the larger context. We are offering up our work—both in
our relationship and in the world—for the sake of the transformation of our families, communities, and society.

Whole mates ultimately must say:

We are offering up our relationship for the sake of the evolution of relationship itself.

Within the context of devoting one's relationship to the Whole, creating love, passion, and success becomes not only about personal fulfillment but also about acting in service and devotion to the love, passion, and success of the Whole.

The phrase *not only* that we deployed above is both precise and potent. The personal is not left behind in any sense, shape, or form. Whole mate transcends and includes soul mate. The whole mate relationship is ultimately intimate and personal—and all of that is in context of and offered into the larger Whole.

The larger Whole does not exclude personhood. The larger Whole is not, as it is often portrayed in myriad sources, the impersonal. Rather, it is the personal *beyond* the impersonal. The larger Whole is the larger Field of Consciousness, which includes the Infinity of Power even as it includes the Infinity of Intimacy. This is why, in CosmoErotic Humanism, the name we utter to evoke the Divine is *the Infinite Intimate*. The Name of God—the Whole—is the Infinite Intimate. To be a whole mate is to be a conscious expression of and in devotion to the Infinite Intimate.

The moment you act in service and devotion to a value beyond your relationship, you transition from soul mate to whole mate. This evolution changes everything. To engage actively in whole mate relationship is to participate in the larger evolution of consciousness. This is what it means to participate—through your love and devotion—in the evolution of love.

Said another way, the evolution of love and consciousness for everyone is pushed just a little bit forward when you and your whole mate evolve your own love and consciousness. Love and consciousness evolve in the lives of actual relationships.

It might seem wild that two individuals and their interpersonal relationship can impact the evolution of love for everyone. Think of it like this: Every action you and your partner take creates a pattern. That pattern ripples through the Universe and makes it just a bit more likely that other couples will repeat the pattern. Over time, the more a pattern is repeated, the more that pattern becomes a common and everyday expression for future couples.

For example, imagine that you and your partner have come up with a new way to have an argument. Instead of arguing for your point of view, both of you vehemently argue for the position that you think best integrates your point of view with your partner's. Let's say that you have been doing this for years, and it really works to help you both get past what would otherwise be intractable arguments. These actions ripple throughout the Universe, influencing the actions of couples everywhere. To be clear, we are not suggesting that other couples will behave in the exact same way as you, but because of your actions, the probability that couples will seek out more evolved ways of arguing will increase.

9.2 Wholeness through Realization of Unique Self and Evolutionary Unique Self

Role mate and soul mate relationship generally take place at the level of what we call separate self, or what has often been called ego self.[59] Separate-self experiences itself as a distinct part, with no ontological or essential relationship to the larger Whole. At the level of role mate relationship, the separate self makes a contract with another separate self to mutually fulfill their roles to ensure their mutual surviving and thriving. At the soul mate level, two separate selves mutually agree to include each other, including their feelings, wounding, and depth, as part of their newly chosen wholeness.

Whole mate emerges from a larger, more whole vision of Self. Whole mate is premised on the realization of *True Self*. True Self is the Field of Wholeness itself. It has also been called the Field of Consciousness. In CosmoErotic Humanism, we call it the Field of Eros, or the Field of Consciousness and Desire. At the level of consciousness that is True Self, one realizes that he or she is indivisible from the larger Whole. There is a softening of ego through contact with the Whole, or even through a fragrance of awareness of the Whole.

The experience of the True Self is twofold, however, as realized through the experiments of the interior sciences. On the one hand, the part realizes that it is indivisible from the larger Whole. On the other, the

---

59 We unpack this theme—the crucial correlation between separate self, True Self, and Unique Self to role mate, soul mate, and whole mate—in much more depth in Whole Mate. See also Sections 3.3–3.4 in Essay One.

part realizes that the larger Whole itself is indivisible from—and quite literally resides in—the part. True Self is the Singular that has no plural. In the scientific experiment that realizes True Self, I realize that I live in the Whole and that the Whole lives in me. In this precise sense, the one who has a fragrance of True Self Realization has access to a prior sense of Wholeness with which they enter the relationship.

The movement from separate self to True Self, however, is not the end of the story of human evolution. It is followed by the triumphant emergence of *Unique Self*. Unique Self is a unique expression of True Self Wholeness. Unique Self is the unique perspective, the unique set of eyes, of True Self, a unique quality of intimacy of every individuated expression of True Self. If True Self is the seamless coat of the Universe, Unique Self is the realization that the coat of the Universe is seamless but not featureless, and that you are its unique feature. If separate self is the realm of the personal or personality, and True Self is the impersonal beyond the personal, then Unique Self is the personal that emerges beyond the impersonal. Unique Self is the unique expression of the Infinite Personhood of Cosmos discretely expressed as you.

But unlike separateness, or separate self, which alienates us from the Whole, uniqueness is the currency of connection to the Whole. In True Self, we realize that the Whole is in the part.

Unique Self = True Self + unique perspective + unique quality of intimacy

Thus, in the experience of Unique Self, the Whole is present in the part. Paradoxically, the more you are in your irreducible uniqueness, the more clearly the Whole shows up in you. However, the part is not only connected to the Whole but is also in devotion, in service, to the Whole.

True Self is the realization that the part is a part of and needs the Whole. Unique Self deepens these early realizations into the knowing that the Whole needs the part. As Unique Self, you realize: I am an intended result of the Universe. The Universe intended my uniqueness.

An entirely novel dimension in the relation of the Self to the larger Whole emerges when the Unique Self realization deepens into the

Evolutionary Unique Self.

As Unique Self, you have unique gifts to give that address unique needs in your unique circle of intimacy and influence. Those unique gifts are the expression of your most fundamental identity, your Unique Self. At the level of Unique Self, you experience yourself as completing something in the Whole, as it shows up in your unique circles of intimacy and influence—something that cannot be completed by anyone else.

At the level of Evolutionary Unique Self, you become more connected to the larger Evolutionary Field of Being and Becoming. You realize that your gifts can be given by you and you alone, and they are profoundly needed and desired, not only by specific individuals in your circle of intimacy and influence but by All-That-Is. Your unique gift, however, not only *completes* the Whole but also *evolves* the Whole.

As Evolutionary Unique Self, you are the personal face of the evolutionary impulse. You are the personal face of the LoveIntelligence of evolution, what we call, in CosmoErotic Humanism, Evolutionary Love. Thus, your love not only completes but evolves the Whole.

In that sense, giving your unique gift is your unique obligation. Literally the same word as *love* in some Semitic languages, *obligation* refers to the unique Outrageous Acts of Love that can be committed by you and you alone. It does not matter what the mission is. It might be to start a soup kitchen, to raise a child, to excel at your chosen line of work, or to do the work of personal transformation. Whether giving your unique gifts happens to be public or private, it does not matter. Rather, the question is, what is your intention in giving your unique gift? If your intention is for the sake of the larger Whole, then you have entered—as Evolutionary Unique Self—into the consciousness of whole mate relationship.

Because Reality is relationship, it is virtually never the case that you can give your unique gift alone. Your partner therefore has the potential to become your whole mate. Your partner is in devotion not just to your mutual personal fulfillment but also to the fulfillment of the most epic and extraordinary view of your Self—your Unique Self and your Evolutionary Unique Self. Therefore, as a whole mate, living the wholeness of your Evolutionary Unique Self, you are filled with desire for a larger wholeness through powerful intimacy with your whole mate.

Your whole mate is devoted to the fulfillment of your Evolutionary Unique Self, or your whole mate might also be your partner in manifesting the *Unique We* of your shared Evolutionary Unique Selves. Either way, you join in evolutionary relationship with the intention that your unique life, love, and gifts are in service to the larger Whole. In this sense, your wholeness comes, at level three, from your relationship to the larger Whole, as it lives in you, and as you live in erotic relationship to it. The part yearns for the Whole, and the Whole longs for the part.

Your Unique Self, like a puzzle piece, is both whole unto itself and seeking a connection to the larger Whole. But it is more than that. Your unique quality of the Whole, your Unique Self, makes the Whole more Whole. This sense of ever-evolving Wholeness is a core truth of the interior sciences, in some sense inexplicable in words; words can stretch toward but not fully hold this paradox.

Whole mates in evolutionary relationships participate in the original Wholeness of Reality. Unique Self is the unique incarnation of True Self, the original Wholeness of Reality itself in person. True Self is the quality of original consciousness that many of the great traditions of the interior sciences referred to as the Divine. Divinity, in the interior sciences that ground CosmoErotic Humanism, is Wholeness desiring more Wholeness. At the inception of the manifest world, particularly at the level of evolved humanity, where the manifest in human form becomes ever-more conscious of its own identity, the original Wholeness becomes—paradoxically—more Whole. The evolved level of humanity is precisely what we have referred to as the movement from the level of separate self to the level of True Self, Unique Self, and Evolutionary Unique Self. More succinctly, this is the transformational movement from *Homo sapiens* to *Homo amor*.[60]

---

60 See Section 3.7 in Essay One.

9.3. The Field of Eros as the Field of Wholeness: From Ordinary Love to Outrageous Love

Role mate and soul mate, in the vast majority of the population, are expressions of separate self and ordinary love:

Separate self: I am a skin-encapsulated ego—a separate self.

Ordinary love: love as the social construct of these last few centuries.

That is utterly insufficient to be the ground of relationship. Whole mate, however, draws from a deeper source of wholeness, even as it is moving toward ever-greater wholeness. This deeper sense of wholeness is the quality of Eros, of what we call alternatively Outrageous Love or Evolutionary Love.

When I love as a whole mate, I am loving from inside—as an expression of—the Field of Eros, the Field of Outrageous Love and Desire. This is the Field of Wholeness itself. This is the Wholeness that David Bohm alluded to in his description of the implicate order.[61] It is the Wholeness that interior sciences across space and time, each in their own language, describe as the Name of God. They came to these descriptions based on their own direct experiments, which yielded direct experiences of its quality.

When I love as whole mate, with a love that consciously participates in the prior Wholeness of all of Reality reaching for its own ever-greater Wholeness,[62] I overcome my separateness. It is not that my separateness disappears, but my separateness lives in paradoxical uniqueness to our union. It is no longer my separateness, which is ultimate and cannot be overcome, but it becomes my uniqueness. I am in my uniqueness but not

---

61 David Bohm, Wholeness and the Implicate Order (2002).

62 On this paradox of wholeness, see Section 11 below. See also Your Unique Self: The Radical Path to Personal Enlightenment, by Marc Gafni (2012), pp. 127–150, and Radical Kabbalah, by Marc Gafni (2010), volume one, where this paradox of human participation in the Divine, which is paradoxically additive to the Divine, is the focus of much of the conversation in parts three through five.

in my separateness anymore. I am in my uniqueness and in union at the same time. My uniqueness both participates in and contains the original Wholeness, even as it makes that Wholeness ever more Whole. This is the paradoxical realization of CosmoErotic Humanism that lies at the core of the interior sciences of Hebrew wisdom, one of its main sources.

9.4. Unique Gender

The third dimension of prior wholeness in whole mate relationship emerges from the birth of *Unique Gender*. Some realization of one's own Unique Gender, at whatever level, is itself an original wholeness that the beloved brings to the relationship. Unique Gender is an expression of Unique Self. But Unique Gender is a consciousness of an entirely different order of power and potency than the balance between masculine and feminine that both sides attempt to achieve in a soul mate relationship. There is a realization that simply making lists of qualities that are ostensibly masculine and feminine does not work any longer. Any list of feminine qualities no longer can be accurately applied only to women. No list of masculine qualities can be accurately applied only to men.

At the level of Unique Gender, there is a realization that the core qualities that used to be applied to masculine and feminine are indeed accurate expressions of a true ground ontology[63] in the nature of the masculine and feminine.[64] London is primarily masculine, and Bali is primarily feminine. London has a different quality from Bali. Receptivity is different from penetration. Autonomy, or independence, is different from communion. However, these qualities can no longer be fairly or accurately described by the words *masculine* and *feminine*. Based on the

---

63 By using the term ground ontology, we mean to convey that some dimensions of these qualities of masculine and feminine are intrinsically real. However, they are not immutable. Rather, they are an intrinsic part of the ground of personhood for most men and women. However, that ground evolves and expresses itself uniquely in every human being. For in every human being, a unique synergy emerges between their original ground qualities, which, although primarily masculine or feminine, also already contain, even in the ground, some dimension of both.

64 See Section 8.

interior sciences of the wisdom of Solomon lineage, we have called these qualities *lines* and *circles*.[65] The lines and circles qualities already exist in Reality in the first nanoseconds after the Big Bang. They are known in science as attraction and repulsion. These same phenomenological qualities have also been referred to as autonomy and communion, or allurement and autonomy.

In popular culture, line qualities used to be exclusively associated with the masculine and men, while circle qualities were exclusively associated with the feminine and women. Now we realize that these two qualities of Reality show up fully in both men and women. Many men are rooted more primarily in line qualities, and many women are rooted more primarily in circle qualities. But there are also many men who do not identify more readily with line qualities, and many women who do not identify more readily with circle qualities. Moreover, every human being has a deeper identity than their gender. And as we noted above, Unique Gender is part of the unique erotic quality of one's Unique Self.

This is the powerful intuition of the transgender, sometimes called the gender queer movement: Your identity is not reducible to your gender. You are something more essential, beneath and beyond your being a boy or a girl. The weakness of the transgender or gender queer intuition is that while your gender identity is rejected as being nonessential, no deeper sense of identity is offered in its place. In the consciousness beyond Venus and Mars, emergent from the best integration of leading-edge thought in the world today, that glaring weakness in the transgender invitation is corrected. You do have a deeper identity than gender. That deeper identity is your Unique Self.

Every human being is a Unique Self, a unique expression of Reality, in terms of their physical anatomy, cellular structure, and interior consciousness. This uniqueness is not an accident but the intention of evolution. Evolution moved through countless levels of emergence, for over 13.7 billion years, in order to produce the Unique Self that is you. You are irreducibly original at every level of your exterior form, your cellular, atomic, and organic structure, and your interior quality and taste.

---

65 On lines and circles, see also Section III.1 in part two.

One expression of your Unique Self is the unique combination and integration of line and circle qualities that make up you. That is your Unique Gender. Unique Gender constitutes a Unique Wholeness. When the beloved comes to the relationship from the place of incarnating their own Unique Gender, they bring a primary wholeness to the relationship.

Now here is the key:

Your Unique Gender is not neutral or weak in their masculine or feminine identity, as soul mates often are. It does not lack distinction. Rather, your Unique Gender is powerfully masculine, powerfully feminine, and powerfully hermaphroditic. It is powerful in whatever form your Unique Gender expression is. Or, said more accurately: Your Unique Gender is beyond old categories of masculine and feminine, beyond Venus and Mars. Your Unique Gender is the unique combination, integration, and texture of all your line and circle qualities. Your lines and circles, in the unique combination that is an expression of your Unique Self, form your Unique Gender.

Your Unique Gender is powerful, distinct, and distinguished. There is nothing anemic, weak, or neutral about it at all. In this sense, your Unique Gender is not some sort of balance between your masculine and feminine. Rather, your Unique Gender is a new emergent that is beyond Venus and Mars—beyond He and She. It is a new emergent that never existed before. It is the new emergent of your unique integration of lines and circles. In this precise and potent sense, your Unique Self is sharply distinguished and distinct. Because of that, it creates polarity with other Unique Genders.

The true martial artist is a great image of Unique Gender. He or she is powerful, fast, and wields deadly force in their blows. At the same time, the true martial artist is graceful, gracious, kind, and surrendered to the larger life force that moves through them. Movies like *Crouching Tiger, Hidden Dragon* capture this vision of Unique Gender, which is the highest expression of martial arts. Other figures of the feminine in the movies of the last decades capture Unique Gender as well. One powerful Unique Gender woman is Katniss Everdeen, the character portrayed by Jennifer Lawrence in the Hunger Games trilogy. She is powerful, fast, and deadly as a warrior. She is beautiful, evocative, and inspiring as a woman. She is neither line nor circle. She is a seamless integration of both lines and circles and can be reduced to neither. In the Hunger Games, she nurtures, and she kills, and she does both equally well. The last scene of the third movie has Katniss holding her baby, but just several short movie minutes earlier, she strides into the main square dressed in leather, assigned to execute an evil leader. There is no dissonance between the two scenes. Katniss is Unique Gender.

At the *He and She* or *Venus and Mars* level of relationship, the polarity that creates attraction is between masculine and feminine. Therefore, role mate relationships tend to have somewhat more polarity than soul mate relationships, because there is more distinction in roles, more differentiation, and thus more polarity. Polarity at this level is based on the model of electromagnetic attraction: Opposites attract and complete each other, creating a larger whole. In this precise sense, there is a dimension of passion and potency that is lost at the soul mate level of relationship, because there is a loss of polarity. There is less polarity because each side has some general sense of having access to some balance of their masculine and feminine. This is true for both men and women, so the sharp distinction between masculine and feminine is neutralized.

But in the whole mate relationship, polarity is restored, because Unique Gender generates a sharply unique expression of life force. This unique expression is in polarity with other Unique Genders, which generates allurement or attraction. The attraction or allurement between two Unique Genders is that same attraction that joins two puzzle pieces. The puzzle pieces are both like each other and different from each other. They complete each other because their differences fit into a larger Whole, even as each puzzle piece is also independent from the other puzzle pieces. There is unique attraction, or unique polarity, between two highly distinct Unique Genders, needing each other to complete each other, even as each is whole unto him- or herself.

To summarize:

1. Level one, role mate: a clear man-woman distinction (different roles). The attraction is between the polarity of those two. Together, they become whole.

2. Level two, soul mate: Formal role mate distinctions fall away, and men and women want to feel like they have a balance to their masculine and feminine qualities. We have leveled intrinsic differences, and now, each side has access to all the qualities. In that sense, they do not necessarily need each other. The goal for each partner is to independently create balance between their masculine and feminine. But nothing new emerges. Level two all too often simply created weak androgyny.

3. Level three, whole mate is a momentous evolutionary leap. It's not just soul mate balancing, but Unique Gender. Each partner is a Unique Self, and an expression of that Unique Self is Unique Gender—their own unique integration of lines and circles. Every Unique Gender is a unique evolutionary emergent. Polarity between you and me is not the same as the old, level-one polarity. It is polarity between two Unique Gender whole mates.

10. The Tragedy of Soul Mates

10.1. From Pre-Tragic to Tragic to Post-Tragic

There are three primary levels of consciousness through whose prisms we experience our lives. We will call these three levels the *pre-tragic*, *tragic*, and *post-tragic*.

At the pre-tragic level, life is good. Life is delightful. Life makes sense. It is ordered and reasonable. Life is clear. Certainty is the life mood of the pre-tragic. Although we experience pain and suffering, yet they are not tragic. We can explain to ourselves and our intimates what happened. We might use religious, psychological, or scientific explanations. Explanation saves our suffering from being tragic. The key dimension of the pre-tragic is clarity.

Let's take two examples that are central to virtually every human being's concerns: suffering or pain, and sexing.

For example, a fundamentalist may live a pre-tragic life because their religion offers a road map to life that claims to explain all of Reality with absolute clarity and certainty. When suffering occurs, the fundamentalist knows exactly why—and generally it has something to do with sin, or a failure to have proper faith or belief.

At the same time, a reductionist materialist, who says that the world has no meaning at all but is rather an expression of randomness and chance, is also pre-tragic, because for them, all is clear as well. Suffering happens simply because the world is random and without meaning. So why shouldn't there be suffering?

Pre-tragic sexuality would include both a premodern, sex-negative narrative (sex is sinful and destructive) and the classical modern, sex-neutral narrative (sex is simply biology, no different than eating lunch). Both avoid the complexity of sexing. They are both perfectly clear. Two opposite positions can be both pre-tragic. Both sex negative and sex neutral—reductionist materialist nihilism as well as religious fundamentalism—are pre-tragic. So was the postmodern, flower-power, sex-positive stance of the sixties.

The second level of consciousness is the tragic. The goodness of life is broken up by suffering, but we no longer feel able to explain it. Perhaps the suffering is more intense than any we have experienced before. Alternatively, our trust in the religions or philosophies of life that undergirded our explanations has been shaken—often irrevocably.

Or, in relationship to our second example, we no longer have a story equal to our sexing. The rules break down. We lose access to our clarity. Our certainties are shattered or merely slip away. Ennui and murkiness displace the aliveness that seemed bound up with our clarities. Our lives feel at best unmoored; our suffering and sexing, once untethered, do not feel free but rather gradually devolve to feeling empty and meaningless. Our lives become, as Faulkner calls it, sound and fury,[66] echoing Shakespeare:

---

66 The Sound and the Fury is a novel by the American author William Faulkner.

It is a tale
Told by an idiot, full of sound and fury,
Signifying nothing.[67]

We are overwhelmed or simply deadened by the tragic nature of life itself. We may continue to function, love, and even be highly effective achievers. But our joy mechanism is broken. We are cut off from the essential goodness and primal aliveness of life. There is no clarity. Uncertainty and confusion are the life mood of the tragic.

Most people live their lives at either level one or level two of consciousness, the pre-tragic and the tragic. Some people move from level one to level two as a result of losing trust in life, usually occasioned by a personal tragedy. Others move from pre-tragic to tragic because they witness the virtually unbearable suffering in the world. In the realm of the sexual, the move generally happens because the old vision of sex negative violates the goodness of the sexual that seems almost self-evident—even as the sexual causes untold pain, tearing apart lives and hearts. In other words, we lack a story of the sexual equal to our experience of the sexual.

Still many others move from pre-tragic to tragic because new information from the sciences shatters their trust in the pre-tragic maps of the traditional wisdom systems. For example, when autopsies reveal that the number of bones in the human body is different than the number claimed by doctors invested in church dogma, our trust in the church sustains a blow from which it does not easily recover. The tragic emerges when the old laws, principles, and values that used to make sense of the world no longer seem sensible. Clarity succumbs to murkiness or even nihilistic intimations. Certainty, and the trust born from it, are broken.

Some individuals, after shifting to tragic consciousness, eventually revert to pre-tragic, either because they find some new, comforting explanation for their suffering based on a superficial reworking of their old beliefs, or because they simply forget their experience of tragedy and fall back into their prior pre-tragic state.

But there is a third level that is available at the leading edge of

---

67 William Shakespeare, Macbeth, act 5, scene 5, lines 29–31.

consciousness. We call this level *post-tragic*. In the post-tragic, a new level of clarity comes online. It is not a dogmatic clarity or certainty. On the one hand, new life models give us access to new depth, which evokes a certainty about the fundamental goodness of our own being and of Reality itself. At the same time, we embrace, from a deeper level of our consciousness, the absolute mystery of Reality.

We experience the ecstasy of true gnosis—based not on dogma but on our direct experience. We embrace the certainty that life matters, that our choices are significant, that Reality is meaningful, even when that meaning is not fully accessible, and even as we gain a new capacity to dance in joy within the uncertainty. We live in the certainty of our own deeper truth, even as we live in the cloud of unknowing, refusing to resolve the mystery and the pain of our confusion with articles of faith that violate our deeper sense of self and life.

Here, at the level of the post-tragic, the person or culture participates in the elemental joy of living once again. This happens when the individual or culture directly reconnects—gains direct access to the core Eros and aliveness of Reality.

In this post-tragic move beyond the complexity of Reality, a second simplicity emerges. There is a new clarity that wells up from second simplicity. It is not the first simplicity of dogma, be it materialist or religious, but rather the second simplicity on the other side of complexity that includes and transcends the complexity—in a direct realization that we live and participate in a Field of Value, that everything matters, and that no joy and no tear is insignificant.

We step beyond *the pain of our guilty feet that have got no rhythm*[68]—and feel not the naïve innocence of the baby but the second innocence of the rebirthed. We cast out the dogmas of secular reductionism and mendacious fundamentalism and re-embrace the tender and fierce joy of our aliveness.

In "A Dialogue of Self and Soul," Yeats wrote of this third level, post-tragic consciousness, in the understated but raw Eros of his verse, which ends with:

---

68 "Careless Whisper" by George Michael.

When such as I cast out remorse
So great a sweetness flows into the breast
We must laugh and we must sing,
We are blest by everything,
Everything we look upon is blest.

What causes the emergence of this third level of consciousness is always the deepening into emotional maturity or wisdom. Part of it may come from in-depth work that the person has done with his or her own wounds. Another part comes from the maturity of letting go. Often, the source is the evolution of a more poignant and potent worldview.

The evolution of consciousness virtually always includes deeper answers to the three questions—*Who? Where?* and *What?*—three great inquiries of CosmoErotic Humanism we explored in Essay One:

- Who are you? Who are we?

- Where are we?

- What do we desire, or what do we want?

In other words, it emerges from a deeper and better narrative of identity, from a deeper and better Universe Story, as well as from deeper and better narratives of desire and power. By *deeper* and *better* we mean narratives that integrate more validated information from the interior and exterior sciences, drawn from all the premodern, modern, and postmodern wisdom streams, synergized into a larger Whole—a deeper and better story of our lives. All these together generate the post-tragic experience of Reality.

Concurrently, as we already implied above, the post-tragic comes from an inherent deepening in the first-person experience of life. It is that deeper first-person experience itself—what is often referred to as wisdom or spiritual maturity—which opens us to ever-wider and deeper stories—Universe Stories, narratives of identity, desire, and power, which respond in better, in more true, good, and beautiful ways, to the primary questions of Who? Where? and What?

To recapitulate: The post-tragic experience of life always comes from some process of joyful deepening. Joy is different from the more superficial happiness. Joy includes and transcends the tragic. We hold the tragic, we cry the tragic, and we laugh the tragic. And we can dance, and we can sing, we are blest by everything, and everything we look upon is blest.

10.2. She Comes in Threes:
The Pre-Tragic, Tragic, and Post-Tragic
in Role Mate, Soul Mate, and Whole Mate

Both the role mate, soul mate, and whole mate trinity and the pre-tragic, tragic, and post-tragic trinity are expressions of a deeper tectonic plate of Reality, which, in CosmoErotic Humanism, we call *trialectics*, or *She comes in threes*. Virtually all its expressions describe the same general core structure of Cosmos through their own unique prism. Many of the expressions of *She comes in threes* can be overlaid on each other and seen as different-angle descriptions of the same phenomenon. For example, first simplicity and second simplicity, with complexity in the middle, are roughly (but not precisely) analogous to first innocence and second innocence, with guilt in the middle.

They are not always isomorphic, they are not always expressions of the precisely same phenomenology, but they always intersect. For example, one might experience pre-tragic, tragic, and post-tragic versions of role mate, soul mate, and whole mate. In other words, there is a pre-tragic, a tragic, and a post-tragic experience of role mate. The same can be said for soul mate and whole mate. But we are rather interested in describing a clear vector, where the two trinities do overlay on each other, deepening our understanding of these three stages of relationship and catalyzing our evolution to whole mate relationship—for the sake of the evolution of intimacy, which responds potently to the meta-crisis. In this potent vector, **role mate is pre-tragic, soul mate is tragic, and it is only whole mate that begins to open the space of the post-tragic.**

You may be surprised to see soul mate, the ostensible holy grail of modernity and postmodernity, being cast as tragic. But that is, in fact, the explosive crux of the entire matter.

Role mate relationship, rooted in role mate consciousness, as it has appeared in history and in large sectors of the population as the dominant relational structure, is pre-tragic. It is pre-tragic not in the sense of being easy or even always joyful. Nor is it pre-tragic in the sense of being the right model of relationship for everyone—before things crash into the tragic. Rather, it is pre-tragic in the sense of being *clear*. In role mate consciousness, the roles are clear. Both sides need each other. There is a form of absolute dependency. Neither side can survive or thrive without the other.

Moreover, these respective roles are divided between masculine and feminine, understood predominantly as men and women. And masculine and feminine are understood, in role mate consciousness, to be the absolute nature of things (not without an intrinsic biological foundation). There is a sense of mutuality of need and dependency at the role mate level that does not spell tragic. Role mates are pre-tragic because they are in clarity. The roles are clearly mandated and, at least from one reality perspective, self-evidently appropriate. The question of why a man needs a woman, or why a woman needs a man, simply does not make sense from the perspective of role mate consciousness. Of course men and women need each other.

The move from role mate to soul mate is a profound evolution of consciousness. The personal conversation deepens, the personal intimacy deepens—feeling each other's feelings, knowing each other's wounding and trauma, being far more attuned to each other's desires, looking deeply in each other's eyes. In a very real, beautiful, and wondrous sense, this is a deepening of the Good, the True, and the Beautiful, which is an evolution of consciousness and love.

And yet there is more than a trace of a deeper fragrance to soul mate consciousness—the fragrance of the tragic. This whiff of the tragic in the scent of soul mate relationships catches us by surprise. Expecting to be perfumed by joy, we are often more than shocked to feel choked for air by the often-harsh odor of soul mate scents.

There is a trinity of void that lies at the center of the whiff of the tragic that animates soul mate relationship. The trinity is formed by:

- the nature of self that is at play in relationship,

- the experience of location and participation—or nonlocation and nonparticipation—in the larger Field of Value, and

- the nature or quality of the love that is at play in the relationship.

It is worth noting our resistance to this possibility at the outset. We are daring to speak heresy. But like all true heretics, we dare speak these words for the sake of a deeper love. In our call to evolve beyond the primacy of the exclusively soul mate quality of relationship, we do not lose access to the wonder of soul mate relationship. Rather, the new level of relationship, whole mate, includes that wonder of soul mate relationship even as it transcends it for a more wondrous, deeper, and more erotic, intimate level of loving.

Let's engage each dimension of the trinity to trace the fragrance of the tragic to its root.

First, we turn to the nature or quality of love at play in the consciousness of most soul mate relationships. This quality of love is what we refer to as *ordinary love*. It is at once real and yet is understood to be—in the social story deeply embedded in our hearts by cultural and psychological conditioning—as mere human sentiment. In other words, ordinary love is what postmodernity explicitly calls a social construct, a fiction, or a figment of our imagination. We say *I love you*, but we are no longer sure what it really means, to whom it applies, or what is its deeper source or ground. We have alienated our love from the heart of existence itself.

Secondly, in most soul mate relationships, the selves of the beloveds are at the level of separate-self consciousness. To be a separate self is related to the third aspect of the trinity—living outside, not participating in—the Field of Value. The separate-self consciousness underpinning most soul mate relationships is usually there either because it is a postmodern soul mate relationship, which, by and large, denies that there is a Field of Value, or, in a premodern (traditional) or even modern soul mate relationship, the human being seems to be a creation of an infinite force that lives outside the created world. In other words, value is commanded, by Source or God, to human beings, who are obligated to fulfill the demands of value but do not directly participate in the Field of Value and therefore do not participate in its evolution.[69]

Classical soul mate consciousness is thus rooted in a separate-self experience of ordinary love, alienated from any experience of an intrinsic Field of Value. It is worth noting that soul mates will often talk about *eternal love*, a borrowed phrase to give their love more depth and gravitas. But this loan of love does not ultimately hold. The loan is called in and found to be bankrupt by most moderns living in open society, because there is no new human Story of Eros and Value in which to locate our experience.

Moreover, the emergence of soul mate consciousness, particularly when it doesn't include a dimension of the prior role mate consciousness, is related to dissolution of the interdependence of the needs to survive and thrive. The core idea is that a woman does not need a man to survive or thrive or to be socially received and recognized. And a man does not need a woman to survive or thrive—or to be socially received or recognized, for that matter. Each beloved desires to have the capacity to support themselves and to pursue their own fulfillment—to survive, thrive, and be socially received and recognized outside their relational devotions. The soul mate relationship therefore becomes another form of fulfillment but is no longer necessary for survival, for thriving, or for social acceptance.

---

69 The sense that value is eternal but never evolving—and imposed on the human being from a source alienated from our very humanity, even if that source is a creator outside of human reality—violates our sense of a good Universe. In the same way, however, the sense that value is purely contrived—just a social human construct, a figment of our imagination—violates our sense of Reality. Either side of this polarity violates our sense of the true nature of Reality. Our deeper sense of Reality is not polarized but paradoxical. We feel that value is intrinsic—real and eternal (eternal in the sense of being beneath space and time)—and yet at the same time, we understand that Reality evolves, and that value evolves with it. We know that the ethics of the kings of England, for example—expressed in the way they treated both their wives and the common folks—are reprehensible by any modern and postmodern standard of value. We know that universal human rights as the right ideal (which did not exist in any real way at the center of the traditional world is an evolution of value, an evolution of consciousness that is real and sacred. Such an evolution is premised on the realization that the human being participates in the Field of Value. See First Principles and First Values.

This is facilitated by a multitude of factors, which include new visions of sexuality; the birth control pill, which disconnects sex and children; changing social mores around having children (bearing and raising children is no longer a social imperative); evolving values and visions around the nature of masculinity and femininity; women surpassing men, in many societies, in most fields of education and in many fields of employment in the marketplace.[70] The intrinsic Eros and value of the mutuality of needs has thus disappeared—at least as the primary factor in the relational play between the sexes.

Since there is no larger Field of Eros in which to locate the soul mate experience, the result is a love that cannot ground itself, a love that cannot *source* itself. The shared purpose of personal fulfillment is simply insufficient when it is decontextualized from a larger shared Field of intrinsic Value and Meaning, including the value and meaning of Eros itself. Love cannot be erotic when it does not participate in the larger Field of Eros.

When there is no Eros, then only pseudo-eros remains. The entire focus of the relationship then shifts to wounding and trauma, indeed the realm of the tragic. But the tragic, at its core, is not the wounding and trauma. In the context of *trialectics* of pre-tragic, tragic, and post-tragic, the tragic is the experience of stepping out of the Tao—the Field of Value, Meaning, and Eros, the Field in which Eros itself is a value, in which love is the Outrageous Love that is not mere human sentiment but the heart of existence itself, and our human love stories are not social constructs but chapters and verses in the Universe: A Love Story. The naked experience of soul mate consciousness, after the early stages of infatuation wear off, evokes the image of the emperor who has no clothes. We feel a Love that is Real, but we cannot ground it in a larger Field. There is a hidden emptiness to our love when it does not participate in the larger Field of Eros, Meaning, and Value. There is a tragic emptiness to our devotion when it does not participate in the larger Field of Devotion. The beloveds become egocentric—not in the way of a healthy ego but in a self-indulgent and self-absorbed sort of way, and this empties the relationship of Eros.

In some sense, the soul mate relationship has become a trinket or

---

70 See Section 2.

trophy of a world whose primary story is the rivalrous conflict governed by win/lose metrics. We seek to augment that story with a sense of personal fulfillment—the soul mate story or the romantic story in its many permutations. But as the poet T. S. Eliot wrote long ago, there is an emptiness to the prostrations of soul mate love. His poem "The Hollow Men" points to the emptiness of our prostrations of love when alienated from the larger Field of Eros.

We are the hollow men
We are the stuffed men
Leaning together
Headpiece filled with straw. Alas!
Our dried voices, when
We whisper together
Are quiet and meaningless . . .
Shape without form, shade without colour,
Paralysed force, gesture without motion; . . .
Waking alone
At the hour when we are
Trembling with tenderness
Lips that would kiss . . .
In this last of meeting places
We grope together
And avoid speech . . .
Between the desire
And the spasm
Between the potency
And the existence
Between the essence
And the descent
Falls the Shadow . . .
This is the way the world ends
Not with a bang but a whimper.[71]

71 T.S. Eliot, "The Hollow Men."

The attempt to articulate personal fulfillment as the goal of human life, even as we empty the Field of Meaning of its intrinsic fullness, is not only the tragic nature of personal soul mate consciousness.[72] The potency is lost. The lips that would kiss, trembling with tenderness, walk alone. In the words of William Butler Yeats, the center cannot hold:[73]

> *Turning and turning in the widening gyre*
> *The falcon cannot hear the falconer;*
> *Things fall apart; the centre cannot hold.*

10.3. The Tragic Nature of Our Choosing

At the level of role mate relationship, the clarity of need owns the day. The self-evident desire—the instinctive need to succeed, to survive, to thrive, at least in some sense—bonds the role mates to each other in a clarity that is not easy but is very much pre-tragic. *I need you* is a very clear reason to be together, and there is a great, self-evident dignity in that.

If role mates say *I need you*, the apparent evolution of consciousness that is soul mate is the move to *I choose you*. It is not that *I need you* disappears entirely. The soul mates feel like they need each other for

---

72 It is also a stale fragrance emitted by the social engineers who dominate so much of the global discourse at this crucial juncture of civilization. We have written in another context about the motivational architecture of cyber-totalitarianism, which we have called TechnoFeudalism, all expressions of the planetary stack and tech plex (see section 1.4 in Essay One). Much more than governance, philosophy, or religion, this has invaded the texture of the everyday human life. There is a constant refrain that talks about a new utopia, in which humans have an enormous amount of leisure time to fill with their creative projects, art, and other fulfillments of their heart's desires. These pronunciations are a part of the utopian promise of the rapidly emergent architecture of ever-expanding, invisible digital dictatorships. But they are not compelling. Indeed, they are not only bland, but they also carry the scent of the ominous. One is reminded of Aldous Huxley's soma, the placating happiness drug that sedates the population to barely notice its loss of meaning, freedom, value, and dignity. It hijacks the beauty of soul mate consciousness as part of its medicinal effect. But love without grounding in the larger field of Eros, Meaning, and Value ultimately turns us into the hollow men and the stuffed men.

73 William Butler Yeats, "The Second Coming."

emotional fulfillment, to ameliorate loneliness, and to share their traumas, life wounds, and stories. But the visceral need of the other to play a structural role in the very core of my surviving, thriving, and core social acceptance fades into the background or disappears entirely. Instead, there is a sense of choosing. This choosing is not present in the same sense in role mates, which were generally orchestrated by social, cultural, ethnic, religious norms, coupled of course with political and economic factors. In soul mate, at least in the way that we tell the story, choice—*I choose you*—is at the very center of the soul mate relationship.

For the role mate, need—*I need you*—is the center of gravity.

For the soul mate, choice—*I choose you*—is the center of gravity.

But the paradox is that we are paralyzed in our attempts to choose. Who do we choose and why? Is it about the truth that we both like Italian food and dancing? Or do we live in a shared Field of Value? Are we in devotion to an Eros and ethos larger than our personal fulfillment mantras?

When the Eros of role mate disappears from the relationship, and in absence of any larger framework to respond to, or at least engage, these ultimate questions, the soul mate relationship not only loses its potency but becomes paradoxically tragic.

We ask: What is the right cause for our choice?

We do not really know. At the level of soul mate, it is all about choice, but the choice has no ground. We say *I love you* but cannot access the Field of Meaning that grounds and aligns our choices in the true nature of Reality itself.

We feel—based on the stories we live in—that our choice is not grounded in the Tao. Our choice has no North Star by which to orient. As such, it is almost impossible to make the right choices, or to feel that the choices ultimately matter.

Choice breathes its dignity—and even its nobility—into us when it is grounded in the wider Field of Value. But when Eros is not a value, then choice has no ground. For choice itself is then no longer a value grounded in the Field of Value. Then, *I choose you* becomes flaccid, fatuous, and confused instead of noble, rapturous, and dignified.

Moreover, we are told by those who reject the Field of Value that choice is not only not a value but an illusion. You think you chose your beloved, we are told, but in reality there were invisible fields of cultural, social, and psychological conditioning that cast your choices in stone before you ever knew what you would choose. Dozens of relationship books are devoted to explaining that our choice of our primary beloved is entirely a function of our early attachment style. They say it has little or nothing to do with any real, conscious, and present choice.

While these voices are partially correct—antecedent cause does impact our choices—we know anthro-ontologically[74] that there is a dimension of the human being that is free. A human being can rise beyond and feel below the field of necessity and causation—and choose, at key moments, with some genuine degree of freedom. That is why being an awake human is connected to being free.

That is why, when personal fulfillment is no longer accessible, we quickly exit our soul mate relationship. We unchoose our choices because we sense that the choices never had ground and gravitas to begin with. Our soul mate relationships have become largely tragic, even as they lose both their potency and passion. We have lost the polarity of authentic need and no longer feel the truth, gravitas, or compelling nature of our own confused choices, if indeed they were choices at all.

In a world in which we have killed all the gods except Aphrodite, to challenge the soul mate relationship borders on heresy or even blasphemy. But we have forgotten how to worship at her altar. Moreover, since we are alienated from the Field of intrinsic Value, Eros itself is no longer Goddess. Like all gods and goddesses, we think Aphrodite to be a mere figment of our imagination.

But we have forgotten that our imagination itself is a figment of God.

---

74 Anthro-ontology is a new field of thought, a methodology, that we have delineated and named as one of the key pillars of CosmoErotic Humanism. It is the notion that clarified human interiors disclose some of the interior faces of the Cosmos. The Anthro-Ontological Method is a core method of radical empiricism, the capacity to know something about Reality, whether we are talking about the nature of the exterior structure of Reality (the First Principles and First Values that guide the physical world, like the values in a mathematics equation describing that exterior world) or something of the nature of Reality's inner value structures—the First Principles and First Values that animate the interior face of Cosmos, like the value of values, including Eros, intimacy, love, goodness, truth, and beauty.

10.4. Whole Mate: I Choose to Need You

There are only two ways to redeem soul mate relationship: to include a role mate dimension, or to evolve to whole mate relationship that includes and transcends both (so that both role mate and soul mate consciousness are redeemed).

Whole mate consciousness is, at its core, a higher level of role mate consciousness, in the sense that it exists in service to a larger Field—a shared purpose. Role mates are in service to the survival and thriving of their family. Whole mates are in service to the larger Whole. The core of whole mate consciousness is the sense of not rooting the relationship in looking deeply into each other's eyes but rather in looking at a shared horizon.

Whole mates both participate in the larger Field of Eros and Wholeness and are in service to the larger Field—to the larger Whole. This may mean the radical support the beloveds give to each other in realizing their Unique Self and Evolutionary Unique Self and in giving their gift to the larger Whole. The beloveds tune and resonate with each other, playing their instruments in the Unique Self Symphony, contributing to the music and melody—the needs of the Whole.

A whole mate relationship may also express itself as a shared gift—given from the space between the beloveds—the unique Evolutionary We Space, the unique Evolutionary Intimacy, from which they give their gift.

If there is a larger Field of Eros that is even implicitly realized between the beloveds, they can access the realization that their love participates in that Field of Eros. They can intend their love for the sake of the larger Field, which can either strengthen it or weaken it.

In all three of these scenarios, and myriad others, whole mates are evolutionary partners for the sake of the Whole.

In role mate, the Field is one's service and devotion to one's immediate circle of biological family with perhaps a few close friends. In whole mate, the larger Whole is wider and deeper than the circle of friends that also happen to contribute to one's survival and thriving. Both beloveds have at least the fragrance of an omni-considerate relationship to the larger Whole.

At the level of role mate, the partners say to one another, *I need you.*

At the level of soul mate, the beloveds say to one another, *I choose you*—but the choice is not grounded in the Tao, so it is almost impossible to make the right choices or to feel that the choices ultimately matter.

At the whole mate level—which includes role mate and soul mate—we move from the *I need you* of role mate, to the *I choose you* of soul mate, to the *I choose to need you* of whole mate. *I choose to need you* reclaims the dignity of need and the dignity of choice. This is not a separate self, choosing in the context of the social construct of ordinary love, outside of any realization of the Field of Value. This is Unique Self and Evolutionary Unique Self, choosing to need as an irreducibly unique expression of the very Field of Value, the Field of Eros, the Field of LoveDesire, LoveBeauty, and LoveIntelligence. On the one hand, I am sovereign and whole within myself. At the very same time, I experience a profound need, a potent desire for ever-deeper and wider intimacies. I desire a relationship with you. I come to that relationship whole—even as, through the relationship, I become more whole. That is the very essence of the whole mate relationship.

11. Wholeness Becoming More Whole

The model for wholeness becoming more whole—or *I choose to need you*—is the very core of the interior sciences.

The Infinite Divine manifests Reality.

Why? Why does the Infinite, Perfect Divine, who is in Her (or its) very nature utterly Whole, choose to manifest Reality and—for the interior sciences—to need Reality?

This is the great question of the philosophers through the ages. In the words of the great German theorists Fichte and Schelling: *Why is there something rather than nothing?*

In the hidden architecture that addresses its own coded nomenclature, these kinds of profound questions of mystery and realization are often called the Names of God.

In CosmoErotic Humanism—a New Story of Value in response to the meta-crisis—we have tenderly and fiercely integrated the leading-edge realizations of the interior sciences into a new Name of God that Reality has whispered in our ear. It captures the deepest integration of the interior and exterior sciences—and that is what the Name of God must do in every generation. This new name is the Infinite Intimate.

Divine Infinity, which is Ultimate Wholeness by nature, desires Intimacy. In the realization of the interior sciences, there is a way in which the Divine becomes more Whole through that new Intimacy. Indeed, Divinity is realized to become more Whole not only through the manifest world as a whole but through contact and realized union with every irreducibly unique expression of the Divine. Every Unique Self—the unique eyes, perspectives, and qualities of intimacy of True Self—is a unique expression of the Field of Wholeness.

What the Infinite Intimate says to humanity—in the deepest realization of CosmoErotic Humanism, emergent from the deepest integration of the interior sciences—is not *I need you*, and not *I choose you*, but rather: *I choose to need you.*

There is a set of anthro-ontological experiments performed by the interior sciences that discloses this set of realizations. It is called *Sod HaTzimtzum*—the mystery of Divine Kenosis. *Kenosis* means emptying out. The Infinite Intimate, which is Whole, steps back, gives itself—Her/Himself—permission to love Reality, and to love all of Reality, and to love madly and desperately, and in that Loving become more Whole.

To say *I love you* is, in its depth, to say *I need you*. There is no true Love without need. That is the disclosure of the Divine, which is the Infinite Intimate.

The act of *I choose to love you* means *I choose to need you*. This is the nature of the Divine—of Ultimate Value. But we participate in the Field of Value, so it is our nature, too.

It is the Ultimate Divine Choice. It is the ultimate expression of Divine Wholeness—and of our wholeness.

But the movement of manifestation of the Infinite Intimate is not only

Divine Choice but also Divine Necessity. It could not be any other way. It is Divine Necessity, even as it is a Radical Choice. The metaphysical argument that has dominated the millennia—between Divine Necessity and Divine Voluntarism—is resolved at a higher level of consciousness in the choiceless choice of *I choose to need you.*

In CosmoErotic Humanism, there are specific terms deployed for the evolving levels of Self, the higher and deeper levels of human consciousness. These are deeper levels of humanity, the possible human who consciously participates in the Wholeness of the Field of Value and Eros. In True Self, Unique Self, and Evolutionary Unique Self,[75] they realize their participation at ever-deeper levels in the Field of Meaning, Value, Eros, and Self.

There are three distinct stages in the realization of the absolute human participation in the Field of Wholeness. These three Selves incarnate the qualities of consciousness that characterize whole mate relationship. True Self is the Field of Wholeness itself. Unique Self is the unique expression of the Field of Wholeness incarnate as you. Evolutionary Unique Self is the core quality of the New Human and the New Humanity, which we have called *Homo amor.*

The new Divine Name, the Infinite Intimate, discloses the realization that Infinity desires Intimacy. It is that stirring of Desire in the Infinite that manifests the Intimate—the manifest Cosmos. The Infinite Intimate joins in potential whole mate relationships with every human being. The Unique Self, the human incarnation of the Infinite Intimate, joins her beloved not only as soul mate but as whole mate. Infinitely Intimate Unique Selves choose to need each other in order to give their respective unique gifts, to love each other and to give a shared unique gift. In either case, whole mates say to each other, I choose to need you. It is not a capricious or arbitrary choice. It is, at a deeper level of realization, a choiceless choice.

Often you speak to beloveds who clearly chose to be together, and they will tell you that it could not have been any different. They needed to be together; it could not have been any other way. This is the paradox of the choiceless choice that is the essential nature of the Infinite Intimate's

---

75 See Section 3.3 in Essay One.

choice, as well as the essential nature of whole mate relationships, which themselves incarnate the Infinite Intimate. The whole mate comes to the relationship whole and yet, paradoxically, becomes more whole through the relationship itself.

Similarly, the Infinite Intimate comes to relationship with the world Whole, for how could the Divine not be Whole? And yet paradoxically, after the Infinite becomes intimate with the world, it becomes somehow more Whole. In other words, there is always more God to come.

The Infinite Intimate, or God, is the world's Whole Mate.

ESSAY THREE

THE NARRATIVE THREAD OF COSMOS: THE EVOLUTION OF INTIMACY THROUGH THE FOUR BIG BANGS

Most of us know that at the center of our personal reality are our relationships, but sometimes we think we make them matter too much or give them too much weight. Yet relationships are not just the core of our personal lives. The exterior and interior sciences together are now awaking to the realization that our personal lives and relationships, on the one hand, and the structure of the Cosmos, on the other, are one. The laws that govern the success or failure of our personal lives are the same laws that govern Reality as a Whole.

We have information from the leading edges of science that has never been available before. This new information gives us access to new insights, new tools, and therefore new hope and new possibility. This information is not dogmatic but tells us something about the core structure of Reality. *"Reality is that which, when you stop believing in it, does not go away."*[76]

---

76 Phillip K. Dick, "I Hope I Shall Arrive Soon" (1985), 3.

It is the new information of the sciences that opens us to the most profound realization that the essential nature of Cosmos itself is Story. This narrative view of Cosmos informs cosmological, biological, and cultural evolution. It is only now that the leading edges of modern science are beginning to realize that there is a direct through line, a narrative thread if you will, beginning, in this current Universe, with the Big Bang and moving all the way from matter (chemistry, physics, and cosmological evolution) to life (biology and biological evolution) to mind (spirituality, psychology, and cultural evolution).

Before we turn to the Four Big Bangs, which we will unfold as the narrative arc of Cosmos—the core of the Universe Story, and particularly of Evolution: The Love Story of the Universe—some crucial contextual notes are in order.

1. Evolution as Crisis and Invitation

In other writings on CosmoErotic Humanism, we will explore distinct plotlines of the Intimate Universe in depth. To simply state them here, evolution evolves to more and more Eros. The plotlines of Cosmic Eros include:

- more and more complexity,

- more and more uniqueness,

- more and more consciousness,

- more and more creativity,

- more and more care and concern,

- more and more intimacy, and

- more and more story.

For the sake of this writing, however, let's just focus on the evolution of intimacy as the overarching vector of evolution's progression. The narrative arc of this evolutionary plotline is the Four Big Bangs. They form the crux of the narrative thread of Cosmos. Central to the emergence of Conscious Evolution is our very recent ability to discern precisely this narrative thread.

One common feature of all evolutionary theories is the idea that evolution is hard, painful, crisis-prone, and existential—a matter of life and death. It is clear that, at key moments, crises occur—cataclysmic events that bring into the Universe something that is totally new and truly unprecedented. As we have discussed in Essay One, there is little doubt that we are in the midst of an evolutionary meta-crisis. This is the first totalizing crisis of the Anthropocene,[77] as humanity and the planet itself are forced into a reconfiguration of intimacies toward higher-order evolutionary emergence. This is a moment of crisis, and yet such a crisis is perfectly in sync with the narrative structure of Reality. Everything we know about evolution suggests that, precisely at such a moment of breakdown, we are poised for breakthrough.

But our choices *matter*. That is exactly what *Conscious Evolution* means. It is the movement to the pivotal role of conscious human choice—evolution in person *as us*—in both ensuring that there will be a future and in designing the quality of that future. Our choices are the leading edge of evolution itself. We are the verbs in the arc of evolution. This narrative arc will become clearer as we outline the Four Big Bangs below.

---

77 The term Anthropocene comes from the Greek roots anthropo, meaning human, and -cene from kainos, meaning new or recent. This term is now being used as a formal unit of geological epoch division, basically suggesting that humanity has so impacted Earth that, from a strictly scientific position, our age constitutes a new geological epoch, a new stage in the history of the planet's basic physical being, especially its atmospheric and chemical composition. The term has deep roots but was brought to prominence by Paul Crutzen, a Nobel Prize–winning atmospheric chemist.

The meta-crisis must shift not only our physical systems and ex-teriors (infrastructure and social structure) but also our interiors—our consciousness, or Eros itself (*superstructure*). And this evolutionary leap will be catalyzed by the meta-crisis that we are in the midst of right now. This crisis has to do *not* only with the geo-history of technology and the limits of the biosphere. It is *not* just about the complexity of the planetary stack. It is, more fundamentally, a crisis of self-understanding.

Virtually every crisis, at its core, is a crisis of intimacy. We are not intimate with ourselves and our world, and as such, we are not in love with ourselves or our world. We need to be in love with our world, our planet, and with our Cosmos. It is because we are not that we are not intimate and in love with each other or ourselves. We need a Universe Story in which we can locate ourselves. We need a Universe Story that meets the depth of our longing and the depth of our knowing—the truth of the interior and exterior sciences.

One of the core sentences of CosmoErotic Humanism is: **Evolution is Love responding to need.** It is the depth of this need, emerging from the meta-crisis of this moment, that can generate such a new Universe Story. Our CosmoErotic Humanism is one model of such a new Universe Story. Only from such a new Universe Story can we articulate a narrative of identity, in which we are literally *in* love, in which we participate in the very fabric of Reality's Eros.

We are in the midst of an unprecedented species-wide identity and relationship crisis, and this is happening during the very decades when the self-inflicted extinction of our species has become a potential reality for the first time. Our Universe Story and its derivative narratives of identity, power, desire, and community have collapsed on themselves, no longer able to claim alignment with any genuine features of Reality beyond the surface structures of what postmodernity calls *social construc-tion*. We no longer know what it means to be human.[78] And for the first

---

78 Don't misread the recent upwelling of fundamentalist religion as a sign to the contrary. This reactive and often violent grasping and entrenchment of tradition is driven precisely by the now inescapable and hegemonic force of the non-stories about the meaning of humanity. The biggest sacrilege—and what looks to fun-damentalist cultures like godlessness—is really the storylessness of postmodern

time, we are aware of this ignorance, collectively.[79] Dogmatic materialism coupled with postmodernism and superficial evolutionary psychology, the conventional narratives of the age, have *de-story-ed* Reality. Together, they reject the notion that we have any intrinsic purpose on the planet, let alone the Universe.

And yet, at the very same time, the leading edges of postdogmatic and postconventional thinking in the sciences, both interior and exterior, have begun to tell a new Story. At the leading edge of thought, there is a growing understanding that consciousness, and the Eros that animates it, as well as our own core self-understanding, are not epiphenomena. Eros and consciousness are not side effects in our lives. They are the main event. Eros, consciousness, our Universe Story, and narrative of identity are not merely supervening or reacting to a more basic biotechnological base. Rather, human Eros (or its lack) and its desire for greater intimacies, consciousness, and self-identity are at the core of everything. It is because of Eros's fundamental and central nature that failures of Eros are driving the global crisis on all levels. We cannot live without Eros, for it is our fundamental nature and the nature of Cosmos. Reality is Eros. When Eros breaks down, pseudo-eros in the form of every kind of substitute gratification seeks to fill the void.[80] Pseudo-eros is the direct cause for

---

culture, which stems in part from its (pseudo-) scientific basis: a nonfoundationalist, open-ended, choose-your-own-adventure worldview that glibly dismisses ancient traditions by citing the latest scientific headline and then dismisses that headline when a newer study is released.

79 It should be said that humanity has never known its true identity and purpose. This is not something we once knew and have forgotten, or something we lost and must now find. Certain cultures have previously been convinced of a particular identity and purpose for all humans, and there have been visionaries who have offered their stunning guesses at the riddle of our being. The difference now is not ignorance—we have always been ignorant—it's that now there is widespread knowledge of our ignorance and an unprecedented groping toward truly new answers that are postdogmatic, postdisciplinary/academic, postconventional, and transnational/ethnic.

80 See A Return to Eros: The Radical Experience of Being Fully Alive, by Marc Gafni and Kristina Kinkaid (2017), pp. 113–130, 178–192. For the original formulation of the distinction between Eros and pseudo-eros, see The Mystery of Love, by Marc Gafni (2003), pp. 24–31.

the collapse of ethos. Formalized succinctly, we can say: All failures of Eros lead directly to a breakdown of identity, which in turn engenders a collapse of ethics.

Our generation is in an unprecedented position to take responsibility for participating in profoundly generative and destructive evolutionary crises. The question is:

Can we understand our crises in a Cosmic Context,
as opportunities for the emergence of the unprecedented,
and as invitations into a higher form of life?

The only effective response to the meta-crisis is, in fact, the movement from unconscious to Conscious Evolution. And Conscious Evolution means, as we noted at the outset, not only the structural realization that we are a direct emergent and expression of evolution. It is not enough to know that evolution lives in us and that the evolutionary impulse beats in our hearts. Conscious Evolution means that we have gathered new information from the sciences, integrating its interior and exterior disciplines. In doing so, we have realized that evolution itself is love in action. And *as* Conscious Evolution, we are, quite literally, *evolution as love in action in person*. Indeed, this is the impulse that moves the project of CosmoErotic Humanism itself and all like-minded meta-projects.

What moves us to gather all the fragments of information—myriad separate parts—into a new larger whole, weaving strands from all the diverse disciplines into a larger embrace, is none other than the same Love that moves the Sun and other stars: Evolutionary Eros itself. And the primary action of Evolutionary Love is the evolution of love itself.

That evolution has now awakened to itself inside of our own identities. *That* is what we refer to as *Conscious Evolution*. We now realize that we are personal incarnations of the Force of Evolutionary Love pulsing fiercely and tenderly in us and as us. So, it is Conscious Evolution from here on out: We are able to know and do too much to pretend otherwise; we must consciously orchestrate the future of the planet and the biosphere. And as we have begun to unpack above, the next step in Conscious Evolution is the realization of the Universe: A Love Story.

The interior sciences remind us that *the inside of consciousness is Love*, or what we are calling *Eros*, which is defined by an incessant drive for ever-deepening intimacy and creativity. And, as we have begun to point toward[81] and will deepen in future writings, intimacy and creativity are the same movement of Cosmos.

As we began to unpack earlier, new intimacy is created by fostering ever-wider and deeper shared identities in the context of (relative) otherness. Separate parts allured together to foster new wholes is the essential movement of both intimacy and creativity. It is the movement of becoming, which characterizes the Story of the Intimate Universe.

2. The Story of the Four Big Bangs

We must come to see that the evolution of the Universe and biological life is not just a fact. It is a story. Evolution is a story about us, who we are, and what we are going through now. The Universe itself is best understood as a Story, not as a mere fact. The Universe is a Love Story. Like all true love stories, and unlike Harlequin romances or romantic comedies, it has been a Story of profound crisis, cataclysm, tragedy, hope, emergence, and creativity.

One of the best ways to summarize the narrative arc of this Story was offered by Pierre Teilhard de Chardin,[82] who followed Charles S. Peirce, as well as cryptic strains in Kant's early metaphysics of nature, and organized his master work according to three epochal emergent properties of the evolving universe: matter, life, and thought. This same

---

81 See, for example, Return to Eros and Homo Amor and CosmoErotic Humanism: First Thoughts, by Marc Gafni and Zachary Stein (2018).

82 Pierre Teilhard de Chardin, The Phenomenon of Man (1959). Originally published in French in 1955.

tripartite division has been rehearsed recently by Holmes Rolston III in his *Three Big Bangs: Matter-Energy, Life, Mind*.[83] We use this framing to tell the Story of Cosmic Evolution, only we add a Fourth Big Bang.

2.1. A First Glimpse at the Elements of the Fourth Big Bang

At the core of the Fourth Big Bang is the planetary phase-shift resulting from evolution becoming conscious of itself in and through humanity. This is the dawning of the age of Conscious Evolution, which intimately co-emerges with the advent of existential risk to the future of humanity itself. Co-emergent as part of the Fourth Big Bang are

- a new Universe Story (the Universe: A Love Story or the Intimate Universe),

- a new narrative of identity (Unique Self and Evolutionary Unique Self), and

- a new narrative of We-Space (Unique Self Symphony).

All of these are key strands in the emergence of the New Human and the New Humanity—*Homo amor*—animated by the evolutionary philosophy of CosmoErotic Humanism.

We stand today on the edge of this Fourth Big Bang and have only a glimmer of the unimaginable horizons it opens. The best image available to capture what is currently potentiated in humanity is the image of a universal, noncoercive human superorganism, constituted as a Unique Self Symphony. A Planetary Awakening in Evolutionary Love through Unique Self Symphonies is core to the emergence of Conscious Evolution and *Homo amor*.[84] This is the plotline of the Intimate Universe, the Universe: A Love Story. Essential to the Fourth Big Bang is the realization of the

---

83 Holmes Rolston III, Three Big Bangs: Matter-Energy, Life, Mind (2010).

84 See Sections 3.6–3.7 in Essay One.

narrative nature of Cosmos, in which we are personally implicated.

The realization of *Homo amor* is that *your story*—the love story of your life, the intimacies of your life in all the realms of your life—are chapter and verse in the Universe: A Love Story.

Key to this vision is precisely the disclosure of the narrative nature of Cosmos, or, said differently, the realization that Reality is not merely an eternal fact but an evolving story. We must tell this story, because understanding that Cosmic Evolution *is* a Story, and being able to see its narrative arc, is an essential part of expanding the self-understanding of humanity during this time of crisis. Importantly, our ability to position the evolution of humanity in the vast deep-time context of Cosmic Evolution emerged only recently. For example, Einstein was initially unaware of and barely able to grasp the breathtaking idea that not only life but the Cosmos itself is evolving. It is, however, precisely the quality of the Universe as a Love Story that is disclosed when we realize that both the perilous reality of our impending self-induced extinction and a breathtaking new vision of humanity's precious and miraculous place in Reality confront us at the very same historical moment.

The future depends on our ability to make sense of the past. This means not only our cultural and social history but also the big history of the cosmological and biological story that led directly to our species and to the cultural story in which we now find ourselves. There is a direct line between cosmological, biological, and cultural evolution, the Story of Reality's emergence from matter to life to mind—our self-reflective and self-creating humanity.

2.2. The First Big Bang

One of the seminal moments in modern science was the *discovery* of the First Big Bang—although, as has been suggested, a better name might be the *Great Flaring Forth*.[85] With remarkable irony, a scientific worldview dedicated to denying the existence of the unmeasurable and questioning

---

85 See, for example, The Universe Story: From the Primordial Flaring Forth to the Ecozoic Era—A Celebration of the Unfolding of the Cosmos, by Brian Swimme and Thomas Berry (1992).

the reality of the immaterial led inextricably to the conclusion that everything in the Universe came into being as a spontaneous explosion of *something* from *nothing*. The mystery school of modern physics tells of many mysteries, but none is more mysterious than this.

Moreover, we are told that in less than a millionth of a second after something exploded out of nothing, intelligent structures began to emerge, structures that would make it possible for the Universe to unfold toward the emergence of ever new and more intricately organized structures, such as solar systems, suns, and planets. In the language of the interior sciences, the Infinite disclosed its intimate nature. The Infinite desired the finite. The Infinite *yearned* for intimacy—to love and be loved. The Infinite acts in the Eternal Now, yet we place these sentences in past tense because we are writing and describing—from within time—the primordial movement from nothingness to something as the yearning for intimacy, which discloses itself as the inception of the Universe and time itself.

In calling the physical structure *intelligent* in the previous paragraph, we *are* taking a stand on the conscious-Universe-versus-materialism debate, but we are *not* endorsing any kind of intelligent-design argument. We are noting, however, that the Universe was born already intrinsically structured in configurations of coherent intimacy, ordered and erotically allured toward increasing complexity and self-organization along certain very specific lines. This could simply be chance, some big cosmic *oops!* But to believe that would be to cling to randomness and chance in the face of obvious Eros and *telos*[86] (or, more neutrally, self-evident structure and purpose).

Again, we are not arguing for intelligent design, which is the idea that there is some purely extrinsic intelligence that designed and built all we see before us. As Henri Bergson was wont to say, *evolution is much more than a plan.* We are arguing that the Universe itself *is* intrinsically intelligent and animated by Eros. We are affirming the self-evident truth that matter itself *is* full of life, meaning, and purpose. These qualities need

---

86 See Sections V.1–V.2 in part two for a deeper conversation on randomness and telos.

not come from outside the Universe; they are its primordial properties.[87]

2.3. The Second Big Bang

As billions upon billions of years passed, a Second Big Bang was being prepared, breathtakingly improbable from the perspective of the sciences that have demonstrated its reality—*the emergence of life from (seemingly) lifeless matter*.[88] From the perspective of CosmoErotic Humanism, the intensification of intimacy between interconnected parts generated life from matter.

The genesis of the biosphere on Earth arouses almost as much radical amazement and wonder as the explosion of everything from nothing. And as many science writers have demonstrated, the sheer statistical improbability of such an occurrence is truly mind blowing.[89] Yet it is a scientific reality that cannot be denied. Earth would come to be entirely encased in life, an explosion of ever-evolving configurations of intimacy, as the surface of the once barren rock was transformed into a teaming

---

87 Moreover, from a nondual perspective, there is no outside or inside to the Universe. Thus, technically speaking, we endorse a form of panentheistic evolutionary nondualism—what we have termed CosmoErotic Humanism—with the understanding that none of those concepts can, by themselves, replace an actual waking up in consciousness that grasps the Ultimate Mystery. Otherwise, all of these terms are just more dualistic concepts (even nondualism, as a concept, only makes sense contrasted to dualism—which is why the great Buddhist sage Nagarjuna denies both terms as being adequate for Ultimate Truth).

88 Matter itself is not actually lifeless or insentient in an absolute sense. It is rather a structure of allurement generating unique configurations of Eros moving to ever-deeper and wider levels of wholeness and coherent intimacies (see Sections II.2 and III.8 in part two).

89 For good overviews of these issues, see The Origins of Order: Self-Organization and Selection in Evolution, by Stuart A. Kauffman (1993), and The Systems View of Life: A Unifying Vision, by Fritjof Capra and Pier Luigi Luisi (2014). For a discussion of the compounding improbabilities involved in the emergence of higher-order life-forms—i.e., beyond the already stupefying improbability of primordial ooze—see Rare Earth: Why Complex Life Is Uncommon in the Universe, by Peter Ward and Donald Brownlee (2003), and Origins: A Skeptic's Guide to the Creation of Life on Earth, by Robert Shapiro (1986). In nonscientific parlance, the term impossible comes to mind when considering these kinds of figures, and yet, here we are.

wilderness of biological diversity. The tendencies displayed in the evolution of the material universe, such as the spontaneous confluence of diffuse matter into organized forms and the emergence of higher-order structures, resulted in even more complexity—coherently intimate configurations—during the evolution of the biological world.

Thus, in the past decades, *emergence* and *self-organization* have become the watchwords of the branches of biology seeking to explain the earliest forms of life on Earth. Emergence appears to be an intrinsic property of the Intimate Universe. Intimacy generates emergence. The Universe: A Love Story is a living process, in which synergies and symbioses—resulting from self-organization—propel matter toward unprecedented new forms. When what were once independent entities reach a certain density of interconnectedness, they spontaneously become potentially intimate elements of a new higher-order coherent whole, and in so doing they can no longer be understood as separate parts. This is the progressive deepening of intimacies, which is the plotline of the Intimate Universe throughout the arc of all the Big Bangs.

2.4. The Third Big Bang

As the evolution of intimacy—the movement toward ever-deeper and wider levels of wholeness—unfolded on Earth for billions of years, a Third Big Bang was being prepared. It is again a seeming miracle from the perspective of materialistic science: *the emergence of self-conscious awareness and human culture.*

Each of the Big Bangs implies the miraculous in the sense of the Latin word *mirari*, from which *miracle* derives. *Mirari* means "to behold with rapt attention." Such attention, sensing a quality beyond that of the merely material, is what our colleague Howard Bloom calls "a material mysticism."

It is not clear exactly when the transition from animal signaling to human language occurred, or when the natural activities of foraging and hunting became tied into the reflective transmission of culture and technology that characterize even the earliest human societies. Aside from the very first microorganisms that transformed the atmosphere of the Earth into oxygen, and thus created the conditions for the possibility of the biosphere, the emergence of human culture is perhaps the most significant moment in the history of the planet.

3. The Narrative Logic of Evolution Lives within Us

There is a narrative logic in the Big Bangs themselves. The physiosphere (matter and energy) fulfills itself in the biosphere. Each stage of emergence leads to the next. This is one of the many expressions of the dialectical paradox of randomness and nonrandomness—holy chaos and holy order—that form the heart of the Universe: A Love Story.[90] As scientist Harold Morowitz points out in his excellent study of evolutionary science, *The Emergence of Everything: How the World Became Complex*, each stage of emergence inherently leads to the next stage.[91]

Each stage of matter has independent value, and that value gradually accumulates with matter ultimately fulfilling itself—triumphing—as life. In a similar sense, each stage of life is inherently self-validating and has inherent value and dignity, even as there is a dimension of life that fulfills itself—triumphs—in the depth of the self-reflective human mind. In other words, from the perspective of the narrative of arc of Cosmos, matter fulfills itself in life, and life fulfills itself in the depth of the self-reflective human mind. Cosmological evolution fulfills itself in biological evolution, and biological evolution fulfills itself in cultural evolution. Or said yet again: The physiosphere fulfills itself in the biosphere, and the biosphere fulfills itself in the noosphere. From the vantage of hindsight, a clear telos emerges.

And yet, the sorting mechanisms for this powerful thrust of life,

---

90 See Section V.1 for a deeper look into this paradox.

91 Harold Morowitz, The Emergence of Everything: How the World Became Complex (2004).

driven by the "creative advance into novelty,"[92] is Darwin's holy idea of natural selection, which includes contingency and randomness. That is the free and open-ended nature of the Universe: A Love Story, which emerges from *Source*—from *no-thing*—as an expression of apparent otherness. The Universe emerges, driven by its own inherent ceaseless creativity, self-actualizing, based on ever-deeper and more complex *in-formation*, which unfolds through spontaneous and free chance interactions, inherently animated by the Tao of an unseen telos.

We can access this pulsing Heart of the Cosmos *anthro-ontologically*. By *anthro-ontology*,[93] we mean, for now, simply the lived truth that the Intimate Universe lives in us, even as we live in it. Human beings are constituted—literally—of all of the previous layers of Reality's evolution. We are made up of both the physical stardust (all of the elementary particles, and all of the previous stages of evolution) and the felt allurement and interior gnosis that live in the core of our being. Echoing evolutionary mystics and interior scientists of the last several hundred years, we might offer "the mysteries are within us" as a succinct, five-word summation of anthro-ontology. It is for that precise reason that we can access the working of the Intimate Universe within our own clarified interiors. Evolutionary Mystic Kook captures the *Anthro-Ontological Axiom of Reality* in a short passage:

It is necessary to explain the nobility of studying the
secrets of Torah,
in conjunction with the requirement to honor the inner knowing of
the human being,
who is the foundation of the world.
And increasingly,
this culture of externality
comes from this formula:

---

92 The notion of creative advance into novelty comes from Alfred North Whitehead: "Neither the God, nor the World, reaches static completion. Both are in the grip of the ultimate metaphysical ground, the creative advance into novelty." Process and Reality: An Essay in Cosmology (1978), 349.

93 For more on anthro-ontology, see First Principles and First Values.

the more that a culture's valuing of externality increases,
the more the human eye fixes on discerning the external,
and the more it disregards inner knowing,
and as a result of this, the true value of a human being dwindles
and declines,
and the liberation of the world depends on elevating the value of
inner knowings,
which emerge and shed light,
by means of the great intimate entry into the depth of interiority,
which itself is the fascinating engagement with the secrets of Torah,
with holiness and purity,
with humility and special courage.[94]

In other words: *The mysteries are within us.* We live in an Amorous Cosmos. And the Amorous Cosmos lives in us.

4. The Dialectic of Freedom and Telos: Moving Toward the Fourth Big Bang

It is the nature of all intimate relationships to be a dialectic of *telos*— patterned order and symmetry—and *surprise and contingency*. Intimate relationship with a person, a body of knowledge, or a community always moves between patterned, symmetrical, intimate order and open-ended curiosity, new possibility, and transformation. All evolutions of love, both personal and collective, take place in this dialectical context of love. There is open-ended freedom and possibility on the one hand and patterned order and regularity that create trust on the other. Without

---

94 Abraham Kook, Orot HaKodesh [Lights of Holiness], vol. 1 (1937), 96.

either side of the dialectic, the intimate Reality becomes undone at every level of Cosmos.

The telos of the progressive deepening of love self-actualizes as life, through the laws of physics and chemistry, guided by the inherent structures of information that literally, in David Bohm's evocative phrase, *in-form* each stage of emergence as the Story of Reality. Reality moves through the stage-by-stage emergence from the physiosphere toward its triumph in the biosphere.[95] Life is the triumph of matter, fulfilling itself in a quantum jump, a second great flaring forth, the Second Big Bang. The Second Big Bang is the emergence and the evolution of the biosphere. But just like the First Big Bang, the emergence of matter and energy from *no-thing*, it is not the product of an inevitable causation from some past set of events that we have measured. The First Big Bang, at least according to the classic scientific story of cosmogenesis, is the emergence of something from nothing. But however we tell the story of the birth of cosmological evolution, it is clearly an emergent. It is not the product of simple past causation.

In the interior sciences, the story is told of *involution* before *evolution*. There was *no-thing* before there was *something*. Infinite *No-thing* sources everything. Indeed, as the new science of relativity informs us, the space-time continuum itself is a product of the Big Bang. Speaking in the metaphors of time, we might say that Cosmos is an invitation from the future. But by future, we mean not a point in time but the intention of Eternity. The code for this radical gnosis of the interior sciences, in the specific language of the interior sciences of Hebrew wisdom, is the four-letter Name of God—*Yod He Vav He.*

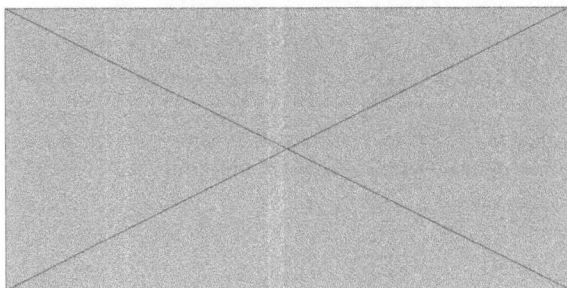

---

95 See The Emergence of Everything: How the World Became Complex, by Harold J. Morowitz (2004).

The classical interior scientists, deploying their own language, declare unabashedly: *Eros is the Name of God*. The first two letters (moving from right to left), *Yod* and *He*, are the masculine and the feminine—not man and woman but masculine and feminine, or rather, two primary forces of Cosmos, lines and circles.[96] The first letter, *Yod*, enters the second letter, *He*. This is called by the mystics *Zivug Matmedet*,[97] literally translated as the *constant Eros* or *allurement* that animates all of Reality. This is an interior structure of Cosmos, which—since the Cosmos is interiors and exteriors all the way down and all the way up the evolutionary chain—also has an exterior expression. The Universe, in every moment, every situation, every person, every entity, every dynamic, is the play between the *line* qualities of autonomy and independence on the one hand and the *circle* qualities of attraction and allurement on the other.[98] The *Yod* entering the *He* is often referred to as *It'aruta De'Leyla*—*Arousal from above*.[99]

The last two letters of the Name of God are the *Vav* and the *He*. The

---

96 On lines and circles, see Isaac Luria's Sod Iggulim ve Yosher (1964). For a discussion of this Lurianic distinction, see Marc Gafni's The Mystery of Love (2003) for a chapter on lines and circles. For classical Kabbalistic texts expressing the masculine-feminine polarity in the name of God, see Pardes Rimonim: Orchard of Pomegranates, by Rabbi Moshe Cordovero (2007), and Gates of Light = Sha'are Orah, by Rabbi Joseph ben Abraham Gikatilla (1998). See Kabbalistic Writings on the Nature of the Masculine and Feminine by Sarah Schneider (2001) for a carefully annotated translation and rudimentary analysis of a classic set of mystical Hebrew texts on this trope.

97 This term is drawn from the interior science of erotic mysticism in Hebrew wisdom, particularly from the writings of the Zohar (for example, Zohar, vol. 3, 120a) and later Isaac Luria. This realization is expressed throughout his lineage in myriad forms with particular emphasis in the writings of Abraham Kook. On the lineage line from Luria to Kook in these regards, the serious reader of interior sciences is well directed to the writings of Tamar Ross, for example, "Overcoming the Epistemological Challenge" (2014).

98 See also Section III.1 in part two.

99 As we will see in the next chapter, attraction, or allurement, is built into the very structure of the universe.

Vav, an obvious phallic expression,[100] enters and is received by the *He*, the Divine Feminine.[101] Interior scientists call this *Zivug She'Eino Metamedet—nonconstant Union.* This union is caused by *It'aruta De'Le'tata—Arousal from below*, the aroused Eros generated by human activism in the realms of the Good, the True, and the Beautiful.[102]

The *Vav* only enters the *He* when human beings—through their own processes of activation—arouse the Divine *Zivug*. For the interior scientists in the Solomon tradition, human beings can realize their capacity to participate directly in the great *Zivug* of Reality and to arouse the Divine *Zivug* by living the unique quality of one's full Eros and aliveness in every dimension of their life.

We add here the dimension of the future. The first letter, *Yod*, is *the point of eternity that calls in the future*. The last three letters, *He, Vav, He*, form the Hebrew word for *present*. The Name of God is thus an equation, which expresses the eternal point that lives in the present, calling it to the future. The entire Name spelled together means: *It will be*. It is Reality called into being from the future—but the eternally becoming future, beneath the space-time continuum.

---

100 It likely originates from the Egyptian hieroglyph representing a mace, taking on a phallic image.

101 He in Judaism is often taken to mean the Name as deference to the ineffable God, or that which cannot be named.

102 The relationship between arousal from below and above to constant Zivug and nonconstant Zivug (Zivug that must be aroused through human action) is complex and varied in different texts, and, while a fascinating study, it is beyond our purview and not necessary for this conversation.

5. The Evolution of Love from Physiosphere to Biosphere to Noosphere

The physiosphere appearing out of *no-thing* is not a product of past physical causation but a necessary and free emergent, a great flaring forth.

In the same sense, the biosphere comes out of the physiosphere—although in no way violating any of the laws of physics or chemistry, yet almost infinitely more than a necessary product of matter and energy. It is a momentous leap into the future, in full integrity with its prior causes but called into being by the future, the infinite point of being that self-organizes evolution into the becoming of tomorrow. The biosphere is thus a new Big Bang, a radically new, emergent flaring forth called into being, self-organized by Reality's inherent eternal future. In other words, life is not a densification of matter, which becomes life. Rather, there is something radically new in life, a dimension that literally flares forth from no-thingness.

In the scientific reading of CosmoErotic Humanism, integrating the exterior and interior sciences, life emerges from the intensification of intimacies between the parts of matter in such a way that the new intimacy flares forth into life. We know this to be true anthro-ontologically—in the depth of our own interiors. For within ourselves we know that the intensification of intimacy is what generates new Eros, new possibility, and new creativity, which in turn births new levels of wholeness. Mathematician and complexity theorist Stuart Kauffman alludes to this understanding of the intensification of intimacy being cause for the emergence of life in more formal scientific terms in the following passage:

> As the diversity of molecules in our system increases, the ratio of reactions to chemicals, or edges to nodes, becomes ever higher. In other words, the reaction graph has ever more lines connecting the chemical dots. The molecules in the system

are themselves candidates to be able to catalyze the reactions by which the molecules themselves are formed. As the ratio of reactions to chemicals increases, the number of reactions that are catalyzed by the molecules in the system increases. When the number of catalyzed reactions is about equal to the number of chemical dots, a giant catalyzed reaction web forms, and a collectively autocatalytic system snaps into existence. A living metabolism crystallizes. Life emerges as a phase transition.[103]

Similarly, the intensification of intimacy within the biosphere generates the awakening of the new depths of self-reflective human consciousness, the emergence of human consciousness and culture. The third level of consciousness does not emerge simply putting together more cells, or life. There is a radically new emergence flaring forth from no-thingness.

The biosphere follows the same dialectical pattern, that of symmetrical order and radical freedom—radical symmetry, law, and order, coupled with radical freedom, spontaneity, and contingency. Life goes through the many distinct stages, which in retrospect present a self-evident sequence of emergence, from single-celled bacteria all the way to hominids walking on the African savanna more than 2.5 million years ago.

At that point, the biosphere fulfills itself in a quantum jump, the Third Big Bang, with the emergence of the noosphere. This is the triumph of the biosphere in the noosphere. Life triumphs itself as it is transcended and included in mind. Here again, like the physiosphere and the biosphere, the emergence of the noosphere, the human world, is not the product of necessary causation from the past. It is, like the previous Big Bangs, radically new, unlike all that came before, and not fully explicable in terms of antecedent causation.

Noos, or mind, is the world of the self-reflective, self-representing human being. This human being

---

103 Stuart A. Kauffman, At Home in the Universe: The Search for the Laws of Self-Organization and Complexity (1995).

- passes down knowledge, which multiplies exponentially,

- speaks language,

- creates art,

- trades,

- creates the superorganisms of culture,

- and continually evolves his/her own interior consciousness,

- even as his/her human organism remains the same.

The noosphere, then, goes through many structural stages of development. These evolutionary stages have been charted along different lines of development, or what we might call *vectors of evolution*. For example, one could trace development of the technological base of society

- from *hunter-gatherer*

- to *horticultural* (early farming with a hand instrument)

- to *agrarian* (later farming with an animal-drawn plow)

- to *industrial* (the Industrial Revolution)

- to *informational* (the age of the computer, telecommunications, etc.)

- to the emergent age of what we might call *exponential tech* (biotech, infotech, nanotech, AI, machine learning, augmented reality, and all the rest).

Another line of development might be communal—the movement

from clans to tribes to kingdoms to great religions and empires, and all the way to nation-states, including both dictatorships and democracies. These communal stages of development roughly correspond to the techno-base stages.

But perhaps the most important line of development is what we might call *the evolution of consciousness itself*. It is the evolution of *worldviews*. This includes both the Universe Story of a particular epoch as well as the consequent narrative of identity that derives from the Universe Story and all the consequent values, including forms of government. This is the *evolution of interiors*. It is, according to Jean Gebser, the emergence from archaic to magical to mythical to rational to integral consciousness.[104]

In parallel to these worldviews is the evolution from early clans and later tribes ruled by a chieftain all the way to modern democracies. All of these are further progressions in what we have called the *evolution of love* or the *evolution of intimacy*. All of these stages of evolution are inter-included with each other, and they are all part of the Third Bang—cultural evolution within the noosphere.

To sum up, evolution moves

- from cosmological (physiosphere, matter and energy, and all of the stages of its evolution from elementary particles to planets)

- to biological (the biosphere and all the stages of life from cells to humans)

- to cultural evolution (the noosphere and all the stages of human development).

Each of these levels of development can be understood as stages in the evolution of intimacy. The progressive deepening of intimacies is the plotline of evolution throughout the narrative arc of Cosmos—the first three Big Bangs. Within human evolution, the Third Big Bang moves

---

104 Jean Gebser, The Ever-Present Origin (1985). Originally published in German as Ursprung und Gegenwart in 1949–1953.

- from the egocentric consciousness of survival clans and early (magical) tribes

- to the ethnocentric consciousness of later (mythic) tribes, empires, and early nation-states

- to the worldcentric consciousness of twentieth-century democracies.

Each of these emergent levels expands the boundaries of intimacy to ever-wider circles of inclusion.

6. The Dark Side of Evolution

Every new structure-stage of development brings in its wake new promise, as well as new potential pathology.

To state it somewhat simplistically, rocks do not get cancers, but animals do. Animals clearly represent an evolution of intimacy beyond rocks. The interior of animals is exponentially more intimate than the interior of a rock: The intimate relationships between all the interior parts and systems of an animal far exceed that of a rock. Concurrently, the interaction of an animal with others evokes more intimacy and love in intersubjective relationships than does the interaction of rocks. That is perhaps why people rarely keep pet rocks, while pet dogs and cats are wildly popular. But at the same time, animals get cancer and rocks don't. The evolution of intimacy from matter to life, from the physiosphere to the biosphere, brings with it a higher level of potential pathology.

The same is true with the evolution of love from the biosphere to the noosphere, and with each progressive widening of Love within the noosphere. Let's just give two examples.

Human beings are capable of far deeper love than animals. While there is clearly pain and suffering in the animal world, there is a broad consensus among scientists that the level of anguish and emotional pain and trauma caused by human relationships exceeds and outstrips the experience of pain and suffering that we witness in the animal world. To cite but one statistic that supports this view, the animal world does not suffer a million suicides a year, which is the rate that the human world is now approaching.

The second example brings us to our main point. Within the human world, there is also a progression of love from ethnocentric to worldcentric consciousness—expanding the circle of love and care from one's own nation or religion to every human being on the planet. This evolution of intimacy is co-emergent with the evolution of technology, which itself is a form of new intimacy between separate parts. Technology connects a distant world.

But worldcentric intimacy—facilitated by new forms of rapid communication and travel in the industrial age, and instant communication in the information age—also generates new pathologies. A world civilization can contract *cancer* in the *body politic*. What, after all, is cancer if not the metastasizing of one cell, or a set of cells, that disassociates from the larger whole of the body and its needs? Just like new structures of intimacy create cancer in the body of the lifeworld in a way that was not possible in a rock, new structures of global communication and intimacy create the possibility of a dangerous cancer in the body politic, disassociation from the larger shared story of the body politic with its protocols, values, and telos.

A brief explanation is in order. Paradoxically, in the world of ethnocentric intimacy, which characterized the major political, social, and religious structures[105] of premodernity and modernity until after World War I, there was a shared story within every ethnocentric group, be it a clan, tribe, kingdom, empire, religion, or nation-state.

---

105 There were, however, intimations of worldcentric intimacy in multiple streams of thought, in both premodernity and modernity, but they were virtually always peripheral to the social, political, and religious power structures as well as to the center of gravity of popular thought.

The good news of that shared story, which included a Universe Story and its corollary narratives of identity, community, power, et cetera, was that it created a potent basis for love, dignity, nobility, honor, obligation, meaning, shared purpose, and shared action within the ethnocentric in-group.

The bad news was that many, although not all, dimensions of the shared story were based on what later turned out to be false dogmas.[106] These made the *other* less than human, allowing all manner of ethical violation, including murder, whenever the *other* refused to comply with the will of the more powerful incursive party. Coupled with those intense shadows were the mistreatment of women and children, the relationship to personal uniqueness, to the body, and to what modernity established as the basic rights of human dignity.

The ethnocentric communities (religions or ethnic groups) were unable to distinguish the genuine depth of insight and destiny, which they authentically shared, from socially constructed surface structures, which were false and simply perpetuated extreme and oppressive forms of in-group/out-group dynamics. Similar lack of discernments between depth structures and surface structures also perpetuated upper-caste- and lower-caste-type dynamics within the ostensible in-group. The result was oppression by the in-group of all who were considered the out-group, the infidels of all forms, and oppression against the lower castes of the in-group.

---

106 Key dimensions of the shared story were based on valid gnosis, derived through the Eye of Consciousness. The Eye of Consciousness is one of the three Eyes that reveal Reality to us: the Eye of the Senses, the Eye of the Mind, and the Eye of Consciousness in its four expressions (with their injunctions/practices): the Eye of Contemplation (Meditative Practices), the Eye of the Heart (Practices of Loving), the Eye of Value (Practices of Ethical Discernment), and the Eye of Spirit (Practices of Rituals, Ceremony, and Sacred Text). Some of these dimensions are the shared universals, derived through direct experiment of the interior sciences, which disclosed crucial gnosis about the nature of self and Reality. Other dimensions of this knowing involved the unique quality of intimacy between the Field of Consciousness and that particular nation, religion, or tribe. That is what we have called the Unique Self of that particular tribe, nation, or religion—the unique quality of intimacy between the Infinite and the finite, which is the story of that tribe, nation, or religion. But inextricably entwined, mixed in, with these valid dimensions of gnosis were all of the ethnocentric shadows.

Beginning with seeds of universalism,[107] the old in-group and out-group dynamics began to fall away. A new worldcentric consciousness, standing for universal human rights, sourced in the dignity of all human beings, struggled to emerge to some extent within significant swaths of the population. It was concentrated mostly but not entirely in the democratic world.

The massive problem was that this new worldcentric consciousness lacked the soil of a shared Universe Story based on a shared Story of Value rooted in First Principles and First Values. After World War II, late modernity stripped away many of the false social constructions of early and middle modernity and premodernity. But it did *not* distinguish between the validated insights of the great lineages of the interior sciences in the traditions—as well as the important gnosis of modernity—and the social construction of both, which generated false or corrupt dogmas. The postmodern moment deconstructed these dogmas but never engaged in the reconstructive project. In other words, postmodernity did not articulate a new shared global Story of Value rooted in evolving First Principles and First Values to replace all that had been appropriately deconstructed. We engage this failure of story in more depth in other writings of CosmoErotic Humanism.

The result was a world of global interconnectivity and the fragrance of potential global intimacy. But there was no interior technology within which to ground the potential vision of global intimacy. The world was *de-storied*. There was a glaring absence of a shared global story that might generate a global ethic for a global civilization. In what seemed like a flash of time, technology had connected everyone. But the connection created not intimacy but heightened alienation. Everyone was crashing into each other. There was no narrative of shared identity to foster a sense of shared pathos and therefore shared purpose and passion.

Without a shared story, the void was filled with the success story, measured by win/lose metrics, which in turn fueled a disastrous model of necessarily self-terminating growth based on perpetual extraction,

---

107 Universalism was sourced in ancient texts but first showed up at the cultural center of gravity of the Renaissance, and only came to more significant political and cultural fruition after World War I.

production, and consumption. The win/lose-metrics success story coincided with far-flung, complicated, and therefore fragile systems of global interconnectivity. These two factors were exacerbated by exponential tech, which made power, including destructive power, available to relatively high numbers of rogue actors.

The failure of a shared global Story of Value rooted in First Values and First Principles was coupled with the win/lose metrics and undermined the articulation of shared codes of honor. Those codes of honor, if rooted in a universal grammar of *ethos*, might have limited the proliferation of destructive exponential tech. The vacuum left by the missing shared global Story generated a high number of rogue nonstate actors as well as rogue state actors with access to technologies capable of destroying the world.

In effect, the progression of intimacy through new technology and the potential global intimacy of the world community was existentially threatened by the new pathology it generated. The global intimacy disorder with multiple rogue players and communities of players engaged in rivalrous conflict degenerated into multipolar traps, races to the bottom, and tragedies of the commons. These types of dynamics pose a genuine set of catastrophic and existential risks to the future of humanity.

In effect, the de-storied world generated the genuine, even likely possibility of cancer in the body politic. This cancer involves both individual human beings and communities of human beings experiencing their identity as separate selves. These are ontologically isolated from the whole, and therefore their Eros derives only from a success story based on rivalrous conflict governed by win/lose metrics. Moreover, the experience of most communities is that they are merely individuals in *random* superorganisms—products of the random walk of evolution.

Even those who profess classical or alternative forms of religion or spirituality are infected with the virus of what is presented as a de-ontologized universe. Although they may live in a particular religion or spiritual view, they are invariably infected with the dogmas of *scientism*.[108] The

---

108 On the notion of scientism and its difference from genuine science, see
       Section I.1.

latter constantly injects its nonscientific, dogmatic materialism into the bloodstream of culture. The result is a new pathology taking hold, side by side with the apparent evolution of love—the promising move from ethnocentric to worldcentric consciousness. A global intimacy disorder sets in, which undermines the promised emergence of a genuine global ethos. For a global ethos cannot emerge without the Eros of a shared Universe Story and narrative of identity. This is where we stand today—at the end of the world born in the Third Big Bang.

7. Crisis Is an Evolutionary Driver: From Caterpillar to Butterfly

It is crucial to realize, however, that the *telerotic* drive of evolution is as strong as it was at the pivotal moments of the First, Second, and Third Big Bangs. The same evolutionary impulse that has driven all the great breakthroughs of evolution is at play right here and now. The evolution of love is not over. It is self-evidently in midplay. Indeed, in this time between worlds and time between stories, the progressive deepening of Love is poised for another momentous leap. As we are poised between utopia and dystopia, the Fourth Big Bang is beginning to emerge.

The Fourth Big Bang follows the inherent narrative logic of Cosmos that is apparent in the first three Big Bangs. Much like the physiosphere fulfills itself in the biosphere, and the biosphere fulfills itself in the noosphere, the noosphere also desires its next stage of evolution.

How does the noosphere fulfill itself?

This is the movement from *Homo sapiens* to *Homo amor*—the emergence of a New Human and a New Humanity based on a new Universe Story. It is not a coincidence but an expression of the intimate nature of Cosmos that the Fourth Big Bang is just now beginning to explode, for, as we described in Essay One, the alternative is a level of existential risk that might well result in the last chapter of the human story.

The image of a butterfly emerging from a chrysalis aptly captures this moment in time, when the noosphere necessarily seeks its own evolution of consciousness. This is the Fourth Big Bang, the caterpillar dissolving, while dormant imaginal discs begin to transform into imaginal cells that generate a butterfly, and not a moment too soon. As always, crisis is an evolutionary driver,[109] and at its core, the crisis is always a crisis of imagination. The old society, convinced that its story is the only possible way society can function *successfully*, kills the attempted emergence of new imagination, which might birth a new Story.

The caterpillar goes through a powerful process before it emerges as a butterfly. It begins with massive consumption. The caterpillar eats as much as a hundred times its weight every day. At a certain point, it is too bloated to continue. This is the beginning of the crisis. So, the caterpillar hangs itself up. Its skin dries into a chrysalis. Inside the chrysalis, the caterpillar digests itself until there is only soup left—with the exception of so-called *imaginal cells*, which have been dormant in the caterpillar's old life. In the process of metamorphosis, they are allured to one another to form highly organized small groups (ten to fifty cells) called *imaginal discs*. Imaginal discs are like blueprints of the future body parts of the butterfly, which begin to form its adult body. The imaginal cells hold the memory of the caterpillar's future—the butterfly. They are the seeds of imagination already present in the old, before it begins to break down. The imaginal cells are not generic; they are holding a unique vision of each dimension of the butterfly that needs to emerge.[110]

The imaginal discs of our world are the voices that see the coming breakdown and are already imagining the possibility of a butterfly—a new world. But the systems of society move in myriad ways to choke the seeds of imagination from the nourishment they need to bloom. The imaginal discs are not resourced. They are marginalized, dismissed as fringe, or even attacked in more aggressive ways. But when the crisis

---

109 See Section V.3.

110 Silvia Aldaz and Luis M. Escudero, "Imaginal Discs" (2010).

they have long predicted finally erupts in the existing society, it will be resolved in the vision of the imaginal discs. The imaginal discs feed on the soup. They literally ingest the crisis and turn it into the evolutionary driver of new life birthed by new imagination. Their willingness to ingest the new reality is the cause for their transformation into imaginal cells.

Just like the old-world systems, the caterpillar's immune system initially fights the imaginal cells and doesn't allow them to proliferate. But as the immune system, together with the whole structure of the old, breaks down, they keep emerging faster and faster. The imaginal cells are driven by the search for new intimacies and new coherences with their partners and co-creators. They begin to intimately link with each other. New configurations of intimacy cohere and emerge. The crisis of imagination is resolved in the imaginal cells coming together in imaginal discs, a precursor of what we call Unique Self Symphonies. With the new intimacy comes a new freedom. The cells are now free to turn to their unique function in the life of the butterfly. The imaginal cells turn into the butterfly, which emerges out of the chrysalis.

This is a compelling archetypal story about how crisis precedes transformation. It is not a fairy tale or myth but a story rooted in scientific facts sourced in nature.

The old system breaks down. New visions begin to emerge, but the old guard shoots them down. We have called this stage of the process, in other essays, the Murder of Eros.[111]

The old guard represents the old level of consciousness.[112] This is the immune system of the caterpillar, which views the new consciousness of the imaginal cells as a threat. The immune system moves instinctively to destroy these harbingers of a next level of consciousness—the butterfly, the next level of humanity. Eventually, however, enough of the imaginal cells are allured together, the old guard dissolves, and a beautiful butterfly emerges from the chrysalis.

---

111 Gafni and Kincaid, A Return to Eros, 471–480.

112 There is also something quite poetic about the role the old guard plays for the new reality, becoming the food that nourishes the growth of new form. We must recognize that there is always a purpose for tradition and the preservative function in times of crisis and radical change.

The chrysalis embodies the core structure of evolution: Crises serve as evolutionary drivers.[113]

A new Universe Story and a new vision of identity begin to emerge in the Fourth Big Bang. At the core of the Fourth Big Bang is the fulfillment of *Homo sapiens* in *Homo amor*.

8. The Fourth Big Bang

Human self-consciousness led to the development of civilizations and eventually our modern capitalist world system.[114] This is, of course, a long and complex story, which goes through many stages. But as culture evolved through various and largely cumulative political and scientific revolutions, a Fourth Big Bang was being prepared. Eventually, culture itself would come to be informed by thinking about evolution. Evolution was becoming conscious of itself in a new way through human consciousness.

This has been a halting, error-prone process. Even today, the majority of the world's population does not believe in anything like a scientifically informed theory of evolution. But even more importantly, those who do trust the science of evolution view it as a theory of origins and not as a

---

113 See Section V.3 in part two.

114 The idea of world systems is essential for any serious thinking about evolutionary futures for the human species. See World-Systems Analysis: An Introduction, by Immanuel Wallerstein (2004). World-systems analysis is a growing transdisciplinary field, encompassing economics, politics, sociology, and history. The modern world system, which began to emerge during the sixteenth century, is the largest functionally integrated unit the human species has ever created. Its existence and continuation have fundamentally changed the very frontiers of human possibility and fundamentally altered the self-regulatory processes of the biosphere. It is the highest-order unit of selection and is unprecedentedly close to literally encompassing all of humanity, something never achieved before by any historical world system. Wallerstein argues that, at this point in geohistory, when there emerges a world system without peripheries or frontiers, an evolutionary crisis ensues, and a fundamentally new world system must be painfully and violently born—one no longer predicated upon endless accumulation, growth, profit, and exploitation.

radical revisioning of what it means to be a human being. Nevertheless, there are good reasons to believe that evolutionary realizations will spread like wildfire in the coming decades and a new species-wide self-understanding will emerge, including new ideas about the nature of the self and human personality and new ideas about the evolutionary function of human collectives and cooperatives.

8.1. Shadows of Early Evolutionary Narratives

The emergent truth of evolution is love in action. When we lose sight of this, the result is potentially disastrous. Evolution disassociated from its intrinsic nature as love in action is open to multiple forms of pathology. Indeed, the first glimmerings of an evolutionary view of humanity and the Universe coincided with one of the most violent and divisive periods in human history. This includes the specter of eugenics that still haunts all attempts to apply evolutionary theory to the social world.[115] These demons cannot be exorcised without having the courage to call them by name and look them in the eye. What has been said again and again, and was perhaps best said by Gould and Kevles,[116] is that these first attempts at applying the biological sciences to the design and governance of society resulted in a nightmare. Evolutionary theory was co-opted by warring capitalist nation-states and used to buttress racist ideologies that perpetuated nationalism, imperialism, and ultimately a global war.

This is all true. But it is important to know exactly why things went so horribly wrong, especially given the optimism expressed by many early pioneering biologists that evolutionary theory would unite humanity, an

---

115 Barbara Marx Hubbard, a coauthor of the first volume of this work, was initially taken by some of the transhumanist arguments in a number of domains and expressed herself inaccurately, in ways that were prone to tragic but sometimes understandable misinterpretation. Her encounter with CosmoErotic Humanism opened her thinking to Unique Self Theory, the centrality of the Evolutionary Eros, and much more, which caused her to recant some of the earlier transhumanist ideas.

116 See, for example, In the Name of Eugenics: Genetics and the Uses of Human Heredity, by Daniel J. Kevles (1985), and The Mismeasure of Man, by S. J. Gould (1981).

optimism shared by many to this day.[117] Two things stand out that should free us from the fear of inevitably repeating the horrors yielded by our progenitors' attempts at applying evolutionary theory in thinking about human systems.[118]

First, these early attempts were based on extremely simplistic ideas about genetic inheritance, selection, and other key aspects of evolutionary processes. Numerous key advances in the biological sciences have recently obliterated such outmoded forms of thought. Yet, despite the simplicity and easily demonstrable inadequacy of their ideas, the early eugenicists had huge ambitions, which, as they should have known, required extremely complex ideas and tools they did not have (which were decades away). They needed a scalpel; all they had was an ax. Why did they run ahead into surgery on the body politic anyway? It appears this was a case of politics trumping science, and of scientists being co-opted by money and power, intoxicated by state-sanctioned violence, and caught up in utopian dreams hatched during periods of profound social upheaval. There is no question that today we have fundamentally more adequate tools and ideas about the nature of evolution. But can we shield them from co-optation by political and economic powers that have no interest in scientific truths and their ethical application, especially during a time of great crisis?

Second, early attempts at applying evolutionary theory to society radically undertheorized human interiority, consciousness, and especially the nature of human personality. They were shaped by a dogmatic version

---

117 Make no mistake: Racism was a major problem throughout the world system during this period and remains a major problem today. The arguments offered here are not intended to downplay this aspect of the historical context. Instead, the goal is to identify the illicit epistemological moves that allowed for the perpetuation of racist ideas by creating the illusion that they were backed by scientific theories and objective measures. When the early IQ testing movement, for example, is simply dismissed as racist without further analysis, we have gained no insight into the mechanisms by which science was made an accomplice in the crime of political inequality. Moreover, we miss the fact that many of these mechanisms are still in play as aspects of contemporary ideology.

118 However, we must always continue to be in touch with this fear of repeating history. And we ought to continue to retell and remember the horrors we wish not to repeat, even if only to honor the victims and to educate the younger generations who might otherwise forget.

of materialism, which ignored interiors. In the language of CosmoErotic Humanism, they failed to marshal the evidence in the interior and exterior sciences that would point to the realization of the Intimate Universe, or the Universe: A Love Story. The Universe is not an ordinary love story. It is an Evolutionary Love Story whose very plotline is the evolution of love. That Love Story moves from cosmological to biological to cultural or human evolution to yet another future breakthrough.

8.2. Awakening from the Shadows: From Unconscious to Conscious Evolution

It is only recently, however, that *we* have awakened from unconscious to Conscious Evolution. We now understand that humanity is directly implicated in the next chapters of the Universe: A Love Story—or else there may be no further chapters for humanity at all. Humanity is the Universe evolving in person. But not only humanity. Every unique human being is personally implicated. Every unique human being is the Intimate Universe in person. Every human love story is chapter and verse in the Universe: A Love Story.

We are finally transcending the desiccating dogmatic claim that the self and its experiences can be understood as artifacts of the racial group or functional purpose. This alienation from interiority and consciousness disabled empathy and ultimately gave ideological justification to state-sanctioned violence of unimaginable proportions. By looking at evolution *only* in terms of *exterior* physical systems (genes, biology, technology), the evolution of individual and collective *interiors* was occluded from consideration. A whole generation was blinded by reductive evolutionary thinking and rendered unable to see *the other* as anything but a vehicle for the evolution of bloodlines.

Today, we not only need a theory of evolution that is qualitatively more complex and adequate in its dealing with the material and external aspects of evolutionary processes, but we also need one that can illuminate the evolution of interiors—the evolution of self and culture. We are called to weave a unified vision of humanity as part of an evolving Universe, one that integrates interiors and exteriors, matter and consciousness, agency and communion. This is the nature of the Fourth Big Bang, in which we are participating as the Universe in person at this very moment. The Fourth Big Bang has three major elements:

- There is the movement from unconscious to Conscious Evolution.

- Essential to Conscious Evolution is the realization of the interior nature and narrative thread of Reality, namely the Intimate Universe and the Universe: A Love Story.

- There is the movement from unconscious to conscious *uniqueness*. The emergence of Unique Self is key to the emergence of the New Human and the New Humanity. The Fourth Big Bang is *the emergence of the New Human and the New Humanity—Homo amor.* *Homo amor* is the Intimate Universe, or the Universe: A Love Story, in person.

8.3. The Heart of the Fourth Big Bang: Unique Selves and Unique Self Symphonies as the Emergence of Evolutionary Intimacy

A fundamental set of insights that guides the emergence of *Homo amor* is articulated in Unique Self Theory.[119] Unique Self Theory understands that one of the central dimensions of the evolutionary process is

---

119 The notions of Unique Self and Unique Self Symphony emerged at the interface of religious scholarship, psychological meta-theory, and evolutionary meta-theory—expressed collaboratively in different forms by Gafni, Stein, and Hubbard. This work naturally integrates with Hubbard's seminal work expressing and exploring Conscious Evolution, titled Conscious Evolution: Awakening the Power of Our Social Potential (2015). For a detailed look at the genesis of Unique Self Theory itself, see the special scholarly issue of the Journal of Integral Theory and Practice, 6(1), which is dedicated to Unique Self Theory. The volume was edited and largely penned by Marc Gafni, with the lead article "The Evolutionary Emergent of Unique Self: A New Chapter in Integral Theory" pp. 1–36. See also Gafni's Your Unique Self: The Radical Path to Personal Enlightenment (2012) and Self in Integral Evolutionary Mysticism: Two Models and Why They Matter (2014) on the core articulation of Unique Self Theory.

uniqueness. That is, evolution produces *the unique*—and, as evolution unfolds, uniqueness increases. This means that the idea of evolution becoming conscious of itself can be reframed in terms of uniqueness becoming conscious of itself. The moral implications could not be more important.

We describe the concept of Unique Self in depth in the first volume of this book,[120] but for the purposes of this essay, we will lay out the basic ideas in schematic form as a series of related postulates:

1. Evolution is a process that moves from simplicity to complexity—and from less consciousness to more consciousness.[121]

2. Greater complexity means greater interconnectivity. Evolution moves to deeper and wider levels of interconnectivity.

3. Reality is interiors and exteriors all the way up and all the way down the evolutionary chain.

4. The interior of interconnectivity is intimacy.

5. Evolution can therefore be thought of as the evolution of intimacy.

6. Intimacy always implies coming together of unique parts.

7. This movement toward greater complexity, consciousness, and intimacy is also a movement toward increasingly unique forms of life.

8. The greater the uniqueness, the greater the potential depth of the new intimacy.

---

120 Gafni and Hubbard, Whole Mate.

121 This is Teilhard de Chardin's notion of law of complexity and consciousness. See his The Phenomenon of Man (1959), originally published in 1955 in French as Le Phenomene Humain.

9. Increases in complexity, consciousness, intimacy, and uniqueness correlate with increases in creativity and Eros as organismic potentials.

10. Evolution is thus the move from unconscious uniqueness to conscious uniqueness.

11. The self-reflective Evolutionary Unique Self—the organism aware of its own evolutionary uniqueness—becomes a possibility with the emergence of humanity and can be thought of as a key attractor in the evolutionary process.

12. Your Evolutionary Unique Self is the *personal* face of a universal evolutionary process. In this way, your unique qualities of personhood beyond ego participate in the evolution of the Universe.

It is necessary to pause here to clarify the meaning of *Unique Self* and to preempt some common objections. Firstly, there is a difference between what is typically referred to as *ego* and *Unique Self*.[122] The term *ego* is typically used with reference to a contracted sense of self, where one emphasizes difference and asserts self over other. Unique Self, on the other hand, can be understood as individuation beyond ego, or beyond separate self.

Separate self is both real and an illusion—both from the exterior and interior perspective. Albert Einstein was referring primarily to exteriors when he pointed to the self-evident truth of the contemporary ecological evolutionary sciences that the notion of a separate self is an optical delusion of consciousness. The interior sciences of the perennial philosophy, across space and time, have pointed to the same validated truth from the

---

122 See Your Unique Self: The Radical Path to Personal Enlightenment, by Marc Gafni (2012), for twenty-six distinctions between Unique Self and Ego. A free copy of Gafni's "Twenty-Six Distinctions between Unique Self and Ego" from Self in Integral Evolutionary Mysticism: Two Models and Why They Matter can be found at https://worldphilosophyandreligion.org/dr-marc-gafni-26-distinctions-between-ego-and-unique-self/.

perspective of interiors. This is understood by Unique Self Theory to mean that there is no consciousness and desire separate from the larger Field of Consciousness and Desire. This knowing is our true identity as True Self—the identity in which every human being must consciously participate in order to know themselves at the most fundamental level. Unique Self is *not* separate self. That would be a *pre–True Self* realization. Rather, Unique Self is a *post–True Self* realization. In other words, Unique Self is the unique perspective and unique quality of intimacy of the LoveIntelligence, LoveBeauty, and LoveDesire—individuated beyond ego, or beyond separate self. To know one's identity is therefore to awaken to one's Unique Self.

This does not mean that Unique Self comes online only after a full realization of True Self. What is required, however, is a general sense or fragrance of True Self. Once one has a fragrance of the larger Field— which one can access just by reading the last couple of points (the part of you that understands the sentences above is your True Self), you can awaken to the realization of your Unique Self. Your Unique Self is the unique expression of the Field of the True Self.

This notion of identity is the most inclusive framework we have around identity. It is supported by the classical sciences, both exterior and interior. Unique Self makes sense for Albert Einstein, for quantum physics, for molecular biology, even as it is a perspective that makes sense in atheistic Buddhism, especially in its Vajrayana forms, as well as in the esoteric realizations of Judeo-Christian, Sufi, Hindu, Confucian, and Native wisdoms. Note that this is different from most typical spiritual and ethical teachings, which suggest *overcoming* or *forgetting* one's personal story—disappeared and outshined by the Absolute—be it the Eternal Fact or the Evolutionary Impulse. Rather, our story is a part of the larger Story. Each unique personal story drives the larger Story. There is no split between personal evolution and the evolution of Reality. You don't overcome or forget your story; you clarify the uniqueness of your story. There is an evolutionary imperative to promote uniqueness. And uniqueness is a relational category.[123]

---

123 Uniqueness is what philosophers call a relational category, which contrasts with an entity category. This means uniqueness describes something that occurs

Unique Selves come together to form Unique Self Symphonies, which is how the Universe optimally and ethically self-organizes and evolves at the level of human culture and personhood. The realization that the Universe inherently self-organizes or self-actualizes based on simple rules emerges from work done during the last half of the twentieth century, beginning with Alan Turing's epic "Morphogenesis."[124]

What drives self-organization at the human level?

In the Third Big Bang, self-organization is driven by different motivational architectures at every structure stage of consciousness. In developmental language, we might refer to the structure stages of the Third Big Bang as *the first tier of human consciousness*, as described in overlapping forms by myriad developmental theorists as aptly recapitulated in Integral Theory.[125] At what developmental theory calls *second tier*, a new structure stage of consciousness recognized in some form by myriad theorists, *uniqueness* is the self-organizing instrument of the Fourth Big Bang.[126] Unique Self Symphony is an emergent form of superorganisms, because it requires

---

between and among things, arising out of relationships, as opposed to being an intrinsic abstract property of a thing in isolation. Uniqueness is not just about difference; it is about differences defined through relations. Charles S. Peirce did the first pioneering work on the differences between relational categories and entity categories. See The Continuity of Peirce's Thought, by Kelly A. Parker (1998).

124 Turing, "The Chemical Basis of Morphogenesis."

125 See the charts in Integral Psychology, by Ken Wilber (2000). For an important critique and up-leveling of the way development is often presented in Integral circles and other forums, see "On the Use of the Term Integral," by Zachary Stein (2014), especially the section "Growth-to-Goodness from Baldwin to Wilber." One of the foundational volumes of CosmoErotic Humanism under preparation, by Stein and Gafni, is titled In a Unique Voice. We intend it to integrate Unique Self Theory and developmental theory, and it will be a key pillar of CosmoErotic Humanism.

126 See, for example, the essay/dialogue by Marc Gafni and developmental theorist Suzanne Cook Greuter in Journal of Integral Theory and Practice, 6(1). We also note the reaction of Don Beck on reading the original Unique Self Book—Your Unique Self: The Radical Path to Personal Enlightenment, by Marc Gafni (2012). Beck remarked, "Your Unique Self is the bible of Yellow," referring to the first structure stage of second-tier consciousness. Most importantly, however, note the chapter on Unique Self Theory in Education in a Time Between Worlds: Essays on the Future of Schools, Technology, and Society, by Zachary Stein (2019)

that we care about everyone's story. It has social justice—the view from everywhere—at its core and leverages the benefits of justice to promote further harmonious evolutionary emergence. Unique Self Symphony is the personal and communal expression of what we call *Evolutionary Intimacy*.

PART TWO

—

REALITY IS RELATIONSHIP

—

I. FIRST NOTES ON SCIENCE, MYSTERY, AND RELATIONSHIPS: THE EMERGENCE OF A NEW SCIENTIFIC WORLDVIEW

1. Beyond Scientism and Religion

Science is one of the key voices that guide and inform us as we unfold the next step in relationships.

In the ancient world, at least in the popular mind, Reality was thought into being by Divine feat, *Deus Ex Machina*, through a waving of the divine wand. The different parts of Reality were thought to be living expressions of Spirit, but Spirit was seen as controlling its own real estate in the world of matter, rather than matter being governed by natural laws or principles. Relationships between parts of the Whole were thought to be ordained by God's Law, but that Law was not seen as being inherent to Reality itself. Creativity was believed to be a property of Divinity that lived outside the world. The job of man was obedience and submission to Divine Law or Grace.

Modern science has its roots in Aristotle, who, continuing the lineage of the pre-Socratics, articulated a new Universe Story. He began to internalize the purely exteriorized Spirit with the notion that concrete

Reality is derived from what he called its immanent form,[127] an idea that gave rise to the scientific method.[128]

The sciences are responses to the worldviews of the ancients. Science is the wisdom that integrates experiments, data collection, and communities, rigorously testing the validity of experimental results. Integral Theory (echoing and adapting Thomas Kuhn, Wilfred Sellars, and others) describes science as a triplicate between *injunction* (experiment), *datum* (recorded observations of the outcomes of the injunction), and falsification in *a community of the adequate* (a community of experts capable of reading the results of experiments). This, according to Wilber, is the same triplicate of the *interior sciences* used to validate findings from interior injunctions like meditation.[129] The notion of the empirical nature of the interior sciences articulated in Integral Theory is common to key strains in Buddhism, Kabbalah, Kashmir Shaivism, Sufism, and other

---

127 In Metaphysics, Aristotle writes (1037a29–30), "For substance is the immanent form from which together with matter the composite substance is said." Or, in a somewhat different translation: "From both these schools, then, we can learn this much, that the contraries are the principles of things; and how many these principles are and which they are, we can learn from one of the two schools. But how these principles can be brought together under the causes we have named has not been clearly and articulately stated by them; they seem, however, to range the elements under the head of matter; for out of these as immanent parts they say substance is composed and moulded." (Translation by W. D. Ross.)

128 Aristotle's hylomorphic account—that physical reality arises from a combination of matter and internal form (what makes matter turn into the things it turns into), in Metaphysics 1036a2–8—was reserved for what became natural philosophy and later the sciences. But Aristotle maintained that there was a more primary being, which is the source and the pursuit of particular substances—compounds of matter and form—rather than particular substances merely being made of particular substances. Aristotle saw this primary being as the object of philosophy and source of wisdom itself (Metaphysics 1064a35–b1). Compare also: "That Wisdom is a science of first principles is evident from the introductory chapters, in which we have raised objections to the statements of others about the first principles; but one might ask the question whether Wisdom is to be conceived as one science or as several. If as one, it may be objected that one science always deals with contraries, but the first principles are not contrary. If it is not one, what sort of sciences are those with which it is to be identified?"

129 See The Marriage of Sense and Soul: Integrating Science and Religion, by Ken Wilber (1999).

esoteric readings of the great traditions.[130]

Science provides invaluable information about the physical Universe and the rules that govern matter. Science has demonstrated, for example, that we live in a constantly creating Cosmos, and that this creative Cosmos generates Reality from its own internal creative process over eons of historical time through an ever-evolving creative drive toward new depth and novelty. In a deep and careful reading of the empirical information, we realize—scientifically, in the interior and exterior sciences—that Reality desires and yearns for ever-deeper and wider forms of Eros and intimacy. The drives for greater Eros and for greater intimacy are primary Values of Cosmos. They express an entire set of inter-included Cosmic Values, which include the desire and drive for ever-greater complexity, consciousness, creativity, uniqueness, love, care and concern, and more.

1.1. Science and Scientism

Science, however, is often confused with *scientism*—a bunch of scientific dogmas, a worldview making dogmatic claims about the nature of the world. Just like religions had their dogmas, which were often at odds with the actual wisdom of religion, science developed its own dogmas. They made claims about the nature of Reality that were not sourced in actual scientific knowledge about the external world. These dogmas also ignored other forms of important experimental knowledge, which revealed truths about the interior face of the Cosmos.

The dogmas of scientism in its most radical forms are:[131]

---

130 On the direct access of the practitioner to the Divine Gnosis, see for example Marc Gafni, Radical Kabbalah (2010), vol. 1, part three. The notion of the validation of the community, however, is missing from Radical Kabbalah, which is very much about the unique individual, who is untranslatable to the community of peers. Instead, it plays a pivotal role in the interior sciences of the Talmud, which understood the role of the community of expert peers to be central in validating the conclusions of interior science. See, for example, on this key topic, Not in Heaven: The Nature and Function of Jewish Law, by Eliezer Berkowitz (2010).

131 These dogmas were once working assumptions built into the foundation of science, and thus seemed to have been borne out through experiments based on these assumptions (although never "proven" directly). This is, in part, why these

- The essential building blocks of Reality are separate tiny particles.

- The particles are assumed to be purely material, with no sentience.

- The particles move according to fixed mathematical laws.

- Matter is purely passive and inert.

- Only humans have thoughts or feelings. The rest of Reality is a dead machine.

Man's job (and it really was man and not woman) was to control nature for the sake of humanity, or at least for the sake of the part of humanity that was thought to be enlightened with Western, Christian, European principles.

To be clear, the core notion that Reality has fixed laws, which can be mapped and, most importantly, measured, was a scientific revolution. It took us out of the world of myth and later supported the modern industrial and informational revolutions. This in itself was very good news and generated the techno-economic base that catalyzed some of the greatest evolutions of Eros and intimacy since the beginning of time, including universal human rights and the aspiration for universal education.

The bad news is that the assumption that Reality is merely material is essentially wrong. So is the reductionist movement in sciences, which understood elements in the Universe as essentially isolated from each other—that is to say, the idea that the most fundamental particle is the key building block of Reality and each particle is separate from all other particles. The vision of Reality as discrete objects that are part of

---

assumptions were mistaken for truths and became dogmatic (even as science itself eventually undermined them). In contrast to the reductive-materialist view that dominates much of scientism today, Galileo and Newton thought that divine wisdom ordained the laws of mathematics and nature. Both men were highly spiritual, with Newton being a profound mystic in his understanding of Reality.

a larger machine with no inherent intelligence is based on assumptions, not on any experimental results. In this view, we are separate from Reality. If you then add the dogma of evolution—not the scientific truth that Reality evolves, but the dogmatic claim that the Universe has no direction other than the survival of the fittest, and so life is inherently predatory—then both our self-image and the world look pretty depressing indeed.

The living, telos-driven Cosmos of Aristotle has been lost to the popular modern mind, because the dogmatic materialism asserted, without sufficient reason or evidence, that only exterior Reality is truly Real. That would mean that subjective interiors, which include love, loyalty, nobility, ethics, values, goodness, beauty, and everything else that makes life worth living, were not ultimately Real. At best, they are just complex neurochemical interactions. All of these critical dimensions of Reality, however, are available to us, but not through dogma, as the old religions often claimed. They are available through the experimental methods of the interior sciences.

1.2. Dogmas of Science and Dogmas of Religion

The interior sciences, which grow out of the most refined esoteric, mystical strains in religions and enlightenment traditions—Kashmir Shaivism, Vajrayana Buddhism, Christian mysticism (like that of Meister Eckhart), Taoism, Hebrew mysticism, Sufism, the nature mysticism of native peoples, and just about every other system that developed and maintained interior practices—have been able to access the knowing that all of Reality is utterly interconnected and that the inner feeling of connection is intimacy.

The great principle of *Reality is relationship*—or more precisely, Reality is *intimate* relationship—was known through introspection (although never expressed in exactly these words), but it wasn't supported by the reductionist views of physics or the reductionist expressions of molecular biology that dominated the sciences of the time. Overlaid on the view of the world as consisting of disconnected particles has been the equally dogmatic view of a brutally competitive and directionless world that emerged from neo-Darwinism—the secular hijacking of evolutionary science.[132]

The dogmatic worldviews, wrongly attributed to pure science, were often hijacked to justify corrupt forms of capitalism.[133] One example would be the robber barons in the United States. These capitalists regularly tried to hijack science through dogmatic scientism to justify their greed and their trampling of individuals, ethics, and integrity in the pursuit of a distorted fulfillment of power—degraded forms of *power over* instead of noble forms of *power for*. Science, they asserted, informed us that dog-eat-dog, brutal competition is simply the law of the jungle.[134] As our colleague John P. Mackey, the founder of Whole Foods, has pointed out, crony capitalism still dominates the preponderance of the marketplaces around the world.

Science was so wonderfully successful at producing knowledge about the physical world that generated life-changing innovation, such as landing on the moon, fiber optics, and genetics, that its authority was clearly and correctly recognized. That was appropriate and good.

---

132 The term neo-Darwinism is not fair to its namesake. Darwin, who could not have known or speculated on genetic mechanisms that are the reductionist wont of neo-Darwinists, explored mechanisms beyond natural selection through small, iterative adaptations. It would be fairer to call the neo-Darwinist movement neo-Mendelism, after the Mendelian genetics, as the movement is based primarily on explaining the evolutionary process exclusively through population genetics.

133 Capitalism is not inherently corrupt. Indeed, it has beautiful and conscious forms. See for example Conscious Capitalism: Liberating the Heroic Spirit of Business, by John Mackey and Raj Sisodia (2013).

134 This neo-Darwinian co-opting is based on a misunderstanding of the idea of evolutionary fitness—the idea of survival of the fittest, which is taken to mean that those most well adapted to their environment survive and reproduce. Darwin did not see evolution as a success story of the fittest in absolute terms, as neo-Darwinian dogma does, but of the relatively more fit as environmental conditions change. Those most fit for a particular environment have failed as conditions rapidly change, as history has shown again and again. But even beyond Darwin, there is a body of work revealing that an evolutionary selection process happens at the level of environmental niches, meaning evolution is not merely about species fitting their environment but environments fitting their ecological zones. Humans themselves can be called a species of niche constructors, meaning humans enact a kind of evolutionary process when we literally recreate environments (the Anthropocene), which themselves change the conditions for fitness.

The problem was that very little distinction was made in the popular or philosophical mind between science itself and the myriad dogmas of scientism. The methods of the interior sciences were also lost to the popular and philosophical mind because Spirit had fallen into disrepute for multiple reasons, including these primary ones:

1. Religion had become the institution of state that inflicted all of the injustice of the previous two thousand years. It was that which Voltaire had in mind at the dawn of the Enlightenment, when the battle cry to throw religion out was *Remember the cruelties!*

2. Religion had overreached and made claims about medicine, astronomy, and many other things that were clearly disproven by science.

3. The popular conceptions of virtually all religions claimed to own truth and God. Each one claimed that their teaching was exclusively true. They made no distinctions between their rituals, for which they claimed exclusive Divine Truth, and the interior wisdom of their legitimate knowledge. They saw everything through their own exclusive prism. When all the religions were gathered and compared, all these issues exploded and undermined the believability of religion. It became clear that religion had lied, claiming knowledge it did not have. Lying always undermines relationship. It became clear that all the religions were claiming to be the only true religion, which obviously could not be correct.

4. Religion's view of a purely external God was not aligned with the new information coming from all the fields of science.

1.3. Science's New Wisdom: Reality Is Relationship

The dogmas of disconnection, peddled by scientism, were often purveyed by leading scientists who made declarations about the nature of life.

Steven Weinberg and Stephen Hawking are two of dozens of examples of this phenomenon, overreaching into fields of expertise that have nothing to do with their own knowledge domains.

This arrogant overreaching of science is part of what caused what philosopher Bertrand Russell described as an unyielding despair settling over the modern mind. He wrote that, according to the popular worldview, man's "growth, his hopes and fears, his loves and his beliefs, are but the outcome of accidental collocations of atoms."[135] In what seems to be "such an alien and inhuman world, can so powerless a creature as man preserve his aspirations untarnished?"[136]

On the one hand, premodern, modern, and postmodern religions hold that their system contains exclusive truth, while all heretics burn in various forms of hell. On the other hand, the dogmatic claims of scientism reject any realization of the Ultimate Value of the Good, the True, and the Beautiful as the inherent Desire of the Intimate Universe. Both sides together have colluded to create a quality of despair that has de-eroticized Reality and produced what we call a global intimacy disorder.[137]

We are not intimate with each other unless we participate in a mutually recognized and felt Story of Value. We are intimate with ourselves only when we recognize our own participation, our own shared identity, *with* and *in* the Field of Value. We are intimate with Reality only if Reality's intrinsic quality bears intimacy.[138] Intimacy is generated by participation in Value, and if such Value does not exist, if Reality is

---

135 Bertrand Russell, Mysticism and Logic, Including a Free Man's Worship (1986), 10.

136 Bertrand Russell, "A Free Man's Logic," in Mysticism and Logic and Other Essays (1919).

137 See Essay One for an in-depth exploration of this topic.

138 For example, on a human level, we create intimacy with a person who shares a similar interior consciousness, who participates with us in the interior Field of Value and Meaning. It is harder to create intimacy with a rock, because a rock does not share the depth of human consciousness, meaning, and value. But if Reality itself had no quality of interior, if it were only material, then these words themselves would make no sense. Words make sense insofar as they are intimate with Reality, and intimacy implies shared identity in the context of otherness that expresses itself in mutualities of recognition, feeling, value, and purpose.

merely material, then intimacy with Reality is not possible. It is the failure of intimacy, birthed by stagnant worldviews such as the scientism that breeds despair and ennui.

All the despair invoked by the scientistic vision of a disconnected and apathetic reality has been deeply challenged, and in many cases overturned, over the last hundred years, as the dramatic new information of the new sciences has been coming online. The new sciences—quantum mechanics, systems science and its daughters, complexity and chaos sciences, molecular biology and systems biology, natural genetic engineering, attachment theory, and more—have given us powerful insights that have grounded the conclusions of the interior sciences in the exterior structures of science.

The core information coming out of the new sciences is the underlying principle of Reality:

Reality is Eros—desiring ever-more intimacy, ever-deeper and wider shared identities in the context of otherness.

The following are three crucial implications of this principle:

- Reality is evolution.

- Reality is relationship.

- Reality is evolution of relationships.

Reality has an inherent direction toward ever-deeper and ever-wider forms of intimate relationship. The direction of evolution is toward deeper and deeper forms of intimacy, and its driver is crisis. Any crisis is a crisis of relationship, in other words, a crisis of intimacy. Crisis in relationship serves as an evolutionary driver to the next level of passion and possibility.[139]

The crisis is resolved through an evolution of intimacy and

---

139 The idea of crisis as an evolutionary driver is explored in Section V.3.

relationship, which yields the next emergent of relationship and intimacy. All the sciences listed above assert, in their own languages, what the interior sciences have always implicitly known: Reality is relationship, or, more precisely:

- Reality is intimate relationship, that is, a relationship defined by shared identity, mutuality of recognition, mutuality of pathos (feeling), mutuality of value, and mutuality of purpose between parts.

- Reality is constantly evolving to ever-deeper and ever-wider forms of relationship.

- Reality is the progressive deepening of intimacies, that is, the emergence of ever-wider and ever-deeper circles of shared identity and mutualities of recognition, pathos, value, and purpose.

We will not be able to engage all of this new information from the exterior sciences, which clearly implies the movement of Eros and intimacy that animates Cosmos, but we want to access at least the fragrance of this new information. We will just touch on some core insights from quantum physics, molecular biology, complexity science, and evolutionary theory. All of these fields capture and express the startling insight that the core structure of Reality is Eros—an ever-deeper contact in an ever-more intimate relationship.

We will not share this insight in the formal, scientific language. Rather, we will share some of the potent personal, political, and poetic implications that emerge from these sources, as they are relevant to the core principle that Reality is intimate relationship.

2. Pan-Interiority of Reality

Science is a modern form of revelation: It reveals facts about the nature of Reality. These facts, however, are not dry, abstract, or merely theoretical. Facts are not only prose but poetry. Facts directly inform the fabric of our understanding of Reality, our Universe Story, and therefore of our place in Reality. In other words, science has downloaded an enormous amount of crucial new information into the source code of culture.

Scientists are the new co-holders of the mystery. At the leading edge of knowledge, the old war between science and spirit is over. It is only primitive visions of science and spirit that are still lost in that outdated battle. Science and spirit—or, more precisely, exterior and interior sciences—give us different truths about different dimensions of Reality seen from different perspectives:

- Interior sciences map subjective interiors. Postdogmatic wisdom masters of Spirit help us map and make sense of what happens on the inside of our hearts and consciousness.

- Exterior sciences map objective exteriors, or what happens in what Plato called, in *The Republic*, the visible and intelligible realms.

New information from the exterior sciences, which we only allude to in this book, is a powerful validation of the interior sciences.

The shocking but not at all surprising news from the frontiers of exterior and interior sciences is that insides and outsides are not separate but connected; more than that, they are *reflections* of each other.

The premodern view was that there was a great chain of being, with Spirit at the top and matter at the bottom—with exterior objects at the bottom and interior subjects at the top. But we now realize that this is, at least in part, an inaccurate map of Reality. Interiors and exteriors are not separate *magisteria*[140] that occasionally overlap. All of Reality is One with two faces. Reality is interiors and exteriors all the way up and all the way down. We refer to this quality of Reality as *pan-interiority*. There is some level of *proto-interiority*, or *proto-consciousness*, at every level of Reality. The great mathematician Alfred North Whitehead, who wrote *Principia Mathematica* with Bertrand Russell, referred to this proto-interiority as *prehension*. This initial spark of interior consciousness is what the physicist Freeman Dyson and the mathematical complexity theorist Stuart Kauffman refer to when they talk about some proto level of free will even at the subatomic level of consciousness.

Clearly, the subatomic level of consciousness is something very different than the experience of interiority, consciousness, and freedom on the human level—or even at any of the levels of the biosphere. Indeed, this is the trajectory of evolution. Evolution moves toward ever-more complex and interconnected exteriors, which possess ever-more profound interiority, freedom, and consciousness. We know that physics can plot the motion of the stars and predict their locations accurately a thousand years from now, but a biologist, brilliant as they may be at molecular biology, cannot tell you where their cat will be ten minutes from now.[141] And of course, freedom is exponentially more pronounced in human beings, whose natural capacity for free choices vastly exceeds stars, atoms, or even cats. Moreover, human beings have the capacity to engage in developmental practice, be it physical, psychological, or spiritual, which greatly increases their interior capacity for choice and freedom.

While interiors and exteriors cannot be reduced to each other, they do point to each other. Exteriors and interiors are inter-included with each other and are always alluding to each other. There is a never-ending feedback loop between interiors and exteriors.

Consider a simple example: You fall in love. This is an interior,

---

140 Magisteria is the plural of magisterium, which, according to Webster's New World College Dictionary, is the "authority, office, and power to teach true doctrine by divine guidance."

141 However, physicists also cannot predict the location of a single particle in the next second. It is only in the realm of classical physics, which deals with large enough objects, that the location of an object is sufficiently determined.

subjective experience. Your body releases dopamine and other neu-rochemicals—the exterior, objective co-expression of that interior. But it would be a mistake (one that is often made) to reduce love to neurochemicals. Love is an interior experience, which is expressed and at times even evoked by neurochemicals. But love is not reducible to neurochemicals. Love is an interior, which, in this manifest world, also has an exterior expression. We stake our lives on our loves, because we realize that our loves are very much not a passing sentiment evoked by a cocktail of neurochemicals (which themselves are supposedly a product of a random and meaningless evolutionary process). Rather, our love participates in the Field of Eros and Value (sometimes called *the Tao* and known by dozens of other names), which is the very Ground of Reality. It is the most real experience we know, and thus it infuses our existence with aliveness, meaning, purpose, and joy, all of which are self-evident in our immediate experience.

The physical, exterior model of Reality as relationship and the interior, psychological, spiritual, and existential models of Reality as relationship are inextricably related. In that sense, it might be said that value is already nascent in the very structure of exterior Reality and its sciences, which already imply visions of what it means to live a good life. Nascent value, personal and collective, is already coded in the sacred autobiographies of atoms, molecules, and cells.

There are patterns that connect and laws that govern both the physics of our interior worlds and the physics of the exterior worlds. Both live in us even as we live in them. We are stardust, we are quarks and atoms and cells, even as we are feelings and insights. In the first volume of this work, we describe one crucial strand in the evolution of relationships that we are in the midst of right now, the evolution of human romantic rela-tionships from role mate to soul mate to whole mate.[142] This evolutionary movement is not only the evolution of your personal relationships. It is also the evolution of our collective relationships at this juncture in history, and it directly participates in the evolution of relationship, which is the core plotline of Cosmos itself.

---

142 For a deeper view of whole mate relationships, see also Essay Two in this volume.

3. From Dualism to Materialism to Evolutionary Science

Science has evolved radically in the last few decades of the twentieth century and has given us dramatic new insights based on new information.

The first insight confronts an old idea (taken as a given in most of modern science) that *matter is dead*. The dogmas of dead matter defined first the dualism of the seventeenth century and then, in their new forms, the materialism of the nineteenth century.

The worldview dominating the emergence of modern science was dualism. The implicit image of the world was that of the living Divine and dead matter. Dead matter was animated only by mediation of the Divine into its inert space. As the old visions of the Divine were discarded in the nineteenth century, the half of Reality that was claimed to be Divine by Descartes and other dualists was lopped off, and we were left with the worldview of dead, inert matter at the center of modern science and culture. The nineteenth-century materialism, which still dominates so much of the scientific establishment, was, at its core, simply dualism with its head cut off. Large swaths of the world population that remained religious have had their trust in the essential goodness of Reality shaken at its core—even if they continued practicing their particular religions.

But in the newly emerging understanding rooted in new scientific discoveries, we live in a *self-organizing Universe*.[143] The Universe has inherent ceaseless creativity, which moves Reality to higher and deeper forms of intimacy and relationship. Nobel Prize–winning chemist Ilya Prigogine was a key player in rejecting the old notion of dead matter.

---

143 It is worth noting that emergence is arguably a much older term than self-organization. See The Re-Emergence of Emergence: The Emergentist Hypothesis from Science to Religion, edited by Phillip Clayton and Paul Davies (2006).

He showed that, long before there were human minds, chemicals could self-organize into complex patterns capable of coordination. There was no human intention or governing body. There was no genetic set of instructions driving them. Rather, Prigogine demonstrated that matter itself has self-organizing properties that guide these complex interactions.[144] It is because of the self-organizing dynamics of matter that "over the course of four billion years, molten rocks transformed themselves into monarch butterflies, blue herons, and the exalted music of Mozart."[145]

The second key insight is the realization that cooperation and relationship are core drivers of evolution. This realization is rapidly being integrated at the leading edges of science. The crucial role of Love as a driver of the selection process (both in Darwin's particular thought and evolutionary theory in general) has been decisively highlighted by thinkers as diverse as Stephen Jay Gould, David Loye, and Geoffrey Miller. As Miller intimated in a personal conversation with this author (I am paraphrasing), any doctoral student today who explains evolution only in terms of survival of the fittest, who missed that the desire to love and be loved are primary forces driving evolution, is dogmatic, anti-science, and fundamentalist.

Miller points out that *sexual selection*, which was pushed aside in the works of mainstream evolutionary theorists in favor of natural selection, is central to the evolutionary process.[146] Sexual selection, at its deepest core, is the desire for erotic, intimate relationship, the desire to love and be loved, and what we are willing to do to get that intimacy and love.

---

144 See Order Out of Chaos: Man's New Dialogue with Nature, by Ilya Prigogine and Isabelle Stengers (1984).

145 Brian Swimme and Mary E. Tucker, Journey of the Universe (2011).

146 Geoffrey Miller, The Mating Mind: How Sexual Choice Shaped the Evolution of Human Nature (2011).

Reality is Eros.

Reality is Fuck.[147]

Reality is Love.

A stream of evolutionary thought that understands evolution as being driven by the desire for deeper and deeper intimacies is finding its way into the mainstream of science. It was initially championed by the likes of historian Peter Kropotkin and the great interdisciplinary geniuses Charles Sanders Peirce and James Mark Baldwin.[148] Mainstream evolutionary theorists like David Sloan Wilson now talk about the existence of altruism all throughout nature.

The science of emergence is now implicit in the understanding of the evolutionary process, which begins with the subatomic world and moves toward ever-greater interconnectivity and complexity, the inside of which is ever-greater intimacy, love, and relationship. We could cite at least half a dozen other major fields of leading-edge science that all point in the same direction, but we think we have said enough to at least introduce this fundamentally game-changing insight.

Human beings are no longer understood to be essentially separate from each other. Human beings reflect the deeper nature of Reality. Reality is relationship—from subatomic particles to human beings (and

---

147 We use the word fuck not in its degraded expression (of objectifying or dehumanizing sex). In fact, we hold that the degradation of fuck is itself an essential dimension of the contemporary crisis of shame and desire. Fuck, while not the only quality of Eros, is a quality that cannot be bypassed without paying a moral price. We have shown in many books that bypassing the quality of Fuck in Eros creates abuse. See A Return to Eros.

148 There are important differences in the concept of evolution toward intimacy in each of these great thinkers. Kropotkin refuted any kind of universal love, arguing instead that mutual aid has practical advantages in the survival and reproduction of species. Baldwin, a friend and contemporary of Peirce, saw evolution operating on the principle of continuously exploring one's environment, which inevitably led to the persistent generation of novelty (read: persistent Fuck generates new configurations of intimacy). Peirce called his theory of evolutionary love agapism—a revering love of Cosmos supporting the development of new evolutionary forms. On the evolutionary thought (rooted in love) of Kropotkin, Peirce, and Baldwin, see Mutual Aid: A Factor of Evolution, by P. Kropotkin (2011); "Evolutionary Love," by Charles S. Peirce (1893); and Genetic Theory of Reality, by James Mark Baldwin (2009).

beyond). Reality, whether in the life of a human being or the life of humanity,[149] and all the way down the evolutionary chain, is the intensification of intimacy and relationship.

Science and Spirit are coming together as never before. Several hundred years ago, science and Spirit split off, disassociating rather than differentiating. Now, they are coming back together in a new embrace. None of the information we shared above was fully available even fifty years ago. Quantum physics and the Hubble and Webb telescopes have begun gathering this information. It has continued to accumulate, much of it coming into focus in the last few decades. The science of emergence, which has unfolded the core principle of the inherent ceaseless creativity of Cosmos,[150] is virtually all based on new information.

4. Telos and Eros of the Self-Actualizing Cosmos

The realization that we live in a self-actualizing Cosmos is one of the most potent new insights of science. The world does not emerge through a wand that is waved once and voilà, it appears. It also does not evolve by blind chance.[151] The world evolves because there is a ceaseless inherent creativity built into every dimension of Cosmos that moves Reality toward more and more complex and conscious forms.

The self-actualizing Cosmos operates according to laws of physics,

149 The evolution of relationship to deeper and wider frames is the core engine of evolution not only for individual human beings but for humanity. See Sections V.1–3.

150 For example, Stuart A. Kauffman writes, "God is our chosen name for the ceaseless creativity in the natural universe, biosphere, and human cultures." See "Breaking the Galilean Spell" on Edge.org (https://www.edge.org/conversation/stuart_a_kauffman-breaking-the-galilean-spell).

151 See Sections V.1 and V.2 for a deeper look at the seeming paradox of order and randomness.

chemistry, and biology, but the move toward self-actualization can also be seen as a constant inner process of Cosmic Genius, interior to matter itself, constantly inventing ever-deeper, more beautiful, and more brilliantly complex systems of matter, life, and awareness.

The whole Universe is coded with the erotic power of emergence. Parts are attracted (or *allured*) to other parts. They do not *fuse* with them, because they are also coded with their own separate integrity. Rather, the parts come together as staggeringly complex wholes combined through the mysterious elixir of evolutionary creativity.

All of the mathematical formulas of physics disclose what could be called the ground melody for this unimaginable symphony of what Oxford biologist Denis Noble calls the Music of Life.[152] A vast, intimate, musical, and mathematical Cosmic Mind is activated that guides the allured parts—sometimes over eons—to form larger wholes. The Universe is an ongoing creative, erotic vortex of supernova-like brilliance, complexity, and interrelationship. This self-organizing process does not begin with life. It begins with the first elementary particles of matter.

For example, *photosynthesis* is, in a very real sense, the deepening of intimacy between the Earth and the Sun. This feat of dazzling creativity has at its core

[a] molecular assembly . . . requiring perhaps tens of millions of years to develop, which has engineered an elegant resonance with sunlight.

Like tuning forks shaped to vibrate in the presence of certain sorts of music, these special molecules, called *chlorophyll*, glow with energy when the light from our Sun falls upon them.

The photons, when captured, lift electrons to a higher energy state, which immediately sets off a cascade of chemical events leading to the creation of powerhouse molecules within

152 See The Music of Life: Biology Beyond Genes, by Denis Noble (2006).

every cell.[153]

This deepening intimacy between Earth and Sun allows life on Earth to directly access the Sun's energy, in order to set off a chain of chemical interactions—uniquely intimate plays of Eros. Together, they sustain life on Earth. This feat of unparalleled creativity—which no team of scientists, aided by the best of artificial intelligence, could even dream of recreating—was innovated over vast stretches of time by a team of primitive organisms that did not even have brains, let alone eyes, hands, or libraries.[154] This is how Reality expresses its inherent and ceaseless creativity.

Cosmologists have written with lyrical beauty about the self-organizing processes of stars. We know that anthills and beehives self-organize in intricate and seemingly miraculous ways. We know that the cells in the body, a hundred times more numerous than stars in our Milky Way galaxy, self-organize intelligently in ways that demonstrate agency and high-level intelligence, exploding the old views of reductionist materialistic evolution.[155]

What we often forget is that self-organization reaches down all the way to the very beginning of Reality. At the core of the self-organizing process of star creation are sets of erotic and intimate relationships between the elementary particles that constitute the nuclei of the atoms that make up the stars.[156] Reality's desire for erotic relationship creates the radiance of stars.

Evolutionary emergence theory, which describes a self-actualizing Cosmos, speaks implicitly of the deep Eros[157]—the profound intelligent

---

153 Brian T. Swimme and Mary E. Tucker, Journey of the Universe (2011), 84–85.

154 Swimme and Tucker, Journey of the Universe.

155 For an in-depth description of these developments, see Evolution: A View from the 21st Century Evolution, by James Shapiro (2011).

156 See Section II.2.

157 See, for example, The Re-Emergence of Emergence: The Emergentist Hypothesis from Science to Religion, edited by Phillip Clayton and Paul Davies (2006); Evolution: A View from the 21st Century Evolution, by James Shapiro (2011); The Music of Life: Biology Beyond Genes, by Denis Noble (2006); and Dance to the Tune of Life:

aliveness deep in nature itself, which is always seeking more and more relationship, recognition, mutuality, and embrace. *Telos*[158] (=direction) and *Eros* (Fuck, Allurement, or Love by any other name) are the nature of Reality.

5. Reality Self-Actualizes through Relationship

Alan Turing, the genius who cracked the Nazi war code during World War II, was essential to the emergence of the new scientific world-view. After the war, he wrote a classic essay, "The Chemical Basis of Morphogenesis," where he laid down some of the foundational principles necessary to understand our world. The core of the new scientific Universe Story is that the Universe operates according to inherent principles of self-organization.

It is what organizes an anthill, a beehive, and flocks of birds flying in precise and complex formation. It is the inherent internal guidance that attracts a hundred billion galaxies and stars to form atoms from particles. It is what tells a cell in an early embryo whether to form a kidney or a heart, and it is the intelligence that knows exactly how to execute endlessly dazzling depth, complexity, and interconnectivity.

For what is the human being if not 37.2 trillion cells[159] in a precisely

---

Biological Relativity, by Denis Noble (2016).

158 This is an ancient Greek term that refers to an end, fulfillment, completion, purpose, goal. It is the source of the modern word teleology. Teleology is the study of purposes, goals, ends, and functions. For example, in the natural science of Aristotle, the telos of a member of a species is the complete and perfect state in which the entity can reproduce itself (so, most animals reach their telos when they become adults). Another example would be the telos of an organ, which is the function it plays in the organism as a whole—e.g., the telos of an eye is seeing.

159 See "An Estimation of the Number of Cells in the Human Body," by Eva Bianconi

calibrated dance of autonomy and communion, self-organized and governed in cellular communities of beauty and wondrous complexity, which defy the farthest reaches of our imagination? Advances in science and technology have given us information that was never available before. The New Universe Story derived from that information is also called cosmogenesis.[160] Reality birthed our Universe at the moment of the Big Bang. The Big Bang is the great flaring forth of Reality: out of the quantum vacuum of nothing emerges everything. In the first nanoseconds after the Big Bang, the entire implicate order of Reality is born. All of the laws of physics and mathematics are already at play. Immense intelligence moves the process from within.[161]

And in the first nanoseconds of Reality, Eros forms the first intimate relationships, for Reality is relational. From both poetic and scientific perspectives, one might say that Reality seeks to self-actualize through relationship—or one might just say Reality is erotic. Who would have ever thought that Reality would self-actualize from molten rock to Mozart, from dirt to Dante, from bacteria to Bach and Beethoven, or from helium to hospitals?

Creativity, however, is not what we once thought it was. We know with some scientific certainty that the inherent creativity of Reality is not like that of an external engineer creating a blueprint that Reality would follow. And yet, Reality is also not without inherent values that

---

et al. (2013).

160 While there are some less credible deployments of the term, it has value, as explored, from the perspectives of science, in some depth by Harvard Astrophysicist David Layzer in Cosmogenesis: The Growth of Order in the Universe (1990). Layzer looks at the emergence of chemical and structural order—the progressive deepening of intimacy in the Universe—in the context of the origin of the Universe, quantum physics, and evolution. One need not endorse the entire work to benefit enormously from the cross-disciplinary depth and detail.

161 In some sense, the laws of chemistry and biology are inherent in Cosmos. Whether that means that the laws are primordial or the laws of chemistry emerge with the emergence of molecules just as the laws of biology emerge with the emergence of cells in the way that Charles Sanders Peirce describes it is beside the point for our purposes. In both cases, the laws are expressions of the First Values and First Principles of Cosmos. See also The Re-Emergence of Emergence; Evolution; The Music of Life; and Dance to the Tune of Life: Biological Relativity.

animate and shape the evolutionary process. The emergence of greater and greater complexity and consciousness is an expression of the deep intimate patterning of Reality.

It was for providing pivotal insight into this intimate process that Ilya Prigogine won the Nobel Prize in the late twentieth century.[162] It is this Reality that the transdisciplinary science of emergence has revealed. But Reality is not following an exterior design in the classical management or engineering model that we have become accustomed to. It is a more organic process.

How is self-organization possible? Think of the incredibly complex process through which a child learns language from their mother or primary caretaker. The child doesn't know the rules of the "code" they are so effortlessly learning (nor do they have any notion of "code" or "grammar"); in many cases, neither does the mother. The language in all its richness emerges anew in the child's being from myriads of small exchanges and gradually re-created patterns.[163]

Creativity emerges from the intensity of the intimacy between mother and child. As we noted above, it is always the intensification of new and unique qualities of intimacy that generates new energy, new life, new creativity, and new possibility. If Mom speaks Chinese, then the child will speak Chinese. Both the child's brain and facial muscles are being constantly sculpted in particular ways depending on what language she is learning.

In a similar fashion, the mother gives the baby radical love. The baby's brain and heart, in their exterior and interior circuits, are being constantly sculpted by the particular languages of love that the baby absorbs from the mother. In other words, the baby absorbs not only mom's exterior language but also her interior language of intimacy. This transmits value, meaning, consciousness, and the radical sense of being welcome—the

---

162 Prigogine won the Nobel Prize in Chemistry in 1977 "for his contributions to nonequilibrium thermodynamics, particularly the theory of dissipative structures," or, said differently, for his work defining how the behavior of open systems far from equilibrium can create new structures through internal self-reorganization.

163 Nowadays, linguists prefer to speak of a child "acquiring" their native language, rather than "learning," because this process is so different from school learning.

intrinsic goodness of existence. This is transmitted from mother to child in infinite small exchanges, which have a massive influence on the interior landscape of the child's consciousness as well as its physical brain and heart.

Here is a key point: this process is not *random*.[164] Instead, it takes place in the context of a Field of intrinsic yet evolving Value, which is inherent to Reality. Every single interaction between mother and child is an expression of an ever-deepening intimacy and constant creativity. This is an expression of—and embedded in—the larger ground or Field of ever-present and evolving intimacy and creativity. The mother, driven by love, is moved to ever-more potent intimacy with her baby, which is constantly creating her Reality. Each act of intimacy is self-validating and independent of any larger goal.

So too are all the processes of the Universe's expressions of constant creativity and intimacy. There is never anything that is merely random. All freedom in the Cosmos exists in the larger context of Reality's desire for Value, ever-deeper expressions of Reality's intrinsic yet evolving First Values and First Principles. All is Eros, value, and creativity seeking expression.

From the very beginning, forming deep relationships has been the implicit goal of Reality and an evolutionary driver of the entire Universe Story. Reality contains an inherent intelligence. Reality is filled with telos.

Reality moves from simple to elegant and complex beyond imagination. When you track the evolutionary story from the first elementary particles to molecular biology, to Shakespeare, to science, to the great sacred texts of human spirit, you are witnessing a dazzling display of intelligence and direction that science has just begun to document.

---

164 See also Section V.1.

6. How Do We Know Anything—and How Do We Know That Reality Is Relationship?

The great German philosopher Habermas writes about different interests (or desires) that drive our will to know.[165] There are three modes of knowing, or knowledge constitutive interests, according to Habermas: *technical*, *practical*, and *emancipatory*.

- Technical interests are concerned with material reproduction, i.e., man's use of tools and technologies to predict and control nature.

- Practical interests are concerned with social reproduction, namely with the intersubjective norms driving cultures and communities.

- Emancipatory interests are concerned with human freedom and autonomy.

Integral Theory, following Habermas's lead, added a fourth interest: *soteriological*, or interest in enlightenment through liberation from suffering and sin. Each interest has its own ways (methodologies) for arriving at true knowledge, or what Habermas, in *Communication and the Evolution of Society*, calls the three primary validity claims.[166]

In this context, it is worth relating Habermas's validity claims to what we call *the three Eyes*. The three Eyes, as we have conceived them in CosmoErotic Humanism, are:

---

165 Jürgen Habermas, Knowledge and Human Interests (1971).

166 Jürgen Habermas, "What Is Universal Pragmatics?" (1979).

- the Eye of the Senses,

- the Eye of the Mind, and

- the Eye of Consciousness.

The Eye of Consciousness expresses itself in four distinct ways:

- The Eye of the Heart, which deploys the feeling of Eros to know Reality.

- The Eye of Value, which discerns value or meaning.

- The Eye of Contemplation, which uses introspection, meditation, and other disciplines of Love to reveal the inner nature of Reality.

- The Eye of the Spirit, which deploys multiple forms of exercises, including prayer, ritual, dance, and more, to know Reality.

These two models do not precisely overlap but naturally illuminate each other.

Habermas talks first about claims dealing with elementary propositions or *truth claims*. These claims are derived from the Eye of the Senses, which uses empirical experiments, and the Eye of the Mind, which uses logic, deduction, and conceptual frameworks to organize facts about objects.

Secondly, there are claims of *normative rightness* or justice that examine the norms and standards for human relationship and conduct. We might say this deploys the Eye of Value.

Finally, there are *sincerity* or authenticity claims, such as through psychoanalysis or myriad other forms of interior work, which deploy the Eye of the Heart and examine the intentions of actors through language and other methods.

We might expand the territory of validity claims to a broader range of the interior sciences and their teachings of liberation, which derive from the Eye of the Spirit or the Eye of Contemplation, using introspection, meditation, and other disciplines of Eros to disclose something of the inner nature of Reality. But they are also correlated to the Eye of the Heart and the Eye of Value, in their unique expressions of the Eye of Consciousness.

All three Eyes (Senses, Mind, and Consciousness in all of its forms) reveal valid knowledge. None have the right to triumphantly colonize or dismiss the others. All three are necessary for true knowing and a whole life.[167] As we have seen, the Eye of the Senses and the Eye of the Mind reveal that Reality is relationship. But when we open the Eyes of Consciousness (especially the Eyes of the Heart, Value, and Contemplation), an even more potent realization reveals itself: Reality itself is born through the desire for relationship. The response to Fichte and Schelling's great question, *Why is there something rather than nothing?*, is: because Reality desires relationship. Infinity desires intimacy.[168]

The Universe itself is birthed by intention. In the words of one great physicist, Sir James Jeans,

> Today there is a wide measure of agreement, which on the physical side of science approaches almost to unanimity, that the stream of knowledge is heading towards a non-mechanical reality; the universe begins to look more like a great thought than like a great machine.[169]

Intention implies desire. The Universe desires relationship. The Infinite desires the intimate. Virtually all of the most subtle and contemplative minds, deploying multiple versions of the Eye of Consciousness, across space and time, cultures and history, whose insights constitute

---

167 This presentation both aligns with and takes significant issue with our dear friend Ken Wilber's original adaptation of the medieval notion of the three eyes, *Eye to Eye: The Quest for the New Paradigm* (2001).

168 See also Section II.9.

169 James Jeans, *The Mysterious Universe* (2017), 154. Originally published in 1932 under the same title.

the highest expression of the interior science of evolving perennialism,[170] agree on one thing:

The intention of Reality is relationship.

Infinity desires a relationship to the finite.

Infinity desires finitude.

The Eternal desires a relationship with the temporal.

This knowing is revealed not by experiment or logic but by opening the inner Eye of Consciousness in its four expressions, plus what we could call the Eye of Outrageous Love.

In the exterior realm, the mysterious desire of Reality to manifest is expressed in the radically amazing notion of the *quantum vacuum*, the existence of which was verified via experiment by Willis Lamb and Robert Retherford in 1947.[171] It tells us that some elementary particles and waves simply leap into existence. It is just the way it is.

There is a realm, which might be called the Infinite or the Ground of Being, which is in no sense the same as, but might be alluded to by, the quantum vacuum, which births particles seeking intimate relationship. This Field, the Ground of Being, which itself generates the quantum vacuum, is a Field of Pure Potentiality. The interior sciences have long held that the world is not just a place filled with things. Rather, every thing and every person, and even Reality itself, emerge from this common Source in both the manifest and unmanifest realms.

This Source—the Ground of Being, or the Field of Pure Potentiality,

---

170 On the CosmoErotic Humanism conception of evolving perennialism, see First Principles and First Values.

171 A quantum vacuum is the quantum state with the lowest possible energy. According to our present-day understanding, it is however never truly empty but rather contains electromagnetic waves, gravitons, photons, dark energy, and virtual particles that pop in and out of existence. Microwave technology invented for radar in the world-war era was co-opted to great avail in physics experiments interested in measuring particle interactions. The Lamb shift experiment was based on a discrepancy between theory (Dirac equations) and experiment in measuring two energy levels within the hydrogen atom. It was discovered that the cause of the discrepancy was interactions between vacuum energy fluctuations (free electrons) in the Maxwell field and hydrogen electrons bound to the proton as they revolved around the proton.

or the Unmanifest—has one quality that we can identify. We have called that quality Outrageous Love or Evolutionary Love. It is the drive toward intimacy that suffuses the whole story from the very beginning. It is this quality that, according to the Eye of Consciousness, holds the mystery of the Unmanifest, the Infinite, which decides to manifest as the finite. The Infinite manifests as expressions of Eros.

7. The Eros of Relationship in Science: From Separate Particles to Space in Between

Let's take a brief look at some of the core structures of finite manifestation through the lens of basic science, beginning with physics.[172] Until the advent of quantum physics, all of Reality was thought to be made up of separate atoms. Quantum physics, using sophisticated mathematics and measurement instruments, seeks to understand the fundamental substrate of Reality. The very essence of quantum physics is that the heart of matter is not made of discrete particles but of probability waves. One common interpretation of these waves says that they only manifest as particles in the moment of their interaction[173] (that is, their relationship).

---

172 In doing so, we have no intention of participating in the popular trend of merging sloppy physics with sloppy spirituality to produce sloppy New Age thinking. We simply mean to look at the most basic and self-evident implications of this hundred-year-old scientific field, which itself has gone through multiple major shifts.

173 The term probability wave was coined by Max Born, one of the early quantum physicists, for the mathematical wave function that describes the behavior of a quantum particle between detections, the detection being the moment of the collapse of the wave function, when the particle acts like a classical particle with a simple location. In the original version of the most accepted interpretation of quantum phenomena, the so-called Copenhagen Interpretation, it is the moment that the quantum particles interact with a macroscopic object that they become

In a word, Reality is Eros.

David Bohm coined the term *implicate order*,[174] describing the *in-formation*—what we have called *configurations of intimacy*—at the core of Cosmos. Ancient realization meets contemporary science more often than we might imagine. The Hebrew word for *thing*, the basic building block of matter, is *davar*. The word *davar* also means *word*. A word is a structure of intimacy—sounds configured uniquely together to convey in-formation about the nature of all things; these configurations of intimacy are building blocks of conversations.

From the perspective of exterior as well as interior sciences, it is accurate to say that we live in a Conversational Cosmos. The interior of the Conversational Cosmos, just like the interior of any conversation, is constituted by value, meaning, consciousness, and information. Each word in this cluster expresses a different perspective on the same empirical phenomena—the conversations of Cosmos that are the basic building blocks of Reality.[175] There is no such thing as an ultimately separate entity. Relationship is the very essence of Reality. Everything exists not unto itself but in the field of possibility—the space in between. One cannot help but be reminded of the erotic mystics and interior scientists who

---

part of the macroscopic realm and their wave function collapses. That can happen, for example, when an electron hits a phosphorescent screen, where it interacts with the phosphor to create a tiny spark. In recent decades, many physicists have pointed out that macroscopic objects are not different from quantum objects. Instead, it is the interaction with any bit of matter or energy that collapses the wave function. Macroscopic objects simply consist of many particles, which provide many more opportunities for interaction than subatomic particles. In this sense, the Copenhagen Interpretation, which is but one of over twenty interpretations under serious consideration, has evolved. Another interpretation is the Bohmian Interpretation that was suggested by David Bohm in 1951, building on the work of Louis de Broglie, one of the founders of quantum physics. In it, the particles are always particles but are guided by a real wave described by the wave function. That guiding wave travels through a field called the quantum potential, and it is part of a universal wave function that connects all the particles of the Universe, regardless of distance. For a simple explanation of the Bohmian Interpretation, see, for example, https://quantumphysicslady.org/glossary/bohmian-interpretation-of-quantum-mechanics/.

174 David Bohm, Wholeness and the Implicate Order (2005).

175 See also Sections II.2–3 below.

realized Divinity as the Infinite Life Force that spoke from the space between the cherubs atop the ark of the covenant.[176]

The Hebrew word *bein*, meaning *in between*, shares its root with the word *bina*. *Bina*, literally translated as *understanding* or *insight*, is a term in the interior science of Hebrew wisdom for what is called the *lumination* of the upper Goddess. It is the creative space between worlds that births the pregnancies of the upper luminations into the lower luminations.[177]

Bina is, as are all the ontologies of the interior sciences of Hebrew wisdom, a structure of the inner worlds in all of their expressions, including the inner worlds on high, prior to manifestation, and the inner worlds that live within human consciousness. For in the realization of the Eye of Consciousness, the Infinite is prior to and not dependent on the finite, yet the Infinite garbs itself and is reflected all through the structure of the finite. As such, it is not surprising that this space in between, like the synapse between two neurons, is the creative space that animates the finite world.

At the most elemental level, you cannot chop matter up into self-contained units. Rather, Reality, even at the level of elementary particles from which we are all formed, is indivisible. Subatomic particles, in the paradox of quantum physics, simply do not exist in isolation. They exist only as a unique expression of a larger field.

The Universe can no longer be understood as a machine. Science has revealed the Universe as a web of interconnected and intimate fields of energy, forces, consciousness, and life. More precisely, Reality is a dynamic web of ever-evolving and ever-transforming interconnected

---

176 Numbers 7:89, NIV: "When Moses entered the tent of meeting to speak with the LORD, he heard the voice speaking to him from between the two cherubim above the atonement cover on the ark of the covenant law. In this way the LORD spoke to him."

177 I am deploying the term lumination in lieu of sefirot, or sefira, which is central to the interior sciences of Hebrew wisdom. Lumination is a translation of the Hebrew term sapir, or sapphire, which refers to the light quality of the sefirot. I do not deploy the terms emanation or illumination, although both are often used. Each has particular drawbacks, and both are used so broadly in metaphysics that the uniqueness of the tree of life and its sefirot is somewhat obscured. Hence, I prefer the unique term lumination.

intimate life forces.

Once contact is made between two particles, they remain in contact through all space and time.[178] From a quantum perspective, there is a virtually Infinite Now of relationship. In this context, everything takes place not in the isolated unit of an alienated particle but in the creative space in between.

The implications of this revolution in physics have not received broad attention for two main reasons. First, the same laws do not seem to apply beyond the quantum level. Second, the ideas are too counterintuitive to be easily grasped by the mind. Quantum physics emerged into its golden years between two world wars, and as the war erupted again, it was almost immediately hijacked for military purposes and modern electronics.[179]

Scientists did not quite know what to do with the apparently on-tological Reality of the space in between, with the fact that an electron was in some sense in touch with everything at once. What did it mean that, at least at the quantum level, an electron was not a set thing until it engaged in relationship with another quantum—for example, as part of a measurement? The math worked at the quantum level and produced results on the material plane, but by then we were off to fight World War II and afterward to build the postwar boom.

After the war, however, a group of physicists, for the most part work-ing independently, began to take the next huge step. What they began to see through anomaly after anomaly in conventional theories was that the quantum level of Reality, and its essential premise that Reality is relationship, was really at play in some form in all of Reality. They began to talk in terms of what they called a quantum field,[180] which underlies

---

178 This has been called quantum entanglement or quantum nonlocality, with theories being developed that suggest that time may be a side effect of quantum entanglement.

179 The Radiation Laboratory was based at MIT and produced as much as half of all the radars deployed during World War II. Microwave technology used in radar was later used in quantum physics experiments to discover phenomena like the Lamb shift, which we discussed earlier.

180 Quantum field theory combines classical field theory, special relativity, and

all material reality. Everything on every level of physical reality began to glimmer with the sense of ultimate interrelatedness. The space in between became central to their investigations.

On the most fundamental level, all human beings are packets of quanta, exchanging information and in relationship with the larger quantum field. Information exchange, which we view as a core quality of relationship,[181] began to be observed in all dimensions of life, including cellular and DNA communications. Even human perception began to be seen as interactions between the subatomic particles in our brain and the larger quantum field.[182] We began to realize that we literally *resonate* with our world. What began to emerge was the vision of *a seamless coat of the Universe*—seamless but not featureless, as all of its features were irreducibly unique. At the same time, every unique feature is in inextricable relationship with the larger quantum field. It is in more than just superficial relationship: The quantum part does not exist outside of its relationship to the field.

Reality is relationship—intimate relationship of shared identity in the context of otherness with mutualities of recognition, feeling, value,

---

quantum mechanics. It treats particles as excitements or excited states (also called quanta) of their underlying quantum fields, which are more fundamental than the particles. A quantum (plural quanta) is the minimal (quantized) amount of a physical entity involved in an interaction—meaning the magnitude of its physical property can take on only discrete values consisting of integer multiples of one quantum. For example, if there are two excitations of the photon field, we can observe them as two photons. And three excitations of the electron field will give us three electrons. The ground state of a photon field—also known as its vacuum state—is the state where all quantum numbers are zero—meaning, there are zero photons. An excited state of a system in quantum mechanics (e.g., atoms, molecules, or the nucleus of an atom) is any quantum state of the system that has a higher energy than the ground state (which is the absolute minimum). These higher-energy states are always integer multiples of the energy of the quantum.

181 Relationships appear in different disguises, all the way up and all the way down the evolutionary chain: interactions between particles and the quantum field, gravity, electromagnetic attraction and repulsion, the strong and the weak nuclear forces, information exchange, sexual attraction, feelings of yearning, et cetera.

182 See, for example, "Experimental Indications of Non-Classical Brain Functions," by Christian M. Kerskens and David L. Pérez (2022).

THE EVOLUTION OF LOVE

and purpose, which transforms parts into new wholes. The Intimate Universe came alive. The truths of *Reality is Eros, Reality is allurement,* and *Reality is relationship* were the subtexts of the sciences. These subtexts remained silent, as the language of science gifted Reality with myriad new technologies but obfuscated the *qualia* of Reality itself.

8. Relationship Is an Expression of the Eros of Cosmos

No Spark is lost from the binding of Unity.
All are ready for the great feast.—Abraham Kook[183]
[The Universe] is diverse because it is divided into mutually adapted subjects and objects.—Pratyabhijna Hrdayam[184]

The core truth that Reality is relationship is not about the politics of relationship; it is about the poetics of relationship. But this poetry is not a mere metaphor or some flight of fancy. Reality is relationship is a core, factual truth. It is true whether you are guided by science or spirit or love. For the first time in history, the deepest insights from the leading edges of science, spirit, and love are all telling the same story.

- Their first shared truth is that **Reality is relationship**.

- Their second shared truth is that **relationships evolve**.

---

183 From Orot HaKodesh [Lights of Holiness], by Abraham Kook (1937), vol., 2, 538.

184 Pratyabhijna Hrdayam: The Heart of the Doctrine of Recognition, by K⊠emarāja (d. 1025, disciple of Abhināvagupta).

- Their third shared truth is that the evolution of the Real, of Reality, is **the evolution of relationships**.

- Their fourth shared truth is that the evolution of relationships is **the evolution of love**.

- The fifth truth is that **evolution has not stopped**. Evolution moves through matter in all of its levels (the physiosphere), through life in all of its levels (the biosphere), and through the depth of the human self-reflexive mind in all of its levels (the noosphere). The motivational architecture for evolution is **the progressive deepening of intimacies**. In other words, the evolution of relationships is what drives evolution.

- The sixth shared truth follows naturally from the first five. It is simple, in the second-simplicity sense,[185] but it is not mere metaphor, or fanciful or wishful declaration, or some form of sweetness-and-light, pollyannish optimism. **When we engage in the evolution of our own relationships in all their forms, we are participating in the evolutionary process.** Or more precisely, we *are* evolution.

It is the evolutionary impulse beating in us that moves us toward the evolution of relationship. This is true personally—in the vectors of our own relationship lives—but it is no less true culturally and collectively. For example, the evolution of relationships from role mate to soul mate to whole mate is not a strange aberrant phenomenon but rather Cosmos doing what it does: evolving relationships and intimacy in response to a crisis in intimacy—to the global intimacy disorder.

When we point toward a new sexual narrative, or a new narrative of desire, which embodies a new vision of relationship, we are not evoking a clever phrase or a new life hack. Those never accomplish much in the

---

185 See Essay Two, 10.1 and 10.2, for an explanation of second simplicity, which is the simplicity that comes after complexity.

long term, even when wrapped in the pretty costumes of bestselling books. Rather, a new sexual narrative—the new narrative of desire—is a source-code shift in the very nature of relationship, one fully aligned with the nature of Reality, for the very nature of Reality is evolution, relationship, and story. And the story of Reality is the evolution of relationships. Or again, said slightly differently, Reality is intimate, Reality evolves, and the evolution of intimacy is the narrative arc of Reality's Story.

The essence of what we are putting forth, through all the writings on CosmoErotic Humanism, is itself the very nature of how Reality evolves. This is how it has always worked. This is the inexorable law of Reality.

Relationship, which we envision as one of the core goods of human life, is in fact an expression of the core Eros and allurement that is the nature of Cosmos itself. We are not merely social animals in some technical, functional sense, although we are that. We are creatures of Eros. We are literally Gods and Goddesses of Allurement.

Relationships always imply allurement, attraction, desire, need, and Fuck. The Fuck can be physical sex, or it can be idea sex. Relationships can be about pleasure, partnership, or both. Relationships can be about joining genes or joining genius or both.

Relationship is always erotic.

Sex models Eros, but Eros always precedes sex—and sex never exhausts Eros.

A simple but accurate way to describe Eros might be as infinitely tender and fierce. In other words: Love + Fuck = Eros.

Eros is the animating energy and generating algorithm of Reality, all the way up and all the way down. To realize that *Reality is Relationship* is to realize that God is Eros—or that what the great traditions called *Hieros Gamos*, the Divine Marriage taking place in every second of Reality, is integral to the source code of Cosmos.

II. FIRST NOTES ON THE CONVERSATIONAL COSMOS: THE AMOROUS COSMOS IS THE RELATIONAL COSMOS IS THE CONVERSATIONAL COSMOS

1. Relationships Are Our Primal Need

We want to live from a deeper place of aliveness, joy, and vitality. A relationship can fill us with all of these—or drain us of all of these. We want to experience our lives as suffused with purpose, creativity, and fulfillment. We want not only to achieve great things but to share our achievements. If we have no one to share our achievements, they often seem meaningless. Being witnessed in relationship is part and parcel of the motivational architecture that drives us to achievement.

In a word, we want to be in relationship. We want to be outrageously[186] in love with our partners, our friends, ourselves, and with life

---

186 Outrageous Love is a term we use to describe a Love that is of a different order and quality than what we call ordinary love. Ordinary love is contrived human sentiment. Outrageous Love is the structure of Cosmos itself. We turn to this distinction later in this book; see especially Sections IV.1–2.

itself. Only the personal love or relationship has the capacity to heal the traumatized stories of our past, and only the personal love or relationship liberates the contraction of our coiled separate self. Only the personal love heals the wounds of the traumatized ego.

It is in relationship that we transcend ourselves—only to find ourselves.

It is not by accident that our shared path of meaning in the world today is the path of relationships. Relationships are not an adjunct of our lives. We hold them to be essential to a life well lived. Whatever our nationality, our stance on religion, our political or spiritual orientation or lack thereof, there is one path that we all walk together: the path of relationships. It can be fairly stated that the one shared spiritual path in the world today is the path of relationships. This path is being walked by atheists, Buddhists, Christians, Muslims, Jews, Hindus, Aboriginals, and everyone else.

Reality is relationship. Relationships are our primal need.

Imagine this scene: You have won the lottery, or you have realized a precious life goal, or you have seen something of dazzling beauty or depth. You rush to your mobile phone to text, email, or share on social media. But you are stopped short by a crushing realization: There is no one who wants to receive your communication. There is no one with whom to share. You are crushed by loneliness.

Based on extensive scientific research, we now know that loneliness, even without physical isolation, far outweighs diet and lifestyle as a predictor of disease and death.[187] We lose our will to live if there is no other being with deep interiors with whom we can exchange feelings, energy, and information. Put simply, if there is no one to talk to—to *really* talk to—life virtually ceases to be worth living.

If we do not have at least one being with whom to communicate, who has an interior quality resonant with our own, our life is a horror

---

187 On the connection between quality of relationships and chronic health, see "Aging Well: Surprising Guideposts to a Happier Life from the Landmark Harvard Study of Adult Development," by John F. Mitchell (2004), pp. 178–179, and Love and Survival: The Scientific Basis for the Healing Power of Intimacy, by Dean Ornish (1998).

of loneliness. We can have everything we need to survive. We can have every material pleasure available to us—delicious food, a beautiful setting, and the most sublime music, coupled with every available form of entertainment. We can have every intellectual pleasure available to us. But if we cannot communicate with another person, interior to interior, then life becomes almost not worth living. Without relationship, life withers and dies. For most people, not being able to talk to another being with an interior sense of self generates borderline or full-on suicidal depression.

We are compelled to foster relationships again and again, even when facing past pain and failure. The imperative to relationship, however, is not merely a *biological* imperative. It is the categorical imperative of all of Reality, from atoms to planets to cells to humans.

Remember the wonderful twenty-first-century movie *Cast Away*. The protagonist Chuck Noland, played by Tom Hanks, is marooned on an island in the South Pacific. He uses his own blood to imprint a face on a Wilson Sporting Goods volleyball. He gives the ball a name—Wilson. He needs someone to talk to, and Wilson is that someone.

He had everything he needed to survive, and even thrive materially, on the island. But despite that, he risked his life to get off the island by setting off in a makeshift raft. He would rather die in search of another human being than remain alone on the island. Chuck is expressing something much deeper than a strange fluke of human beings who can't stand to be alone. He is expressing a core imperative of Reality, the drive to relationship. He knows that the lack of (fulfilling) relationship is literally a form of death. In the language of the erotic mystics of the Talmud in the third century, *havruta o mituta*—either relationships or death.[188]

---

188 Babylonian Talmud, Tractate Ta'anit 23a.

2. Conversation Happens between Edges of Desire

From the perspective of CosmoErotic Humanism, we live in a Conversational Cosmos; our lives are a series of conversations.[189] Chuck, cast away on an island, is desperate for conversation. Although in objective terms he has little chance of surviving the open sea on his makeshift raft, the call of subjectivity entirely overwhelms the objective. Without the experience of conversation—meeting another interiority—life isn't worth living. This is not an abstract postulate but our own direct experience of reality. In the concentration camps, the prisoners whose interiors had collapsed, who had resigned themselves to the horror, often lost their capacity for conversation. They went silent—a silence of absence, in which the cries of suffering were silenced by the deafening intensity of pain that muted all conversation.

What is a conversation? It is the place of encounter. Encounter happens between edges. The edge of my face meets the edge of your face. We are face to face, which is the position of authentic conversation.

---

189 At the turn of the twenty-first century, I partnered with a close friend at the time, Erica Fox, in the realizing of her dream of opening an institute for spirituality and negotiation under the auspices of Harvard Law School. The first event opened with a public dialogue between me and Bill Ury (the author of Getting to Yes, with Roger Fisher and Bruce Patton, 1991) in a packed hall at the law school. Then, I had a key conversation with Erica and Doug Stone (one of the authors of Difficult Conversations, 1999). In that conversation (2003 approximately), I unpacked an early version of the new Story of Value to Doug and Erica, and as part of the new Story I formulated an early notion of the Conversational Cosmos, which has later been refined over the years, in multiple teachings. To the best of my knowledge there are three of us who have expressed some notion of the Conversational Cosmos: myself, Howard Bloom, and David Whyte. Howard and I have discussed the term and its implications extensively over the years and will publish together on this term as part of our larger shared work on what we might call honest readings of science that disclose the Amorous Cosmos. Our thoughts on the Conversional Cosmos are somewhat related to David's but in more important ways also radically different. The formal term was first coined and published by Howard.

In an authentic conversation, I need to be in my own voice. I need to find the singularity, the aloneness of my voice. I need to feel the contours of my desires held in the qualities of the voice that is uniquely mine. My voice is the quality of unique desire that is my identity.

At the edge of my identity, which is the edge of my desire, I yearn for contact with you. This is the nature of Eros—the experience of radical aliveness, desiring ever-deeper contact and ever-greater wholeness.[190] Contact happens through conversation. But my desire is not just for contact with you in any generalized sense but with *the edge of your desire*. If you are lost inside of your desire, we cannot make contact. If you are alienated from your desire, we cannot make contact. It is only when you are both *inside* your desire and *at its edge* that you open to my desire. In the space in between, contact happens.

The image of reality preferred by the lineage of Solomon is two sensually entwined cherubs atop the ark of the covenant in the inner sanctum, called the *Holy of Holies*, of the temple in ancient Jerusalem. In the language of the sacred text, it is the place of meeting—the empty space *in between*, from which the word of the Divine emerges. Conversation takes place in the empty space between the cherubs.

Contact is conversation. The movement of Eros is to contact through conversation, which generates deeper contact and greater wholeness. All of Eros is conversation.

The sexual models the Erotic, which is why the interior sciences often understand sexing as conversations: Upper lips meet upper lips, and then lower lips begin to speak, evoked by *tongue*. Indeed, the very word *tongue* (in both Hebrew and English), can refer to language—the structure of consciousness that arouses and capacitates conversation. All conversations are erotic conversations.

The primary Hebrew term for sexing is *Yada*. *Yada* means "to know," in the sense of carnal knowledge. Carnal knowledge is where the edge of my desire meets the edge of your desire, in the space in between the cherubs, from where a new *gnosis*—the word of God—emerges. Sexing that ignores the desire of the other is not conversation. Communication

---

190 See Essay One, Section 2.4, for a more detailed definition of Eros.

is communion; intimate communion is the conversation of desires that meet at the edge and create a new gnosis. In the language of the text, Adam and Eve transcend their loneliness in the gnosis of sexing, which is intimate communion.

Sex is contact at the edge of identity. My identity is the unique quality of desire that fills me. I am desire.[191] The only way to embody the fullness of my own unique desire is to realize that the name of God is Desire[192]— and that there is no *local* desire, even as there is no *generic* desire. To be a Unique Self[193] is to realize that I am not separate from the larger field of Desire, even as I am a unique incarnation of that very field. Therefore, my identity is my unique configuration of desire.

Desire expresses allurement to a value or set of values. Therefore, the clarification of desire generates the clarification of value. In other words, desire is a conversation around value. All desire is the desire for a deeper conversation around value, and Conversation itself is a value of Cosmos. That is what we refer to when we talk about the Conversational Cosmos.

3. Conversational Cosmos: The First Whispers of Conversation

Once pointed out, the conversational nature of reality becomes self-evidently true in the human realm. But according to both the interior

---

191 This identity between the human being and desire is the core of A Return to Eros.

192 See Essay Three, Section 4, for a conversation on the name of God in the lineage of Solomon.

193 See Essay One, Section 3.3, for an analysis of the name of God.

sciences and exterior sciences,[194] this is the nature of reality all the way up and all the way down, in every dimension of reality. From a scientific perspective, we live in a Conversational Cosmos.

There are conversations taking place between subatomic particles that become atoms, between the atoms that become molecules, between molecules that become macromolecules, between macromolecules that become cells, between simple cells (prokaryotes) that become more complex cells (eukaryotes) and then multicellular organisms and be-tween organisms and organs within an organism—all the way up the evolutionary chain. These conversations are based on shared values, shared meaning, shared telos, and shared story. These four overlapping elements are often referred to in the exterior sciences as *information*.

In the next two sections, we'll explore the conversations happening on the most fundamental levels of Reality, between subatomic particles. Later throughout the book, we'll turn to conversations between atoms, molecules, and cells.

3.1. Quarks: Beloveds Who Are Never Separate from Each Other

Let's go back to the beginning of the Universe.

In the first nanoseconds after the Big Bang, gazillions of quarks explode as Reality. Quarks are called elementary, or fundamental, par-ticles because they are the essential building blocks of the Universe. They are not divisible into other particles—the intimate communion that constitutes them is not, in the current understanding of science, subject to separation into separate parts.[195]

---

194 For the exterior-science perspective of the Conversational Cosmos, in formal terms, see "Conversational (Dialogue) Model of Quantum Transitions" by Pavel V. Kurakin, George G. Malinetskii, and Howard Bloom (https://www.academia. edu/33106632/Conversational_dialogue_model_of_quantum_transitions). On the Conversational Cosmos in a more conversational tone, see The God Problem: How a Godless Cosmos Creates, by Howard Bloom (2016), pp. 409–452.

195 This description is rooted in the so-called Standard Model of particle physics. It was developed in stages throughout the second half of the twentieth century,

When trying to understand the subatomic world, it is crucially important to disengage from the image of particles as tiny balls or specks of matter, which is almost inevitably invoked in our minds by the very word *particle*. A particle is a *part* that is not *apart*; it *participates*—through its irreducible uniqueness—in the larger field of reality. Quarks, protons, neutrons, and all other particles are best thought of as sets of relationships, or allurements. Quarks, for example, which make up 99.9 percent of ordinary matter, could be seen as fast-moving, dancing points of allured energy. Professor Frank Wilczek, Nobel laureate of 2004 and one of the world's most eminent theoretical physicists,[196] discovered that the mass of a proton comes entirely from the *arrangement* of the quarks and not from the quarks themselves.[197] In an essay in *The New York Times*, MIT physics graduate Dennis Oberbye writes about Wilczek[198] (we added the italics for emphasis):

> Nowadays physicists—those coldblooded reductionists—are
> telling a . . . poetic but no less mathematically rigorous tale. It
> is a story not of a clockwork world but an entangled interactive
> world *whose constituents derive their identities and properties*
> *from one another in endless negotiation*—a city, in one physicist's
> words, of querulous social inhabitants. In other words, they

---

by many scientists worldwide. Although the Standard Model has demonstrated some success in providing theoretical predictions that were later confirmed experimentally, it falls short of being a complete theory of fundamental interactions, as it leaves some physical phenomena unexplained.

196 Frank Wilczek is known, among other things, for the discovery of asymptotic freedom, the development of quantum chromodynamics, and the discovery and exploitation of new forms of quantum statistics. See, for example, his Longing for the Harmonies: Themes and Variations from Modern Physics, with Betsy Devine (1989), and Fundamentals: Ten Keys to Reality (2021).

197 Quoted from "In the New Physics, No Quark Is an Island," by Dennis Oberbye (2001): "'The arrangement of the quarks' means their movements and the relationships between them. Their movement creates kinetic energy, which is, according to Einstein's relativity theory (E=mc²), equivalent to mass."

198 Oberbye, "In the New Physics."

are telling a tale about *relationships*. . . . Particle physics, Dr. Wilczek and his colleagues like to point out, is not really about particles anymore, but about their mathematical *relationships*—in particular symmetries—aspects of nature that remain invariant under different circumstances and viewpoints.

In the language of CosmoErotic Humanism, particles are fundamental configurations of Eros and intimacy in a larger Field of Allurement.

Quarks are so relational that they are never found in isolation. They first appeared in the Universe as the so-called *quark-gluon plasma* (*gluons* are quanta of energy that bind quarks together). Once the Universe cooled down a bit, they entered into even more intimate relationships with each other, in groups of three, within (what we now know as) *neutrons* and *protons*. We use the word *intimate* here not poetically but precisely—according to the terms of our intimacy equation:[199]

1. They have a shared *identity* (as a neutron or a proton) while retaining relative otherness as distinct quarks.

2. They *recognize* each other; we know this because they enter into relationships only with particular *types* of other quarks: A proton is made up of two *up* quarks and one *down* quark, and a neutron is composed of two down quarks and one up quark (*up* and *down* are two of six distinct "flavors" of quarks).

3. They converse and *feel* each other through *gluons*, the carriers of the strong nuclear force that binds them together.[200] In the

199 Intimacy = Shared Identity × [Relative] Otherness × Mutuality (Recognition + Feeling + Value + Purpose). See also Essay One, Section 2.3.

200 The strong force, which binds the quarks together, is weak when the quarks are close (it even drops to zero when the three different color charges of the quarks get close to one another) but increases steadily when you try to separate them, making it impossible to isolate a single quark. This property of the strong force, which is known as asymptotic freedom, is a surprising, counterintuitive property, which is not found in any of the other fundamental forces. That is why the theory

language of CosmoErotic Humanism, we might say that gluons are
intimate love notes between quarks.

4. Their shared field of *value* is constituted by the laws of physics and
mathematics they all obey, as well as their mutual drive to become
parts of larger wholes.

5. And finally, they have a *shared purpose* as neutrons and protons,
which go on to co-create all known chemical elements of the
universe and, ultimately, biological life.

In the interior sciences, the configuration of intimacy at the level of
elementary particles is characterized as two beloveds making love, who
do not ever separate from each other (in the Aramaic of the *Zohar, Teri
Rein DeLo Mitparshin*). This is called, in the interior sciences of Hebrew
wisdom, the *Zivug* of *Abba* and *Imma*—the *Sefirot* of Wisdom (*Chochma*)
and Insight (*Bina*) in the Kabbalistic Tree of Life. These are the higher
Sefirot in the Tree of Life.[201]

3.2. Intimate Conversations within Atoms: No Electron Is an Island

It is now 380,000 years after the Big Bang. A proton, neutron, and electron, in particular configurations, are coming together to create a new
whole called an atom. Howard Bloom writes about the emergence of the
first atoms in the Universe:

Electrons do indeed discover that their inanimate lusts match
the loneliness of protons perfectly. And electrons and protons

---

describing the strong force, called Quantum Chromodynamics (QCD), has to be
simulated on huge computers. See, for example, "Solving the Mysteries of Quarks,"
Phys.org, May 26, 2005, https://phys.org/news/2005-05-mysteries-quarks.html.

201 The Kabbalistic Tree of Life consists of ten Sefirots (the word usually mistranslated
as "spheres" but uniting three related meanings: mispar, "number," sipur, "story,"
and sappir, "light").

do glump together. They do pair up in proton-electron two-somes. What's worse, when electrons discover how naturally they fit around protons, the result is a radically new set of properties. . . . It's the handful of properties we call an atom: hardness, durability, and the ability to play with others in the sandbox of space, to team up in ways this cosmos has never seen before.[202]

While electrons and protons are stable on their own, a neutron has about a fifteen-minute life span outside of the nucleus of an atom, that is, outside of its relationship to a proton. If it does not establish a relationship, it loses its wholeness as a neutron and decays into a proton, an electron, and an antineutrino. But once it creates a relationship with a proton to form the nucleus of an atom, it can last as a neutron for billions of years.

All the particles within an atom are in unique relationships with each other and in constant intimate conversations. The messages between the atomic nuclei and the electrons dancing around them take on the form of *photons*—the carriers of the *electromagnetic force*.[203] The nucleus of an atom consists of protons and neutrons.[204] The electromagnetic force would have repelled protons from each other, because they are positively charged. However, at the very close distances inside the nucleus of an atom, the so-called *residual strong force allures* protons and neutrons together. When three quarks are bound together in a proton or a neutron, almost all of *the strong nuclear* force carried by the gluons goes toward binding the quarks together. However, a tiny fraction of the force acts outside protons and neutrons and allows them to have a conversation that generates a new whole, the nucleus of an atom. The messages in

---

202 See The God Problem, chapter 2.

203 If we could magnify the simplest hydrogen atom so that its nucleus (in this case only one proton) were the size of a basketball, then its lone electron would be found about two miles away).

204 The most common form of hydrogen has no neutrons, but this should not obscure our discussion.

this conversation take on the form of *mesons* (quark-antiquark pairs).

Said differently, there is a constant interplay between forces of allurement and autonomy between particles and an exchange of energy between the protons and neutrons within the nucleus of the atom. We might also say that neutrons and protons are aroused to be in conversation with each other.

All matter is made up of atoms and their relationships. And all atoms are made up of relationships: the strong nuclear relationships between the quarks (and their intimate relationships and conversations), the residual strong nuclear relationships between the protons and neutrons (and their intimate conversations), and the electromagnetic relationships and conversations between the atomic nuclei and electrons.

An atom is a new emergent whole: It is more than the sum of its particles. The particles themselves are changed and transformed in that relationship, in a way that is essentially not so different from how we are changed and transformed in an intimate relationship.[205] As the quantum gravity theorist Lee Smolin formulated it: "It can no longer be maintained that the properties of any one thing in the universe are independent of the existence or nonexistence of everything else," and "No electron is an island."[206]

3.3. Wholeness Implies Conversation

Both protons emerging out of conversations between quarks and atoms emerging out of conversation between protons, neutrons, and electrons

---

205 See, for example, Gravity, Special Relativity, and the Strong Force, by Constantinos G. Vayenas and Stamatios N.-A. Souentie (2012), Gauge Theories of the Strong, Weak, and Electromagnetic Interactions, by Chris Quigg (2013), and Particles and Nuclei: An Introduction to the Physical Concepts, by Bogdan Povh et al. (2008). See also "The Four Forces," by T. Thacker (1995, https://webhome.phy.duke.edu/~kolena/modern/forces.html#005), "The Color Force" by Lena Hansen (1997, https://webhome.phy.duke.edu/~kolena/modern/hansen.html). For a simple summary, see, for example, "What Is the Strong Force?" by Jim Lucas, LiveScience (2022, https://www.livescience.com/48575-strong-force.html).

206 Lee Smolin, The Life of the Cosmos (1997).

are what Arthur Koestler called *new holons*.[207] A holon is a set of parts that come together to participate in a larger whole. The emergence of holons is a structural quality of Cosmos. In a holon, each part is both individuated and has the wider identity of the larger whole. This is the core of our definition of intimacy (see Essay One, Section 2.3). In effect, a holon is a *conversation*—an act of communication generating communion, or wholeness.

Proton, neutron, and electron are allured to each other. They are desperate to talk. In conversation, they form a shared identity—they are now an atom. They obviously recognize each other. They feel each other, so they have shared pathos. But they also have a shared value. It is the shared value of wholeness itself, and what each of them brings to the table to generate the new configuration of intimacy. This, in turn, creates new vectors of possibility—a shared purpose. The reality of shared value is the premise for shared purpose.

If they were not communicating through some sort of conversation around value, they would have no reason to integrate; they could not come together in the pattern of intimacy we call *atom*. Only shared value can evoke the underlying codes of communication. There needs to be a conversation—an exchange of meaning. Conversation is absolutely intrinsic to Cosmos. Wholeness always implies conversation, which always implies meaning and value.

The notion of conversation blurs the line between two forms of meaning or value, *instrumental* and *intrinsic*. A conversation may have a purpose, but it can also be self-validating—valuable for its own sake. In other words, conversation is a mode of activity that is both intrinsically valuable, in and of itself, and extrinsically, instrumentally valuable for other purposes. It is this blurred distinction that makes conversation a core structure of reality, all the way down to quarks. It is critical to understand that this is the core of science. Reality is holons—conversations—all the way down and all the way up. This is not a regressive animism but the realization of an Intimate Universe, a CosmoErotic Universe.

This conception of conversation as both intrinsic and instrumental is, in part, what animates the notion of Leela, or Divine Play, of the

---

207 Arthur Koestler, The Act of Creation (1964).

great traditions. Play is both infinitely serious and pure play at the same time. Similarly, conversation is both serious and playful. It is valuable for its own sake and is somehow accomplishing something. What is the most basic structure of reality? Multiple forms of serious yet playful conversation in pursuit of some open-ended expression of value. In this realization of the nature of conversation, we begin to get a fragrance of the paradoxical relationship between contingency, randomness, and design—one of the big unanswered questions in evolutionary thought. To hold this paradox, we simply need to look at the nature of conversation.[208]

I have often been in deep conversation with a close partner. We have never prepared a script for the conversation. There is never an outline or talking points. There is a sense of utmost seriousness in the conversation, and yet there has always been a sense of play, the sense of Leela, a sense of delight for its own sake. And yet, if you were to read the transcript of the conversation, you would think that we had spent weeks orchestrating it. In retrospect, it looks as though the conversation followed a script, planned and carefully designed. And yet it is also fully filled with spontaneity—contingency and surprise. The conversation is not random but rather free and open.

What we are saying is that conversation is the structure of evolution itself. This is the nature of conversations all the way up and all the way down the evolutionary chain. That is the interior of what is now exteriorized as information theory. One of the core weaknesses of some key strains in information theory is the attempt to take the music out of the conversation and reduce it to its mechanics. It is the attempt to transform conversation—the exchange of meaning—into a purely causal, mechanistic process. But value and meaning that are the substrate of every conversation are beyond the category of causality.

3.4. All Conversations Are About Value

At the earlier levels of reality (as in the conversations between quarks or atoms we just described), the conversation seems to be more scripted than

---

at the later levels. In other words, the first-person experience of freedom and choice with regard to desire and its clarification is more veiled. Yet it is still present, in the form of proto-desire, or what Whitehead called prehension.[209] However, Reality evolves. Indeed, we might see Reality as the evolution of Eros itself. The evolution of Eros is the evolution of desire. The evolution of Eros is the evolution of conversation, for desire is, at its core, the lonely self-desiring intimate communion. Communion emerges from conversation, and all conversation is a conversation around value.

Why do we have conversations, which are the root of all occurrences? Why does something occur in the world? Is it because of causality or is it because there is agency?

This is what Whitehead was exploring. In the end, we understand that everything is rooted in prehension—a proto-consciousness, a *Tao*, a Field of Value, in which all things arise. At the most foundational level of atomic particles, prehension may look a lot like causality, and yet even these fundamental conversations are exchanges of information—value and meaning. Value expresses itself in the material and the biological through conversations. Without this realization, all our conversations lose their meaning, and we are left in a crisis of meaning, which at its core is a crisis of Eros—a crisis of conversation.

All through Reality, conversations have had meaning, from the beginning of time, and all of those conversations—between particles, between atoms, between molecules and macromolecules, between single cells and multicellular structures—continue in us. All of those conversations live in me. I am physically constituted by meaningful conversations. I am constituted by conversations around value.

That is why we are all desperate for conversation. That is why everyone understood Chuck in the Tom Hanks movie *Cast Away* we invoked above. Nobody said, "Huh? That's really weird. Why is he doing that?" Everyone got it. There was a universal anthro-ontological recognition of the rightness of it.

We now begin to understand the root of mental crises. We are told that there is no inherent value, and therefore there is no shared value. But the

---

209 See Process and Reality: An Essay in Cosmology, by Alfred North Whitehead (1978).

essence of conversation is shared value. If there is no shared value, then there is no conversation—and there are also no heroes, and no love stories. What the Conversational Cosmos says is that there *is* a conversation to be had, and declarations to be made. Both our words and actions matter, and our words *are* actions. You can be a hero in every conversation.

Conversations are always, at least implicitly, about value. The Eye of Value, which illuminates every conversation, discloses value through our own deepest heart's desire. In opposition to the Eye of Value, you have the eye of anti-value, which actively seeks out the sacred to destroy value. The natural strategy of the eye of anti-value is to destroy conversation. The eye of anti-value desires—a pseudo-Erotic desire—to destroy all of the deepest conversations you could have.

The Eye of Value is art. The eye of anti-value is advertising.

The Eye of Value is Eros. The eye of anti-value is pseudo-Eros.

The Eye of Value is depth. The eye of anti-value is clickbait.

So much of what we are attempting to do in this book, and all of our writing, is articulation of a new language for value. The old ways of making arguments don't even work anymore. We are in a new stratum of language and justification that, at its core, is a new language of value. We need to move beyond the *nowhere*, where you can live from an assumption that there is no Field of Value, to a place where we can fiercely contest values, but *from within* the Field of Value.

In medieval times, God was everywhere. In modernity, God is nowhere. *Messiah* means that God will be everywhere, again. That is the messianic transformation of the assumption behind all the conversations: We reclaim, at a new level of consciousness that integrates all sciences, that conversations about value are real, and that they only take place within the context of the Field of Value.

3.5. Messiah Is Conversation

When I meet the depth of experience, I cannot but respond. I erupt in song. It might be a song of praise, a love song, an ecstatic song or melody of grief and pain—but the bursting of a song wells up from the conversational demand of the intimate moment; it is quite different from silent introspection. The messianic moment is demarcated by song, for nothing can hold the fullness of eruption other than the conversation between finitude and the Infinite, for which prose is insufficient. Only poetry and song can begin to even allude to that ultimate conversation.

But for the lineage of Solomon and many other interior sciences, song is not merely a human trope. It is not just about adding the bird song or the whale song either. *All* of Reality is song, and each unique discretion of infinity has its own finite song. Nachman of Breslav writes that every distinct blade of grass has its own song. This realization is the premise of *Perek Shira*, an ancient work called *chapter of song*. The work, comprised of six short chapters, is attributed by some to Solomon, by others to his father David or perhaps their descendant Judah the Prince of the second century. At its core, it is understood by all to be the lyrics for the song of all of Reality—the song of the rock, the song of the field, the song of the trees, the song of the earth, the song of the sky, and all the way through the elements of the biosphere. By *song*, the text means something like: Reality is sentient, Reality is coded with unique qualities of meaning, and every dimension of the Real has a unique song. *Song* is taken to point to value, to unique qualities of intimacy, that both evoke and incarnate a uniquely intimate conversation with Reality.

The interior sciences deploy the term *Messiah* as a code word for conversation. The Hebrew root word for the word *Messiah*, according to interior scientist Nahum of Chernobyl, is *siach*, the same as in "conversation":

> Every person who is a God wrestler must prepare a palace for
> the part of Messiah that is of his soul. Then the complete form
> of Humanity/Reality will be whole. . . . Messiah is related
> to the word *maShiach*, meaning conversation . . . and when
> thought unites with speech wholeness is realized and the
> Messiah arrives.[210]

What the interior sciences describe as *Messiah* is in effect what

---

210 Nahum of Chernobyl, The Light of the Eyes: Homilies on the Torah (2021), 633–34.

CosmoErotic Humanism calls the New Human and the New Humanity. For the interior sciences of the great traditions, Messiah is not a single person but the emergence of a new consciousness in humanity. It is the natural progression of evolution itself. Relationship, which is the structure of Reality itself, is defined or expressed in terms of the deepening capacity for *conversation*, itself the basic unit, or monad,[211] of Reality.

In conversation, desire meets desire. Desire is our edge; it is the realization that we are not self-contained in our autonomous vessel. We are longing for communion—we are filled with the urgent desire for conversation. We yearn for intimate unions, recognition, mutuality, and embrace. Desire is our edge. The edge of our desire is not a desire in its superficial form but our deepest heart's desire to speak, and be heard, and to witness our beloved.

Conversation is desire. Messiah is the harmony of all desire and conversations. When all conversations at the edge synergize into Unique Self Symphonies,[212] we begin to smell the fragrance of Messiah. In effect, Reality is the evolution of love, which is the evolution of conversation, which is the evolution of intimacy.

But Messiah is not an omega point. It is not the final conversation but the culmination of what is possible in the sublunar theater—and then we begin again, at the next level, in the next place, on the next journey.

---

211 The term monad comes from ancient Greek, μονάς (monas) unity, and μόνος (monos) alone. Originally, it was conceived by the Pythagoreans. For them, the Monad is the Supreme Being, Divinity, or the totality of all things. For Gottfried Wilhelm Leibniz (and other philosophers of the early modern period), however, there are infinite monads, which are the basic and immaterial elementary particles, or simplest units, that make up the Universe (Discourse on Metaphysics and The Monadology, 2005). We are using monad in something approximating the first sense in the sense of the implicate order of wholeness of being that defines and allures Reality to its own evolutionary becoming.

212 See Essay One, Section 3.5.

4. Eavesdropping on the Conversational Cosmos

One of our key intellectual partners and our dear friend, Howard Bloom, with whom we have been in deep conversation for many years, speaks of the Conversational Cosmos from the perspective of the classical exterior sciences.[213] We speak of—or perhaps eavesdrop on—the Conversational Cosmos from the perspective of the interior sciences. We refer to the Conversational Cosmos by different names: *the Intimate Universe, the Amorous Cosmos, the CosmoErotic Universe, the Universe: A Love Story,* or *Evolution: The Love Story of the Universe.*

The conversation between the interior science and exterior science is critical, for reality is interiors and exteriors all the way down and all the way up the evolutionary chain.[214]

The following text is derived from a conversation between Howard Bloom and myself. I had just introduced to him the key ideas around *Reality is relationship, Reality is evolution,* and *Reality is the evolution of relationship.* Howard was profoundly aligned with this view, to which he, from his self-described perspective of a materialist mystic,[215] then offered

---

213 Bloom, The God Problem (2016).

214 See Section I.2.

215 Howard views his role as maintaining his materialism, and from there speaking into the classic scientific discourse. Howard's materialism, as it has emerged in dozens of conversations between us over some seven years, has little to do with the kind of neo-Darwinian reductive materialism that is fashionable in the scientific community. Rather it more closely approximates what the seminal sage of Kashmir Shaivism Abhinavagupta called vimarsa, which itself discloses a kind of pervasive panpsychism, as the material body of all existence. New Materialists like Karen Barad have written importantly if partially in this regard. I have looked with some care at this set of issues over many years in multiple conversations with the sensitive teachers of Kashmir Shaivism, our dear friends Michael Murphy, Sally Kempton (Swami Durgananda), and Michael Schumacher (Swami Chetanananda). Worth reading in this regard is the work of Loriliai Biernacki, The Matter of Wonder:

his exterior science view of the Conversational Cosmos in support. We deploy different language and take issue on multiple fronts. But we both see the truth of *Reality is evolution, Reality is relationship, and Reality is the evolution of relationship* as the fundamental pattern of Cosmos. Howard, as an expression of his own early training, uses words like *sociality*, while we use words like *intimacy, Eros,* and *desire*—but we are looking at the same patterns of Cosmos. Our empirical descriptions overlap and fructify each other. In the following section, my words in the language of CosmoErotic Humanism are interspersed with Howard's, without identifying who the speakers were, in order to show the common nature of Cosmos toward which we are pointing.[216]

- The intimate configurations of communion that animate Cosmos—what empiricists sometimes call the sociality of the Cosmos—begins when the first particles emerge, in the very, very, very first blast of the Big Bang. The first particles are inherently conversational. These particles cannot exist without each other. They cannot exist without creating a society, and if they don't make it into one of these twosomes or threesomes, they are over and out. How do the twosomes and threesomes get together? They converse with each other. They pick up the signals of attraction and repulsion from each other, and then they act on them. There is an exchange of meaningful information that leads to new emergence. This Universe, from its very first instant, if it's anything like the axioms that are used by corollary generators, has inherent in it everything that will happen until the very end, in that first microflash of a second.

- Imagine entropy as things continually falling apart. When you were a child, you would put a Slinky at the top of a staircase—if

---

Abhinavagupta's Panentheism and the New Materialism (2023), who in part sees Abhinavagupta as a kind of materialist mystic, in which the split between the purely material and the purely mystical, or matter and what matters, virtually disappears.

216 Howard's voice in these texts is drawn from our conversation and leavened with pieces of his writing, or phrasing, particularly from The God Problem.

Slinkys were still something that you had in your house—and you watched it. You would put one end on the first stair going down, and you watched the Slinky go down stair after stair after stair. That's what is supposed to happen to the Cosmos under the rules of entropy.

- Entropy is not a valid idea. It is not borne out by any aspect of the Cosmos whatsoever. In fact, the impossible is the real perception, in the reality of this Cosmos. Because the Universe is like the Slinky footage being run in reverse. So, the next step up is invisible at any given point in time. It is implicit, meaning that from the very time of the very first particles, that staircase for the Slinky run in reverse is already there. All the stuff in the Universe is in the process of discovering its way toward the next invisible stairstep up. But when it comes to these quantum leaps, when it comes to these phase transitions, when it comes to the transition from quark soup to protons and neutrons, those stairsteps, a proton and a neutron, are not at first visible.

- The Universe does not show randomness as the primary driver of Cosmos,[217] and it doesn't show randomness, especially at that first sliver of a second of the Universe's existence. A random Universe would be a gazillion particles, a gazillion different kinds of particles, with no necessary coherence, no necessary relationship between them, even though they all sprang from the mother of the space-time manifold. But quite the opposite is what emerges. What emerges is a universe of inherent and necessary coherence. And it emerges in stairsteps.

- Stairstep number one: the emergence of quarks.

- Stairstep number two: quarks showing social properties and glomming together in groups of two or three, what we call in

---

217 See also Sections V.1–2.

CosmoErotic Humanism configurations of intimacy. Without which the quarks disappear.

- Stairstep number three: These threesomes turn out to have astonishing emergent properties—the emergent properties of protons and neutrons.

- This is but one snippet—but one expression—of what we are describing in CosmoErotic Humanism as the evolution of relationships.

- The evolution of relationships is, first, the evolution of the relationships between quarks.

- Next is the evolution of the relationship between the neutrons and protons.

- Way, way down the road, we have the evolution of relationships in a really big way, when we have electrons, protons, and neutrons getting together. We have described this just above, and it is about 380,000 years later.

- A hydrogen atom is based on what you could call a perpetual conversation between an electron and a proton. That's a staggering emergence of a new kind of relationship that produces whole new emergent properties, radical supersized surprises, emergence that makes absolutely no sense based on prior causation. New wholes are clearly called by the music of the future; they are not merely the result of mechanical process of the past. It is rather emergence based on the evolution of new forms of relationships that are called forth by the inherent value structure of Cosmos itself. The magical ingredient that we cannot leave out if we are honest empiricists is the supersized surprise. Indeed, emergence is the fairy dust of science.

- This is what we describe as *Intimacy generates Emergence*. The radical amazement, the wonder of Cosmos, is that ever-deeper intensities of intimacy themselves generate new configurations of intimacy, which are in effect both the catalysts and expression of new emergence. The electrons and protons can get together, and out of nowhere, out of *no thing*, all of a sudden, the properties of hydrogen, helium, and lithium come into existence, and we couldn't have predicted them by knowing the properties of electrons and protons (and neutrons). This is the *creative advance into novelty* emergent form, the lure of becoming which is core to CosmoErotic Humanism.[218]

- Now, with this in mind, let's turn to the *valence*, or *value*, of subatomic particles as it appears in chemistry and physics. The valence of an electron is negative, and the valence of a proton is positive. Now, if we were to go to the *Oxford English Dictionary*, we would see that the root of the word *valence* is the same as the root of the word *value*.[219] Valence is also part of the cluster of words that includes valor, valiance, *valentes*, and valentine, all of which, like valence, are rooted in value, which itself is self-validating.

---

218 The particular phraseology appears in various guises in the writings of Alfred North Whitehead, but the basic notion is also central to multiple other heterodox theorists of evolution from the proto-evolutionary theories of Luria to the writings of James Mark Baldwin and especially Charles Sanders Peirce. See also Essay Three, Section 3.

219 Valere means both to be strong and to be of value, to be of worth. It goes from Latin valere to Old French valor, which is connected to worth. A valorous knight is not just strong but represents value; he is saving the damsel. Then it goes to Middle English, and then to value. A violation of value arouses political will. Will is aroused by value. The knight accesses their valor because their valor is connected to their values. That root is related to the root of the word will. This is a willful Universe. The word will in the original Hebrew—ratzon—is an Eros word, which is drawn, among other sources, from the Song of Songs. The Song of Songs is an erotic expression of Reality that declares its insides are lined with love—in other words, Reality itself is Eros. The Song of Songs is understood by Akiba—the central figure in the transition from the Jerusalem Temple to the oral law—in one text as participating in the ontology of the Holy of Holies of the Jerusalem Temple and in another text as being a sufficient basis to guide the moral world if the Torah had never been given.

- At the outset of the *Song of Songs*, the lover says to her beloved, "Draw me after you, and I will run toward you."[220] The word for *run toward you*—in Hebrew *rutza*—shares its etymological root and meaning with the Hebrew word *ratzon*—which translates as *will*. In other words, *draw me after you*, meaning allurement, and at some point, when the intensity of the intimate allurement becomes sufficiently potent, I will run after you. I will surrender my lower will to you and allow myself to be taken over by the deeper ErosValue—the erotic will of Reality—moving through me, which arouses me to you, generating a new and unique configuration of intimacy and Eros that overwhelms all separation and boundary and generates new emergence in Reality.

- This text is central to the Song of Solomon. The song, however, is far from being a love song only about a particular love between human lover and beloved. Instead, it understands itself, together with an entire current of esoteric texts in the interior science of Hebrew wisdom, as describing the very source code of Reality itself, all the way up and all the way down the evolutionary chain, or some version of what used to be called the great chain of being. The core text of the *Song of Songs* is *Tocho Ratzuf Ahava*, "*Its insides are lined with love.*" Or, said differently: Reality is Eros.

- Reality is Eros all the way down and all the way up, and a core quality of Eros and its allurements is will. Will is an expression of desire. And desire, in its clarified form, is simply the will toward value. In other words, the amorous desire of the Cosmos, the evolutionary will of Reality, always reaches for—desires—ever wider and deeper value. This notion of value is inherent in Reality from the first nanoseconds of the Big Bang. Value evolves—that is clear. But value at its core is not a human construction but an intrinsic property, the valence of Reality itself.

- There are certain principles, certain relationships, that are in the Universe, very near the very beginning, and then they show up over and over again, level after level of emergence. Value is one of them. There is a primitive precursor of *valentes*—of will—at the very beginning of the Universe. The fact that this Universe spurts out space, time, and speed—that's *valentes*. That's the precursor of will in its later forms—precursor of the will that's in you and me.

- Now, we need a couple of Herbert Spencer's terms here. Herbert Spencer talks about differentiation and integration. Indeed, that is the title of chapter 15 of his work *First Principles*.[221] What does that mean? That means that we all have unique personhoods and need to, in some way, demonstrate our uniqueness. Personhood is deeper than personality. It is not an accidental feature of the mechanical cosmos that developed a random new application. Personhood is the unique conversation that is every being and most potently incarnate in every human being.

- When you enter a new group, you have two jobs:

- The first is to show that you blend in. In other words, to feel your common identity. This is the first dimension that generates the communion (through integration) within the larger group.

- And the second is to show that you stand out. In other words, to feel your irreducible uniqueness within the group. This is the second dimension that generates communion (through differentiation) within the larger group.

- But then: Once you have differentiated, when you are coming together in a whole, the whole that you make—the society that you make—has radically new emergent properties. And this dialectical tension between our uniqueness and our sameness is the key to

---

221 Herbert Spencer, First Principles (1880).

intimate communion at every level of Reality, from matter to life to mind. Indeed, this dialectic of sameness and uniqueness is an expression of what we call, in CosmoErotic Humanism, two First Principles and First Values of Cosmos, allurement and autonomy, or what are also sometimes referred as autonomy and communion.

- A lump of dirt is a social relationship. Or said more clearly, it is a configuration of intimacy—of intimate coherence. A lump of dirt is composed of atoms and molecules in intimately configured relationship with each other. (And, if it is soil on Earth, it may even include hundreds of millions of microorganisms living in intimate communion.)

- A single bacterial cell is a relationship at a whole different level of intimate communion. It builds on all the intimate relationships between the organic molecules inside of it, which make up the different parts of the cell, the DNA, the RNA, the amino acids, and proteins; but then it adds a radical new dimension of self-replication and self-actualization. If we were to musically compose the dazzling complexity of intimacies between myriad parts in insanely intricate, allured erotic unions of shapes and forms, we would understand that a single bacterial cell is a musical symphony of intimacies that would shame Mozart.

- A bacterial colony is a relationship of a radically new kind generating an ever-higher and deeper level of intimate communion. It is a community of bacterial cells in communion; the cells communicate and support each other in locating or generating the optimal life conditions for the whole community. You and me, two human beings, again, we are manifestations of relationship that produce dramatic differences, dramatic new things. But we are in the same continuum of intimacy, conversation, and relationship.

- Herbert Spencer called this progress. Another name for it might be the evolution of intimacy, or the evolution of love, or, most simply, the evolution of relationship. Clearly, relationship is a core plotline of Cosmos, even as it is equally clear that the evolution of relationship, or what we also refer to as the evolution of intimacy, is a core plotline of Cosmos.

- In the language of CosmoErotic Humanism, we say that there is a wholeness that can generate more wholeness. In other words, a level of wholeness has been achieved through intimate communion between the parts. But that wholeness does not cease desiring. Wholeness is allured to ever-deeper and wider intimate communions, which means ever-more profound conversations that generate ever-deeper and wider wholeness. This is precisely the Eros equation that we referred to above:[222] Eros = the experience of radical aliveness, seeking, desiring, moving toward ever-deeper contact, ever-greater communication conversation and communion, and ever-greater wholeness.

- The new wholeness is of a kind that you never imagined before. That's why these are supersized surprises. In between differentiation, integration, and progress lies the supersized surprise. This form of social organization, of intimate communion, produces a whole new kind of Reality, a previously unimagined new kind of Reality. What emerges is a new configuration of Eros, intimacy, and desire, a new level of conversation, which is what we call in evolutionary language a new emergent.

- The allurement to higher intimacies is fundamental to cosmos. One relatively early incarnation of this phenomenological reality of Cosmos is a wave. A wave is constantly recruiting new water molecules and then abandoning them, and recruiting a whole bunch of new ones, and so on and so forth all the way across the ocean. It never has the same constituents for more than about fifteen seconds. The matter that makes it up is always changing.

---

222 See Section 2.4 in Essay One.

Yet it retains its coherence because there is some sort of tenacity to larger configurations of intimacy.

- The wave is a result of intimate patterns of relationship that are evoked by the inherent nature of reality. But if you just looked at it as relationships, you wouldn't see the wave. You can describe the wave with equations. It is this kind of relationship that can be described with simple equations, that persists. It has its own will, and yet it is nonmaterial.

- Human beings are part of a continuum with the wave of evolving patterns of intimacy. But of course you and I are not just the water molecules in that wave. We are constantly changing, unlike the water molecules. But even though we are constantly changing, we are forming a part of some larger pattern that seems to have been inherent from the beginning. I mean, how can we go from people who lived in societies of thirty-five to a hundred fifty individuals eleven thousand years ago to people who live in a society of a billion today? And it's a largely coherent society, even while we are so individually fluid.

- So, the question is, how does reality generate coherent complexity? In our reading, Alan Turing's essential response in "Morphogenesis"[223] is simple first rules.

- Yes, I came to a similar conclusion as Alan, based on a somewhat different set of scientific axioms of reality. There are three or four simple rules that are largely scientific but which have value implications.

- These simple first rules are similar to what we call in CosmoErotic Humanism First Principles and First Values. But in CosmoErotic Humanism, the simple first rules address not only exteriors

---

223 Turing, "The Chemical Basis of Morphogenesis."

but also interiors. Indeed, it would not be inaccurate to say that complexity theory operates based on the iteration of simple First Principles and First Values in exteriors, while the evolution of culture and consciousness is animated and driven by the iteration of simple First Principles and First Values in interiors. We have identified, in CosmoErotic Humanism, some eighteen First Principles and First Values.

- We might also talk about these as learning algorithms of the Cosmos. One example of a learning algorithm is very much akin to Herbert Spencer's: First, reach out and explore; then, rush together again and consolidate; then, reach out and explore again. Fusion and Fission is another way to express the same simple first rule of Cosmos. So, those are the two fundamental learning rules of the Cosmos, and probably rules at the very beginning of the Cosmos—the simple rules, the First Principles and First Values, are what we might call the axioms that kick-started the Cosmos.

- In CosmoErotic Humanism, we say it something like as follows: Differentiation is the drive toward ever-deeper irreducible uniqueness, a form of autonomy, while integration is the allurement toward ever-greater, deeper, and wider intimate communion. Allurement and autonomy are both First Principles and First Values, which are themselves the plotlines of Evolution: The Love Story of the Universe. Indeed, Eros itself is not allurement but rather the precisely calibrated dance between allurement and autonomy.[224]

- The big thing to not lose track of is the things that we do not have sufficient words for and that science has not really grappled with— things like the wave, which is a self-sustaining pattern that is not dependent on any individual group of material things. Those are the stairsteps, those larger patterns that emerge only when there

---

224 See Chapter III.

are enough of us getting together. Those are the invisible stairsteps, and those are all about relationship, except there is something bigger than relationship at work. It's about the evolution of these new properties that we can derive. It's also about the next stairsteps up, which are not things over which we have a choice. These new patterns are what we have called in many conversations a memory of the future, called forth by inherent Eros of Cosmos itself.

5. Intimacy Generates Emergence

Great literature is often about great people—often those who are willing to risk everything, including fame, fortune, and reputation, for the sake of relationship with their beloved. The beloved may well be another human being—family, friend, partner, or lover—or it may be a beloved of an entirely different nature. It may be an animal; there is an entire literature of love stories between human beings and animals.[225] It may be a group, a society, a tribe, an army unit, a sports team, or a group of old friends. It may be a set of values, a religion, a society that stretches across

---

225 One beautiful example of this genre is the film My Octopus Teacher, which came out several years after the core of this text was written. It is a love story between a masculine and muscular South African diver, Foster, and an octopus. He describes with enormous depth and beauty the subtle love that developed between him and an octopus that he met in his deep-sea dives. Wikipedia describes the movie as follows: "The film shows Foster's growing intimate relationship with the octopus as he follows her around for nearly a year. They form a bond where she plays with Foster and allows him into her world to see how she sleeps, lives, and eats." Here is some of the language that the diver uses to describe their love: "My relationship with the sea forest and its creatures deepens . . . week after month after year after year. You're in touch with this wild place, and it's speaking to you. Its language is visible. I fell in love with her but also with that amazing wildness that she represented and . . . and how that changed me. What she taught me was to feel . . . that you're part of this place, not a visitor. That's a huge difference."

space and time. It may be a country, a body of knowledge or gnosis, or a set of intrinsic values of Cosmos expressed in a cause. All of these are subjects of relationships with whom we may be in intimate communion.

Equally profound is the capacity to be in relationship *to yourself*. That is not as simple as it seems. In most of the great interior sciences, the essential movement of Reality is when *subject* becomes *object*. Divinity expresses herself as subject and can reflect on herself as an external object. The same principle is true at the highest reaches of human development. For American developmental psychologist Robert Kegan, a new level of consciousness and depth is obtained when the subject of one level of consciousness becomes the object of the next level of consciousness.[226] This is a form of evolving relationship to self. Let's deploy two examples to illustrate what we mean by *subject becoming object* as a form of relationship to self.

Newborn babies cannot discern between what is their bodies and what is not. They cannot discern between different parts of their bodies. They *are* their bodies. Their bodies are subject. It takes several months until they start to voluntarily move their hands and watch their movements with their eyes. This is a nascent realization: *I am not my body; I am in relationship to my body*. And it takes even longer until they understand that they cannot make their caretakers come and go, nor can they move their caretaker's hands. This is the nascent realization of separation individuation—self and other:[227] *I am not other; I am in relationship to other*. These realizations emerge when one day, they, the babies, are able to discern between themselves and their hands, or themselves and their bodies. They have made their bodies object: *I can look at, and talk about, my body. My body is part of who I am, but it doesn't exhaust my whole me. My body is an object inside of my whole me (my subject)*. Similarly, they distinguish between self and other: *I am not merged with my mother or caretaker.*

Another example of subject becoming object is the psychological

---

226 Robert Kegan introduced his subject-object theory in his books The Evolving Self: Problem and Process in Human Development (1982) and In Over Our Heads: The Mental Demands of Modern Life (1994).

227 See the work of Margaret Mahler (MS 1138 in Manuscripts and Archives, Yale University Library. https://archives.yale.edu/repositories/12/resources/).

process often called *shadow work*. A quality that is in shadow cannot be seen. It has been dissociated *within* the subject, whether it is a negative quality or a wondrous positive quality. It is a split-off part that cannot be made object, so it remains an unconscious subject and is thus invisible. Because the shadow quality is split off, it will then be projected into second and third person. For example, take the quality of anger or rage, which lives in the first person of the subject but is split off or disassociated. Instead of recognizing ourselves to be angry, we project the anger onto someone else. There is a failure of intimacy with self, which causes the projection of the self-experience onto someone else. This dynamic expresses as: *I am not angry, but you seem to be angry,* or: *All the other people out there are angry.* Anger is simply not recognized as being part of one's own self, the subject. Rather than becoming a healthy object inside our own subject, the shadow part is dissociated and projected onto another subject that then becomes an object.

The person onto whom we have wrongly projected the split-off anger—our own split-off shadow quality—can no longer be accurately felt. That person becomes to us not a subject we can relate to but an object, a thing. Our relationship with that person thus devolves from what Martin Buber famously calls an *I-Thou* (subject to subject) relationship to an *I-it* (subject to object) or *it-it* (object to object) relationship.

The reason it would be an object-to-object relationship is because by splitting ourselves off from our own anger, we become nonintimate with ourselves. We reduce ourselves from a subject that we can accurately feel to an alienated object. When we evolve or deepen our consciousness, the split-off quality can be returned to the light. We can take our projections back and recognize our projected shadow as part of our own self or subject. The alienated quality becomes a part of our whole being. More formally, it becomes an object, which we can see and therefore act on, shape, or direct, *within* our subject—our own felt sense of our full self. This is because we can now *see* the split-off quality within our self and therefore act upon it, perhaps to transform, activate, redirect, or even honor it, depending on what the precise nature of quality might be.[228]

---

228 To cite one example: Many years back, I was working with a wonderful CEO of a major firm, who was a decent and kind man with genuine integrity. But he

Whichever one of the myriad forms of relationship we are referring to, the fundamental facts remain the same:

Reality is relationship.

Reality is evolution.

That means that the evolution of Reality is the evolution of relationships.

That is true not only on the macro level of history, from quarks to humans, but also in your life. The more you evolve, the better quality of relationships you will want. The more we evolve, the more we are willing to risk everything not just for a relationship but for an even deeper relationship. Or even better, if at all possible—and it sometimes is and sometimes is not—to deepen the relationships we already have.

Relationships are expressed in conversations. The evolution of relationships is the deepening of conversation. At the core of an extraordinary life are always extraordinary relationships, which are constituted by extraordinary conversations.

Remember the old adage: *If a tree falls in a forest and there is no one there to hear it, does it make a sound?* Let's rephrase its implications more overtly in terms of relationship: *If something momentous happens to you and there is no one there to share it with, did it happen?*

But it is even more than that. Relationships are not only about sharing—they are about creating or synergizing new life through our coming together. Sometimes, that new life is a baby. At other times, that new life is new depth, new truth, new goodness, and new beauty in the

---

was always having conflicts with his management team. The conflicts were often intense. He would not back down, and they seemed incongruous with his persona and personal ethic in other dimensions of his life. After a short series of talks, we excavated an early set of memories, when his father, who started the company, would say to him, "Don't let the management team take advantage of you. You have to show them who is in charge, or they will ride all over you." This was a mantra from his father that he had forgotten in his conscious mind. But when we recovered it, we realized almost instantly that, when he engaged his management team, he was not directly engaging them. Instead, his communications and positions were in fact directed toward proving to his father that he was a worthy successor to him. This entire dynamic had been in his subject. When we recovered it, it became object. He was not in relationship with this part of himself. And once he realized it, he was in relationship and had the capacity—if he so chose—to evolve the relationship.

Cosmos that was birthed by our relationship. It is new relationship, new intimacy, that generates all novel emergence. Or, said simply: *Intimacy generates emergence.*

6. Invisible Patterns of Intimacy

Giacomo Rizzolatti discovered another core expression of *Reality is relationship* in the realm of molecular biology. He called his discovery mirror neurons.[229] Humans and other primates, he claimed, make use of mirror neurons to read emotions as well as behaviors in others.[230] He

---

229 Giacomo Rizzolatti and Laila Craighero, "The Mirror-Neuron System" (2004).

230 The first animal in which Rizzolatti and his colleagues studied mirror neurons was the macaque monkey. What they called a mirror neuron is a neuron that fires both when the monkeys act themselves and when they observe the same action performed by another. In other words, the neuron mirrors the behavior of the other, as though the observer were itself acting. Researchers have found such neurons in human and primate species, as well as in birds. However, the function of these mirror neurons in humans is a subject of much speculation. To date, there have been no widely accepted neural or computational models put forward to describe how mirror neuron activity supports cognitive functions. While many researchers in the scientific community have expressed their excitement about the discovery of these mirror neurons, there are also scientists, such as Hickok, Pascolo, and Dinstein, who have expressed doubts about the existence and role of the so-called mirror neurons in humans. For example, Gregory Hickok published an extensive argument in 2009 against the claim that mirror neurons are involved in action understanding. The name of his paper is "Eight Problems for the Mirror Neuron Theory of Action Understanding in Monkeys and Humans." He concludes that "the early hypothesis that these cells underlie action understanding is likewise an interesting and prima facie reasonable idea. However, despite its widespread acceptance, the proposal has never been adequately tested in monkeys, and in humans there is strong empirical evidence, in the form of physiological and neuropsychological (double-) dissociations, against the claim." In the preface to his The Myth of Mirror Neurons: The Real Neuroscience of Communication and Cognition (2014), Hickok writes, "The international debate over mirror neurons and indeed the nature of human cognition

and one of his young postdoctoral researchers were shocked to discover that some of the exact same sections of the brains of macaque monkeys that activated when they performed an action were also activated when they watched someone else performing that action. Other scientists, including Stephanie Preston and Frans de Waal,[231] have independently argued that the mirror neuron system is involved in empathy.

Their research suggests that when you watch someone else in a moment of joy or pain, you are having the same experience, at least in terms of the neural activations in the brain. This applies not only to the sensation of physical pain but also to the emotional aspect of the experience. We activate each other's neural circuitry all the time. In fact, as Rizzolatti's and others' work makes clear, perceiving Reality is in no sense an individual affair. It is a result of shared neural circuitry. Neurons externalize, in our physical brain circuitry, the felt sense of others.

In some sense, in order to perceive and understand another, we merge with them for a moment. We recreate their experience as if we were having it ourselves. We have a core human capacity rooted in our neural circuitry to literally feel into the experience of another, whether through mirror neurons or other mechanisms.[232] There is a partial intimacy. For a

---

has intensified. Mirror neurons are no longer the rock stars of neuroscience and psychology that they once were and, in my view, a more complex and interesting story is gaining favor regarding the neuroscience of communication and cognition."

231 Stephanie D. Preston and Frans B. M. de Waal, "Empathy: Its Ultimate and Proximate Bases" (2002).

232 While experts like Gregory Hickok doubt that complex capabilities in humans (and in somewhat different form in primates), like empathy, imitation, social learning, et cetera, can be explained by mirror neurons alone, there is no doubt that these abilities exist. In chapter 8 ("Homo Imitans and the Function of Mirror Neurons") of his book The Myth of Mirror Neurons: The Real Neuroscience of Communication and Cognition (2014), Hickok writes, "Here we have a potential behavior that mirror neurons might support, not simple imitation (mimicry), but some form of social or imitation-like learning. But what kind of social learning could mirror neurons support in the context of the experimental paradigm that led to their discovery? . . . Macaques reach for and grasp things all the time and they observe their own actions visually. Pretty soon, an association builds between the execution of an action and the (self) observation of that action. Poof! Mirror neurons are born. Now, when the animal sees the experimenter execute an action similar to those that

moment, there is, in our experience, a shared identity between ourselves and the person we are observing. The simple act of reading a novel opens a window to the implicit intimacy between us that connects us in a way that is accessible to almost every human being.

This is the same process that Alfred North Whitehead saw taking place between elementary particles. The subatomic particles have what he calls prehension, a very elementary feeling in which the perceiving thing apprehends aspects of the perceived thing.[233] It is that ability to feel each other that allows them to enter into the bond of intimate relationship. The same process in ever-more evolved forms takes place all the way up the evolutionary chain. For Reality is relationship, an intimate relationship, all the way down and all the way up the chain.

At the human level, the boundary between you and others (especially those in your circle of intimacy) is blurred. Those boundaries are mediated by a complex mix of neural firings originating from inside and outside your head. That is why we might be watching a movie and alternatively sobbing tears of pain or tears of joy depending on the scene playing out. As Rizzolatti's student Christian Keysers notes, "Watching the movie scene in which a tarantula crawls on James Bond's chest can literally make us shiver, as if the spider crawled on our own chest,"[234]

---

the monkey has previously executed, the cells fire because of the preexisting association built on self-observation. It's got nothing to do with understanding. . . . I'm suggesting an associative account of mirror neurons similar to the one Arbib and Heyes promote, but with a different source of the association: the experimental training itself rather than self-action to other-action sensorimotor generalization. The mirror neuron research team may have inadvertently trained mirror neurons into the monkey's brain. Hopefully, future experiments will be designed to test this hypothesis." See also "Schema Design and Implementation of the Grasp-Related Mirror Neuron System," by Erhan Oztop and Michael A. Arbib (2002), and "Where Do Mirror Neurons Come From?" by Cecilia Heyes (2010).

233 Prehension was not conceived as a cognitive process at the level of basic particles but rather an unconscious apprehension. It may be thought of as more of an inherent reflex of what has been called proto-feeling or proto-touch that connects ostensibly alienated particles. See Whitehead, Process and Reality.

234 Christian Keysers at al., "A Touching Sight: SII/PV Activation during the Observation and Experience of Touch" (2004), 335.

because, in a very real sense, we are experiencing the physical sensation of a tarantula crawling across our own chest, along with the emotions that go with it.

The more we love the other, the more actively our empathy is aroused. Eros expresses itself in our psyche and in the physical structure of brain circuitry. Even just seeing another's emotional state is enough to trigger an emotional response in ourselves. American neuropsychologist Allan Schore has discovered that mothers and their babies often have interlocking brain waves. This phenomenon of relationship is referred to as brain-to-brain entrainment, right-brain-to-right-brain nonverbal communication, or interbrain synchronization.[235] They are so deep in relationship that, from the perspective of brain waves, the prefrontal cortex of the mother becomes the prefrontal cortex of the baby. There is an emerging body of research, using dual EEG,[236] showing evidence that the EEG brain-wave patterns of the mother synchronize with the EEG pattern of the baby in a variety of states.[237] When they separate, their brain waves diverge, only to recalibrate and resonate once again with each other when they come back together.

This kind of entrainment is not limited to mother-baby pairs, however, but is inherent in many forms of relationship, including, to some degree, two strangers who are paired for an experiment.[238] Partners even seem to be able to send brain signals from isolated rooms to each other. The person

---

235 See Allan Schore, "The Interpersonal Neurobiology of Intersubjectivity" (2021) and "Right-Brain-to-Right-Brain Psychotherapy: Recent Scientific and Clinical Advances" (2022).

236 Dual-EEG research is simply research involving two or more subjects wearing electroencephalograms and looking at the correlation patterns between subjects performing a variety of tasks.

237 See, for instance, the project "Using 'Naturalistic Dual-EEG' to Measure Mother-Infant Brain-to-Brain (b2b) Synchrony in Socially-Mediated Learning," led by Victoria Leong and Samuel Vincent Wass, researchers at the University of Cambridge (https://gtr.ukri.org/projects?ref=ES%2FN006461%2F1).

238 On neural synchrony between strangers, see, for instance, "Brain-to-Brain Entrainment: EEG Interbrain Synchronization While Speaking and Listening," by Alejandro Pérez et al. (2017).

whose brain is receiving the brain signal will imitate the brain pattern of the sender. The partner and sender to do not need to know each other, and there is no contact between them other than mental intention.[239]

All these invisible patterns of intimacy—as well as those yet to be discovered—are exterior confirmations of the core truth: Reality is relationship. Reality is Eros.

7. The Fellowship of the Ring

J. R. R. Tolkien's epic Lord of the Rings trilogy—*The Fellowship of the Ring, The Two Towers*, and *The Return of the King*—is all about one theme: Reality is relationship.

Tolkien's books, and the movies based on them, found their way into the world to a real degree, independently of the contrived marketing machines of studios and publishing. Tolkien's books have sold somewhere around six hundred million copies—powered in great part by their own inherent momentum.

At each key moment in this story, there is a dialogue clarifying the most essential structure of Reality as radically committed relationships. It is about relationships between two individuals and about relationships in the context of the group. It is about whether the Fellowship of the Ring has the integrity and potency necessary to stand against corruption and evil.

---

239 The following are three related studies from the late 1990s that participated in generating this field of inquiry: "The Electricity of Touch: Detection and Measurement of Cardiac Energy Exchange Between People: An Exploratory Study," by Rollin McCraty et al. (1998); "An Experiment on Remote Action Against Man in Sensory-Shielding Conditions," by Mikio Yamatomo et al. (1996); and "Biophoton Emission of the Human Body," by S. Cohen and F. A. Popp (1997). See also "EEG Correlates of Social Interaction at Distance," by W. Giroldini et al. (2015), "Electroencephalographic Evidence of Correlated Event-Related Signals between the Brains of Spatially and Sensory Isolated Human Subjects," by Leanna J. Standish et al. (2004), "A Direct Brain-to-Brain Interface in Humans," by Rajesh P. N. Rao et al. (2014), and "BrainNet: A Multi-Person Brain-to-Brain Interface for Direct Collaboration Between Brains," by Linxing Jiang et al. (2019).

The Ring is most powerfully described as *precious*. Gollum, the emotionally and physically twisted figure, who was formerly a hobbit, once possessed the Ring. He is both madly devoted to it and degraded by it. Gollum rasps in whispers again and again through the text *"My Precious"* in his reaching for the Ring. The Ring, *My Precious*, represents anti-precious or anti-value. Or, said slightly differently, the Ring is Anti-Eros.

Eros is the core value of Cosmos. According to the Eros equation, Eros is the experience of radical aliveness, yearning for ever-deeper contact and ever-greater wholeness. In other words, Eros itself is about contact between parts and generation of wholeness—right relationship between parts—in other words, *ethos*. Eros is ethos. In their deepest expression, there is no split at all between the erotic and the ethical.

Eros *is* ethos.[240] Or said slightly differently, Eros is Value exponentialized as the Infinite Value that suffuses Reality. Nothing exists outside of the circle of Eros as Value and Value as Eros. Eros *is* ethos, and ethos, or Value, is the *Ought* implicit in Reality that suffuses all of Cosmos. This is what we refer to in CosmoErotic Humanism as *ErosValue*.

The Ring, however, was forged by the corrupt Lord Sauron to dominate and bind all other rings in blind submission to his power. It experiences itself as being outside the circle of Eros and Value. This is the optical delusion of consciousness that is generated by the Ring. The Ring promises ultimate power and freedom—not authentic power or freedom, but the freedom from the *Ought* of Eros and Value, from *ethos*, from the Obligation and Joy of Reality. The Ring of power is the evil of cancerous

---

240 Naturally, Eros and ethos appear at different levels of evolving consciousness. Level one of Eros is often an explosion of Eros that is not yet clarified by ethos. There is a second level, in which ethos constrains Eros, demanding its clarification and appropriate context and expression. There is then a third level, where Eros and ethos disclose their fundamental identity. True Eros—when it is clarified, when one accesses, at the level of human Eros, one's deepest heart's desire—is always the highest expression of Eros and ethos as one. When the clarification of Eros at level two does not take place, then the natural explosion of Eros at level one reappears, in many distressing disguises, as pseudo-eros—showing up whenever the experience of emptiness and void is too powerful to bear, and there is no genuine Eros that the person has the capacity to access to fill the hole. That happens, in other words, for anyone not constantly engaged in the wondrous work of self-transformation and clarification.

independence from the larger Whole, which not only is alienated from the Whole but hates the Whole and Wholeness.

The Ring of power, in the myth of the Lord of the Rings, like in the interior science of Hebrew wisdom, has quasi-autonomy in the sense that it has its own motivational architecture toward abusive power in its most pseudo-erotically degraded forms. In other words, the Ring is pseudo-eros so exponentialized that it feels like Eros herself, with powers of seduction that are similarly exponentialized.

In other words, the pseudo-eros of the Ring is so radically exponentialized that it feels like Anti-Eros—Anti-Value, which presents as Eros herself—as Value herself. That is precisely why evil crusades attract support and followers. Said succinctly: Anti-Eros presenting as Eros is the ultimate expression of pseudo-eros.

A flashback in the movie shows how the Ring is rediscovered at the bottom of a riverbed by a young diver. Within moments of his discovery, however, the young man's friend, entranced by the ring's precious, raw Anti-Eros, its seductive potency, kills him to gain its possession.

The biblical story of Cain and Abel has the same theme. Judas betraying Jesus is the same story. And every Asian, native, and western tradition has its versions of the same tale of betrayal.

The betrayal of intimate friendship manifests the very nature of the Ring. Anti-Eros rears its head to destroy the authentic Eros that is the very nature of Reality, whose narrative arc is the progressive deepening of intimacies, a series of love stories, all the way up and down the evolutionary chain.[241] The response to Anti-Eros can only be Eros of the most potent form. This is the Fellowship of the Ring. Thus the Ring, Anti-Eros, can only be undone by the Fellowship. Gandalf and the warriors Legolas and Gimli, together with Boromir, son of the steward of Gondor, and Aragorn, the not-yet-recognized king, as well as the hobbits Frodo, Sam, Merry, and Pippin are at the core of the Fellowship. Others are key beloveds. Arwen, the beloved of Aragorn; Galadriel, the Elven priestess; Elrond,

---

241 One of the constituents that define a story is some dimension of freedom, a sense of choosing, at least to some degree. It is for that very reason that Eros, by its very nature, must entertain the possibility of Anti-Eros. Otherwise, Reality would not be a story but a tech manual. See Temple, First Principles and First Values.

father to Arwen and leader of the Elves; Faramir, brother of Boromir; Theoden, king of Rohan, and his daughter Eowyn and nephew Eomer are all central beloveds in the story, each with their role to play in supporting the Fellowship. It is only the bonds of love and loyalty between the Fellowship that will allow the Ring to be dissolved and Eros restored.

When the Fellowship is threatened, the Ring gains ascendancy. When the Fellowship is strong, the way is opened to the dissolution of the Anti-Eros of the Ring. If the Fellowship is broken, then the bonds of trust and love in relationship are betrayed, Eros—Value itself—is broken, and the Ring grows strong.

One of the core motifs of the New Story of Value we are telling in CosmoErotic Humanism is the demonstration that Reality is Eros. This is not different than demonstrating that Reality is Value. Eros is the right relationship, rooted in ethos (the right valuation of the parts), which then generates a larger whole. In other words, to say *Reality is Value* or *Reality is Eros* is absolutely identical to declaring *Reality is ethos* or *Reality is relationship*.

In Tolkien's trilogy, the truth of *Reality is relationship* is incarnate in the Fellowship of the Ring. Indeed, virtually all great literature and the lyrics of virtually all popular music revolve not around philosophical inquiry or doctrinal issues of faith or psychological personality analysis but rather around intimacy and relationship—the longing, the betrayal, the pain, the ecstasy, and the joy. For Reality is relationship—all the way down and all the way up the evolutionary chain.

In the trilogy, seduction by the Ring is the original sin, heralding the destruction of the characters' reality. Because Reality is relationship, the rupture can only be fixed by repairing and restoring relationship. But it cannot be simply a restorative repair, where relationship goes back to its prior status. After the shattering, a new and more whole vessel of relationship must emerge. This evolutionary deepening of the relationship, forged in the outrageous pain and Outrageous Love of our lives, is the goal of the quest. The quest, which seeks liberation from the Anti-Eros, the ultimate pseudo-eros of the Ring, is not only about returning to Eden or restoration. It is about the radical deepening of relationship, the yearned-for utopia of relationship that is our grail. In other words, for the Fellowship to thrive, relationship (the Fellowship) has not only to continue but to evolve. Reality is not only relationship. Reality is evolution, and Reality is the evolution of relationship.

It is in the ever-deepening and evolving integrity of the Fellowship's intimacy that hope for Reality lies. The hobbits are carriers of the great power of relationship. They lack fighting skills. They have no political power to speak of. They know no magic. They have studied no great wisdom texts, and they command no armies. But they understand, with the unvarnished depth of pure wisdom, that all of Reality is relationship. And life in the Shire, the hobbits' home, is about the natural deepening of relationship in the context of the everyday nature of living. The hobbits incarnate a certain innocence, not of a naïve kind but rather *a second innocence* of the kind that comes after tragedy and loss. They live the simple truth: *Reality is relationship.*

In the third book, *The Return of the King,* it is the depth of love between the hobbits Frodo and Sam that allows Frodo not to be destroyed by the Ring. The true trial in that book is: Will Gollum (the hobbit who committed the original murder to take possession of the Ring) succeed in destroying the bonds of friendship between Frodo and Sam? For a time, Gollum succeeds in doing just that. He convinces Frodo that Sam has betrayed him and seeks only to steal the Ring for himself. This is precisely the nature of Anti-Eros as the ultimate pseudo-eros. It persuades the Fellowship that the original sin of betrayal has been committed, when in fact there is only radical love and loyalty. Pseudo-eros imitates Eros, as in, for example, the twisted and tragic nature of Gollum's feigned outrage at Sam's presumed betrayal of Frodo.

Without Sam, Frodo cannot find his way. He winds up shrouded like a mummy in the suffocating web of a cruel spider. He is about to be killed. He cannot complete his mission to destroy the Ring. Reality will be destroyed.

The turnabout in the last moment happens through the recovery of their Fellowship. Sam and Frodo restore the integrity of their relationship; hope and possibility are reborn. In that moment, each recognizes their unique singularity. Sam realizes that only Frodo can carry the Ring, and that Sam cannot share that burden with him. But Sam says to Frodo:

Come, Mr. Frodo! I can't carry it for you, but I can carry you.

Frodo realizes the truth of this, and in this new partnership, their love—the Fellowship of the Ring—deepens and evolves.

The books and their movie versions are sprinkled with dialogue that would be easy to miss but that carries the deeper intention of the whole story. It is only in knowing that Reality is the integrity of relationship that the Fellowship of the Ring can save Reality.

Because of the limitations of space, we will share only four short scenes from just one of the movies, *The Return of the King.* But these scenes sufficiently represent the essence of the realization we have described to this point. The scenes all take place at a moment of possible death. Every great wisdom tradition says that the moment right before our death is a moment when the veils part and truth is revealed for a fleeting moment. What is truly Real comes to the foreground, and everything else recedes.

The first scene is a dialogue between two great fighters, the Dwarf warrior Gimli and the Elf prince Legolas. It takes place at a moment when their deaths seem imminent.

Gimli: *Never thought I'd die fighting side by side with an Elf.*
Legolas: *What about side by side with a friend?*
Gimli: *Aye. I could do that.*

The second scene is in the same battle, led by their friend Aragorn, the returning king. The king is an archetype of Unique Self. The Unique Self is the one who fully incarnates their unique configuration of intimacy—their unique expression of LoveIntelligence, LoveBeauty, and LoveDesire. This is the one who decides to move through the trauma and demons from the past in order to claim the full power of their unique destiny. That is what it means to be king.

Historically, the realization of Unique Self was thought to be limited to kings and queens. Everyone else was expendable. It was the king and queen who were uniquely called, needed, and chosen by Reality. In this era, we now realize that greatness is democratized. We are all Unique Selves. We are all—in potential—kings and queens—the democratization of royalty.

The realization of the Intimate Universe is the realization that every human being is a unique configuration of intimacy—intended, recognized, chosen, love-adored, desired, and needed by All-That-Is. Every person has their unique instrument to play in the music of the Unique Self Symphony.

Moments before the battle, in which Aragorn's army is outnumbered and, from the look of things, will be unable to triumph, Aragorn gives a classic speech. It is the speech of the Unique Self king. It is about one thing only: Reality is relationship. Aragorn speaks of the potency and power of the love that binds friends. He rides before the men and shouts these words:

> *Sons of Gondor! Of Rohan! My brothers!*
> *I see in your eyes the same fear that would take the heart of me.*
> *A day may come when the courage of men fails, when we forsake*
> *our friends and break all bonds of fellowship. But it is not this day.*
> *This day we fight! . . .*
> *By all that you hold dear on this good Earth, I bid you stand! Men*
> *of the West!*

We now turn to scene three. After the Ring has been destroyed, Sam and Frodo are stranded on a slab of rock in the midst of volcanic eruption. They seem once again to face certain death. Frodo turns to Sam and says poignantly but powerfully:

I'm glad to be here with you, Samwise Gamgee, here at the end of all things.

Who are you truly with at the end of all things? You are with your friend. If that is so, then Reality—Relationship and Love—triumphs over death. If that is not so, then you are dead already, so death matters little.

In the same moment, before what seems to be their impending death, Sam remembers what he wished to have done in his life. He does not wish for wealth, power, or any other achievement. He wishes for relationship. Sam remembers the relationship that never happened, the girl he would have married. He can see Rosie Cotton dancing. *She had ribbons in her hair. If I ever was to marry someone, it would have been her. It would have been her.*

Another key relationship in the trilogy is that of two other hobbits from the shire: Merry and Pippin. They are separated at a key moment in the third movie. It marks an imminent danger to the very survival of Reality as they know it. That danger is marked by what seems to be the breaking of a core relationship between friends.

> **Pippin**: *But we'll see each other soon? Won't . . .*
> **Merry**: *I don't know.*

And after those words, the entire tale of *The Return of the King* unfolds. After a battle where Merry is wounded by a dark foe, the end is marked with these simple and unpretentious words between Merry and Pippin when they are reunited.

> **Merry**: *Are you going to leave me?*
> **Pippin**: *No, Merry. I'm going to look after you.*

The entire trilogy ends with the reuniting of Aragorn and Arwen—the king and queen. But theirs is far from an ordinary love story. Theirs is quite an Outrageous Love Story. What is most potent is that they are not role mates having children and surviving. They are not merely soul mates staring deeply into each other's eyes. They embody a new station in the evolution of love—an evolutionary relationship. They are whole mates. Their love is intensely passionate and personal, but it is not just about them. Their love is in service to the larger Whole.

Perhaps the best way to close this meditation is to return to Frodo and Sam, with whom we began. They are at the beginning of their mission. Their relationship is suffused with loyalty and love. But it's not just about them. They are pulled by a purpose that is larger than them. They are whole mates in evolutionary relationship.

> **Frodo**: *It would be the death of you to come with me, Sam, and I could not have borne that.*
> **Sam**: *Not as certain as being left behind.*
> **Frodo**: *But I am going to Mordor.*
> **Sam**: *I know that well enough, Mr. Frodo. Of course you are. And I'm*

coming with you.

8. Reality Does Not Only Create Relationship: Reality Is Relationship

We live in a CosmoErotic Universe, an Intimate Universe, an Amorous Cosmos. The subatomic and atomic world, which constitutes all dimensions of Reality, is animated by the Field of Intimate Allurement and Autonomy, the Eros-suffused conversation. In this Field, desire for new configurations of Eros and Value—Eros as Value and Value as Eros—defines the evolutionary movements of Reality. Evolution is the Love Story of the Universe.

There is both radical continuity and discontinuity between the levels of Reality, from matter in all of its levels, to life in all of its levels, to the depth of the human self-reflective mind in all of its levels.[242] The drive of a neutron toward feeling, sensing, or prehensing a proton in the space and creating a new reality, in which both are inter-included in a larger whole, the nucleus of an atom, is part of the essential structure of Reality. As mentioned above, this is the only way that neutrons can survive for more than fifteen minutes without falling apart: A neutron that is not in intimate conversation with a proton will decay within fifteen minutes. In other words, the neutron really *needs* the presence of the proton in order to be itself. In effect, the proton says to the neutron: *Your need is my allurement.* This is a sentence birthed by the mutuality of pathos that is core to our intimacy equation; it expresses shared identity in which we feel each other in multiple loops

---

242 This is the principle of continuity and discontinuity of value all the way down and all the way up the evolutionary chain, and in the inception of the evolutionary chain, a core tenet of CosmoErotic Humanism. See Temple, First Principles and First Values.

of ever-deepening feeling: I feel your need and I am allured to fulfill it.[243] We come into the depth of our identity in the context of relationship. It is relationship that evokes our *I-ness*.

Great traditions classically speak about the Infinite Divine from the perspective of *power*. Divinity is the Infinity of Power. However, the deeper realizations of the interior sciences evoke the Divine as the Infinity of *Intimacy*. Indeed, in CosmoErotic Humanism, we evoke a new Name of God—*the Infinite Intimate*.

Reality creates relationships. But even more fundamentally, Reality *is* relationship. The basic process of Reality is that an individualized part of Reality reaches out to another part. Each part prehends, senses, or feels the presence of the other, and both parts create a new whole. The new whole is, in multiple ways, greater than each of the parts and has new qualities that neither of them has on their own, but neither loses their individual integrity in the larger whole. This process is the essence of Reality itself.

In Arthur Koestler's terms, the new whole that is formed from this process may be called a *holon*.[244] This is an entity that is simultaneously a whole unto itself and a part of a larger whole. A holon has two characteristics:

1. The whole is greater than the sum of its parts.

2. The parts do not lose their integrity in the larger whole.

This process has also been called *synergy*. Alfred North Whitehead called the process or the occasion of one part reaching to feel and receive the

---

243 To be clear, we are not suggesting a magical animism. There is no equivalence between the human experience of allurement and need and the experience of allurement and need at the subatomic level. There are obvious radical discontinuities between the structure of consciousness of an atom, an amoeba, a plant, a fish, a dog, and a human being. But there is also a fundamental underlying continuity, as all the above are animated by ever-evolving levels of interiority or consciousness. At the atomic level, that might be a form of proto consciousness, what Alfred North Whitehead called prehension and Abraham Kook called the Ratzon of the Domem, the elemental will that lives in the ostensibly inanimate.

244 Arthur Koestler, The Act of Creation (1964). See also Section II.3.3.

other part prehension:[245] One subject prehends a second subject. Prehension could be described as proto-touching or proto-feeling. In prehension, one subject prehends another subject and then adds something emergent to form a new whole. This is the property of Reality that he called *creative advance into novelty*.[246] As Whitehead demonstrates, this relational process is the wondrous essence of Reality that keeps repeating itself at more and more evolved levels, all the way up the chain of matter, life, and human culture.[247]

That essential structure of Reality is always evolving within a trajectory of telos, reaching toward ever-deeper and wider expressions of the core values of Cosmos itself. It is precisely this quality of Reality that caused life to spread across the planet at every stage of emergence. The expanded network and depth of relationship, the progressive deepening of intimacies, and the evolution of intimacy are the essential methodologies of evolution. **The evolution of life is literally the evolution of relationships.** As Fritjof Capra, a philosopher of science and a systems theorist, put it, "Life did not take over the planet by combat but by cooperation, partnership, and networking."[248] Read: *by relationship.*

---

245 In philosophy, prehension is taken to mean the reaching or grasping of a part toward another part, event, or entity as a mode of perception, though not necessarily cognition.

246 "Neither the God, nor the World, reaches static completion. Both are in the grip of the ultimate metaphysical ground, the creative advance into novelty." See Whitehead, Process and Reality, 349.

247 Whitehead, Process and Reality, 349.

248 Fritjof Capra, The Hidden Connections: Integrating the Biological, Cognitive, and Social Dimensions of Life into a Science of Sustainability (2004), p. 231. See also Capra's The Web of Life: A New Scientific Understanding of Living Systems (1996). Capra published The Web of Life in 1996, a year after our friend and colleague Ken Wilber published his magnum opus Sex, Ecology and Spirituality (1995). Wilber's book integrates more philosophical ground (while remaining readable) in that he deals directly with issues of epistemology—how we know what we know. Wilber adapts and expands on Jürgen Habermas's framework of communicative action based on three types of speech acts and validity claims, developing the four quadrants—an epistemological framework that recognizes the co-validity of different spheres of knowing: subjective and objective, individual and collective. Wilber recognizes that the worlds that these spheres of knowing point to tetra-arise—that is to say, they all arise together, and any attempt to absolutely prefer one over another is an epistemic

9. The Evolution of God: As Above So Below

There is a knowing in the interior sciences of Hebrew wisdom, hermeticism, and many other traditions—a realization that *as above so below*. By *above and below*, we are not referring to the above and below of the great chain of being, with matter at the bottom and Spirit at the top. It also doesn't mean that there is a structural analogy between the upper and lower words, however one interprets that innocuous phrase.

In CosmoErotic Humanism, we understand *as above so below* as referring to interiors and exteriors. Manifest Reality is—as above so below—*participatory*. The finite human being participates in the interior structure of the manifest Divine, even as Infinite Divinity participates in the manifest structure of finite humanity.[249] Just as neutrons only retain their identity by entering into relationship with protons, so Infinite Divinity only expresses the depth of identity by entering into relationship with the finite. The interior sciences describe this truth of becoming one's unique identity only in the context of right relationship as the essential process of Reality's manifestation—in other words, the

---

confusion. Capra later reissued a more complete work of The Web of Life in 2014, together with coauthor Pier Luigi Luisi, under the title The Systems View of Life: A Unifying Vision (2014). This is an excellent edition, which implicitly unpacks the Eros in systems theory in animating the structure of Reality. One of Capra's updates is an important chapter—chapter 13—on the relationship of science to spirituality. In it, Capra responds effectively to Wilber's early critique of The Tao of Physics (Capra 1975), which in certain passages seemed, in Wilber's readings, to reduce mysticism to physics. For a sophisticated reading of Wilber's critique of apparently reductionist strains in ecological theory, see "Ken Wilber's Critique of Ecological Spirituality," by Michael Zimmerman (2001).

249 A distinction is drawn in all of the interior sciences between the Infinite that has no quality, that is beyond any words or quality, and the manifest Divine, which garbs Herself in quality or story. This is called—to cite but one example—Ein Sof, the formless-beyond-description Divine, and Sefirot, the Divine Luminations, Divinity disclosed in the language of human quality and story.

Personhood of the Infinite. Said more bluntly, in the realization of the interior sciences, there is some way in which God becomes *more* God through entering intimate relationship. Of course, by *the Personhood of the Infinite* we do not mean a white-bearded god in the sky but rather point to the primordial Face of Reality, which is personal, and understand it as a manifest expression of the Infinite Personhood, which is the second-person Face of Cosmos.[250]

In some mysterious sense, when Infinity enters relationship to finitude, a new dimension of God emerges—what we might even call, audaciously, *an evolution of God.* These words, which can barely be spoken without trembling in joy, are expressed in the interior sciences in manifold ways, including the formulation of Meir Ibn Gabbai, in his realization of *Avodah Tzorech Gavoha*—God Needs Your Service.[251] In the writings of Abraham Kook, this notion of the evolution of God, although almost never explicitly stated, is a major structural theme.[252]

For Kook, as for all of lineage masters of a key branch of Hebrew wisdom, the core structure of Reality is *Tzimtzum, Shevira,* and *Tikkun.* Loosely translated:

---

250 On the first-, second-, and third-person Faces of Cosmos, see Tears: Reclaiming Ritual, Integral Religion and Rosh Hashanah, by Marc Gafni (2014), introduction, and especially the subsection "The Three Faces of God—The Second Sacred Methodology."

251 For example, Arthur Green, in his essay "God's Need for Man: A Unitive Approach to the Writings of Abraham Joshua Heschel" (2015), writes that "in his summary of kabbalistic teaching, 'Avodat ha-Kodesh,' Rabbi Meir Ibn Gabbai, who lived in the Ottoman Empire in the early sixteenth century, offers a great synthesis of Jewish mystical wisdom in the generation immediately preceding that of Moshe Cordovero and Yizhak Luria, who were to make such great additions and changes to that tradition. The key theme of the work, repeated frequently throughout, is ha-'avodah tsorekh gavoha (lit.: 'service is a need on high'), that worship, including the life of the mitzvot, fulfills a divine need."

252 On the evolution of God, see also Soul Prints: Your Path to Fulfillment, by Marc Gafni (2002), chapter 6, Section "Keeping God's Soul Print Alive." A key collection on the sources on the evolution of God can be found here: https://www.marcgafni. com/evolutionary-kabbalah/. For a conversation on the evolution of God, mediated through Abraham Kook, as an expression of this radical motif in the Hebrew wisdom lineage and in Unique Self Theory, see Your Unique Self: The Radical Path to Personal Enlightenment, by Marc Gafni (2012), pp. 113–133.

- *Tzimtzum* means *Divine Withdrawal.*

- *Shevira* means *shattering* or *breaking*, what is called *the breaking of the vessels.*

- *Tikkun* means *fixing* or *repair*, but not simply *restorative* repair but *evolutionary* repair, fixing, or rectification.

Tzimtzum is the Divine Kenosis, in which Divinity manifests Reality not by thrusting forward but by emptying Herself (Herself, Himself, Itself, etc.) *out* of Reality. This allows for Reality's manifestation. However, the Divine Kenosis is not *ontological*, meaning Divinity cannot empty itself out of Reality, or Reality would disappear. Rather, it is epistemological or—said simply—the Divine Kenosis *appears* as if Reality is devoid of the Divine, and it requires a process of *noticing*—waking up or contemplation—to realize the full suffusion of Reality with the Divine—Value, Meaning, Truth, and Beauty.[253]

This intensity of the Infinite in the space of finitude, or manifestation, causes the second step, *shevira*, the breaking: The vessels of the manifest world shatter because they cannot hold the intensity of Infinite Presence. Broken vessels are spread throughout Reality.

Humanity liberates the sparks from the broken vessels in a process of *tikkun*. Tikkun, evolutionary rectification, is the process of evolving God. As my friend Abraham Leader, scholar of the interior sciences, has pointed out, *tikkun* means, in many sources of the interior sciences, not restorative repair but evolutionary rectification—a new whole emerges, greater than the sum of the parts. The *tikkun* takes place through the human being who participates in the Divine.

---

253 Another master of the Hebrew wisdom tradition, however, Nachman of Breslov, comes along and says we must take the void seriously as an ontological possibility, even if it is not an ontological Reality. It is only then—after sitting deeply in the void—that we attain the realization that the void is real but not Real. Or said slightly differently, the void is real but not true. Nachman demands our capacity to live in the radicalness of paradox. We must take radically seriously our own human experience that tells us, at our most painful and devastating of times, that the void is real. And only then do we realize that the void is not Real, and that Divinity suffuses everything and every person.

If the human being becomes more whole, God somehow, impossibly and paradoxically, becomes more Whole. Remember, Divine Kenosis is only apparent but never Real.[254] Thus, finitude, including humanity, participates in the Divine. When we generate, through a process of *tikkun*, a New Human and a New Humanity, both individually and collectively, we generate a new Face of the Divine that is somewhat more complete than the original God. In some mysterious sense, it is when Infinity enters relationship to finitude that a new dimension of God emerges. In other words, all of Reality, including the Divine, the Ultimate Real itself, becomes more Whole through relationship, through new intimacies.

The human being becomes intimate with her- or himself, with the beloved, and with Reality—and directly with the Infinite Divine in both first, second, and third person:

- The Divine as it lives in the human being (first person).

- The Divine in the sense of the Infinite Personhood of Divinity that knows our name (second person).

- The Divine in the sense of the third-person manifest Divine that we meet in all the sciences.

In the intimacy between the Infinite and the finite or, as Plotinus wrote, the intimate communion between the lonely one and the lonely one, the Divine becomes more Whole, more fully God, and the human being becomes more whole, more fully human.

Once we understand that the human being evolves the Divine even as the Divine is Eternal, and that the Divine holds us even as She lives in us, we understand the notion of *eternal and evolving values*. This notion is at the very heart of the new theory of value and the New Story of Value in CosmoErotic Humanism, which is so critical in responding to the

---

254 In other writings, we have said: It is real but not Real. Meaning, it is real in our experience, and we need to deal with it on that level, but it doesn't have Ultimate Ontology. It is not Real.

meta-crisis. We call this new theory of value evolving perennialism.[255]

---

255 For a discussion of the evolving perennialism, see First Principles and First Values.

III. FIRST NOTES ON ALLUREMENT, AUTONOMY, AND EVOLUTION OF DESIRE: INTIMACY IS A DANCE OF ALLUREMENT AND AUTONOMY

1. Relationships Are Configurations of Allurement and Autonomy

Goodness, truth, beauty, and everything we hold precious in the world are born from the play between the two elemental energies of Cosmos, which we call *lines* and *circles*, coming into *right relationship* with each other.

Right relationship always births new creation, new creativity, and new forms of goodness, truth, and beauty. New forms of the Good, the True, and the Beautiful emerge. New forms of Love emerge. Love itself evolves. The LoveIntelligence of evolution is no less than the Possibility of Possibility. As we awaken to ourselves as expressions of evolutionary consciousness, our relationships participate in the evolution of love.

Lines and *circles* are terms deployed extensively in the interior sciences of Hebrew wisdom. They are sometimes thought about as men and women, He and She. Here, however (as in many passages in the interior sciences themselves), these terms refer not to man and woman—nor even to masculine or feminine gender—but rather to core principles of Cosmos that are inherent in Reality for billions of years before the emergence of sex and gender.

These principles live in every man and every woman. In every man and woman, there is a unique constellation of both line and circle qualities. Each person has a Unique Gender[256]—a unique combination and integration of all the essential qualities of circles and lines.

These two forces live at every level of Cosmos, from subatomic particles to us. As one core expression of these two essences, the circle is the force of attraction, seeking intimacy and communion, while the line is the force of independence and freedom from any constraint. Sometimes these are called *attraction* and *repulsion*. At other times, they are called *centripetal* and *centrifugal* force. Still other writers have called them *communion* and *agency*. In CosmoErotic Humanism, we generally refer to these qualities as *allurement* and *autonomy*. They are in play from the first nanoseconds of the Big Bang. They are at the core of every relationship, all the way down and all the way up the evolutionary chain.

Relationships are not *just* attraction or allurement. Rather, relationships are the precise *calibration* of attraction, connection, and allurement on the one side and autonomy and independence on the other. In the space between attraction and repulsion, freedom and connection, allurement and autonomy, relationship is born.

- If there is too much allurement, there is fusion, or merging. Distinction and autonomy disappear. There is no relationship.

- If there is too much freedom or repulsion, there is alienation and rupture. Connection and intimacy disappear. There is no relationship.

Neither allurement nor repulsion is good or bad. The precise balance between these two forces is the dance of relationship, upon which all of

---

256 See Gafni and Hubbard, Whole Mate, chapter 6 (entry 9), chapter 7 (entry 2), and supplementary essay 3, for an unpacking of this concept.

Reality depends. Relationships happen in the space in between. From subatomic particles to the most advanced human beings, Reality is a dance between these line and circle principles.

Not only do all creativity, aliveness, and Eros depend on the way these principles dance together, but the existence of Reality itself depends on the tempo and timing of their dance steps. It is the elegance of the play between these two forces that evolves matter and births the galaxies, the stars, and the entire process of life out of which we emerge. If you removed the force that moves toward communion or the force that moves toward autonomy, neither matter nor life would have emerged.

Lines and circles are qualities of Essence that live in Reality. Both circles and lines live in every single dimension of Reality—including, of course, every single one of us. For the interior sciences, a moment of perfect relationship is one that has the exact right balance between these qualities of Essence. Such a moment of relationship births new Reality.[257]

This is the great dance of Reality. This dance of relationship dynamics is going on all the time.

- The Universe flares forth with a massive expansion, or inflation, that carries matter apart for billions of years. This is a powerful directional force of expansion, independence, freedom, and penetration of space.

- At the same time, there are other, equally fundamental forces at play in the Universe. One of these forces we call gravity. *Gravity* is a name we give to one of the forces of attraction that pull things together. This attractive force pulls matter together to form galaxies and stars.

---

257 This is what Isaac Luria, the greatest of the Renaissance Kabbalists, meant when he said that, in every moment, the human intention is Leshem Yichud Kudsha Berik Hu U-Shekhintei—for the sake of uniting the Shekhinah, the feminine force—with Kudsha Berik Hu, the masculine force. Luria speaks here of lines and circles. When the moment is loved open, it is by the person who is in right interior relationship between their line and circle qualities.

The entire unfolding of Reality as we know it is based on the play between the two forces of Eros, allurement and autonomy, captured in the first set of terms in our definition of intimacy as shared identity in the context of relative otherness (in Essay One, Section 2.3).

According to Ilya Prigogine, for a system to enter into its own creativity, it needs to pull away from the larger enveloping system.[258] As long as a system is tightly held within a larger system, it is dominated by it. Its intrinsic potential can only come forth when it becomes free enough to allow something new to be born from its own depths. For example, the early Universe existed as a dark plasma *fog*, or cloud; as the Universe cooled, it fractured into helium and hydrogen clouds, which then moved to fracture into smaller clouds. This was a move from communion toward autonomy that birthed the galaxies, which, in due course, birthed us.

What caused this movement away from communion that separated the original cloud? To our best knowledge, it was caused by a series of *pressure waves* passing through the original dark cloud, where photons were mostly interacting with electrons and protons, without being able to travel far (hence the darkness of the early Universe).[259] These waves—fluctuations in the density of matter—have their origin in the birth of the Universe itself. They were the force of autonomy, always balanced with the gravitational drive for communion, which broke the Universe apart at the exact right time and in the exactly right way to birth galaxies.[260]

---

258 Ilya Prigogine, Thermodynamic Theory of Structure, Stability and Fluctuations (1971).

259 Physicists were able to measure the remnants of these waves in the cosmic microwave background and trace them back to the time when the foggy plasma Universe started condensing into first large-scale structures.

260 Ashley Balzer writes on the NASA website (2020): "There were tiny fluctuations of about one part in 100,000. What few variations there were took the form of slightly denser kernels of matter, like a single ounce of cinnamon sprinkled into about 13,000 cups of cookie dough. Since the clumps had more mass, their gravity attracted additional material. It was so hot that particles couldn't stick together when they collided—they just bounced off each other. Alternating between the pull of gravity and this repelling effect created waves of pressure—sound—that propagated through the plasma. Over time, the universe cooled and particles combined to form neutral atoms. Because the particles stopped

The precise dance between attraction and autonomy is at the heart of the creativity of the Cosmos.

2. The First Intimate Relationships in the Universe

In the first microseconds of Reality, relationships began. Subatomic particles called quarks were drawn to other quarks—not just any quarks, but those to which they had a particular allurement.[261] Protons and neutrons were born. From the start, in the very beginning of time and space, the Universe reached for relationship.

An image to describe the beginning of Reality might be a large and wildly chaotic singles bar. Of course, this singles bar was driven by the inherent intelligence of Cosmos rather than by the human self-reflective choice that would not emerge for billions of years. In this original relationship scene, subatomic particles would collide, ceaselessly churning and interacting with one another. They would then scatter apart, only to collide with different partners—millions of collisions in each instant, the first great colliding of lines and circles. The first stable relationships between quarks (protons and neutrons) appeared within a few minutes after the Bing Bang.

Only a few minutes later, the dynamics in our singles bar change. When a single neutron interacts with a single proton, instead of each going its own way and scattering, they remain bonded together, forming

---

repelling each other, the waves ceased. Their traces, however, still linger, etched on the cosmos. . . . While the waves no longer propagated, the frozen ripples stretched as the universe expanded, increasing the distance between galaxies. By looking at how galaxies are spread out in different cosmic epochs, we can explore how the universe has expanded over time." https://www.nasa.gov/universe/nasas-roman-space-telescope-to-uncover-echoes-of-the-universes-creation.

261 See Section II.3.1.

the first heavy hydrogen nuclei.[262] At first, the forces of other attractions would tear these early relationships apart. Other particles, exerting powerful attractive forces, would undermine the stable relationship. But as the Universe began to expand and cool, these early couples began to survive and stay in relationship. This early phase of the Universe, which lasted between ten seconds and twenty minutes after the Big Bang, is known as *primordial nucleosynthesis*.

In about one hundred million years, stars were formed. We once thought they were eternal objects we gazed at in wonder as they lit up the night sky. Now we know that they are stories with inherent plotlines, self-organizing processes of evolving intimacy that go through clear stages of emergence and transformation.[263] A star begins as a large cloud made up of gas and dust, which breaks into fragments over time. As these fragments (clumps of matter) collapse under the force of gravity, their temperature increases, and a "protostar" is born. Eventually, after millions of years, the pressure and temperature squeeze the nuclei of hydrogen atoms together to form helium. This process, called nuclear fusion, prevents the star from further collapse. The new star achieves the state of maturation—a stable configuration of the line principle (internal pressure from the nuclear fusion, which pushes matter *outward*) and the circle quality (gravity, which pulls it *inward*). It is only by a star holding both its line and circle qualities (and not identifying exclusively with either) that new intimacy and relationship is born.

Eventually, as the star runs out of hydrogen, it begins to die. Its further destiny depends on its mass: Smaller stars become white dwarfs, which may later become novae. Stars over eight solar masses, however, are destined to die in a titanic explosion called a *supernova*. It is within the supernovae that all of the heavier elements are formed—including carbon, which is essential to the emergence of life itself. It is the creative tension between the line and circle forces that keeps a star in existence for billions of years.

---

262 Normal hydrogen nuclei only consist of one proton. The heavy hydrogen nuclei, consisting of one proton and one neutron, are also known as deuterium nuclei.

263 See, for example, https://science.nasa.gov/universe/stars.

The same dance between attraction and autonomy expresses itself as the precisely right rate of expansion needed to manifest a Universe in which life is possible. If the rate of expansion had been off by even a trillionth of a second, then life could not have emerged. The rate of expansion—the velocity of matter moving outward toward autonomy—is in a perfect dance with the force of attraction, the move toward closeness and communion. This not only allows the world to exist; it is essential to the very process of life, ever evolving to higher and higher levels of complexity and depth.

A technical word in science for the balance of the line and circle forces is *homeostasis,* meaning the capacity for a system to tend toward stabilization. Homeostasis is the internal balance or wholeness a system achieves by creating right relationship between its opposing tendencies. It is the play between these line and circle forces from the very beginning that creates the wholeness that both sustains stability and births ever-new creativity and aliveness. It creates not only aliveness but intensified intimacy between parts, which generates a new wholeness that we call life itself.

The Intimate Universe is a reality of physics. This dance of relationship, or evolving intimacies, takes place between elementary particles, atoms, cells, and more, all the way down and all the way up the evolutionary chain to human beings.

3. The Intensification of Intimacy across All Realms of Cosmos

We live in an Intimate Universe, where relationships are everything. The deepening of intimacy and relationships is the core movement of Cosmos. The transformation of relationships is the core driver of Reality itself on all levels.

Reality desires more intimacy. Evolution is driven by the desire of Reality for more intimacy and can be fairly described as the progressive deepening of intimacies. Evolution always desires more intimacy. Intimacy is a structure of identity rooted in a quality of feeling. The intimacy equation we introduced in Essay One is intended to describe the motivated behavior of internal Reality:

- Intimacy = Shared Identity in the Context of [Relative] Otherness × Mutuality of Recognition × Mutuality of Pathos × Mutuality of Value × Mutuality of Purpose.

As we shall see, it applies across all realms of Reality. Its truth is accessible through a confluence of exterior and interior empirical verifications. It is a truth that is visible to the naked eye, even as it lives inside of our own lived interior Reality.

From the ménage à trois of quarks at the inception of the Universe,[264] new and deeper structures of intimacy continually evolve and emerge, all the way through the subatomic, atomic, molecular, and first cellular stages. This is the evolution of intimacy:

- Atoms desire, feel, and are allured to each other. Atoms become intimate with each other and form molecules—deeper and wider wholes.

- Molecules desire, feel, and are allured to each other. Molecules become intimate with each other and form increasingly complex molecules.[265]

- The intensification of intimacy between the macromolecules generates the momentous leap from macromolecules to cells.

- Single cells desire, feel, and are allured to each other. Single cells

---

264 See Section II.3.1.

265 See Section III.8 for examples and details.

become intimate with each other. This evolution brings about the emergence of a stable relationship between cells, which produces the first multicellular organisms.

Evolving intimacies unfold all the way up the evolutionary chain. The dance of Eros and intimacy also takes place between celestial bodies. To take one example of this dance, there is an erotic, intimate relationship between the Earth and the Sun. It is the precision of that Eros that gives every single one of us life. Here is just one small dimension of the dialectical dance between autonomy and communion that forms the intimate, erotic relationship between the Earth and the Sun.

The surface temperature of the Earth cannot change too far in either direction, or life will become extinct. For a very long time, deep into the last century, life on Earth was thought to be a blessed result of the Sun being at precisely the right distance from Earth—ninety-three million miles away. However, recent scientific discoveries of nuclear fusion and new knowledge of the structure of stars show that this is not exactly true. We now know that over the past four billion years, the Sun's temperature has increased by 25 percent. That change should have destroyed all life on Earth. But as you are reading this sentence, you know that this did not happen.

The riddle is, why are we alive? The answer to this riddle is radically amazing: The Earth intimately co-evolved with the Sun to allow us to remain in the narrow sliver of right relationship that allows life to flourish. Photosynthesis—plants drawing carbon dioxide out of the atmosphere and emitting oxygen—changed Earth's atmospheric composition over time. The Earth got cooler as the Sun got hotter. This staggeringly complex and perfectly timed process defies imagination. It is what allowed the Earth and the Sun to live together in intimate communion of right relationship.

Reality is a complex configuration of closely interwoven intimacies that are always deepening each other. For example, the energy you use to read these words comes in great part from your last meal. Your last meal is in large part the result of the energy of the Sun. The Sun's energy is poured out in the form of photons and absorbed by plants. The plants then transform the energy from the Sun and the seemingly inanimate matter of the Earth into food. Thus, your ability to read these words results from the Sun energizing you this very second. The Sun itself draws its energy from the fusion of hydrogen nuclei,[266] which source their energy in the birth of the Universe. In this very precise sense, the energy that birthed all of Reality is energizing you in this very instant.

The emerging awareness of these interwoven intimacies awakens us to the realization that we live in an Intimate Universe. More than ever before, we have eyes to see dazzling complexity and beauty at play in the physical world. This new shocking view of Reality's naked beauty and depth is *itself* a new capacity for intimacy that has been evolving even in the short span of our lifetimes. This is just one more example—among thousands that we know of—that shows that ever-deepening intimacy and relationship are essential features of the Cosmos. That is what we mean when we say that we live in a CosmoErotic Universe, or when we talk about *the Universe: A Love Story*. From whatever angle we examine Reality, it reveals its CosmoErotic Nature:

- Reality is relationship.

- Reality is Eros.

- Reality is Fuck.

---

266 The high pressure and temperature in the Sun's core are what cause hydrogen nuclei to separate from their electrons. The hydrogen nuclei then fuse to form helium nuclei. During this fusion process, radiant energy is released. It is actually a much more complex chain of nuclear reactions called a proton–proton chain, in which four protons (four hydrogen nuclei) are transformed into a helium nucleus, consisting of two protons and two neutrons (making use of protons' capacity to decay into neutrons by emitting a positron and an electron neutrino). This whole proton–proton fusion chain can only occur if the kinetic energy (i.e., temperature) of the protons is high enough to overcome their mutual electrostatic repulsion. The conversion of hydrogen to helium, however, takes a long time. The complete conversion of all the hydrogen that was initially in the core of our Sun is calculated to have taken more than ten billion years. See Stars and Galaxies, by Lauren V. Jones (2010), pp. 65–67; "The Proton Type-Nuclear Fission Reaction," by Ahmad Ishfaq (1971); and Nuclear Physics of Stars, by Christian Iliadis (2007).

- The Cosmos self-actualizes toward higher and deeper levels of Eros, intimacy, and relationship.

We begin to realize that Earth is not just an inanimate ball upon which we and all living organisms reside. The Earth is a creative space of relationships. The Whole has inherent intelligence that constantly deepens its intimacies and evolves its relationships. The telos, or direction, of the Universe is not just to sustain existence. It is the creative birthing of ever-deeper levels of aliveness, goodness, truth, and beauty—the core values of the Intimate Universe. Reality is constantly on the move, seeking to perpetuate and even deepen—to evolve—the aliveness, value, and wholeness of its existence.

4. New Intimacy Births New Aliveness

In the language of the interior sciences of Hebrew wisdom, *b'chavivuta talya milta*, "Reality depends on Eros and intimacy."[267] The source adduced here deploys the Aramaic word *chavivuta*, derived from three distinct Hebrew words—*chibah, chesed,* and *ahavah*—which all have somewhat different fragrances of meaning but all are accurately rendered as Eros and intimacy. The words *Reality* (*milta*) and *depends* (*talya*), in the Aramaic text, refer to the structural nature of Reality. Another text, *olam chesed yibaneh*, "the world is built from Eros and Intimacy," is drawn from a much earlier source. Chaim Vital, a key interior scientist of the sixteenth century, understands the text to mean that all of Reality is built on the core structure of Eros and intimacy. The *Song of Songs*, the ultimate text of the interior sciences in their own

---

267 Zohar, Idra Zuta, Vol. 3.128a. See Yehuda Liebes, "Zohar and Eros" (1994; https://liebes.huji.ac.il/files/zoharveros.pdf, Hebrew) and Studies in the Zohar (1993), on different understandings of the term chavivuta, "love," in the key Zohar passage.

self-understanding, says *tocho ratzuf ahava*, "its insides are lined with Eros and intimacy."[268]

We live in an Intimate Universe—a Universe in which Reality is relationship. When we realize this, much about relationship dynamics begins to become clear. We understand why we are driven to seek out intimate relationships time and again, even after multiple apparent failures. This is not pathology. It is rather the life force alive in us, as us, and through us. The drive to bond, to be in relationship, is a biological imperative, the exterior expression of the interior drive for more intimacy, more contact, more wholeness, and more life, which is the desire that animates and drives the Cosmos. Quantum physics, systems theory, and complexity theory have shown us that the principle of self-organization and the drive to relationship are deeper than even biology. The drive for Eros and intimacy is the nature of Reality itself, beginning with the first elementary particles, only nanoseconds after the Big Bang.

It is not good for the human being to be alone,[269] proclaims a classic ancient text on human relationship. *Good*, in this text, is not a moral statement. It rather refers to the correct nature, or what we might call the rightness of things.[270] It is a violation of Reality to not be in an inti-

---

268 This insight from the lineage of Solomon is one of the sources of the interior science equations we have developed for terms Eros and intimacy (see Sections 2.3–2.4 in Essay One), along with validated insights of the classical interior sciences of premodernity, as well as the leading-edge exterior and interior sciences of modernity and postmodernity.

269 Genesis 2:18: "The Lord God said, 'It is not good for the man to be alone. I will make a helper suitable for him.'" This translation (New International Version) does not capture some of the meaning we elicit from the original Hebrew; for example, the meaning of the word good, or in what is meant by a helper suitable for him (we might alternatively translate this segment as an opposite equal in strength).

270 The Hebrew word used in Genesis 2:18 for good is ⬚ōw⬚ (alternatively, tobh or tov). The word is versatile, much as good is in English; it can mean good in an aesthetic, ethical, pragmatic, theoretic, spiritual, or technical sense. Verse 18 is describing how it is not good that man be alone, and so God sees to it to give man a counterpart. Most interpretations of this verse indicate that God creates the human to be naturally social. Tobh is thus taken to mean something like natural, as in it is unnatural for man to be alone. When we speak of nature, we speak of what is just so, as it relates to things and beings of the world (rightness of things),

mate relationship that is good. In fact, your world disintegrates if your relationships disintegrate. We now know that this is true not only about your world or ours. It is true about the world as a whole. The world is a series of intimate relationships, all the way up and all the way down. It is the fierce and tender Eros of intimate relationship that constitutes Reality.

Our own existence, for example, depends on organisms at the bottom of the Pacific Ocean as well as on the Sun's photons. If the intimacy between elementary particles were to lose integrity, then Reality would literally collapse in on itself.

We live in an Intimate Universe. New forms of intimacy and relationship birth new life,[271] new aliveness, and new creativity at every stage of evolution. This is how the new intimacy between cells birthed the multicellular life that birthed entirely new forms of creativity and emergence, ultimately leading to us.

For example, what gives rise to the lizard mind that is so different from the rock that it runs across? They are both composed of the same chemical elements. How is the lizard's animal mind birthed? The unique configuration of intimacy that is the DNA of the lizard organizes billions of cells. If we trace the unique pattern of intimacy backward, we first find amphibians, then, further back, fish, then the first multicellular organism, and then, even further back, the first single-celled organism—when there is no sense of even a glimmer of what will later become the animal mind.

Even before the first single-celled organism emerged, there was an early group of molecules, held together in an intimately configured meshwork of chemical reactions—in other words, unique sets of allurements generating unique intimacies, which in turn generate unique qualities of Reality. The molecules intensified their intimacies generating new qualities of Reality until the depth of relationship, the new quality of intimacy, burst forth as life.[272]

---

or what is true about Reality.

271 Here, life refers both to the emergence and evolution of biological life and to the Living Universe as a whole. The Universe is alive and conscious (or sentient) all the way up and all the way down.

272 How exactly life first emerged on our planet is still a mystery—the Second Big

Think about it this way:

Within the Story of Value rooted in the Eye of Consciousness merged with the Eye of the Mind and the Eye of the Senses,[273] the Name of God is *the Infinite Intimate*. God is not only the Infinity of Power but also the Infinity of Intimacy. The Infinity of Intimacy merged with the Infinity of Power is the Creative God Force, the very Eros of Reality—the Infinite Intimate. It is that Infinite Divine Quality that births that Intimate Universe as an expression of itself, its essentially Intimate Nature. That is what the interior sciences mean when they describe the Universe in the Aramaic texts as *Leit atar panuy meneih*,[274] "There is no place devoid of the Intimate Infinite Personhood of the Divine."

In the stunning logic of the interior sciences, intensifications of intimacy are the creative force that births new Reality. They birth new qualities of intimacy at every level of existence, including the human level. These radical moments of emergence reveal the living nature of the Living Universe, which births more and more life through ever-deepening intimacy.

5. Intimacy Is Not Merely Closeness

The currency of Eros and intimacy is made up of two coins: autonomy and communion, or attraction and repulsion, or allurement and autonomy. Intimacy is not simply an insatiable drive for closeness and communion. Rather, intimacy is the dance between autonomy and independence on the one hand and closeness, attraction, and communion on the other.

On the human level, once we really access this truth, argument and

---

Bang, a supersized surprise (see Essay Three).

273 See Section I.6.

274 Tikkunei Zohar, Tikkun 57, Tikkun 70 (Zhitomir edition [1865], 122b).

conflict stop being the death of a relationship. The need for alone time is no longer a threat. We begin to realize that too much communion does not create the ground for intimacy. Intimacy and Eros in all of its forms require a precise, stunning dance between closeness and separation, between sameness and otherness. If you are too close or too far, passion dies. It must be, as the old Goldilocks fairy tale goes, *just right.*

From the very beginning, Reality moves toward the formation of relationships that work. For a relationship to work, you need a mixture of sameness and difference.

In the original Genesis text,[275] the first couple is described as *ezer kenegdo,* an expression well translated as "helpmates who oppose with equal strength." This is the principle of polarity and paradox, one of the First Principles and First Values of Cosmos. Tzadok[276] calls this principle *tachlit hanigudim,* literally "the apex of opposition," the principle of opposites joined at the hip that is at the heart of Cosmos. Opposites attract. Opposites are allured to each other. Difference and distinction coupled with attraction and communion are the ingredients of passionate relationship. Erotic passion, a mixture of fierce and tender Eros, is what births new life, new ideas, and new consciousness.

We live in a CosmoErotic Universe filled not only with pairs but with multiple models of oppositional allurement, often referred to as *coincidentia oppositorum,*[277] which generate a larger whole—for example, the *lines and circles* we have discussed above. Lines and circles later express themselves in the form of masculine and feminine—polar opposite energies that are allured to each other both intersubjectively (between two subjects) and intrasubjectively (between two forces within one subject).

---

275 Genesis 2:18: "The Lord God said, 'It is not good for the man to be alone. I will make a helper suitable for him.'"

276 Tzadok is a primary student of Lainer of Izbica; see Radical Kabbalah, by Marc Gafni (2010), Book 2, pp. 315–333.

277 Coincidentia oppositorum is a Latin phrase meaning coincidence (or unity) of opposites. It is a neo-Platonic term attributed to fifteenth-century German polymath Nicholas of Cusa in his essay "De Docta Ignorantia" (1440). Psychiatrist Carl Jung and the philosopher and Islamic studies professor Henry Corbin, as well as Jewish philosophers Gershom Scholem and Abraham Joshua Heschel, also used the term.

In reading the texts and laws of physics more carefully, the nature of intimacy reveals itself more deeply. Attraction is based not only on polarity but also on sameness. Sameness and support, mixed with counterforce and polarity, create attraction. Everything with a similar property called *mass* allures. This is what we refer to as gravity. The most potent attractions, however, at all levels of Reality, are based on the precise measure and mixture of polarity and sameness (for example, the fundamental strong force we mentioned in Section II.3.1–2).

6. Allurement Is Primary and Mysterious

Theoretically, we could live in a Cosmos in which elements only drift apart. There is no theoretical reason—other than Eros—for the Universe to be structured as a Field of Allurement, whose evolution is animated by desire, seeking contact and forming greater wholes.

At the human level, Eros is the force that attracts us to other people, places, or ideas—while keeping our personal autonomy/integrity, without merging us into an undifferentiated union or fusion. But when we step out of our own experience and take a wider scientific view, we realize that this force of attraction is operating at every level of Reality. At the level of galaxies, we call it gravity. At the level of subatomic particles, we call it strong nuclear force. We are part of the Universe. We are an expression of the same laws that apply everyplace.

Of course, love evolves. Eros evolves. Love gets wider. At the human level, this means that it includes more and more people. Love gets more and more conscious, moving from instinct to choice. Love gets deeper, both through the intimate practice of communication and through our awareness of each other's depth, grandeur, and fleeting fragility. Love becomes more awake and poignant. But it is the fundamental force of Love and attraction that suffuses and drives every level of Reality.

Love (or allurement, or Eros) is the force that propels the Universe forward. The drive of Eros for intimacy creates new qualities of relationship, which in turn generate new wholes, new coherent intimacies.

As the newborn Universe expanded and cooled, the innate erotic drive for intimacy and relationship moved the negatively charged electrons and the positively charged hydrogen nuclei (consisting of a single proton) and helium nuclei (consisting of protons and neutrons) to come together to form the first atoms. In the words of one science writer, our dear friend and collaborator Howard Bloom, protons and electrons *yearn* for each other. Bloom identifies as a stone-cold atheist and a materialist mystic at the same time. When he describes the implicit yearning between protons and electrons 380,000 years after the Big Bang, he is not asserting interiors based on dogmatic faith. He is describing what is present empirically.[278] Oppositely charged particles draw each other together. The positively charged nuclei relate with the negatively charged electrons in a Field of Allurement.

The allurement or Love between protons and electrons is mysterious, even though we can describe it scientifically as electromagnetic attraction. Like gravity and all the other forces, electromagnetic attraction simply *is*. We can label or describe it, but we cannot *explain* its essence. Nothing external to the protons and electrons is forcing them together. There is no exterior electromagnetic charge of attraction forced upon them from the outside to push them together. Rather, they are drawn together as the most authentic expression of their innate nature. This core polar attraction evolves and changes shape all the way up the life chain of Reality.

It is critical to get the wonder and mystery of it all. It did not *have* to be this way. As scientists point out, we can clearly imagine how things could be different. There is no theoretical reason, from the perspective of science, that the Universe should have the quality of Love, or the exact configuration of allurement and autonomy that allows for all the beauty, complexity, and creativity of the Universe. There is no known reason for the CosmoErotic Nature of all of Reality. The drive to connect and to bond did not need to be a central driving force of the Universe's inherent creativity.

---

278 Bloom, The God Problem, 39–40.

We can easily theorize a Universe that takes the form of trillions upon trillions of disconnected particles. Each particle could be completely independent of every other. Imagine for a moment a world without this quality of Eros, which includes both the forces of attraction or allurement and the forces of repulsion or autonomy.

Remove the strong nuclear force, electromagnetic attraction, gravity, chemical attractors, and all the allurements that make up the biological and human worlds and the galaxies would break apart. The stars would go dark. The Earth would disintegrate. All the mineral and chemical compounds would dissolve. Mountains would simply evaporate. The human world would dissolve as well. Even if the physical structures did not collapse, all motivation to do anything would be lost. All movement would cease because nothing and no one would be interested in anything or anyone else. The world would simply go dark. When it goes dark, there is no reason to write a book or to read a book. There is no pull to do or be anything. We are no longer drawn to anything. Remove Eros, or Love, and the binding energy of Cosmos all the way up and all the way down—the entire structure of Reality—simply disintegrates.

The world is driven in every moment by attraction, interest, fascination, and enchantment, as well as the drive for autonomy—the integrity of each part of a larger whole. These are all qualities of the core Love that lights everything and everyone up. Love—or Eros, or intimacy—is the precise calibration between attraction and repulsion, allurement and agency, communion and autonomy.

The Universe as we know it is precisely the opposite of that imagining. We live in a Field of LoveIntelligence and LoveBeauty. Like a fish in water, we may be unconscious of that Field until the new insights from the practices of the interior sciences wake us up.

7. The Interior Experience of Allurement

Love, with its qualities of allurement and intimacy, expresses itself externally. Particles, people, and ideas come toward each other. Bodies, both celestial and human, are held in a stable orbit because of their intimate relationships—their intimate allurement to each other. As we know from our human world, relationship is not merely structural, not merely a system of *its* (which is how systems theory is all too often presented). Relationship implies allurement—an ultimately compelling *interior* feeling or experience.

To get a sense of what a world suffused by Eros feels like, we turn to Irish poet, author, and priest John O'Donohue. These lines speak of the alluring drive to relationship as it shows up in our human world of love. As you read, feel into the truth of the primary force of attraction that suffuses all of Reality. This first passage speaks to the inexorable power of allurement that draws us, and all of Reality, into relationship:

> There is a lovely disarray that comes with attraction. When you find yourself deeply attracted to someone, you gradually begin to lose your grip on the frames that order your life. Indeed, much of your life becomes blurred as that countenance comes into clearer focus. A relentless magnet draws all your thoughts towards it. Wherever you are, you find yourself thinking about the one who has become the horizon of your longing. When you are together, time becomes unmercifully swift. It always ends too soon. No sooner have you parted than you are already imagining your next meeting, counting the hours. The magnetic draw of that presence renders you delightfully helpless. A stranger you never knew until recently has invaded your mind; every fibre of your being longs to be closer.[279]

---

279 This and other excerpts in this section come from Beauty: The Invisible Embrace, by John O'Donohue (2004).

The second passage points toward the enormous creativity and new possibility that emerge through the power of allurement and relationship:

Huge differences may separate us, yet they are exactly what draw us to each other. It is as though forged together we form one presence, for each of us has half of a language that the other seeks. When we approach each other and become one, a new fluency comes alive. A lost world retrieves itself when our words build a new circle. While the call to each other is exciting and intoxicating in its bond of attraction, it is exceptionally complex and tender and, handled indelicately, can bring incredible pain. We can awaken in each other possibilities beyond our wildest dreams. The conversation of togetherness is a primal and indeed perennial conversation. Despite the thousands of years of human interaction, it all begins anew, as if for the first time, when two people fall in love. The force of their encounter makes a real clearance; through the power of Eros they discover the beauty in each other.

The final passage that you are about to read below is about making love. But when we really understand the nature of allurement as it lives in Reality, we get that Reality is making love all the way up and all the way down. Lines and circles are making love in every moment of existence. As you read the next short passage, feel into this quality of making love, taking place in every instant at every level of Reality. That is what it means to wake up to the realization that we live in an Intimate Universe. O'Donohue expresses, in the language of the poet, the core Dharma of the new narrative of desire, what we have called, at the human level, Sex Erotic.[280] In this new narrative of desire, sex models the Eros that animates and infuses all of Reality.

The instinct, rhythm and radiance of the human body come alive vividly when we make love. We slip down into a more ancient

---

280 On this new sexual narrative, Sex Erotic, and the limitation of the four classical sexual narratives, see Gafni and Hubbard, Whole Mate, chapter 8. See also Gafni and Kincaid, A Return to Eros, chapter 1.

penumbral rhythm where the wisdom of the body claims its own
grace, ease and joy. . . . However, when we understand that the
body is in the soul, intimacy and union seem unavoidable because
the soul as the radiance of the body is already entwined with
the lover.

O'Donohue writes with the ear and pen of the poet. We are always in his debt when we read him. He writes in a religious idiom that is rooted not in dogma but in something much more potent and sensuous—both in the interior and exterior sciences.

We now realize that the body is not merely a home for the soul. In some profound sense, the body and the soul are one. From the exterior sciences, we know that the allurement that drove all of the previous levels of evolution literally lives in the body—from subatomic particles to atoms to molecules to cells to multicellular organisms, all held in relationship by erotic allurement.

The erotic mystics understand that the vessel of the body is the highest form of light, higher in its essence than even what used to be called the soul.[281] The quality of allurement that has every cell in the body falling into rapture in every moment is the quality of Eros alive in the incarnate body. While Eros, or what some would call Spirit, does not depend on the body, it fully suffuses and animates the body. Spirit *becomes* body; it is not merely housed *in* body.

With that crucial caveat, we return to O'Donohue, describing the Eros of lovemaking in a way that expresses the Dharma of Sex Erotic: sex as Cosmic Eros, incarnate, dancing, as body.

The force of their encounter makes a real clearance; through the
power of Eros, they discover the beauty in each other. . . .Stretching

---

281 This theme is implicit throughout the cosmology of the interior sciences of
    Lurianic Kabbalah. One of the masters in this lineage, Schneur Zalman of Liadi,
    and much later Kalonymous Kalman Schapira of Piasczena, formulate it with the
    phrase Gavoha Shoresh Ha-Keylim Me' Shoresh Ha'Orot, "Higher is the root of the
    Vessels than the Root of the Light." Said simply, the light, which derives from the
    highest sources, falls to the lowest sources—not to the manifest light but to the
    manifest vessels.

*across the distance towards each other, they begin to awaken all
the primal echoes, where nothing can be presumed but almost
everything can be expected.*

When we truly understand the Cosmic Force of Eros as love in the
body, then *intimacy and union seem unavoidable because the soul as the
radiance of the body is already entwined with the lover.*

8. Evolution of Intimacy from Atoms to Life: Chemical Reactions as Dynamics of Desire

Eros is always bringing distinct elements together in ever-more complex
configurations of intimacy. Eros drives the evolution of relationships,
which is the evolution of love and intimacy. Eros is both the urge to
merge and the urge to *emerge*. Eros reaches for *being* even as it is the
force of *becoming*.

The conversation about the next evolutionary leap in relationships is
of utmost importance, for it is from the right relationship between different
parts of the microcosm that the overall shape and direction of Reality is
formed. The whole is shaped directly by the nature of relationship between
its most microscopic parts. The creative allurement between particles that
come together in stable relationships and form the new wholes we call
atoms makes possible the next leap of the self-organizing Universe—the
emergence of galaxies and stars, and then the emergence of the heavier elements and molecules within them, from which planets eventually emerge.

Molecules are formed because atoms are allured to each other. This
is a more advanced level of Reality and relationship than the relationship

between particles in an atom (described in Section II.3.2). In most of the known elements, e.g., hydrogen (H), lithium (Li), and sodium (Na), the orbital electron shells of the atoms are incomplete, and this is what makes them relationship hungry.

Let's look at this longing for relationship in some more detail.

The erotic dance of the electrons around the atomic nucleus is usually described by the orbital model, originally developed by Niels Bohr in 1913, in which electrons occupy different *orbital shells*. The orbit of an electron is not really an orbit; it is a cloud of possibilities. In other words, instead of a specific location within an atom, an electron has a cloud of probabilities to be found in different locations at the moment of interaction.

These clouds have different shapes. For example, for so-called s-electrons, the cloud of possibilities is like a sphere; for p-electrons, it resembles a dumbbell; for d-electrons, it's more like a dumbbell embraced by a donut (we'll spare you further details). Each orbital shell contains one, two, three, or four subshells depending on how close it is to the nucleus:

- The innermost shell has one subshell for s-electrons,

- the second, two subshells (for s- and p-electrons),

- the third one, three subshells (for s-, p- and d-electrons), et cetera.

The s-subshell can hold a maximum of two electrons, the p-subshell a maximum of six, the d-subshell a maximum of ten.[282] Each electron occupies the lowest energy subshell available (which generally means closest to the nucleus).

If the outermost shell of an atom has partially filled s-subshell or p-subshell, then the atom is really hungry for a configuration of intimacy that would complete them. It is allured to other atoms with incomplete shells. For example, oxygen has eight electrons: Two of them fill the innermost s-subshell, two occupy the second s-subshell, and the remaining

---

282 In total, the nth shell can hold $2n^2$ electrons.

THE EVOLUTION OF LOVE

four become p-electrons (with dumbbell-like orbital clouds), thus leaving two p-slots in the second, outermost shell empty. These empty p-slots make oxygen really relationship hungry.

The electrons in the outermost incomplete shell of these atoms are called their *valence electrons*. In order to fill this outermost shell, the atoms have to give away their valence electrons, accept electrons from other atoms, or share their valence electrons between them. In the language of CosmoErotic Humanism, implied directly by the empirical sciences, the atoms with incomplete outermost shells *desire* to share electrons with other atoms, in one way or another. Their capacity to be allured by other atoms is called valence or valency.[283] As we said earlier, valence means the desire for a particular value.[284] In this case, at the level of atoms, the desire of atoms is literally for the value of feeling whole and complete. That value is reached by the sharing of their electrons in a process known by science as *chemical reaction*. *Chemical reaction*, however, is but a technical term that can easily obfuscate our sense of the creative and erotic play that is really going on here. What does this well-known term actually point toward?

A chemical reaction describes a dynamic of desire between two elements that are allured to each other, desiring ever-deeper contact and ever-greater wholeness. A chemical reaction, in other words, means that there is an inexorable desire between parts that moves them toward some form of union—similar to when there is *chemistry* between human beings. The difference is, of course, the degree of choice that is at play in relationship to the powerful forces of desire. For example, the molecule of water is formed by allurement between one atom of oxygen (with its

---

283 Atoms with positive valency desire to share their own electrons, while atoms with negative valency are electron hungry (they need extra electrons to feel complete).

284 In the Oxford English Dictionary, the root of the word valence is the same as the root of the word value. That root is related to the root of the word will. Valere means both to be strong and to be of value, to be of worth. It evolved from Latin valere to Old French valor, which is connected to worth. A valorous knight is not just strong but represents value; he is saving the damsel. Then it goes to Middle English, and then to value. A violation of value arouses political will. So, will is aroused by value. The knight accesses his valor because his valor is connected to his representing value. See also Section II.4.

two "empty slots" in the outermost shell) and two atoms of hydrogen, which have only one electron each. In a water molecule, these two electrons from hydrogen are shared with the oxygen atom and complete its outermost shell, so everyone is happy and whole (a covalent bond).

The formation of simple molecules through covalent bonds between atoms opens the evolutionary pathway to *macromolecules*. In other words, you cannot just throw a bunch of atoms together, add some energy, and hope they will magically transform into a macromolecule. Rather, at first, some atoms come together—feeling incomplete and being allured to each other—to form a molecule. Then, two or more molecules (or one molecule and another atom) come together to form a more complex molecule through intimate, erotic conversations (sharing and exchanging photons and electrons). They are excited to form a new identity, a new whole, in the context of their relative otherness. They recognize and feel each other, and they share values and purpose together.

Let's look at the specific macromolecules called *nucleotides*, the building blocks of the most famous macromolecule, DNA—the code of life. Each nucleotide is a unique configuration of intimacy between three distinctive groups of simpler molecules (Figure 1). At the center is a five-carbon sugar molecule ($C_5H_{10}O_4$). It is called deoxyribose and is made up of five carbon atoms, four of which are arranged, together with one oxygen atom, in a pentagonal shape.[285] Carbon, oxygen, and hydrogen form this complex shape with many covalent bonds, because this is how the atoms in intimate relationship with each other feel most complete and whole.

For example, carbon has six electrons. Two of them fill the innermost shell. The second shell has space for eight electrons, but only four of them are filled by the remaining electrons. This means that a carbon atom desires to form four covalent bonds with other atoms, but it can fulfill this desire for completeness through a variety of different configurations of intimacy. In the deoxyribose (Figure 2), the carbon atom 1' is bonded

---

285 In Figure 1, the carbon atoms and simple configurations of carbon and hydrogen found at the vertices of the pentagon are not indicated by letters; see Figure 2 for a more detailed representation of deoxyribose.

with the carbon atom 2', one oxygen atom, one hydrogen atom, and one OH group (a configuration of one oxygen atom and one hydrogen atom). The carbon atom 2', in its turn, is bonded with two other carbon atoms (1' and 3') and two hydrogen atoms, et cetera. If you explore Figure 2 in further detail, you will notice that each of the five carbon atoms enters a different configuration of intimacy to form the overall pentagonal structure—a still more complex configuration of intimacy (with its own potential for even more intimacy).

At the left side of Figure 1, you see a phosphate group ($PO4^{3-}$), which is made up of one phosphorus atom and four oxygen atoms and is bonded with the carbon atom 5' of the deoxyribose. It is an *ion*, that is, an incomplete molecule. An ion is either missing one or more electrons (and is therefore positively charged) or it has excess electrons (in which case it is negatively charged). Ions therefore strongly desire to bond with each other, but they often do so by so-called *ionic bonding* rather than by *covalent bonding*. That means that they experience a strong allurement to each other, which in this case is called *electrostatic attraction*, without fully sharing the electrons. This is a different form of intimacy—something analogous to polyamory versus monogamy. Atoms in covalent bonds are really committed to their one partner, while ions can move more easily from one beloved to another. The charge of the phosphate ion in Figure 3 is three times negative, meaning that it needs or desires three other ions with a positive charge. The phosphate's ion desire for bonding is essential to the formation of DNA with its famous double-helix structure and therefore to the emergence of life as we know it.

Finally, there is a *nitrogenous base*, an intimate configuration of carbon, hydrogen, and nitrogen. The nitrogenous base is the unique (*differentiating*) part of a nucleotide. There are four nitrogenous bases, adenine, thymine, guanine, and cytosine, which intimately partner to form the rungs of the DNA and the basic alphabet of the DNA code (see Section V.2). The whole nucleotide is named according to the nitrogenous base it contains (in Figure 1, it is adenine: $C5H5N5$). This four-letter alphabet is what gives rise, at some point in the evolutionary story, to what we can only refer to as a deepening of the relationship bond—an intensification of intimacy. This intensification of intimacy creates the staggering result we call life. Life as we know it emerges out of this world of ever-deepening, stable relationships between complex molecules.

This evolutionary leap of emergence discloses the inherent intelligence of the self-actualizing Cosmos[286] from which cellular life is born. Cellular life itself evolves through more and more interconnected forms of right attraction and stable relationship. Relationship is the elixir of evolution. Reality as relationship continues to evolve into more and more sophisticated and beautiful forms:

- Molecules awaken to form complex molecules.

- Gradually, we move up the chain of transformation, and eventually cells awaken to what we now call life.

- Reality then moves from single-celled to multicellular organisms. This is a dramatic evolution of relationships that eventually births plants, reptiles, mammals, and finally human beings.

Each new level adds to but often does not eliminate the previous level. This is the order of unfolding as described by evolutionary theorists, which is also implicit and, in a close evolutionary reading, already extant in the primary sources of Hebrew wisdom—the first chapter of the book of Genesis.[287]

---

286 See The Self-Actualizing Cosmos: The Akasha Revolution in Science and Human Consciousness, by Ervin Laszlo (2014).

287 Gerald Schroeder, Daniel Matt, and many others, from both the sciences and the humanities, have written about the evolutionary structure of the Genesis narrative; see God & the Big Bang: Discovering Harmony Between Science & Spirituality, by Daniel Matt (2014), and The Science of God: The Convergence of Scientific and Biblical Wisdom, by Gerald Schroeder (1997).

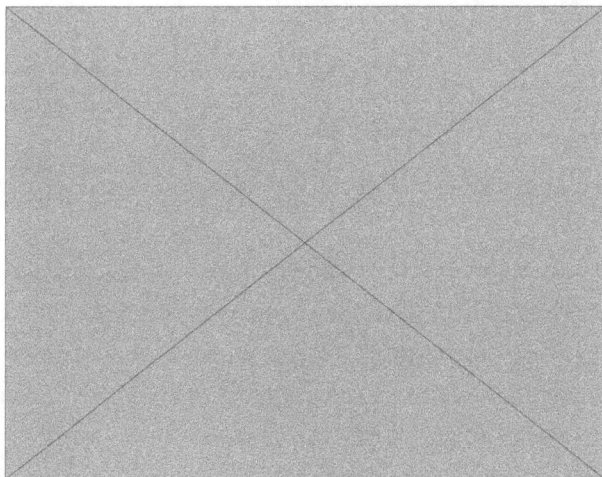

Figure 1. Chemical structure of deoxyadenosine monophosphate.[288]

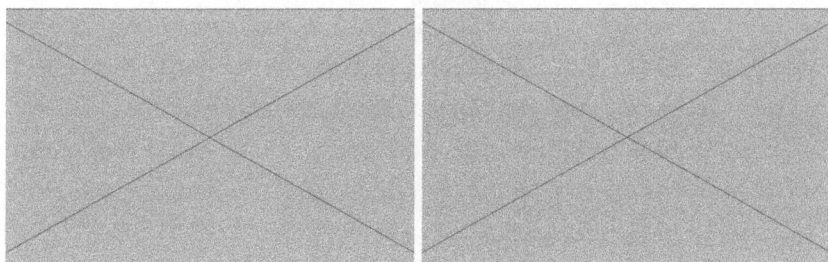

Figure 2. A schematic of the deoxyribose sugar molecule (left) versus the ribose sugar molecule (right).[289]

288 Image by Cacycle (public domain).

289 Images from David J. Russell, "Modeling Biological Structures via Abstract Grammars to Solve Common Problems in Computational Biology" (2010).

9. Evolution of Desire and Passion

The key words of this chapter—*allurement, desire, erotic, intimacy*—evoke a distinct feeling tone beyond the cognitive processing. They are overlapping, inter-included terms that are, at the same time, distinct *qualia*.[290] We have defined the terms intimacy and Eros precisely through their respective interior science equations (see Essay One, Sections 2.3–4). We have described *allurement* in depth, and we have begun to describe its sister term, *desire*.

Reality, by its very nature, desires and is allured toward the actualization of ever-deeper, new forms of erotic intimacy. The evolutionary record shows that Eros births sex. Before any sex, there are twelve billion years of Eros in the self-organizing Universe, driven by principles of ever-deepening configurations of erotic intimacies. They manifest all cosmological evolution and the first stages of biological evolution, all driven by the precise, polar dance between line and circle energies (autonomy and allurement).

All of evolutionary emergence is marked by passion. It is a quality of aroused Eros, expressed in the tender and fierce Fuck that animates Cosmos. There is an urge to merge, balanced precisely by an urge to individuate. There is a powerful inherent drive to reach beyond oneself and make intimate contact with another being without getting so absorbed in the other that you disappear. For both the interior scientists of the great traditions and the poetic scientists of evolutionary emergence theory,[291] the yearning force of passion and desire is the central driving force of Reality. The ability for passion to fulfill itself in ever-more profound, potent, and beautiful forms is one of the vectors of evolution.

---

290 Qualia are conscious, subjective phenomena arising in the individual.

291 See The Re-Emergence of Emergence: The Emergentist Hypothesis from Science to Religion, edited by Phillip Clayton and Paul Davies (2006).

Twelve billion years or so into the process, sex is introduced into Reality. Sex makes the line-and-circle-dance dramatically more distinct. It begins with sperm and egg and evolves to phallus and vagina. This new evolutionary leap in relationship creates the dizzyingly complex and beautifully erotic symphony of intimacy that science calls *meiosis*.[292] This symphony of intimate communion is birthed from the forming of a stable relationship bond between cells.[293]

The male stickleback fish has a red belly and blue eyes. He lives his desire in the courtship dance. If his dance is favorably received by the female, she will deposit her eggs in his nest. He can then quickly move in and fertilize them. From the human perspective on intimacy, this would be a date that would literally leave something to be desired. The man completing the mating dance to the woman's aroused satisfaction, followed by the woman depositing her eggs with almost no direct contact[294] with the man and then leaving, and him then fertilizing the eggs she left behind, just does not make the grade from the human perspective. But it is a dramatic leap forward from the splitting of bacteria into two as the first form of asexual reproduction in single cells. That is precisely the point. Reality is the progressive deepening of intimacies, characterized by both continuity and leaps of discontinuity, all the way up the evolutionary chain. The evolution of intimacy is inextricably bound up with the evolution of consciousness. It will be another hundred million years of relationship history before the passion to merge deepens into the

---

292 Relationship births first mitosis and then meiosis into Reality. While mitosis, which is the process of cell division, is an earlier evolutionary emergent—all the different types of cells in a body can undergo mitosis—meiosis is the process of producing eggs and sperm in sexual reproduction.

293 It is clear that meiosis emerged over 1.2 billion years ago. However, there is currently no consensus among biologists on how sex arose in evolution, what basic function sexual reproduction served, and why it was maintained, given the evolutionary disadvantages of sex. (Among the most limiting evolutionary disadvantages of sexual reproduction is that an asexual population can grow much more rapidly with each generation than a sexual one.) See, for example, The Evolution of Sex, by J. Maynard Smith (1978).

294 There is some limited contact in the mating of stickleback fish, which seems determinant in the eggs' deposition.

formation of sex organs as lizards evolve from their fish and amphibian ancestors.

The coming into being of phallus and vagina allows the fulfillment of desire through an actual sensual interaction between bodies, in which communion, for a brief moment, overcomes otherness and autonomy. Reptiles are able to consummate their passion through a fleeting intermingling of bodies. The emergence of this new form of fulfillment literally changes the course of evolution. Relationships, however, have not come even close to reaching a dead end.

For example, the dance of intimacy between plants and their pollinators has generated a fascinating diversity of strategies to lure the pollinators in. Using sweet scents, bright colors, and perfectly designed forms, the blooms entice their pollinators with the promise of a scrumptious feast. Flowers provide visual clues and formations, through their shapes and sizes, which allow pollinators to make contact.

Some flowers also have nectar guides that contain patterns visible from the air, thus showing pollinators the way to the sweet spot. Plants pollinated by beetles, for instance, have large open blooms, making for a wider landing area to accommodate larger guests. Irises are prolific producers of flowering petals that take an enormous amount of energy to stay in competition with nearby flowering plants, in hopes of alluring the services of bumblebees. Flower receptacles and displays uniquely vary from gullets and spurs to flaps and tubes. With a narrow tubule and a long tongue, the right pollinator and the right plant part, contact is made. The propagation of new life continues.

We have all been delightfully intoxicated by the scent of a flower. Flowers use potent aromas to allure their pollinators as well. Those with alluring fragrances are often those that are quite plain in their appearance. Some flowers exude scents that can be detected at a distance of over a mile away.

Food produced by flowers is also a major attractor for pollinators. Nectar is primarily a sugar water that contains amino acids and minerals. Plants dependent on pollinators with high-energy diets, such as hummingbirds, produce massive quantities of nectar. Pollen, high in protein, is produced by flowers in large amounts to ensure an appropriate feast.

Along with the need for sustenance, pollinators also need to reproduce in order to propagate the next generation of their species. The warty
hammer orchid of Australia takes advantage of this evolutionary impulse
to reproduce by mimicking a chemical scent identical to the pheromone
of the female thynnid wasp. In addition, the orchid's labellum or lower lip
is shaped like the body of the female wasp. The male wasp tries to grab
the faux female and fly off with her to mate, but instead, he crashes into
the flower, releasing its pollen. The male thynnid wasp is a rather randy
guy, and his constant desire to make contact through mating over and
over is advantageous to the warty hammer orchid by causing its ongoing
pollination and propagation.[295]

The emergence of mammals is yet another momentous leap in the nature of relationships. Mammals develop relationships of such depth that,
in some cases, they remain together their entire lifetimes. Relationships
that began their manifest journey in the primary subatomic attraction
between subatomic particles, microseconds after the Big Bang, have now
realized their inner desire at a whole different level of joy and fulfillment.

D. H. Lawrence's "Whales Weep Not!" is an ode to the wonder of
this new emergent level of relationship:[296]

And they rock, and they rock, through the sensual ageless ages
on the depth of the seven seas,
and through the salt they reel with drunk delight
and in the tropics tremble they with love
and roll with massive, strong desire, like gods.

Relationships are the key dramas and traumas of our lives. But that
does not begin, just deepens, at the human level. In the words of Brian
Swimme and Mary E. Tucker, "All animals live in the great drama of
their passions."[297]

---

295 See "Coevolution and Pollination," by Joe Arnett (2014), and "Mimicry: The Orchid
and the Bee," in the PBS Evolution Library.

296 Tucker and Swimme cite this poem in their Journey of the Universe (2011).

297 Ibid.

It may well be worth spending time watching the male bowerbird.

Every morning when he awakens, he dedicates virtually all of his life energy to building the most alluring nest that he can. He finds twigs and binds them together. He may find a straw thrown away by campers in the area. He passionately searches the entire area for the highest-quality building materials that he can find. He then becomes an architect of both beauty and function. He arranges and rearranges his materials until they appear in a way that he considers perfect. He might even use natural dark pastes to paint some of the walls of his house.

Where did he learn all this? It comes from intimate patterns stored in his DNA. To be more poetically and scientifically precise, his DNA contains the common wisdom of his lineage of life. It is the expression of a unique configuration of biological intimacies that are known as bowerbird, as well as his irreducibly unique expression of that unique lineage. All of this uniquely formed and configured intimacy and its wisdom is passed on through the accumulated erotic LoveIntelligence of Reality from his wisest surviving ancestors. Endowed with all this embodied wisdom, the male bowerbird moves to allure his beloved in building the beauty of his nest, driven by the erotic passion for joining, the drive for intimate relationship. It is that mysterious passion that moves him to erect the most beautiful home as part of the line's mating call to the circle.

Some male spiders, in their own unique expression of this same process of evolutionary Eros and passion, learn to dance and to play the strings of their web as a primitive musical instrument. That is part of the spider's mating call.

Dance takes place on water and inland. Stickleback fish dance in the water, while cranes dance on the shore. Male peacocks use the stunning display of art and color in their tail feathers to attract their circle.

All these activities are driven by allurement, the primary drive for relationship, often at the expense of survival. They can take away energy from survival activities or even be life threatening. This is not ordinary love, which is all too often a strategy of the ego, seeking survival, comfort, and some level of security. This is what we call Outrageous Love, the Evolutionary Eros that drives All-That-Is.

10. Relationships Require Transformation, Transformation Requires Sacrifice

Evolution is a series of transformations. This notion of transformation in relationship as key to generating a new quality of intimacy is central to myth as well. The classic images of the beauty and the beast, or the princess and the frog, are expressions of the need to generate a new quality of self to emerge a new quality of intimate relationship.[298] Evolution itself, at all levels, is a series of transformations that generate new wholes—new configurations of intimacy, new shared identities in the context of otherness.

To transform means to change form, appearance, or structure. A structure is the intimate pattern of the component parts in a system. The process of evolution in nature is through transformation, where changes in structure take place at many levels. Nature's Eros expresses in energy, coded with unique intimate patterns of potential emergence, and transforms from one configuration of intimate coherence to another. Eros is the force that drives nature. Nature, from the smallest atoms to plants and animals and through all her ecosystems, is driven by energy transformers and transporters. Everything within nature—ourselves included—functions by receiving energy, transforming that energy into new coherent, intimate forms, and then holding/storing it until it is called upon to be used as a driving force. One common example of transformative nature is sunlight to plant to chlorophyll to animals, including humans. Eating a salad is an act of energy transformation. The salad's

---

298 See also the myths on the frog king, the swan maiden, the werewolf, the vampire, the leopard man, et cetera.

energy, stored in the leaf's chlorophyll, is transformed through the process of metabolism and stored inside the body.

Transformation always involves some dimension of sacrifice—a surrender, a kind of *Kenosis*, which invokes a higher possibility.[299] At its core, this surrender is the surrender of freedom—of myriad alternative vectors of possibility. But it is a surrender that births new possibility and new freedom. This is an expression of the First Principle and First Value of Paradox: Opposites are joined at the hip.[300]

All relationships require personal transformation of both parties for attraction and bonding to be present. A neutron does not form a stable, passionate relationship with a proton without transformation. Both the proton and the neutron must undergo transformation for the bond of relationship to occur. Each has to give something up in order to receive the other. There is a vector of possibility, which is reconfigured when the proton and neutron enter a relationship. In this sacrifice of possibility, intimacy is formed. The new shared identity is in effect a new cauldron of intimacy, which births new possibility. The new possibility can only be born in the wake of a sacrifice, a Kenosis, an emptying of Infinite Freedom. This is what births new freedom in the context of new intimacy—new shared identity and new mutualities of recognition, feeling, value, and purpose—that coheres a proton and a neutron into an atomic nucleus. Both proton and neutron give up part of their mass. When this happens, a flash of heat and light explodes into Reality.[301] It is—very literally—the light of new relationship.

This sacrifice, or Kenosis, is what the interior sciences referred to as *Tzimtzum*, the contraction of the Infinite itself to make room for other in a new shared identity. This is the paradoxical play that is the cause of

---

299 In the interior sciences of Hebrew wisdom, all creativity comes from the void. This process is called Tzimtzum—Divine Withdrawal and Contraction—Kenosis—as the mechanism of the creative act. This is, for the interior sciences, the model of all forms of creativity.

300 See First Principles and First Values.

301 This mass, which by Einstein's mass-energy relation $E=mc^2$ is released as energy, is known as binding energy. The Sun and other stars use this process of nuclear fusion to generate thermal energy, which is later radiated from their surface.

ever-evolving intimate coherence, from atoms to molecules to prokaryotes to eukaryotes all the way up the evolutionary chain.

Ultimately, at the leading edge of human evolution, Reality discloses
what we refer to as nondual humanism, or CosmoErotic Humanism.
This is a new intimacy, a new shared identity between the human and
the Divine. The human being sacrifices their sense of being a separate self, only to be reborn as True Self, and then to be reborn again
as Unique Self—an irreducibly unique emergent of the Infinite Field
of Consciousness, Personhood, Desire, and Creativity. (This Field is
sometimes referred to as God.) The human and the Divine realize their
ontic identity of wills—*unio mystica*, the shared identity between the
human and the Divine.

11. Deeper Configurations of Intimacy Generate Transformation

At each stage of its unfolding, Reality creates new transformations
through new and deeper relationships—what we have called *intensifications of intimacy.*

A deeper relationship can mean simply a deeper communication
between parts, which creates the possibility of greater complexity and
consciousness. But at certain pivotal moments in evolution, there are
jumps—what Stephen Jay Gould called *punctuated equilibrium.* At these
moments, not only is there a deeper communication that sustains the
intimacy of the relationship, but the very purpose of the relationship
changes. There is a whole new context for relating. The new relationship
expresses a deeper intimacy, guided by new communication codes, and
serves an entirely new purpose.

New contexts for relating create new qualities of intimacy.

Procreation is a core function of Reality. At each stage of evolution, the modes of sex and procreation emerge from progressively deepening forms of intimacy. Procreation begins with asexual reproduction, one bacterium splitting into two, and moves to sexual reproduction, with two partners relating on some level. Sexual reproduction means that line and circle, masculine and feminine essences, relate to each other in a new way in order to create new life.

The way sexuality happens deepens at many points in the evolutionary process, which allows for ever-more complex and conscious offspring. But the original biological purpose of sexuality seems to remain reproduction.[302] That is the context for relating.

At some point, this context changes. It becomes clear that the purpose of relating is not only to produce new offspring but also to foster intimacy between the partners that will keep them together.[303] This is a new context for relationship that may have been implicitly there already, but now it becomes somewhat more explicit. It is not only that the new communication codes and new forms of reproductive processes generate offspring with more complexity and consciousness. The new context for relating is no longer purely for procreation but to create sustained intimacy for life.

At some later point, these deepening intimate relationships might take on an additional new purpose—for instance, to care for offspring for some period of time. The new commitment to care for offspring is another new context for relating. Sexuality might then serve the purpose

---

302 At least, that is the understanding of evolutionary theory, as we can see that most animals confine sex to a brief period around the time of the female's ovulation. The animals themselves, and maybe even early humans, probably didn't know that. They related and had sex because of the pleasure it brought. See, for example, "Sex Makes Babies," by Holly Dunsworth and Anne Buchanan (2017).

303 Humans are quite unusual in their continuous practice of sex throughout the year. Most female animals are advertising their ovulation period with bold visual signals, odors, or behaviors—and animals only have sex in that time period. In contrast, humans (and a few other primates) have no means of detecting when they themselves or their partners can be fertilized (or didn't, until modern scientific times). Their concealed ovulations may have directly led to their continuous practice of sex, which indirectly led to a new context for their sexual relationship.

of sustaining intimacy so that the couple, together, will care for the child or children.[304] When this kind of relationship appears at the human level, we call it a *role mate* relationship.

At a later stage of evolution, the sexual act might be uncoupled entirely from procreation and might be said to serve purely the intimacy between the partners. We call this a *soul mate* relationship at the human level of existence. The notion of soul mate moved to the center of culture in full force only in the second half of the twentieth century, but its roots go back very far, well before even the Industrial Revolution, all the way back into the medieval period and even into ancient history. This new context for relating, soul mate relationship, evolved the very nature and quality of intimacy.

Beyond soul mate relationship, we are now pointing to another new emergent context for relating. In this new context, the intimacy in the couple might serve to connect them to the larger Evolutionary Eros coursing through them, in order to awaken a wider connection to the large Whole. The context for relating has now become the awakening of the evolutionary impulse in the couple, so that their partnership can uniquely contribute to the evolutionary process itself. We call this new context for relating a *whole mate* relationship. It is a relationship that experiences itself as part of the larger Whole and is in service to the larger Whole (see Essay Two).

It is at this station of relationship that the lover experiences sexual

---

304 This new evolution seems to be closely related to the earlier one. There are two possible evolutionary explanations for both of these changes in context. One is the father-at-home theory, developed by University of Michigan biologist Richard Alexander and graduate student Katharine Noonan. The other is the many-fathers theory, developed by anthropologist Sarah Hardy of the University of California, Davis. Both explanations seem to be valid but operated at different times in our evolutionary history. It looks like concealed ovulation arose at a time when our primate ancestors were either still promiscuous or living in harems. At such times, the ancestral woman distributed her sexual favors to many males. As a result, none of those males, who otherwise would often kill the babies of their competitors, wanted to harm the baby—and some may actually have protected or helped feed it. In a later evolutionary period, the women then seemed to have used their concealed ovulation to pick a good man (monogamy) and to entice or force him to stay with her and provide lots of help for her baby.

arousal as an arousal not only to sex but to the entire Field of Desire and Arousal. Desire is no longer local but an expression of the larger Field of Reality, what we have called Eros, Evolutionary Love, or Outrageous Love. This new quality of desire can be referred to as supra-sexual arousal. Supra-sex is a term for the erotic arousal of shared creativity that defines whole mate relationships.[305] Like in earlier stages of evolution, each one of these new levels of emergence requires new forms of communication and reshapes the culture codes, which connect cells, internal organs, and partners themselves, in order to fundamentally transform the entire context for relating. Not only do these new contexts change the purpose of the relationship, they also expand the very possibilities of purpose, or telos.

---

305 Supra-sex is a term we sourced from A New Model of the Universe, by Pyotr Ouspensky (1997), chapter 7. Ouspensky differentiates three types of sex: infra-sex—sexual ignorance, disgust of sex, arrested development or degeneration, perversions, abnormal sexual desires or abnormal sexual abstinence, indifference to sex, and disharmony between sex and other aspects of life; normal sex—sex harmonized with other psychological functions and other aspects of life, sex that builds energy and awareness and that inspires; and supra-sex—sex subsumed into mystical consciousness such that normal sex ceases and sex becomes an inner transformation and union intimately tied to one's life purpose and calling, a kind of spiritual intercourse.

IV. FIRST NOTES ON REALITY AS AN OUTRAGEOUS LOVE STORY: EVOLUTION LIVES IN US

1. The Future of Reality Rests in Our Hands

The greatest revelation of modern science is that the Universe is not merely a fact but a story. A fact simply exists. A story is going somewhere. A story has direction, a plot, and a purpose. The leading edges of evolutionary science add a crucial dimension that takes this one step further: The Universe is not merely a story; it is a love story. Love moves Cosmos toward higher and deeper expressions: from atoms to amoebae to plants to animals to humans.

This distinction between human beings and animals is crucial and is often lost by critics of *speciesism*, a term used in philosophy regarding the treatment of individuals of different species.[306] While human beings

---

306 This term has several different definitions in the relevant literature (see, for example, "The Speciesism Debate: Intuition, Method, and Empirical Advances," by Jereon Hopster [2019]). In most definitions, speciesism involves treating members of one species as morally more important than members of other species. Others define speciesism as discrimination or unjustified treatment based on an individual's species membership, while again others define it as differential treatment regardless of whether the treatment is justified or not. Richard Ryder, an English writer, psychologist, and animal rights advocate, who originally coined the term,

can justifiably be considered more advanced than animals in certain vectors of evolution, this should not be used to legitimize animal abuse.[307] But the criticism of speciesism, in a way bordering on the absurd, often effaces all hierarchies, failing to distinguish between dominator and holistic hierarchies.[308]

Each new emergent level is capable of more love and more complex relationships. For example, molecules are more complex than elementary particles, and they have capacity to form more complex relationships.[309] Much higher up the evolutionary chain, the internal systems of the first mammal (called *Morganucodontids*) were more complex than those that make up an amoeba, and it had more capacity for forming and participating in relationships than does an amoeba (which reproduces asexually, by division). Similarly, there is greater complexity in the internal organ systems of a human being (most obviously in their brains) than those of the first mammals, and a human being has a deeper capacity to love and a greater capacity to engage in relationships. However, the human capacity to love is not fixed or static. Rather, it has grown and evolved over time. Early humans had a felt sense of care and concern only for themselves and their survival clan. Now, the most evolved humans have a felt sense of care and concern that includes all of existence.

Such moves from simplicity to complexity are part of an evolutionary story. This story tells of the evolution of love. At its core, the evolution of love is the evolution of relationships. The entire evolutionary unfolding of Reality is the story of moving to higher and deeper levels of intimacy.

---

defined it as "a prejudice or attitude of bias in favor of the interests of members of one's own species and against those of members of other species" (quoted by Peter Singer in Animal Liberation [1990]).

307 To be clear, we are very much against this form of speciesism.

308 Dominator hierarchy is a term introduced by Riane Eisler in her book The Chalice and the Blade (1988). It is a pathological type of hierarchy that Eisler uses to distinguish from healthy hierarchy.

309 See Section III.8.

As we gaze in wonder at the stars lighting the night sky, we often think of them as eternal, unchanging objects. However, science now tells us that stars are characters in stories with inherent plotlines moving them in clear directions. Stars are guided by a self-organizing process, and they go through clear stages of emergence and transformation. We are part of the plotlines of the stories of stars; they gave birth to almost all the chemical elements that constitute our bodies and sustain our existence. Stars are our ancestors; we are literally stardust. In fact, everything in Cosmos, including stardust, lives in us: Subatomic particles, atoms, molecules, cells, and everything else literally live *in* us and *as* us. Not only are we at home in the Universe, but the Universe is also at home in us.

We are beginning to understand that evolution literally awakens *as us* in person. Our creativity, for example, is not separate from the creativity of all of evolution. Evolutionary creativity awakens and expresses itself through us. Essentially the same creative process is at play in cosmological evolution (of atoms, stars, galaxies, and planets), biological evolution (of cells, plants, animals, and mammals), and human evolution (from prehistoric to modern man).

The creative process is one through which all of Reality is driven to engage in deeper forms of relationship. Relationships exist across the spectrum of Reality—in and between celestial bodies, chemical compounds, cells, plants, animals, humans, and everything else. Human beings are a conscious expression of the Universe's self-organizing power to engage in relationships.

The evolutionary story is driven by the evolution of relationships—including the evolution of the way we do relationships in our lives. In the first volume, we unpacked the next great step in evolution's path, the next great level of relationship—whole mate, or evolutionary relationship.[310] In taking our relationships to the next level, we become essential actors in the process of evolution. We participate directly in the evolution of love.

This means that the future of Reality literally rests in our hands. We

---

310 Gafni and Hubbard, Whole Mate; see also Essay Two.

can consciously direct the path of evolution. Waking up to this truth is what it means to wake up to Conscious Evolution. Conscious Evolution simply means that we realize that the evolutionary process lives in us and that we are active agents in its unfolding.

Because the evolutionary process lives in us, we have great power. We can destroy everything or we can create a world of goodness, truth, and beauty beyond anything we have yet seen.

Evolution means that Reality is not just a fact; it is a story.

Reality is not an ordinary story. It is a love story.

But it's not an ordinary love story. Reality is an *Outrageous* Love Story—or what leading-edge science might call an *Evolutionary Love Story*.[311] *Outrageous Love* is not merely a human strategy or sentiment but what Dante, a great poet and erotic mystic, described as the heart of existence itself—the love that moves the Sun and other stars. It is the love that *steers the stars*.[312] Outrageous Love is, echoing the phrase of another erotic mystic and philosopher of science, Alfred North Whitehead, the inherent and incessant movement toward God by the inherent and incessant persuasion of love.[313]

The next stage of relationship always emerges from the creative engagement between different wholes desiring ever-deeper contact and ever-greater wholeness, be it quarks, atoms, molecules, cells, animals, human beings, or ideas. New insights, which generate new structures

---

311 We explore the concept of Outrageous Love in great depth in Whole Mate. See also "Evolutionary Love," by Marc Gafni and Ken Wilber (2012); The Radical Path of the Outrageous Lover: The Path and Practice of Outrageous Love, by Marc Gafni and Kristina Kincaid, an early draft of which is available online (https://www.one-mountainmanypaths.org/outrageous-love-books); and A Return to Eros, especially chapter 1.

312 This phrase is taken from the medley "Aquarius/Let the Sunshine In," written for the 1967 musical Hair and released as a single by the 5th Dimension. The song intuitively captures the dawning of this phase shift in human history, what the song refers to as the Age of Aquarius.

313 On Alfred North Whitehead, see Religion and Scientific Naturalism, by David Ray Griffin (2000). Whitehead understood, consonant with our vision of the Intimate Universe, that the nature of Divine Love, as an expression of Divine Power, is, at least for the duration of history, persuasive and not coercive.

of culture and consciousness, often emerge from an integration of the leading edges of science and wisdom available in the world at this moment in time.

Relationships are an expression of Love—the force of allurement that moves that which is separate to come together.[314] The next stage in the evolution of relationship is, in effect, the next stage in the evolution of love.

2. Between Ordinary and Outrageous Love

Outrageous Love differs from the ordinary love as radically as Infinity differs from a number, however large. For the lover at this level of consciousness, the beloved is all of Infinity, just like the mother is all of Infinite Reality to the baby. To hear our mother or beloved utter the magical *Yes!* is to hear the evolutionary *Yes!* of all of Reality.

At the moment of the Big Bang, there was this great and mysterious *Yes!* to relationship that birthed all of Reality into existence. It is that evolutionary *Yes!* that the lover feels personally addressed to them in the successful dance of intimacy. To love one's way to enlightenment is to cultivate one's lived center of gravity in Outrageous Love and not in the cultural construction of ordinary love. Rabindranath Tagore speaks of Outrageous Love when he says:

> Love is the only reality and it is not a mere sentiment.
> It is the ultimate truth that lies at the heart of creation.

---

314 This usage of the word love aligns with Paul Tillich's reading of love. In being a force that brings together what was once separate, love is seen as a re-unitive force. See Tillich's Love, Power, and Justice: Ontological Analyses and Ethical Applications (1954).

THE EVOLUTION OF LOVE

Outrageous Love can often move human beings (and other species) to stand for Love, even at the expense of individual survival. From our perspective at least, other species seem to be doing so relatively unconsciously, while the human being, potentially, can do so consciously.[315]

We can feel the difference between the two types of Love, ordinary love and Outrageous Love, in our own lives through the Anthro-Ontological Method. Hold your beloved in an embrace with ordinary love and you will not quite find a place to rest. Embrace your beloved with Outrageous Love and you rest in the Eternity and evolution that live in that moment. When a baby is crying,[316] pick the baby up with ordinary love and the baby quiets for only a moment or simply goes on crying. But hold the baby with Outrageous Love and the baby melts into your arms with infinite pleasure and spacious, relaxed delight. Your arms have become the arms of God, the Universe, Eternity, and evolution coming together as you—as your embrace. If you hold hands with your beloved in the consciousness of ordinary love and your hands get a bit clammy, you are almost dying to take your hand back. Hold hands in the consciousness of Outrageous Love and time stops as you melt into Eternity.

To say it all in one sentence: We live in a CosmoErotic Universe. From elementary particles to human beings, it is relationship and attraction all the way up and all the way down. Lines and circles are coming together, all the way up and all the way down. All of it is moved not by ordinary love but by Eros, Evolutionary Love, or what we are calling Outrageous Love.

---

315 This isn't to say that humans don't also act instinctually in ways that sometimes threaten their own survival for the sake of others, as when someone leaps out in front of oncoming traffic to save a stranger or loved one without conscious thought or choice. It is also not to undermine the depth of interiority and choice that exists in animals. But because we lack first-person reports about the interiority of animals, we cannot draw definitive conclusions.

316 Of course, we are not talking about crying out of hunger or pain but out of the need for touch, contact, or Love.

3. Love Is Eternal and Evolving

Love is Eternal. It is the unchanging essence that animates, suffuses, and sustains Reality. It is the force of evolutionary allurement that is ever-present in the Cosmos. Love is the creative cause of evolution. Love is the internal quality of both Being and Becoming.

Love, or Eros, evolves all of Reality, *including itself*. The force of Eros—the experience of radical aliveness, desiring, seeking, and moving toward ever-deeper contact and ever-greater wholeness—drives evolution.

But *how* Eros expresses itself in Reality also evolves. For example, it means one thing to love your partner in ancient China and quite something else in contemporary France. To cite one example, deep communication between beloveds was almost unheard of in the ancient world, while the desire and demand for such communication is, at least to some degree, a given in modern relationships.

Love is eternal and evolving. Love is eternal in the sense of being underneath time and space and not subject to change. And yet, as it enters the manifest world, Eros itself evolves.

A while ago, I was watching a scene in a movie whose name I cannot recall with my partner Kristina, about a Chinese patriarch who had a beautiful love with his wife. Their son had disobeyed the father in a key family issue. The mother supported her son. According to the law of the time, she might have been put to death. Instead, her husband slaps her three times and then hugs her. She tearfully thanks him for the depth of his love. It was clear that in fact they loved each other very deeply. This was the best that love had to offer in that moment. Today, if a man slapped his wife three times in punishment, she would be well within her rights to call the authorities to report domestic violence and have him jailed for assault.

What has changed?

Love has evolved.

Love today cannot express itself in any form of physical violence between partners. In the first century BCE, however, when the family was an inviolable part of identity, before the recognition of individual rights, before the emergent recognition of equality between men and women, three slaps at a particular time, instead of the more severe, mandated punishment, might have been experienced as an act of love. The change in how our love languages and love acts transform and deepen through time, both in their depth of feeling and in our mode of action, is precisely the evolution of love.

You can access these two ontological qualities of Love—being and becoming—through the Anthro-Ontological Method.[317] As erotic mystic Abraham Kook intimated time and again, *the mysteries are within us.* That means that, to find the structural ontology of Cosmos, of being and becoming, you simply have to access the quality of Love—or Eros— that you feel in the realms of your own experience. You observe Reality alive in you.

In some profound way, beyond the purview of this meditation, all science works because we are cosmic humans. We can access the cosmos because the cosmos and all of its laws and mathematics quite literally live inside of us. You *are* evolution—all of it, from the first quarks to stardust, cells, organs, feelings, cognitions. All of evolutionary history is awake and alive in you right now. This scientific insight augments the realization of the interior sciences that all of consciousness lives indivisibly inside of you. This is the premise of analytic meditation, a core Tibetan practice, which involves the tracing of value itself back to its source inside of our own direct experience.[318]

You can *love your way to enlightenment,* because you can trace your own experience of love to the nature of Reality itself. The Love, or Eros,

---

317 As we have said earlier, anthro-ontology is a new field of thought, a method- ology that forms one of the pillars of CosmoErotic Humanism. It is the notion that clarified human interiors disclose some of the interior faces of the Cosmos. The Anthro-Ontological Method is a core method of radical empiricism, the capacity to know something about Reality.

318 This is how the Dalai Lama explained it when I first met him in 2015.

that lives inside of you—when you trace it back to its root—is the true nature both of the Self and of all of Reality. Reality is Eros. And knowing the true nature of self and world is precisely the meaning of enlightenment. That is one dimension of the Anthro-Ontological Method:

1. Clarify your own phenomenological experience.

2. To check yourself, compare it to others who have clarified their experience.

3. See if those others are not just local to you but exist around the globe.

4. Finally, see if they exist not only around the globe but across time.

Through these four steps, you will discover the royal road to ontology. The interior face of the cosmos lives in you, as you, and through you. This is the Anthro-Ontological Method.

With all this in mind, let's return to Love as a quality of both being and becoming. Trace this truth inside of your own interiors.

- You are in love. Simply spending time with your beloved, not doing anything, you bask in the quality of love. That is the Love that is a quality of **being**.

- You move toward your lover, filled with ecstatic urgency, the urge to merge, to make contact, and become intimate, to share ecstatic, intimate identity in the context of otherness. That is the Love that is a quality of **becoming**.

Your desire to deepen, expand, and enrich the quality of your Love, both in *being* and in *becoming*, is *the evolution of love itself*. From the perspective of the interior sciences, it is a stirring in the Infinite that births the Force, the LoveDesire and LoveIntelligence that birth Cosmos. This is the arousal of the becoming quality of LoveDesire and LoveIntelligence.

But we can now also see, from classical, exterior science, that the very nature of Reality is the gradual, progressive deepening of complexity and interconnectivity, whose *interior* is the progressive deepening of intimacy. This progressive deepening of intimacy is motivated by LoveDesire and LoveIntelligence. Beginning with the first quarks, all the way through the next emergence of Cosmos, the biosphere, and then the birth and evolution of humanity, Reality is best defined as the ever-deepening evolution of new configurations of ever-deeper, more conscious, and more potent intimacy.

4. Evolution of Intimacy and Love at the Human Level

When a new level of complexity and intimacy emerges, the dynamics of the preceding level do not disappear. An atom is one level of Reality—a re-lationship, or configuration of intimacy, between quarks, gluons, hadrons, electrons, et cetera.[319] Then, at a certain point of the Evolutionary Love Story, atoms started to be allured to each other and form molecules.[320]

The human being is more than the sum of previous parts. That means, for example, that all the laws that govern the interactions between atoms, molecules, and cells still apply at the level of human beings, for the human being is made up of atoms, molecules, and cells. But the human being is more than a collection of atoms, molecules, cells, and even systems of organs. At the level of consciousness called *human being*, there is also a new set of laws that govern interactions between human beings. But if the drive for intimacy and relationship is built into the very structure of the Cosmos itself, then how important and thrilling it is to be alive at a moment when we can consciously evolve to the next level of relationship!

---

319 See Section II.3.1 and 3.2.

320 See Section III.8.

It is not just that Reality is relationship. The evolution of Reality—not just the evolution of life, but of all of Reality—depends on the evolution of relationship. The evolution of relationship is the evolution of deeper and wider forms of Love. It is the evolution of Eros, which includes the evolution of intimacy.

At the human level, deeper forms of Love or Eros mean loving more intensely, with more depth, understanding, and commitment. Wider forms of Love or Eros might mean loving more parts and wider dimensions of the beloved. Or it might mean loving more than just my family or even just my tribe—widening the circle of Love to include all human beings, or even a felt sense of love for all sentient beings, or sentience itself, including all animals.[321]

It is also wider and deeper self-love. If you turn inward, then to love more deeply means to gain a deeper understanding of your unique identity, quality, and purpose. To love yourself more widely means to love more parts of yourself.

This deepening of erotic intimacy is what drives the evolution of all of Reality. The trajectory of evolution is the evolution of relationship, which is the evolution of love, which is the evolution of intimacy.

Evolution = Evolution of Relationships = Evolution of Love = Evolution of Intimacy.

This equation is built into the very structure of Reality itself.

The process of deepening or evolving love, for example at the human level, can be understood as moving through four distinct levels, or the four circles of love, correlated with the evolution of human consciousness and identity. The two are intimately related. Human consciousness and identity grow from *egocentric*, to *ethnocentric*, to *worldcentric*, and, if we so

---

321 This trajectory we just loosely described is the movement from egocentric to ethnocentric to worldcentric to cosmocentric. Of course, the order in these kinds of things is often not linear. For example, a person might love their pet very deeply, extending love to their animal and yet not loving all human beings—and often also not the animal they have for dinner. In other words, their love of their animal might be a form of egocentric or ethnocentric love and not an expression of cosmocentric love of all life even beyond the human being.

choose, to *cosmocentric*. This is a fourfold expansion to ever-wider circles of love that takes place for individual human beings and for humanity as a whole.

At the level of egocentric consciousness and love, the individual identifies solely with itself. Egocentric love includes the individual and everyone he or she needs to survive. The challenge of egocentric consciousness and love is that it is limited to a small circle and based solely on survival. For many people, egocentric consciousness and love is primary. It is real and even sacred, but it is also limited.

Egocentric consciousness and love expand to ethnocentric consciousness and love as the individual expands their smaller circle to include a larger group. They begin to identify with the larger group, community, or nation they are part of. The critical dimension here—and the key to understanding the limitation of ethnocentric love—is that these groups are rigidly defined. Other people must worship at the same altar, share the same ethnicity, or cheer for the same sports team to be included in the individual's love. The individual's sense of loyalty, care, and compassion expands beyond those it needs for survival, but again, it is significantly limited.

Ethnocentric consciousness and love, then, expand to worldcentric consciousness and love. The individual begins to identify with all human beings, regardless of race, sex, class, or creed. At the level of worldcentric consciousness and love, the individual is in relationship not just with his or her group, community, or nation but with every human being on the face of the planet. The individual does not lose his or her special connection to romantic partners, family, or tribe, but his or her core identity organizes around the entire human family, regardless of the former rigid group distinctions.

Worldcentric consciousness and love expand to cosmocentric consciousness and love. This is love fully awakened in human beings living at the leading edge of evolution. At this level of consciousness and love, the individual profoundly identifies with all of Reality. He or she has a felt sense of love, care, and concern for all of Reality. Cosmocentric consciousness and love expand and deepen to include all of the planet and all of the Universe. The individual recognizes

- that we live in a self-organizing Universe of extreme beauty and dazzling complexity,

- that the Universe has direction, purpose, and creativity, and

- that the Universe evolves to wider and deeper expressions of relationship and love from the subatomic level to the level of human beings and beyond.

This is being recognized at the leading edges of science, psychology, and spirituality all around the world. The evolution of love is happening in front of our eyes.

The movement to wider and deeper levels of consciousness and love is the evolution of relationship. Each new level of relationship is a completely new emergent. Like putting on a new pair of glasses, an evolution in relationship reveals lines of connection and intimacy that were once invisible and undistinguished.

With each new emergence of relationship, we witness a new emergence of love. When we experience the expression and evolution of love at any level of consciousness, we experience the Force of Love that has lived in the Universe since the Big Bang. This Love is the drive to ever-higher levels of union and embrace that animates the entire evolutionary process.

As Love evolves, three things happen:

- There is a wider sense of identity.

- There is a broader circle of love.

- There is an expanded circle of care and concern that expresses itself through action.

At each level of relationship, our identities, breadth of love, and intention of action widen, deepen, and transform.

In our current emergence and expression of Love, human consciousness is in full bloom. It is the perfect time to consciously participate in evolution. We can begin to choose our direction, our identity, and the nature of our relationships. Our natural instincts can merge with conscious choice. For example, we can choose to widen our circle of love. We have done this in the past, and we can do it again, right now.

5. We Live in an Intimate Universe. The Intimate Universe Lives in Us.

A wondrous precision in the dance of Reality takes place across and at every level of Cosmos. We live in an Intimate Universe. That is both prose and poetry. Intimacy lives at every level of the Cosmos. While interior scientists sense this to be true with the Eye of Consciousness, exterior scientists have now shown it to be true with the Eye of the Senses and the Eye of the Mind.[322] Intimacy at the heart of the Universe is visible in its inherent intelligence and stunningly precise timing, which constantly manifest new and deeper levels of emergence and wonder. This led physicist Freeman Dyson to comment,

> *The more I examine the Universe and study the details of its ar-*
> *chitecture, the more evidence I find that the Universe in some sense*
> *must have known we were coming.*[323]

Dyson does not mean that humans were in any sense present at the beginning of time. He points to the radical telos and self-organizing intelligence of Cosmos that holds us in every moment. He speaks the

---

322 On the Eye of Consciousness, the Eye of Senses, and the Eye of the Mind, see Section I.6.

323 Freeman Dyson, Disturbing the Universe (1979), 250.

truth of us living in the Intimate Universe.

We can truly live in the Universe because we are part of the Universe.

The Intimate Universe tells us that we are at home in the Universe.

The Intimate Universe tells us that we are welcome in the Universe, and that our intimacies are at home and welcome in the Universe. Indeed, our intimacies are the very stuff of the Real.

Our intimacies *are* the Universe. We are welcome.

Zhang Zai, a luminary of Chinese Neo-Confucianism, anticipated the realization that not only do we live in the Universe, but the Universe lives in us.

> *Heaven is my father and Earth is my mother, and even such a small creature such as I finds an intimate place in their midst. Therefore, that which extends throughout the universe I regard as my body and that which directs the universe I consider as my nature. All people are my brothers and sisters, and all things are my companions.*[324]

To say the same in evolutionary terms: All of evolution lives in us. Elementary particles, atoms, stardust, molecules, cells, and multicellular organisms all live in us. More than that: Living in us is the memory and capacity of all of Reality's greatest productions. Our DNA contains the records of every great advance that life has made over billions of years. All of the most brilliant innovations produced the radical ways in which the genius of the self-organizing processes of life lives in us. To realize that all of evolution lives inside of us is one of the core ways we wake up to the realization that we live in an Intimate Universe.

---

324 This oft-cited quote is part of the so-called "Western Inscription"—a brief statement that philosopher Zhang Zai wrote on the western wall of his study—which became one of the fundamental and most inspiring expressions of the ethical views of the Confucian revival of the Tang and Song dynasties. Here is another translation, by B. W. Van Norden, from January 13, 2006: "Yang is the father; yin is the mother. And I, this tiny thing, dwell enfolded in Them. Hence, what fills Heaven and Earth is my body, and what rules Heaven and Earth is my nature. The people are my siblings, and all living things are my companions" http://facultysites.vassar.edu/brvannor/Phil210/Translations/Western%20Inscription.pdf.

Evolution is not outside us. We are not separate from it. Evolution takes place inside us. The evolutionary impulse, the creative impulse for transformation, lives in us and as us. That is the force of evolution, which lives in us and as us.

We feel it in our drive to survive.

We feel it in the drive for contact that is our sexuality.

Sex is an expression of the evolutionary impulse. The sexual models the Erotic. When we get the elemental truth that sex is an expression of Evolutionary Eros, the core of sexual shame disappears. It is that same erotic force that drives creativity and innovation in all fields of life. We feel it in our drive for transformation and for the emergence of ever-higher levels of complexity, consciousness, relationship, creativity, and love.

The sexual models the way we want to *live in Eros* in all of the non-sexual dimensions of our lives. If we exile the erotic to the merely sexual, if we do not innovate and transform in every dimension of our lives, then we begin to ask the sexual to fulfill all of our erotic needs. Sex can never do that. When sex becomes the only arena in which we are innovating and transforming, it becomes distorted. Innovation and transformation mean breaking old boundaries and creating new identities, both within us and in the exterior world.

Our nature is to be engaged in this kind of sacred evolutionary boundary breaking in every dimension of life. When we exile all of our boundary-breaking creativity and transformation to the sexual realm, sex collapses under the weight of an erotic burden that it cannot bear.

6. We Are Stardust, and Why It Matters

Transformation, or new emergence, takes place in the external world in myriad forms. It takes place in the inner realms as the transformation of our consciousness. This leads to the transformation of our identity and the transformation of our relationships, both in our lives and in the whole Cosmos. In this exact sense, we can say that at the very core of the evolutionary process is the evolution of intimate relationships.

The way we live our relationships directly affects the very course of evolution. That is not surprising, because the core structure of Reality is intimate relationship.

The bards of relationship singing in the sixties, Joni Mitchell and Crosby, Stills, Nash, and Young, were pointing to this evolutionary truth in their song "Woodstock":

We are stardust,
We are golden,
We are billion-year-old carbon.[325]

Both the interior science texts and the evolutionary story of cosmo-genesis make the same point. The original Genesis text reads,

Let us make a human being in our image.[326]

An insightful commentary asks the obvious question that arises from within the folds of the text. If God is One, then who is God talking to in the text, when the Divine Voice mythically proclaims, "Let us make a human being in our image"? In the third century CE, the proto-evolutionary wisdom masters responded to this query with something akin to *the God you don't believe in doesn't exist.* God is the LoveIntelligence, LoveBeauty, and LoveDesire of Reality. In this text, God turns to all of physical reality (the stars and the galaxies) and to all of biological reality (plants, fish, and animals) and says, "let us *together* birth a human being."[327] What this stunning literary image means for us is that all the

---

325 Crosby, Stills, Nash & Young, "Woodstock (We Are Stardust)," Déjà Vu (1970). Original song composed by Joni Mitchell.

326 Genesis 1:26.

327 Multiple passages in the Midrashic literature on Genesis 1 express this idea; for example, Midrash Rabbah 8:3.

old relationship forms that came before us live in us. The dance, the passion, the desperation for the *Yes*, the polarity of opposites, the mating calls, the drama and trauma, the need to sacrifice and transform to create relationship—all of that is alive in us.

What might it mean *to be stardust*? Essential elements that form our bodies—carbon, magnesium, calcium, and phosphorus—come from the explosion of stars in supernovae. And what is a chemical element other than a configuration of intimacy between its parts? Elements form everything—all of matter. An atom is the smallest part of a chemical element that can exist, a pure substance that cannot be broken down into a more basic element by chemical reactions.[328]

Each chemical element has its own unique fingerprints. More accurately, each atom in an element is a primal configuration of intimacy between electrons, protons, and neutrons, in a particular configuration of Eros. An atom can also be a core part of a larger whole—a molecule containing two or more atoms. The configuration of intimacy in an atom generates the character of the element, just like the configuration of intimacy between two people generates a particular character or quality of relationship—in a way that's both similar to atoms (continuity) and radically emergent (discontinuity).

Almost every element (except for hydrogen and helium, along with traces of lithium and beryllium, which were already formed during the Big Bang)—every atom in your body and everywhere else—is birthed inside of stars and supernovae, by subatomic particles creating stable intimate relationships with each other. When you breathe oxygen, you breathe because of the creations of these stars or supernovae. The life you live is possible because of the gifts of stars. The air we breathe, the food we eat, the compounds out of which we are composed are all new emergents of intimate configuration born from stars and supernovae. A star is a womb of hyperintense, hyperintimate, interconnected, and complex creativity, which births all the next stages of Reality, which all

---

328 Atoms can of course be stripped of their electrons or broken down by nuclear forces. Through the latter, they are actually transformed into more basic elements. But they were long thought of to be the most basic units that couldn't be divided into smaller units anymore. The Greek word atomos means "'indivisible."

live, literally, in us.

Understanding that all these leaps in the evolution of intimate relationships live in us transforms our relationship to evolution. It ceases to
be just a theory *out there* and becomes the essence of our very being. It is
beyond essential for the emergence of *Homo amor* to access an embodied
sense of the truth of this idea, because only then can we impact the future
course of evolution. Only then do we get that the evolutionary impulse
beats our hearts and that **the next steps in the evolution of love will
happen in and through our own relationships.** Only then do we realize
that the next great possibility in relationship is evolution speaking to us
through our own deepest yearnings.

Evolution did not stop with learning how to transform atoms into
molecules, or molecules into macromolecules, or macromolecules into
cells. All these evolutionary leaps of emergence are expressions of intensifications of intimacy. They are the mechanism of the mystery—the engine
of evolution. The engine did not stop when Reality moved from matter
to life, or when Reality moved from life to the depth of the self-reflective
human mind. It is alive in us, as us, and through us, ready to take its
next steps.

7. New Configurations of Intimacy as the Engine of Evolution

The Intimate Universe lives in us both on the most elemental of physical
planes and in the realms of value, intelligence, meaning, and patterns
of intimacy.[329] The Universe never forgets. Every innovation that was

---

329 The realms of value, intelligence, meaning, and patterns of intimacy are in some
 sense enfolded in the physical planes.

needed for more life and value to evolve has emerged in the cosmos and lives inside of us as an expression of the creative intelligence of nature. To the best of our scientific knowledge, the Universe has never forgotten a new insight that served the deepening of beauty, goodness, and life.

- The Universe learned how to eat sunlight (photosynthesis) and has never forgotten.

- The Universe learned how to form complex molecules from simpler atoms and has never forgotten.

- The Universe learned how to manifest multicellular organisms from single cells and has never forgotten.

All three examples are breakthroughs in intimate relationships. Each was born from new configurations of intimacy that generated new wholeness, greater than the sum of the previous parts. New forms of relationship create the deeper intimacy that fosters these mind-bending results. And all of these new configurations of intimacy are aligned with, and literally constitute, the fabric of Eros that is the very essence of our very human existence.

The memory of ever-deepening intimacy lives in us every day. If evolution living in us, as us, and through us were to forget its deepened intimacies, we would all be quite literally dead.

Every new breakthrough that allows for deeper intimacy or new relationship at the cellular level is recorded in DNA as unique sequences of nucleotides.[330] When you ask what DNA is, a scientific response might be:

Deoxyribonucleic acid (DNA) is a molecule that contains the biological instructions that make each species unique. DNA, along with the instructions it contains, is passed from adult organisms to their offspring during reproduction.[331]

---

330 See Section III.8.

331 National Human Genome Research Institute, "Deoxyribonucleic Acid (DNA)

The description in a standard science text might then go on to say:

DNA is made up of a chain of molecules called nucleotides.
Each nucleotide contains a nitrogenous base, a sugar group,
and a phosphate group. Four possible nitrogenous bases
can be present in DNA: adenine (A), thymine (T), guanine
(G) and cytosine (C). The order, or sequence, of these bases
determines what biological instructions are contained in
a strand of DNA. The complete genome [the entire set of
DNA instructions found in a cell] for a human being contains
about 3 billion bases and about 20,000 genes on 23 pairs of
chromosomes.[332]

The formal definitions, while utterly necessary for science, tend to
obfuscate a deeper reality. What is actually happening in every living cell
is the emergence of unique configurations of intimacy and allurement that
birth new forms of unique life. The emergence of DNA, with its miraculous capacity to record all evolutionary breakthrough and inventions in a
seemingly simple alphabet of four "letters" of nucleotides that can be read
by life to create more life, can be fairly described as the Second Big Bang.[333]

For example, when we eat, food is oxidized, and the energy released
in the process can be used or stored in our bodies, in our blood and
flesh. That elemental process of transformation keeps us alive. A key
catalyst in this process is a protein called cytochrome c.[334] This protein

---

Fact Sheet" (2020), https://www.genome.gov/about-genomics/fact-sheets/
Deoxyribonucleic-Acid-Fact-Sheet.

332 Paraphrased from National Human Genome Research Institute, "DNA Fact
Sheet" (2020).

333 See Essay Three, in particular Section 2.3.

334 "Cytochrome c is functionally involved in the electron transport chain of mitochondria. That electron transport is part of the pathway for synthesis of ATP. The
role of cytochrome c is to carry electrons from one complex of integral membrane
proteins of the inner mitochondrial membrane to another. . . . The electron donor
is cytochrome c-1. The electron acceptor is cytochrome c oxidase. Both of these
integral membrane proteins have binding sites for the peripheral membrane protein

is found in plants, animals, fungi, and many unicellular organisms. David Goodsell writes:

> Food is not oxidized in a fiery flame, however. It is oxidized in many slow steps, each carefully controlled and designed to capture as much useable energy as possible. Cytochrome c oxidase controls the last step of food oxidation. At this point, the atoms themselves have all been removed and all that is left are a few of the electrons from the food molecules. Cytochrome c oxidase . . . takes these electrons and attaches them to an oxygen molecule. Then, a few hydrogen ions are added as well, forming two water molecules. The reaction of oxygen and hydrogen to form water is a favorable process, releasing a good deal of energy. In our familiar world, hydrogen and oxygen combine explosively. In our cells, however, the energy is carefully harnessed by cytochrome c oxidase to charge a battery, or perhaps more correctly, to charge a capacitor.[335]

Evolution first learned how to use oxygen in this carefully controlled and efficient way eons ago; before it did, oxygen was deadly poison to living organisms.[336] This breakthrough (or rather series of breakthroughs) has been recorded in DNA and passed down to us. But how did this breakthrough happen in the first place?

Nature is creative. The Universe emerges according to the inherent intelligence of self-organization.[337] Most wondrous, sophisticated, and complex forms emerge way before there are any human brains even remotely on the horizon. There is an inherent, ceaseless creativity built into Reality. To put it another way, matter itself is creative. However you

---

cytochrome c." Philip L. Yeagle, The Membranes of Cells (2016).

335 David Goodsell, "Molecule of the Month: Cytochrome c Oxidase—Cytochrome Oxidase Extracts Energy from Food Using Oxygen" (2000).

336 See Section V.3.

337 See Sections I.1–5.

phrase it, the result is the same. Reality, by its inherent nature, generates new creative possibilities.

It is standard in evolutionary science to refer to the emergence of these new possibilities as chance or random, but a deeper view reveals that they are anything but random.[338] Rather, the natural creativity of living cells is always generating new possibilities and new configurations of intimacy. There is nothing random about that. It is rather nature, or matter, being its creative self. That is the radically amazing nature of matter. There are inherent values of Eros, intimacy, uniqueness, and creativity, all of which are constantly at play, as what we describe, together with scientist and philosopher of science Howard Bloom,[339] as the search engine of Cosmos, always desiring, seeking, moving toward ever-deeper, wider, and more intense intimacies. This is the telerotic nature of matter itself that animates Cosmos.

At some point, it generates the uniquely coded configuration of cytochrome c, which serves life's deepening by allowing the organism to use the oxygen in the atmosphere to transform the food they ate into blood and flesh. This became possible due to unique new forms of intimacy and relationship based on new communication protocols within the cell. The DNA of life-forms possessing and utilizing cytochrome c recorded these new communication patterns, which catalyzed the deeper intimacies in the body and remembered them. In other words, the memory of that pattern lives in our DNA and produces the cytochrome c protein that allows us to successfully eat.

Evolution lives in us.

---

338 See Sections V.1–2.

339 See Section II.4.

8. Memory of Evolution within Us

Brain research from the second half of the twentieth century points to evolution living in us in a dramatic and easy-to-access way. The brain has at least three very distinct layers. Some layers appear to have evolved earlier than others. Each time a new layer emerged, we did not lose the old layer. As always happens in healthy emergence, each new layer of the brain is connected with everything that came before, transcending and including it, and the previous layers are transformed in the process.

The triune model was popularized in the 1960s, but triplicate psycho-physiologies date back as early as fifth century BCE. Paul MacLean first introduced the concept of a triune brain in a paper in 1949 and developed this theory in his 1990 magnum opus, *The Triune Brain in Evolution*.[340] The three regions of the brain in his model are:

---

340 His theory has since been revised by other brain researchers. One of the common ideas associated with the triune brain model is that each layer emerged in a distinct evolutionary period. However, MacLean's "hats-on-hats" model is a deeply questionable simplification, given recent advances in neuroscience. From an evolutionary perspective, the three layers often made big evolutionary advances through reconfiguration of their relationship with each other, rather than simply by stacking layers with specialized functions on top of each other. See "Rethinking Mammalian Brain Evolution," by Terrence W. Deacon (1990). For an evaluation of MacLean's triune model of the brain, see Appendix One, "MacLean's Triune Brain Concept: In Praise and Appraisal" in The Reciprocal Modular Brain in Economics and Politics: Shaping the Rational and Moral Basis of Organization, by Gerald A. Cory Jr., ed. (1999). According to newer research, the neocortex, as the outermost layer of the brain, is further divided: lengthways into two cerebral hemispheres connected by the corpus callosum (discovered by psychobiologist Roger Sperry and colleagues in the early 1960s; in 1981, the Nobel Prize for Medicine was awarded to Sperry for his groundbreaking work), with each of the hemispheres being divided into five lobes—frontal, parietal, temporal, occipital, and insular—with the frontal lobe further divided into the motor cortex (involved in planning and coordinating movement), the prefrontal cortex (responsible for higher-level cognitive functioning), and Broca's area (essential for language production); see, for example, "Heritability and Cross-Species Comparisons of Human Cortical Functional Organization Asymmetry," by Bin Wan et al. (2022), for

- The reptilian or primal brain—the basal ganglia.

- The paleomammalian or emotional brain—the limbic system.

- The neocortex, the neomammalian or rational brain, including its most recent emergent, the frontal lobe, containing the prefrontal cortex responsible for higher-level cognitive functioning.

We can feel the influence of each of the different layers of the brain acting on us in different ways.

- When we experience the fight-or-flight response, we are experiencing the reptilian brain.

- When we have a craving for fatty or sugary food, we are experiencing the needs of our mammalian brain.

- When we plan out our lives or think about the nature of good and evil, we are deploying our prefrontal cortex, which is responsible for higher-level cognitive functioning.

All of the earlier brains live in us. Each layer is necessary. If one of the previous levels were missing, the new and ostensibly more advanced level would not work. All the previous levels represent an epoch of evolution living in us.[341]

---

an analysis of differences in brain asymmetry, or this easy-to-read summary of the study: "The Hemispheres Are Not Equal," Max-Planck-Gesellschaft (https://www.mpg.de/19224941/0915-nepf-the-hemispheres-are-not-equal-how-the-brain-is-not-symmetrical-149575-x). See also "A History of the Lobes of the Brain," by Stephanie M. Casillo et al. (2020), and "The Triune Brain in Antiquity: Plato, Aristotle, Erasistratus," by Chris Smith (2010).

341 It is worth repeating: We are using the triune model here as a good introductory model to first learn about the structure of the brain, but we are not following its original form of stacking one layer on top of another layer, which is problematic if we want a deeper understanding of neurodynamics and neuroevolution. In line with our models of evolution as Love in action, it is the new configurations of intimacy

Deepening this same theme, your lungs were first developed in fish. Your sight went through about sixty different prototypes in earlier life-forms until it was incorporated in human beings in its present iteration. The way some leading-edge evolutionary scientists talk about evolution living in us is through sentences like "we see only because the Earth has long been inventing the sense of sight."[342] They mean this not just as poetry but as the prose of science. The first glimmer of sight began with early bacteria that are responsive to the presence of light. The eye first appears in the fossil records of around five hundred million years ago. Trilobites, the extinct distant relatives of modern lobsters, horseshoe crabs, and spiders, existed for approximately 300 million years, from about 500 million years ago to about 240 million years ago. It was inside of them that evolution constructed what could be called Eyes 1.0.

According to evolutionary biologist Ernst Mayr, however, this is not the common ancestor of every eye. There have been at least forty independent eye projects initiated by Reality.[343] Each one has unique features. Many previous iterations of eyes, and everything evolution learned from them, live in us.

From the hydrogen atoms that come from the birth of the Universe and are energizing you right now to all the levels of your brain, all of the Universe is alive in you. This is the nature of Reality self-organizing to ever-higher levels of complexity and consciousness. This is but the slightest sliver, just a fragrance of what we mean when we say that evolution lives in us.

---

between the layers that point toward our further evolution.

342 Swimme and Tucker, Journey of the Universe, chapter 6, "Seeing and Sensing."

343 Ernst Mayr, What Evolution Is (2001), 205.

V. FIRST NOTES ON THE ENGINE OF EVOLUTION: EVOLUTION IS DRIVEN BY EROS AND CRISIS

1. Eros Is the Telos of Cosmos

All is known, and permission is given.
—Third-century Talmud

In Section IV.7, we talked about the emergence of a particular molecule essential for our ability to eat and derive energy from food, *cytochrome c.* Here is how Tucker and Swimme describe this process:

> Life's capacity to adapt depends on the occurrence of random changes in the DNA molecule. Different patterns of nucleotides appear by chance, which lead to different proteins within the cell. Possibly millions of such proteins were generated in this way before one molecule, later named cytochrome c, enabled its possessor to survive, which led to the genetic patterns for cytochrome spreading throughout the population. This two-step process—where a vast number of trials are conducted and where the successful trials can be remembered genetically—is what enables us to calmly munch on a slice of bread and transform it into tissue of our hearts.[344]

---

344 Swimme and Tucker, Journey of the Universe, 59.

This description is based on the hypothesis that has long been standard for virtually all evolutionary science: Variations in DNA emerge through random mutations, and those most successful at helping their possessors survive and procreate spread throughout the population by natural selection. The way this hypothesis is often presented, it might seem that the only alternative to complete randomness of mutations is the intelligent design by an all-powerful Creator-God. The religious folks, including some leading scientists among them, seem to line up on the intelligent-design side, while the reductionist materialist folks, including many leading scientists among them, seem to line up on the random-mutations-plus-natural-selection side.[345]

The prima facie assumption of materialists is that there is no inherent intelligence that invests (or even suffuses) Cosmos with order, telos, and direction. The idea of telos is generally perceived as an unscientific heresy. If there is no telos, evolution can move in any one of myriad directions over vast amounts of time, and which way things happened or will happen to turn out is meaningless in any sense of Ultimate Value. It could have just as easily been utterly different. This is the mood of reductionist materialism. It is a mood that is, as Carl Jung pointed out, both contagious and, as he understood so well, insidious to mental health. This, however, is the mood that animates writers like Daniel Dennett, Christopher Hitchens, Richard Dawkins, and the standard assumptions of much of the old-school mainstream academy.

Just as the mood of materialism embraces apparent contingency, a superficial read of the religious mood seems to reject contingency altogether. The notion that the Divine Cosmos doesn't know what is going to happen just doesn't make any sense to this side of the conversation. Most religious folks start the conversation with a prior position that puts God in a severely limiting box. God's role is caricatured as exclusively that of an omniscient king who is fundamentally transcendent to Cosmos—whose relationship to Cosmos is to impose order. Naturally, they view order as evidence of Divine Design and disorder as the enemy. Any expression

---

345 Of course, there are also many exceptions, including biologists who actually study molecular genetics.

of disorder needs to be justified, solved, or explained away.

At the same time, the reductionist materialist folks are hell-bent on explaining the evolutionary process as ultimately rooted in randomness. But anyone who has seriously read the best of the intelligent-design literature or looked at the world through the eyes of contemporary sciences without prejudice knows that the levels of design demonstrated are enormously compelling. But it does not sway the reductionist materialist folks, because their nonempirical, dogmatic, a priori position is that there is no organizing Force in Cosmos. They are therefore compelled to see any apparent design as the expression of chance and randomness. However, the evidence that the pathways of evolution are not fully predetermined, that chance and contingency have their role in the process, is also compelling. Just as the materialist folks ignore evidence of design, the religious folks ignore evidence of contingency. The materialist folks focus on the information that seems to point to randomness at the very heart of Reality—Reality is finding its own way; surprises abound. They conclude that the level of contingency is mutually exclusive with any obvious prior Divine Design that created the world deus ex machina. The process of self-organization is taken to be both inherent to Reality and random—not driven by any transcendent causes (which are caricatured as the dogma of the religionists).

The resolution of this seemingly intractable dilemma, which seems to stand in the way of articulating a shared story, is not simply to pick which intuition appeals more innately to one's sensibilities. The contradiction itself is only apparent. The conversations become so polarized that they stop taking place. There seems to be no room for shared language. The Conversational Cosmos breaks down.

Much needs to be said to uncover the biases of each side in the conversation, which are well beyond the limited scope of this discussion. For now, we will point to only one bias shared by both sides: the caricature of the Divine as a purely omniscient king imposing order, for whom contingency is treason. This leads the materialists to deny the spirit of design, and religionists to deny the spirit of contingency, both of which are obviously misaligned with quite a lot of validated information.

But as interior scientist and evolutionary mystic Abraham Kook points out, the contradiction between contingency and elegant order only exists if you are blindsided by your belief in a God who does not exist (Kook reminds us in his writings again and again that the God you don't believe in doesn't exist). Spirit is not only the beauty, symmetry, and order of Cosmos. For Kook, who is not a liberal reformer but an orthodox practitioner suffused with the texts and intuitions of the Hebrew wisdom tradition, one Face of Spirit is the inherent process of evolution itself. Indeed, Kook writes audaciously that "evolution aligns with the science of the inner mysteries more than any other discipline or *gnosis*."[346] For Kook, matter inheres within consciousness—the pan-interiority that we described earlier, in Section I.2. For our purposes, however, we need only realize that there exists a deeper model of relationship between contingency and design than that of a Divine Overlord external to Cosmos and imposing his or her or its will on it.

Here is an example. I have regular meetings with partners and close colleagues. There is an inner circle I have met with for over a decade, often on a weekly basis.[347] The meetings are never preplanned. There is no formal itinerary, no designated or designed program. These meetings are filled with radical surprise. They are defined by contingency. At the

---

346 See Gafni, in Your Unique Self, chapter 8.

347 Within our community we refer to the weekly conversation described here as Holy of Holies. The term Holy of Holies, in the original Hebrew Kodesh Kodashim, is the formal term that designates the inner space of the Jerusalem Temple, where the famous Ark of the Covenant was said to dwell in ancient Israel. Two other terms deployed in the Talmudic and Kabbalistic literature for this space are Omka Da'Omka, the Deepest of the Deep, and Lefnay u Lefnim, the Inside of the Inside. The Holy of Holies is not, at its core, a physical space but a quality of consciousness. Indeed, in the interior sciences of the Holy of Holies, its measurements, as described in the sacred text, are impossible. It is in this space beyond measure, the space of intensified presence, in which the human being and God meet and realize their ontic identity of wills. The core of that consciousness is Eros. At the center of the Holy of Holies is the Ark of the Covenant. Above the Ark are two erotically entwined cherubs, childlike figures of joy and innocence. In the original sacred text—the Torah—the voice of God is described as emerging from the empty space between the cherubs. The emptiness of the space is, however, paradoxical. On the one hand, it is the space in between, in which Divinity has stepped back to allow for dialogue with humanity. On the other hand, it is empty in the sense that nothing superficial is there. It is a place that is beyond measure.

same time, they are not in any sense arbitrary. Indeed, they are filled with elegant order and inherent design. Pieces, strands of conversation, and themes weave themselves together in a larger whole that would have taken months of painstaking planning had we tried to plan them (and it is doubtful that such predesign could yield that level of elegance, nuance, and depth). The meetings are ultimately meaningful and often disclose depth and originality in an always surprising and often shockingly beautiful fashion.

In the Eros of the meeting, the apparent contradiction between elegant design and contingent surprise disappears. The mediating factor between these two apparent opposites is the telos of First Principles and First Values, which animate, direct, and suffuse the conversation invisibly. The First Principles and First Values of Eros were often spoken about only in the first meeting (which might have taken place a decade before), and never reiterated in the weekly meetings. But they are always there, even if not spoken.

They are, to borrow an image from one great wisdom tradition, the Tao that cannot be spoken, which is the only Tao. The Tao talks about *nonbeing*: This is a chair made up of measurable qualities, but it is nonbeing that creates the chair. By nonbeing, Taoists mean what we are referring to as the First Principle and First Value of Eros: the radical intimacy of Cosmos desiring ever-deeper and wider intimacies. But notice again that the Tao that can be spoken is not the Tao, which means it is not going to be detectable by the instruments of science because it is not measurable in that sense. But it is fully present. This is the Tao of Eros, which is always present. Its unspoken nature, or silence, is not the silence of absence but the silence of presence.

That is the nature of a genuine sacred conversation. Conversation is the erotic structure of Cosmos. Conversations, exchanges of inherent design, proto-interiority, and freedom define Cosmos from its inception. It is in this sense that we join Howard Bloom in referring to Reality as *the Conversational Cosmos*.[348] They take place at every level of evolution, including, of course, the complex, intimate interactions between

---

348 See Section II.3.

macro-molecules within a living cell that is constantly responding to its environment.[349] Just like our sacred conversations, these interactions are governed by the First Principles and the First Values of Cosmos—a creative advance into novelty, always seeking for deeper intimacies and more radical aliveness. In a word, they are animated by Eros. As we suggested in Section IV.7, this is exactly how evolution makes its discoveries, which serve the life's desire for more life, and records them in the language of DNA (or, in the more conventional language, comes up with "successful mutations" that serve survival and procreation).

All the way down and all the way up the evolutionary chain within the Conversational Cosmos, randomness and contingency are, paradoxically, seamlessly interwoven with elegant order and telos. Your mind-body at all levels is in a constant exchange of information with the Cosmos—you are in constant conversation with Reality.

In truly sacred conversations, which are free and open, we are filled with surprise, spontaneity, and freedom, and there is also inherent telos and direction. Such is the nature of the Conversational Cosmos in general. It is guided by First Principles and First Values, not imposed by an external God alienated from reality but emergent from within inherent plotlines of the living Cosmos, far beyond the stale naturalistic/supernaturalistic split.

In effect, the First Principles and First Values of Eros, Intimacy, Desire, Relationship, and their evolution *are* the telos of Cosmos. The plotlines of the *Telerotic* Cosmos include the movement toward ever-wider and deeper creativity, transformation, intimacy, love, relationship, and uniqueness. Each one of these is part of the virtually self-evident telos of Cosmos, which has self-actualized from matter to life to self-reflecting mind (through all the distinct levels of each), always continuing to evolve. It is within the context of this telos—these First Values and First Principles—that the Reality of Cosmos unfolds. In this context, there is no contradiction between freedom and necessity, between randomness and design, between contingency and order.

Eros is full suffusion and presence on the one hand and full freedom

---

349 See, for example, The Biology of Belief, by Bruce H. Lipton (2016).

on the other—living in dialectical relationship. That is the core nature of the Eros that animates Cosmos. Radical presence, which animates, suffuses, seduces, invites, and even subtly directs us, lives dialectically with contingency, freedom, and surprise—with the Possibility of Possibility inherent in every moment. This is not a contradiction but rather the paradoxical nature of Cosmos itself, where, as philosopher/scientist Howard Bloom often states, *opposites are joined at the hip*. In the Eros of Cosmos, we directly experience randomness and contingency on the one hand and elegant order, direction, and design on the other, living together in a higher embrace.

And all the way down and all the way up the evolutionary chain of the Conversational Cosmos, randomness and contingency are seamlessly interwoven with elegant order and telos.

2. Beyond Randomness

The idea of *randomness* (or more precisely, *random mutations*) plays such a crucial role in the mainstream theory of biological evolution and its popular understanding that it is worth taking a closer look at it. In so many ways, the idea of blind chance replaces the idea of God in what is considered—all too often—the modern scientific worldview. In the neo-Darwinist model, random errors in the process of DNA reduplication—not intimate conversations within living cells—are the engine of biological evolution.

How has this hypothesis come into being and become so prevalent in science?

The first step in the emergence of neo-Darwinism was the Darwin-Wallace idea of biological evolution as a series of gradual, incremental changes favored by natural selection. But for natural selection to work, it must have something to select *from*: If, say, there is some variation in the length of a giraffe's neck in a certain population of giraffes, then it might favor those with longer necks because they can reach for higher branches of trees for food, and so the population as a whole might drift toward longer necks. This is, the theory goes, how the giraffe's neck must have evolved from the normal-length neck of its moose-like ancestor. Or, to continue our cytochrome c example from Section IV.7, if some organisms have more efficient chemistry for food processing than others, they would be more likely to live longer lives and have more descendants—so the new feature would be gradually propagated throughout the population by natural selection. The question is, however, how do these useful innovations first appear in the population? Darwin and Wallace didn't have that information, but when the double helix of DNA was discovered (and, to some extent, understood), it seemed like science had finally cracked the secret of life, reducing biology to chemistry (however complex). Here is how it was supposed to work:

A single strand of DNA is a string of nucleotides with four possible nitrogenous bases: adenine (A), thymine (T), guanine (G), and cytosine (C).[350] In the double-helix DNA molecule, the nitrogenous bases point inward, toward the opposite strand, each connecting with a complementary base to form so-called *base pairs* (A connects with T, and G with C). It can be therefore seen as a very long array composed of four chemical "letters" (A, T, G, and C)—a set of inherited instructions on how to grow a biological organism. On the other hand, even before the discovery of DNA, biologists had come up with the notion of *gene* as a fundamental unit of heredity; once the DNA alphabet was discovered, it seemed natural to assume that genes were simply certain smaller arrays of the nucleotide letters. In other words, it was hypothesized that a DNA molecule can be thought of as a string of discrete, atomistic "genes" with specific functions in the life of a biological organism. The variation in observable features of biological organisms (like the length of their necks) would then correspond to minor differences in the gene (or genes) responsible for this feature; if a longer neck gives an organism an advantage in terms of survival and procreation, the corresponding gene variants are more likely to pass to the next generation—and so the average length of a giraffe's neck becomes longer and longer over time.

---

350 For a description of the chemical structure of nucleotides, see Section III.8.

Richard Dawkins's bestseller *The Selfish Gene* (1978) gives the genes an almost God-like status: The whole of life is supposed to have been shaped by the selfish desire to multiply, while the organisms serve as mere biological machines built for just this purpose. However neat this model might be, one problem is, in the words of James Shapiro, "that molecular genetics has made it impossible to provide a consistent, or even useful, definition of the term gene."[351]

He continues:

> The modern concept of the genome has no basic units. It has literally become "systems all the way down." There are piece-meal coding sequences, expression signals, splicing signals, regulatory signals, epigenetic formatting signals, and many other "DNA elements" . . . that participate in the multiple functions involved in genome expression, replication, trans-mission, repair, and evolution.[352]

In other words, our understanding of genome has followed the same path as our understanding of the Universe: A simple atomistic model was replaced by a far more complex and fascinating model in which *conversation* is disclosed as the basic unit of Reality.[353] In the language of CosmoErotic Humanism, the DNA molecule is constantly engaged in complex intimate conversations with itself and its environment within the living cell (and therefore with the larger environment of the cell) and even in conversations between conversations ("conversations all the way down"). Instead of neat bead-like genes on a string, there are complex interweaving conversations biology is barely beginning to understand.[354]

---

351 J. Shapiro, Evolution, 193.

352 Ibid.

353 See Section II.3.

354 To be clear, there is nothing wrong in starting with a simple, neat model as a working hypothesis. But difficulties arise if the model persists even in the face of glaring contradictions of evidence; it is at this point that it becomes a hurdle to our thinking—a dogma rather than the useful tool it was supposed to be.

But the hypothesis of *gene* was such a wonderful fit to Darwin's idea of gradual evolution through natural selection, and it seemed to offer a simple answer to the crucial question of where *innovations* come from. Since DNA was assumed to be the only carrier of hereditary information,[355] the innovations *must* happen in DNA; and since any idea of inherent *telos* (or purpose) seemed to be in contradiction with the fundamental assumptions of science, these innovations *must* occur purposelessly—in other words, randomly.[356] It looks like the *only* source of innovation possible under these assumptions is accidental copying errors in the process of DNA replication, so that the sequence of letters in the new DNA strand would be slightly different from the old one. In DNA replication, the two strands are separated, and each serves as a template for the creation of a new complementary strand (that is, a new T has to be newly assembled for each A, a C for each G, and vice versa). This extraordinary feat is accomplished with the help of quite a few other complex molecules at multiple replication sites at the same time. Replicating a human DNA, for example, involves copying almost three billion base pairs and takes a few hours. Accidental errors are quite possible in a process of this complexity (and in fact, cells have some highly sophisticated mechanisms to safeguard against them).

If there were atomistic genes "for" some features of the organism (like, for example, the length of its limbs or the sharpness of its eyesight), the accidentally created new variant could allow the carriers of the mutation (and its descendants) to run faster or see farther—both

---

355 The new information of evolutionary science reveals growing evidence of nongenetic inheritance; however, these mechanisms are dependent on DNA sequence information. See Evolution in Four Dimensions: Genetic, Epigenetic, Behavioral, and Symbolic Variation in the History of Life (rev. ed.), by Eva Jablonka and Marion J. Lamb (2014), and "Understanding 'Non-genetic' Inheritance: Insights from Molecular-Evolutionary Crosstalk," by Irene Adrian-Kalchhauser et al. (2020).

356 It is essential to draw a distinction between different meanings of the word random that are often fused (and confused) in discussions of this topic. It can be given a precise mathematical sense (which would involve certain assumptions about the distribution of probabilities in a set of actual or hypothetical events), or it can simply mean something done without conscious decision, purposelessly or accidentally.

potentially adaptive mutations, allowing predators to hunt (or their prey to avoid them) more successfully. That's where natural selection would kick in, allowing them to live longer and have more kids of their own. The "selfish gene" would have, quite accidentally, built a better machine for survival and multiplication. That's exactly how Tucker and Swimme describe the mechanism behind the appearance of cytochrome c in the quote that opens the previous section.

But is it really possible that the whole variety of fine-tuned complexity, beauty, and intelligence of life has evolved due to accidental errors in DNA replication? In his many popular books, Richard Dawkins insists that it only *seems* to a naïve mind that this cannot possibly be the case; it is simply difficult, he argues, for the human mind to grasp the miraculous power of natural selection, which effortlessly turns accidental copying errors into what seems like design over long periods of time. Might he be right?

Before we turn to this question, it is essential to note that the idea that the biological evolution is shaped by random mutations plus natural selection is, and has always been, a *hypothesis*, not a scientific fact confirmed by evidence; indeed, it is a hypothesis that cannot, in principle, be confirmed by evidence:[357] Seeming randomness can always turn out to be just a measure of our ignorance; if something appears random, it might be because we simply don't (yet) see the underlying causes. Interestingly enough, even though this kind of hypothesis cannot be confirmed, it *can* be falsified. To oversimplify, there are two ways to do this. One is to show that it is mathematically impossible for the evolution to have happened in this way in the given time frame; the other is to find empirical evidence for *other* mechanisms of genetic innovation (in other words, to study what actually happens rather than to stick with the first working hypothesis and turn it into an article of faith). The neo-Darwinist hypothesis of random mutations as the sole engine of evolution has been falsified in both ways.

In his book *Evolution 2.0*, Perry Marshall succinctly summarizes

---

357 Even if this hypothesis had been formulated in precise mathematical terms, it couldn't be confirmed by statistical methods.

mathematical (in particular, information theory) arguments against this hypothesis.[358] From the perspective of Claude Shannon's information theory, accidental copying errors are equivalent to *noise* in information transfer; they increase *entropy*—in other words, *destroy* order and information (that's why cells have enormously sophisticated mechanisms to guard against any copying errors). If this process is allowed to go on for a long time, this doesn't *increase* the likelihood of more order, complexity, and diversity; quite the opposite—all it can do is create more and more disorder. The idea that it can be the only source of genetic innovation is akin to the idea that printing errors are the sole source of the evolution of literature.

Can natural selection reverse this tendency? No, it can only slow it down, by weeding out some of the noise. More precisely, it might have had a chance to make use of these accidents if it were capable of "testing" them one by one, on the microlevel—that is, if it had a way of knowing that an accidentally modified nucleotide might turn out useful to the organism in the long run. But it can only work on the organism *as a whole*, not on the microlevel—and even the smallest genomes contain hundreds of thousands of nucleotide pairs! That's why the idea of genes "for" some specific organism features is essential for the whole theory: It implicitly suggests that natural selection can immediately "test" each tiny mutation, because it becomes visible to it as a specific feature of the organism (without destroying any of the other sophisticated biological processes).

This point is (perhaps accidentally, but brilliantly) illustrated by Richard Dawkins himself. In *The Blind Watchmaker* (1986), he describes a remarkable computer experiment to illustrate the plausibility of the neo-Darwinist hypothesis. A computer starts with a random sequence of letters, which it randomly changes at every step, one letter at a time—and in only forty-three iterations, it "evolves" into a sentence: METHINKS IT IS LIKE A WEASEL. The problem with this experiment is that in order to model "natural selection," the program actually compared each iteration *with the goal sentence!* If the new string was closer to the goal than the previous one, the iteration was used as the basis for further

---

358 Perry Marshall, Evolution 2.0: Breaking the Deadlock Between Darwin and
Design (2015), 281–302.

"evolution"; if not, it was discarded. In other words, he had to introduce telos into the process in a rather dramatic and radical way—as though the natural selection might have had in mind something *exactly* like a giraffe (or a *Homo sapiens*, for that matter) as its "goal" and was able to compare all accidentally occurring variants of DNA with the "final" DNA needed to grow giraffes (or human beings).

But even more compelling than the information-theory argument, molecular biology has, in the meanwhile, found a variety of other mechanisms of genetic innovation, none of them "random." This doesn't mean that they are deterministic either (that is, their result is not predetermined); instead, there is the same interplay of order and contingency we have described in Section V.I.

James Shapiro writes:

> In combination, cytogenetics and molecular genetics have taught us about many processes that lead to biological novelties "independently of natural selection"—hybridization, genome duplication, symbiogenesis, chromosome restructuring, horizontal DNA transfer, mobile genetic elements, epigenetic switches, and natural genetic engineering (the ability of all cells to cut, splice, copy, and modify their DNA in nonrandom ways).[359]

In all these processes, we can discern the same interplay of orderly constraints (First Principles and First Values) and contingency and spontaneity as in the sacred conversations between human beings. Instead of the human self-reflective mind, they are guided by the inherent intelligence of living cells. In fact, Shapiro insists on using the term *cognition* to describe complex information processing involved in intimate conversations within and between cells. Far from being passive victims of random mutations, cells are capable of intelligently editing and evolving their DNA—that is, literally, *their source code*—foreshadowing our own task of evolving the source code of consciousness and culture

---

359 Shapiro, Evolution, 61.

in response to the meta-crisis.

3. Crisis Is an Evolutionary Driver

Crisis in relationship is an evolutionary driver for new forms of relationship. Of course, this very big idea is totally obvious in our lives. What moves us to a new relationship? What moves us to transform our existing relationship or even ourselves? It is almost always dissatisfaction with the old relationship.

Sometimes the real issue, the crisis, is not in the relationship but in ourselves. In that case, changing or even transforming the relationship will not help. What we need instead is to engage in our own personal transformation. In those cases, even if we move on to a relationship with another person, or change the form of the relationship, the core crisis dynamics will likely remain the same. Instead, the crisis in relationship drives us to engage in deepening our relationship with parts of *ourselves*, in order to become the kind of partner we need to be to live the kind of relationship we want to live.

At the same time, it is often the case that our dis-ease with relationship comes from a deeper source. The crisis is in the essential structure of our intimacy. There is something in the structure of relationship that we are living in that no longer works. It no longer works because our sense of identity has evolved, our Universe Story has evolved, the economy has evolved, or our values have evolved. More often, it is some combination of all of these. The old structure of intimacy can no longer meet our most authentic needs or desires.

Such is our contemporary situation. It is this dynamic that is generating the contemporary crisis in relationship examined in depth in Essays One and Two in the first part of this book. And it is the same dynamic that is generating the global intimacy disorder that can only be healed by a New Universe Story—a new narrative of intimacy, of identity, of power, and of sex. But for now, we need to realize that this relationship crisis is not a problem in the usual limiting sense of the word. Rather, this crisis in relationship is—as crises in relationship have always been—an evolutionary driver to a higher form of relationship. The move from role mate to soul mate to whole mate is an expression of the evolution of intimacy. A new structure of relationship emerges based on a new context of relating. This is a core expression of the evolution of love.

But it is not the first time life on Earth faced an existential risk. Indeed, it was an early existential crisis that gave rise to life as we know it. Life on Earth, in the form of single-celled prokaryotic organisms, appeared almost four billion years ago. Almost two billion years later, over the course of another billion years, entirely new configurations of intimacy emerged. Some simple single-celled organisms, known today as *prokaryotes*, gave up their single status and entered relationships. A series of crises led to the emergence of the complex cells known as *eukaryotes* (and eventually to the emergence of all multicellular organisms inhabiting Earth now). This key transformation in the history of life was called forth by the so-called oxygen crisis (also called the great oxygenation event, the great oxidation event, the oxygen catastrophe, the oxygen revolution, or even the oxygen holocaust).[360] This story is an early example of two core principles:

- Crisis is an evolutionary driver.

- All authentic crisis is, at its root, a crisis in relationship—a crisis of intimacy.

Let's briefly summarize the seven steps of this chapter in the evolution of relationships, which we will then discuss in greater detail:

---

360 Lynn Margulis and Dorion Sagan, Microcosmos: Four Billion Years of Microbial Evolution (1986), chapter 6, "The Oxygen Holocaust."

- Step 1: Cells, in their need for food (energy), learn to access the Sun's energy through the process of photosynthesis, using hydrogen as fuel.

- Step 2: As the free-hydrogen resources on Earth start to get depleted, cells respond to the crisis by learning to fuel photosynthesis with an almost inexhaustible source of hydrogen, water (H2O).

- Step 3: The use of water for photosynthesis releases free oxygen into the atmosphere. This leads to the greatest crisis of early life on Earth, the oxygen crisis, because oxygen is a deadly poison to the early cells (which haven't yet learned to breathe).

- Step 4: Some of these early cells learn to breathe oxygen. For these first aerobic cells, life starts to flourish again. Yet, for the rest of life, the crisis is still a disaster.

- Step 5: The thriving aerobic cells start to invade other large prokaryotes. Over many generations, this leads to symbiosis—a configuration of intimacy we now know as cells with *mitochondria*. These are the first ancestors of eukaryotes, cells that can breathe oxygen through their mitochondria. In the process, evolution invented *symbiogenesis*—the emergence of a new life-form from symbiosis between two different species.

- Step 6: Once symbiogenesis is invented, it happens over and over again, ultimately leading to the emergence of the eukaryotes that we know today. Life on Earth is thriving once again. The growing skill sets of these cells include motility (the ability to move around), sexual reproduction, and DNA repair.

- Step 7: Finally, the single-celled eukaryotes come together in mutual support. Over many generations, they become more and more intimate and even dependent on each other. They give up their single status in a whole new way: The first eukaryotic multicellular organisms emerge.

These early relationship crises were not resolved within the lifetime of the organisms. Rather, relationship learning took place over millions and even billions of years. Hundreds of millions of years lie between the first simple cells learning to use the energy of the Sun and the first cells able to breathe oxygen, and then the first more complex cells called eukaryotes, and finally the first multicellular eukaryotes. This long journey reveals a two-step pattern:

1. The erotic drive for relationship leads to a crisis in relationship.

2. The crisis in relationship leads to the emergence of a next level of relationship.

All of the complex life-forms on Earth today are descendants of the first multicellular organisms that emerged from this series of crises and creative play in response to them. Each crisis led to deepening of intimacy and, ultimately, the emergence of a new level of relationship. That is exactly the mechanism that has been, and still is, the evolutionary driver all the way down and all the way up the evolutionary chain.

Let's now take a closer look at each of these steps.

Step 1: Early Photosynthesis

Early in evolutionary history, single-celled prokaryotic bacteria learned to convert the light of the Sun into energy through photosynthesis.

When molecules absorb light, the electrons of their atoms get excited (that is, they jump into a higher energy state). Normally, that energy is simply dissipated when the electron jumps back to its normal state. Yet evolution came up with a complex, multilayered configuration of atoms and molecules that makes it possible to store energy in the form of *adenosine triphosphate* (ATP), a molecule known as the cell's energy storage medium, found today in all life-forms.

A detailed description of the configuration of intimacy that makes this possible is well beyond the scope of this book; all we can do here is give you a glimpse of its dazzling complexity so you can join us in admiring the ingenuity of our earliest ancestors. What has to be in place for a cell to be able to absorb light and store its energy?

The first element is *porphyrin*, which consists of four pyrrole rings linked to each other by carbon+hydrogen groups; each pyrrole ring is a structure containing one nitrogen and four carbon atoms. This configuration of intimacy keeps an iron atom in its center through its interaction with the four nitrogen atoms. The presence of this iron atom allows this configuration to enter into more complex patterns of intimacy, with a protein or with an oxygen molecule; a protein can also be bound covalently to the side chains of porphyrin. Since first invented, this structure has been remembered, reused, and creatively modified by all kinds of life-forms—including us. Some of the relatives of these early porphyrin compounds circulate in our blood today, carrying oxygen to our cells and giving our blood its red color.

Secondly, you need an *electron transport chain*, a series of protein complexes and other molecules, which are capable of transferring electrons from one element to another, along with a transfer of protons. This happens through a series of so-called *redox* reactions, in which the loss and gain of electrons happen at the same time. The energy from these reactions creates an *electrochemical proton gradient* that drives the synthesis of the ATP molecule.

The ATP (adenosine triphosphate) is a nucleotide.[361] It consists of adenine, a sugar molecule (ribose), and a triphosphate group (that is, its phosphate group contains not one atom of phosphorus, like the adenosine we described in Section III.8, but three, along with oxygen and hydrogen). In the metabolic process, this molecule changes into adenine diphosphate or adenine monophosphate and releases energy. This is how Sun gives energy to life.

Notice how all parts in this multilayered configuration retain their own integrity while sharing identity with other parts of the same whole; the elements converse with each other through sharing and exchanging electrons and protons while fulfilling a shared purpose (absorbing and storing energy) in service of life (shared value)—exactly as described in our Intimacy Equation, which we repeat here for the sake of convenience:

---

361 We described nucleotides in Section III.8.

Intimacy = Shared Identity × [Relative] Otherness ×
Mutuality (Recognition + Feeling + Value + Purpose)

This is but a fleeting glimpse of the intimate conversations between particles, atoms, and molecules that allowed the early bacteria to retain the light energy from the Sun and creatively deploy it in their lives. The insights achieved in these chemical conversations many eons ago laid the foundation for life on Earth as we know it.

Step 2: Hydrogen Crisis

These single-cell bacteria had a constant hunger, a virtually insatiable desire for hydrogen they needed for photosynthesis. Where did they find it?
Lynn Margulis writes:

> Piecing together evidence from my colleagues, I suspect that bacteria first removed the hydrogen (H_2) they needed for their bodies directly from air. Later they took up the hydrogen sulfide (H_2S) belched up from volcanoes. Eventually, blue-green bacteria wrenched hydrogen atoms from water (H_2O). Oxygen was expelled as a metabolic waste product. This waste, at first disastrous, eventually powered life's continued growth. New wastes test life's tolerance and stimulate life's creativity. The oxygen we need to breathe began as a toxin; it still is. The oxygen release from millions of cyanobacteria resulted in a holocaust far more profound than any human environmental activity.[362]

The bacteria were desperate to continue living, even when they were running out of their special hydrogen source. They were fulfilling the desire for life—a clear interior telos, a desire for a particular value built into the structure of the CosmoErotic Universe. In response to the shortage of hydrogen, some early ancestors of cyanobacteria learned to split the water molecules into hydrogen and oxygen and use this hydrogen

---

362 Lynn Margulis, Symbiotic Planet: A New Look at Evolution (1998).

for photosynthesis. As a byproduct of this process, oxygen was released into the atmosphere.

Step 3: A Crisis of Relationship between Prokaryotes and Oxygen

Oxygen is a very reactive atom; it is the second-most electron-hungry element. In other words, it has an intense desire to be in relationship, at first with other oxygen atoms but then also with other atoms and molecules that desire to share their electrons. Said differently, oxygen has great *erotic chemistry* with a lot of other elements and molecules.

As a result, oxygen can damage cells, especially the early anaerobic cells, by creating relationships with all kinds of molecules that are vital to those cells and their reproduction. Oxygen quickly enters intimate relationships with most of the gases in the atmosphere. It also oxidizes minerals, dramatically changing the minerals in the soil to new, oxygen-bound compounds of these minerals.

These intimate processes slowly transformed both the lithosphere—the solid, outer part of Earth—and the atmosphere made up of the gases around it. As long as there were enough metals and gases for the oxygen to be intimate with, it did not build up in the atmosphere. Over tens of millions of years, the freed oxygen was absorbed by atmospheric gases, metal compounds, and minerals in rocks, as well as by living organisms, in small amounts.

Over time, however, more and more of the highly reactive, relationship-hungry oxygen was released into the atmosphere. In other words, the great new skill of photosynthesis began to poison the Earth's atmosphere.

This high amount of free oxygen was deadly to all the early *anaerobic* organisms—organisms that hadn't yet learned to be in a thriving intimate relationship with oxygen. The atmosphere had become so filled with oxygen that all of life was dying. There were times when the atmosphere was so filled with this highly reactive, relationship-hungry oxygen that the early bacteria would literally burn up in flames.

According to a 2013 study,[363] these early prokaryotic bacteria[364] had even developed multicellularity already, more than a billion years earlier than the later evolutionary emergents that we call eukaryotes. These early and simple prokaryotic cells without a nucleus had already deepened their relationships to each other so much that they could become a new whole—a multicellular organism. But that only sped up the process of the transformation of the atmosphere, which became extremely rich in oxygen. Today, we are rightly worried about an increase in atmospheric carbon dioxide from 0.032 to 0.033 percent. About two billion years ago, the Earth saw an increase of atmospheric oxygen from about 0.0001 to 21 percent. Imagine that level of environmental crisis!

To deal with this crisis, most bacteria burrowed themselves deeply in the mud at the bottom of the oceans, where the oxygen couldn't reach them. Relationship was in crisis. For a long time, cells did not know what the next step was.

Step 4: Becoming Intimate with the Oxygen

The only way for life to flourish again was to evolve a new form of relationship with oxygen, and in order to do so, it had to transform itself—as it always does—through creative play of DNA molecules re-organizing themselves. As Lynn Margulis and Dorion Sagan say in their book *Microcosmos: Four Billion Years of Microbial Evolution,*

> Microbial life had no defense against this cataclysm except the standard way of DNA replication and duplication, gene transfer, and mutation.[365]

Some prokaryotes developed a new form of relationship with

---

363 Bettina E. Schirrmeister et al., "Evolution of Multicellularity Coincided with Increased Diversification of Cyanobacteria and the Great Oxidation Event" (2013).

364 Descendants of these anaerobic bacteria still exist in oceans, waters, and even hot springs today.

365 Margulis and Sagan, Microcosmos (1986), 99–113.

oxygen—aerobic respiration, using it to create the ATP molecule (adenosine triphosphate) described in Step 1. In the words of Margulis and Sagan:

> Aerobic respiration, the breathing of oxygen, is an ingeniously efficient way of channeling and exploiting the reactivity of oxygen. It is essentially controlled combustion that breaks down organic molecules and yields carbon dioxide, water, and a great deal of energy into the bargain. Whereas fermentation [which was the most common way of ATP production up until this point] typically produces two molecules of ATP from every sugar molecule broken down, the respiration of the same sugar molecule utilizing oxygen can produce as many as thirty-six. Pushed—not, probably, to its breaking point, but to a point of intense global stress—the microcosm did more than adapt: it evolved an oxygen-using dynamo that changed life and its terrestrial dwelling place forever.[366]

Through creatively evolving their DNA, these microscopic organisms learned to grow faster, breed faster, and live faster.

> The newly resistant bacteria multiplied, and quickly replaced those sensitive to oxygen on the Earth's surface as other bacteria survived beneath them in the anaerobic layers of mud and soil. From a holocaust that rivals the nuclear one we fear today came one of the most spectacular and important revolutions in the history of life. . . . In one of the greatest coups of all time, the cyanobacteria invented a metabolic system that required the very substance that had been a deadly poison.[367]

The new oxygen-breathing, aerobic cells had established a new relationship to the oxygen, which allowed them to flourish and procreate in an oxygen-rich atmosphere. Although the anaerobic species didn't vanish

---

366 Ibid.

367 Ibid.

from the Earth completely, they were no longer the dominant form of life on Earth and were vanquished to low-oxygen environments such as the bottom of the oceans.

Cyanobacteria were now able to both do photosynthesis, which generated oxygen, and breathe oxygen, which consumed it. Not surprisingly, they exploded into hundreds of different forms.

> But most significant, cyanobacteria's continuing air pollution forced other organisms to acquire the ability to use oxygen, too. This set off waves of speciation and the creation of elaborate forms and life cycles among them.[368]

Today, our atmosphere is still relatively rich in oxygen, with us, together with almost all multicellular life on Earth, being descendants of these early oxygen breathers.

Step 5: Symbiogenesis—From Cell Invasion to a New Level of Intimate Relationship

In the midst of this ongoing crisis, the move from crisis in relationship to a new level of relationship occurred again. Different types of bacteria intensified their intimacy through entering into symbiotic relationships:

> With the invention of aerobic or oxygen-using respiration, prokaryotes had tapped into an energy source far beyond their ability to fully exploit. Unaware of the global power they were generating, the respiring bacteria flourished in their local niches all over the globe for hundreds of millions of years. But as the level of atmospheric oxygen was rising up to 21 percent . . . a new kind of cell formed. This was the eukaryotic cell with its key feature, the nucleus, and its important secondary characteristic, oxygen-using cell parts known as mitochondria.[369]

---

368 Ibid.

369 Ibid, 115.

Through a process of what is now known as *symbiogenesis*, two different species of prokaryotes became so intimate with each other that they started to become one—a shared identity with shared purpose, values, feeling, and recognition—the first eukaryotic cell.[370] At first, however, these new relationships were not friendly at all. A cell of the oxygen-breathing species invaded another type of a larger, anaerobic cell and began to change its interiors. In the beginning, this may have often killed the larger cell and, with it, the invader itself. In other cases, the larger cell may have succeeded in killing the invader.

But at some point, after lots of creative experimentation, the intimacy between these two cells deepened in such a way that they became dependent on each other. The original oxygen-breathing cell became part of the larger, anaerobic cell it had invaded. Together, they became a new whole—a new type of cell—that was now able to breathe oxygen. It did so through what is now called its *mitochondria*.

Mitochondria are the descendants of the early oxygen-breathing bacteria in a new intimate relationship with the larger, originally anaerobic cell, of which they are now literally a part.

Let's turn once more to Lynn Margulis and Dorion Sagan for some more details of this story:

> The predatory precursors of mitochondria invaded and exploited their hosts, but the prey resisted. Forced to be content with an expendable part of the prey (its waste) instead of the entire body of the prey, some mitochondria precursors grew but never killed their providers. Time wreaked its changes on both parties. Animosity became interchange. . . . Eventually some of the prey evolved a tolerance for their aerobic predators, which then remained alive and well in the food-rich

---

370 See, for example, "Lynn Margulis and the Origin of the Eukaryotes," by Athel Cornish-Bowden (2017). While there is great agreement among biologists that eukaryotes first arose as the result of a merger of two prokaryotic cells—one of which appears to have been a member of a subgroup of archaea, whereas the other partner appears related to alpha-proteobacteria (which formed the mitochondria)—there are different theories about how exactly this merger happened. See, for example, "The Merger That Made Us," by Buzz Baum and David A. Baum (2020).

interior of the host. The two types of organisms used the products of each other's metabolisms. As they reproduced inside the invaded cells without causing harm, the predators gave up their independent ways and moved in for good. . . . As the predator made itself at home, it gradually lost some of its DNA and RNA.[371]

Once again, we see a precise calibration of allurement and autonomy—competition and cooperation—driving the evolutionary process.

Now, mitochondria are totally dependent on the rest of the cell. They share the host cell's genes which code for the production of some of their proteins, including some of the enzymes required for the replication of their own DNA and RNA. The cell uses the energy that mitochondria derive from oxygen, and the mitochondria use the organic acids which were the prey cell's waste materials. When these processes cease, we and all other composite beings die.[372]

These new configurations of intimacy and relationship—shared identities in the context of relative otherness—were the first eukaryotes. They emerged about 1.5 billion years after the first appearance of life on Earth. It was a huge evolutionary step. Life on Earth exploded and flourished once again.

Step 6: Ever-More Complex Eukaryotes

Over another long period of time, the deepening of intimacies through symbiogenesis continued, and eukaryotes acquired more and more new skills.

Another attempt to enter a new form of relationship between yet another prokaryotic cell and our first eukaryote was followed by another

---

371 Ibid., 127–135.

372 Ibid.

crisis of relationship. It led to another long process of evolution—learning to create and sustain another new type of intimate relationship. Step by step, that was the way different organelles of these newly emergent eukaryotic cells were formed: invasion followed by crisis and a successive deepening of intimacy, until a new shared identity was formed. That process is known today as serial endosymbiosis.[373]

Like mitochondria, which emerged from the very first merger, the so-called chloroplasts emerged from another episode of symbiogenesis. This time, our early eukaryotes were invaded again by prokaryotic cyanobacteria. These cyanobacteria transmitted their ability to turn sunlight into food to the eukaryotes. These new eukaryotes became the ancestors of plants on Earth.

After a lot of creative, erotic, and intimate experimentation and relationship-learning through crises, the increasingly complex eukaryotic organisms acquired other organelles. Apart from the ability to breathe oxygen to produce the usable energy of ATP, eukaryotes learned to move around and repair their DNA.

Meiosis and sexual reproduction were next to appear on the scene. Currently, there is no consensus among biologists on how sex in eukaryotes arose in the process of evolution, what basic function the sexual reproduction served, and why it is maintained, given the basic evolutionary disadvantages of sex.[374] It is clear, however, that it evolved over 1.2 billion years ago. Sex was, as we already noted above,[375] a major advance in the evolution of relationship, which is the evolution of love and intimacy. It was also a breakthrough in the evolution of *uniqueness*: Instead of being essentially a clone of its only parent, now each new organism has a unique recombination of its parents' DNA.

---

373 The theory was developed by Lynn Margulis; see, for example, Margulis's *Symbiotic Planet: A New Look at Evolution* (1998).

374 Among the most limiting evolutionary disadvantages of sexual reproduction is that an asexual population can grow much more rapidly with each generation than a sexual one. See, for example, *The Evolution of Sex*, by J. Maynard Smith (1978).

375 See Section III.9.

Step 7: From Single Cells to Multicellular Organisms

The next step in evolution—multicellular eukaryotic organisms—occurred only recently in evolutionary terms, about six hundred million years ago. Communities of cells were transformed into new wholes, in which they were able to specialize to perform different biological functions for the sake of the whole organism—again, an interplay of allurement and autonomy that drives evolution and leads directly to plants, animals, and human beings.

The inherent self-organizing LoveIntelligence, LoveBeauty, LoveDesire, and LoveValue (or what we have called ErosValue) of Reality moved life to a whole new order of intimacy, relationship, and wholeness. New forms of ecstasy and passion that had never existed before were born directly from this evolution of relationship.

To sum up, the crisis of intimacy and relationship known as the oxygen crisis initiated the first mass extinction on planet Earth. Almost all life was dying. From that crisis emerged new forms of life that were not poisoned by oxygen but energized by it. Life flourished once more. And not only did life continue, but it kept evolving—pulled by creative Eros and pushed by crisis. Each of the steps was huge, happening over a period of hundreds of millions or even billions of years.

> As Stonehill College astronomer Chet Raymo points out, the difference between the new cells and the old prokaryotes in the fossil record looks as drastic as if the Wright Brothers' Kitty Hawk flying machine had been followed a week later by the Concorde jet.[376]

And yet, the Amorous Cosmos, the Telerotic Universe, didn't stop there. From anaerobic to oxygen-breathing prokaryotes, to eukaryotes, to meiosis, to multicellular eukaryotic organisms, to plants, to animals, to us, we went up the evolutionary chain. Crisis in relationship leads to

---

376 Margulis and Sagan, Microcosmos (1986), 99–113. See also Biography of a Planet, by Chet Raymo (1984), 72.

transformation and evolution—to a new level of intimate relationship. Breakdown in relationship leads to breakthrough in relationship.

Director Steven Spielberg tried to evoke something of a bygone era in his famous movie series *Jurassic Park*. The question is, what happened to the dinosaurs? Or said differently, what allowed for the emergence of human life, and what did that have to do with the extinction of the dinosaurs?

Dinosaurs ruled the world for over 150 million years.[377] The only mammals were small, scruffy creatures who stayed in burrows and came out mostly at night. They were terrified of the dinosaurs. Then, on one fine spring day, disaster struck. An asteroid, ten miles wide, traveling at a speed of fifty thousand miles per hour, crashed into Earth. It hit just off the coast of Yucatan Peninsula. The impact was greater than that of all the nuclear weapons in the world detonated at once, with equally deadly effect.[378] The impact of the meteor and the earthquake aftershocks, wildfires, dust in the atmosphere, and tsunamis were of imagination-defying proportions. Most dinosaurs were wiped out. Only a group of small meat-eating dinosaurs, ancestors of birds, remained and continued their evolution. Life on Earth was critically compromised. It was a bad day for evolution, or so it seemed.

But it was precisely this breakdown that allowed for the breakthrough of mammalian and, later, human life. Reality responded with new configurations of intimacy, new forms of life evolving and taking center stage. With their main predators gone, mammals were able to emerge from their burrows, ultimately reaching their apex in the mammals we recognize today, including human beings.

Crisis initiates transformation. Transformation means new life, which means new configurations of intimacy.

---

377 For comparison, evidence suggests Homo sapiens have likely only been around for 300,000 years at most, modern human civilization (if we begin with the Sumerian civilization) for 6,000 years, modern industrialization about 250 years, and the information era about 50 years.

378 A 2019 study suggests that the impact of the meteor that wiped out dinosaurs was as powerful as ten billion World War II nuclear bombs. See "The First Day of the Cenozoic," by Sean Gulick et al. (2019).

4. The Universe Can Be Trusted

The Universe can be trusted to follow certain patterns of evolution. Knowing this is how we begin to *relax* into Reality while at the same time feeling the urgency of our own personal lives—because the trustworthy Universe of course includes us. We, too, are trustworthy expressions of evolution, and this is part of what makes the world a trustable and honorable place. But before we turn to our own lives, let's unpack this new gospel.[379]

The Universe can be trusted to come to the edge of breakdown—and from breakdown, it can be trusted to open a new pathway to breakthrough. Crisis always produces new potential and new possibility.

The Universe can be trusted to break down because evolution meanders. It does not move in a straight line. Evolution engenders crisis. The more things evolve, the more dangerous the crisis. To give a stark example, technology has evolved from bows and arrows to nuclear weapons. Nuclear weapons have the capacity to end human life on Earth. Bows and arrows did not.

The same insights can be expressed differently: The Universe can be trusted to move from crisis to transformation.

Crisis is always an evolutionary driver. And evolution is always driving in the direction of greater intimacy and deeper relationship. Knowing that crisis precedes transformation tells us, for example, that the contemporary crisis in erotic relationship is birthing an entirely new level of relationship. New possibilities for potency and passion are born from the pressure of the crisis seeking new possibility. That is precisely the story of the great oxidation event we just shared.

The Universe can be trusted to move from simple to complex. That

---

379 Etymologically, gospel means good news. That the Universe is honorable and can be trusted is the good news. This is the new gospel of science, which for some supersedes and for other others complements the old gospels.

is how breakthroughs appear. The Universe moves from simple forms to more complex and progressively deeper forms.

The dual capacities for breakdown and breakthrough are directly related to a third feature of Reality that can be trusted: The Universe is ceaselessly creative. It will always bring forth newness. The creative advance into novelty is one of the core stable features of Reality.[380]

The fourth way the Universe can be trusted is that the Universe never leaves any level of erotic depth behind. Complex forms have more layers of depth:

- A quark has one layer of depth.

- A proton (as well as a neutron) is a larger whole that contains quarks as its parts. That is a second level of depth.

- An atom is a larger whole that contains protons, neutrons, and electrons as its parts. That is a third level of depth.

- A molecule contains both atoms and their constituents (protons, neutrons, electrons, and the constituents of the protons and neutrons: quarks). That is a fourth level of depth.

And so it continues all the way up through the cosmological world, into the biological world, and into the human world. A human being is almost infinitely more complex than a quark. But the human being contains all the previous levels of depth, which include all of the major properties of all the previous levels—plus one: the level of the human being.

The fifth way the Universe can be trusted is to move toward ever-greater uniqueness and consciousness. Uniqueness is the natural corollary of complexity; consciousness is the interior of both uniqueness and complexity. The more complex and unique something is, the more potential there is for consciousness. For example, the first mammal[381]

---

380 See Whitehead, Process and Reality, 349.

381 It is now believed to have been Morganucodon.

is both more unique and more complex than an amoeba and more conscious. A human being is both more complex and unique than the first mammal and more conscious. By *conscious* we mean simply the capacity for awareness of self, of the world, and of others, with increasing levels of depth.[382]

There are two very powerful expressions of the evolution of consciousness that are relevant to our discussion:

First, evolution awakens and becomes conscious of itself through us. For the first time in history, in the last several hundred years, we have become aware that the world is evolving. Thanks to Charles Darwin and Alfred Wallace, we realized that the biological world is evolving. More recently, we have realized that the Cosmos itself is also evolving.[383] But

---

382 Here, it is essential to distinguish between complicated and complex systems. In complex systems, there is allurement between the parts. Parts are intimate with each other; that is, a shared identity is generated between the parts with mutualities of recognition, feeling, value, and purpose. Complicated systems are nonintimate without inherent allurement between the parts. More complicated does not necessarily mean more of the integrative and self-aware consciousness that we swim in as humans. Complexity is the quality of many component parts having local interactions based on rules that are not necessarily endowed by an ostensibly higher-order source but rather emergent from the inherent First Values and First Principles embedded in a Story of Value that are activated repeatedly, in a way that generates a collective result of emergent order. Think ant colonies or the swirl of a New York City borough. Complicated is a feature of hyperobjects (see Hyperobjects: Philosophy and Ecology after the End of the World, by Timothy Morton, 2013), like climate change or the globally distributed computational infrastructure of the internet and the devices we use to connect to it. These kinds of hyperobjects, emerging from many interactions among conscious beings themselves, have less of the kind of consciousness that a human has—a multilevel self-aware consciousness—and yet are products of many human agents and machine intelligence. So, we qualify our statement by saying that greater organismic complexity generally means greater organismic consciousness, but greater collective complexity (or rather complicatedness) does not necessarily mean greater collective consciousness. There is, however, the possibility of collectives becoming wholes (and therefore truly becoming complex) that emerge with their own form of proto-organismic consciousness, thus leaping onto a Darwinian evolutionary trajectory—for instance, the emergence of life from autocatalytic networks of peptides that eventually became self-replicating compounds.

383 Charles S. Peirce was perhaps the first to recognize that even the seemingly immovable laws of physics we measure today must have necessarily arisen over

we have also awakened to the realization that culture is evolving. In other words, shared consciousness is evolving.

The second expression of the evolution of consciousness, which is even more dramatic, comes about when we realize that evolution is not a process happening somewhere out there. Evolution happens through us. As we awaken and evolve, both as individuals and collectives, we become both the catalyst for and the expression of culture's evolution. It is our Unique Selves and our Unique We that are the vehicles for the evolution of consciousness.[384] We move from unconscious to Conscious Evolution.

To sum up, the Universe can be trusted to evolve to ever-higher levels of consciousness and uniqueness.

The sixth way the Universe can be trusted is that it evolves to ever-higher levels of Love and Eros. The interior of complexity is consciousness. The interior of consciousness is Eros, Creativity, Love, Fuck, Allurement, and Desire. All these qualities of Eros taken together generate more connectivity between parts that come together to form larger wholes and greater interconnectivity within each whole.

For example, the evolution of love takes place when we expand our

---

time as cosmic habits subject to natural selection ("The Fixation of Belief," 2000). As our measurement instruments get more precise, experimental evidence reveals that even what we view as universal constants (gravitational waves and nuclear decay rates, for instance) show variations; see "Experimental Evidence That the Gravitational Constant Varies with Orientation," by Mikhail L. Gershteyn et al. (2002), and "Perturbation of Nuclear Decay Rates during the Solar Flare of 2006 December 13," by Jere H. Jenkins and Ephraim Fischbach (2009). Lee Smolin has developed a theory of cosmological natural selection, which he calls the fecund universes theory ("Precedence and Freedom in Quantum Physics," 2012, and The Life of the Cosmos, 1999). The evolution of the Cosmos itself is already implied by Einstein's realizations of relativity. Einstein himself was shocked by the notion of an evolving Cosmos and changed his mathematical formula through what he called the cosmological constant to cover up this ostensible indecency. This was soon realized by other scientists as the Hubble telescope and other forms of investigation came online. Einstein himself acknowledged his cover-up and is said to have called it "my biggest blunder." See, for example, My World Line, by George Gamow (1970), p. 44, and Exploring Black Holes: Introduction to General Relativity, by Edwin F. Taylor and John A. Wheeler (2000), p. 11.

384 See Essay One, Section 3, on the concepts of Unique Self and Unique We. These concepts are also explored in depth in Whole Mate.

circles of felt love, care, and concern from egocentric to ethnocentric to worldcentric to cosmocentric circles of intimacy:

- At the first level, I might only care about and love my immediate circle upon whom I depend for survival.

- At the second and higher level, I might expand my circle of love and caring to include my entire people, or tribe, or religion. At this level, I have widened my identity to include a larger circle of love and intimacy.

- At the third and still higher level, I might expand my circle of love and care to include every human being on the face of the planet.

- At the fourth level, I might expand my felt sense of love and care to include all animals on the planet and the planet as a whole as well.

Each level is an expansion of our circle of love and intimacy. This kind of evolution has taken place in culture through the course of history. It also takes place in the life of every individual. How far one is able to evolve depends on the person. The Universe can be trusted to evolve Love.

5. Toward Ever-Greater Intimacy and Ever-Deeper Eros

Let's recapitulate some of the key strands we have woven together in these pages.

We have already seen that Eros, Intimacy, Love, and Fuck are core qualities of Cosmos. We have explored how the forces of allurement and autonomy draw parts toward merger and emergence to create larger wholeness.

The drive toward relationship is an essential feature of Reality. This erotic drive lives in human beings, as it does at every level of Reality. Parts are allured toward each other. We refer to allurement by different names: When describing the relationship between celestial bodies, we call it gravity; when describing the dynamics of attraction and repulsion of subatomic particles, we call it electromagnetism as well as the weak and the strong nuclear forces.

It might seem that calling the force of allurement *gravity*, or *electromagnetism*, or *weak and strong nuclear forces* explains it. It does not. Scientific theory has brilliantly elaborated on how all of these forces operate at every level of the physical world, from the cosmic to the sub-atomic to the human. But the quality of allurement itself is *primary*. It is a mystery that reveals a deeper truth about Reality than either gravity or electromagnetism can capture.

There are many theories in physics that explain gravity—for example, a *graviton* as the carrier of the gravitational field. This postulated but not yet empirically confirmed quantum is analogous to the well-established photon of the electromagnetic field. Like a photon, it would be massless, electrically uncharged, and traveling at the speed of light. A *quantum* is not simply a particle but a part of a quantum field,[385] which can be seen as *quanta* (quantized packages of energy often referred to as particles) when the field is excited—for example, when interacting with other quanta from

---

385 The quantum field theory combines classical field theory, special relativity, and quantum mechanics. It treats particles as excitements or excited states (also called quanta) of their underlying quantum fields, which are more fundamental than the particles. A quantum is the minimal (quantized) amount of a physical entity involved in an interaction—meaning the magnitude of its physical property can take on only discrete values consisting of integer multiples of one quantum. For example, if there are two excitations of the photon field (also known as electromagnetic field), we can observe them as two photons. And three excitations of the electron field will give us three electrons. The ground state of a photon field—also known as its vacuum state—is the state where all quantum numbers are zero—meaning there are zero photons.

a different quantum field.[386] The remaining questions are:

- What is underneath these quantum fields?

- Why do they have the features and qualities they have? What is underneath these qualities?

- What are the simple rules—the First Values and First Principles—governing these fields?

The answer is there is allurement on the one hand and autonomy and integrity on the other. They can be expressed as the integrity of the quanta and in what physicists call *coupling* (that is, an intimate relationship) between the fields. There is nothing underneath these qualities. There is nothing more primary or fundamental. They just are. In that sense, they are revelatory of the nature of the Universe just as it is.

Think for a moment about the one hundred billion galaxies dancing through space that astronomy has only recently revealed. What literally holds Reality together is this quality of allurement, or what Charles Saunders Peirce called *Evolutionary Love*.[387] Allurement, which is always in dialectical tension with autonomy, integrity, or uniqueness, is encoded within all the laws of physics, mathematics, chemistry, and everything else. We often refer to this quality of Cosmos as *Outrageous Love*. Outrageous Love is the quality of intimacy that binds the Cosmos and everything in it together. For the erotic mystics, it is also the quality of Source that births Cosmos.

Allurement is what tells us that we live in an Intimate Universe.

---

386 According to quantum field theory, electrons don't directly interact with electrons, and photons don't interact with photons. Instead, an electron (which is an excitement of the electron field) is the source for an electromagnetic field (or photon field). As both of these fields are quantized in what physicists call the coupling between these fields (or we might call it their intimate relationship), an electron (a quantum of the electron field) can get excited by absorbing a photon (a quantum of the photon field).

387 Peirce, "Evolutionary Love" (1893).

New scientific instruments of modernity are able to observe the quality of allurement as it plays in the objective world. The intimacy that exists between the Sun and the Earth is the direct result of allurement.

Allurement is the quality that draws the seemingly separate parts into relationship. It is a profound and powerful energy that suffuses all of matter, life, and culture at every level of Reality. It is allurement that draws clouds of hydrogen atoms into relationship to form a star. It is the mystery of allurement, operating at the human level, that accounts for the mystery of $1 + 1 = 1$, meaning that two parts $(1 + 1)$ are able to form a larger whole that is one (1).

This quality of allurement, or Outrageous Love, literally shapes the Cosmos on every level, whether we are talking about galaxies, stars, planets, subatomic particles, cells, plants, animals, or humans. CosmoErotic Humanism, based on the core principles of allurement, as well as the insights of all the other exterior and interior sciences, draws all these levels and dimensions of Cosmos together in relationship. CosmoErotic Humanism, with its methodology of anthro-ontology, tells us more than that, however. Not only does Outrageous Love move all of these levels together in relationship, but it also moves them toward higher and higher *levels of relationship.*

The exterior sciences reveal that the desire for deeper intimacies between celestial bodies, elementary particles, cells, amphibians, and other animals is a driving force of evolution. As we have seen, at each higher level of relationship, there is more love—more intimacy, more interconnectivity, more depth, and more unique expression. This evolution of love amplifies exponentially on the human level. All of it is driven by allurement, by Eros, by the incessant drive of Outrageous Love to ever-deeper levels of creativity. The movement of Outrageous Love always drives Reality to higher and deeper levels of relationship.

The Outrageous Love that drives Reality to higher levels of relationship between celestial bodies, galaxies, and elementary particles is the same quality that allures us humans to higher levels of intimate relationship. It is a movement toward relationship, and it is an attraction to aliveness. Evolution moves toward more and more aliveness generated by emergence, which itself is motivated by the desire for new intimacy. The progressive deepening of intimacies continues all through what we call the Four Big Bangs—cosmological, biological, and cultural evolution, followed by the emergence of a New Human and a New Humanity—*Homo amor*, the fulfillment of *Homo sapiens*. The evolution of relationships—which is the essential plotline of the evolutionary story—continues through every one of the Four Big Bangs. We call them Big Bangs, as each of them is a huge explosion of something completely new—a new emergent—into Reality that cannot be explained only by what came before.[388]

The evolution of relationships depends directly on the evolution of identity; breakthroughs in evolution depend on the drive toward more and more Eros, as well as on crisis as the evolutionary driver. As identity evolves through every level of consciousness, so too does the nature of relationship. Crisis at one level of consciousness births a new level of consciousness. The new level of consciousness co-arises with a new level of identity and a new level of relationship.

This is true at all stages of evolutionary unfolding:

- An atom is a new identity, greater than the sum of its subatomic parts, even as it has a deeper interiority or consciousness and a deeper set of relationships.

- A cell is a new identity, greater than the sum of its previous molecular parts, with a deeper interiority or consciousness and deeper relationships.

On the human level, the same set of principles applies. It is One Cosmos, and shared principles of Evolutionary Love and the evolution of love apply across all levels of Reality.

From the exterior perspective, this evolution of consciousness expresses itself on the human cultural level in the move from hunter-gatherer to farmer to industrialist to programmer; ultimately, it may move

---

388 We are borrowing the term from H. Rolston III (Three Big Bangs: Matter-Energy, Life, Mind, 2010), but we are introducing a fourth Big Bang. For a more detailed look at the Story of the Four Big Bangs, see Essay Three.

entirely beyond societal roles altogether.

From the interior perspective, this evolution of consciousness and identity on the human cultural level is the move from archaic (early survival clans) to magic (tribes) to mythic (empires and great religions) to mental (modern science and democracy) to integral structure of consciousness. Each new level of consciousness births new structures of relationship.

CONCLUSION

THE GREAT INVITATION

1. A Brief History of Human Community

The evolution of relationship to deeper and wider frames is the core engine of evolution, not only for individual human beings but also for humanity as a whole. Humanity's basic evolutionary movement is to ever-wider circles of relationships. Widening and deepening the nature and reach of our relationships is the essential movement of Cosmos, from subatomic particles all the way up to new visions of a harmonious global community. It is all rooted in relationship. The closer we get—literally, as well as psychologically and spiritually—the more potential there is for creativity, evolution, passion, power, and possibility.

- When a star is born, simple atoms are brought into very close proximity to each other. Through this intensification of intimacy, known in science as compression, different kinds of stars and supernovae produce more than a hundred new elements.

- When individual cells intensify their intimacy by staying in close connection, new forms of relationship are formed, eventually giving birth to plants and animals.

- New forms of community and civilization emerge from people getting close to each other on all levels. Each level of deeper closeness brings with it new creative explosions of new power, potency, and passion.

In the next few paragraphs, we will briefly tell the story of the intensification of relationship and intimacy as it appears in ever-deepening communities of relationship.[389]

1. Families and Clans. Even before the emergence of language, we start with clans made up of groups of families. There are no more than a few dozen individuals. Everyone has a clear role, and that role supports the survival of the clan. Everyone within the clan loves and is kind to each other. Others are seen as a threat, unless a relationship is worked out that makes another group an ally or friend of the family or clan. The family, or clan, makes a living by being hunter-gatherers. This is the status quo for hundreds of thousands and perhaps millions of years.

2. Tribes. Symbolic language appears within the past half-million years (its early forms were likely much simpler than the modern human languages). Language contributes to the emergence of an entirely new level of intimacy. Intimacy in clans was based primarily on the more primitive motivators of shared fate and the struggle to survive. New levels of moral code and shared beliefs, enabled by language, weave a new fabric of intimacy beyond what was possible in clans.

Deeper intimacy is also fostered by collective ritual and the sense of invisible lines of connection within the tribe, rooted in magical beliefs. Language makes possible deeper levels of expression and, therefore, new modes of intimacy, not only in the wider space of the tribal culture but also in the more private space between partners.

Being part of the tribe is core to identity. There is a larger intimacy with the whole tribe. The worst punishment is to lose that larger intimacy—to be shunned from the tribe. The size of the tribe is larger than

---

389 This section directly draws on two overviews, which we thankfully acknowledge: Thank God for Evolution: How the Marriage of Science and Religion Will Transform Your Life and Our World, by Michael Dowd (2008), chapter 16, and Journey of the Universe, by Brian Swimme and Mary E. Tucker (2011), chapter 9.

a clan, reaching up to several hundred people. This new wider form of intimacy and relationship transcends and includes clans. Tribes include clans but add a whole new emergent level of intimacy.

3. Kingdoms. In the last seven to ten thousand years, a new level of relationship and interconnectivity has been enacted in the form of kingdoms. These are far larger than tribes. In part, this is made possible by the first forms of recorded communication, including records for collecting debts and administering justice. The earliest forms of writing also facilitated the creation of social structures guided by a central authority.

This new larger field of intimacy and relationship transcends and includes both tribes and clans. Kingdoms include the structures, interactions, and felt sense of connection between clans and tribes but adds new emergents: the ability to record debts through primitive records, which enables tracking of people, events, and alliances and keeping records of laws, punishment, and ritual obligations. All of this allows for the emergence of a new level of governance, but it also fosters a larger sense of relationship and identity. Some people now feel identified with and responsible for not only their family, clan, and tribe but for the entire kingdom.

4. Early Nations and Empires. The next and far wider field of intimacy and relationship is early nations and empires: for example, the Roman Empire, a huge state that included several kingdoms.

This new intimacy is enabled by the emergence of more intricate forms of writing and mathematics. This allows for much deeper levels of cooperation and complexity in government, administration, and precise expression. Ideas, laws, instructions, and governance can all be clearly written out and transmitted to a very wide variety of people. This new large class of readers and writers can then administer as well as protect and provide for a much larger swath of land and much larger groups of people. The recording of shared narratives and the articulation of principles of ethics, justice, and law enable the creation of vastly larger in-groups of people.

Identity moves past geographic region or bloodline affiliation. One can join the empire, in theory if not always in practice, based on pledging allegiance to the principles of the empire. This is a huge leap forward in creating larger fields of relationship and intimacy. Empires and states transcend and include all the features of clans, tribes, and kingdoms, plus all the new emergent features of empires and states.

5. Democracies, Corporate States, and Global Markets. This new level of relationship and intimacy is a momentous leap beyond anything that came before. It is facilitated, in part, by the emergence of science and industrialization. It makes full use of the printing press. All this enables precise and nuanced communication between millions of people, who are easily connected to each other and able to subscribe to a shared vision.

In all of the previous levels, there was always an in-group and an out-group. As intimacy evolved, the in-group got progressively bigger, and it was more possible to join, while the out-group got smaller. The Roman Empire was much bigger than a kingdom. It was also easier to become a citizen because you simply had to accept and pledge loyalty to the principles of the empire. But democracies and global markets are far easier to join than the Roman Empire. Citizenship is an inalienable right in a democracy, and anyone who has the capacity is welcome to play in the global markets. Everybody, at least in potential, can become part of the government, which decides on the frameworks for the markets and the general rules inside of the given system.

At all the earlier stages, it was very hard to take the perspective of the stranger. The person in the out-group was considered to be of an almost different order of being.[390] Empathy with the out-group was not generally possible. At this new level of intimacy, the value of every individual is asserted in a way that has never been done before. This is the basis of democracy. Individuals choose their leadership, and every citizen has a vote. This is, in and of itself, a fundamental evolution of love, recasting the fabric of intimacy and the nature of relationship in a profound way.

For the first time in the world, there is a recognition that, at least in theory, there should be no out-group. This emerges from a dramatic evolution of intimacy and relationship, in which people are able to identify with all other human beings, whether or not they are part of

---

390 A notable exception is Hebrew wisdom's insistence on loving the stranger. This was the first seeding of consciousness with a higher vision of love beyond the in-group.

their particular religion, country, or race. This leads, for the first time in history, to the abolition of slavery in all the countries that have adopted democracy. Democracy is, on all of these counts, a revolution in relationship and intimacy.

Democracies transcend and include families, clans, tribes, religions, and regional kingdoms. All of these features remain in some manner. Family loyalty, for example, does not disappear in a democracy. But it no longer commands the same level of loyalty it did when it was the exclusive measure of identity. The old intimacies remain, even as they are dramatically transcended by the new and wider intimacies. The new intimacy is being a citizen with inalienable rights in a self-governing democracy. This creates a new level of relationship, which in turn catalyzes whole new possibilities for personal relationships and love.

Until now, in all of the forms of society we have seen, relationship between partners was some form of **role mate relationships**. The partners each had roles prescribed by the clan, tribe, kingdom, empire, or religion. To be in a good relationship meant to be good role mates. It may have also meant to raise children in accordance with the social and spiritual dictates of society. At each level of new emergence, new roles emerged. These roles were almost exclusively dictated by an external set of laws, obligations, and expectations, imposed by society on the individual. To live a good life was to fulfill your role in the best way possible, according to society's dictates.

In the new industrial democracies, a whole new set of factors fanned the first flames of **soul mate relationships**. They were still far from primary. Role mate relationships were still the determining factor in personal intimacy. But the winds of change were in the air: If you are choosing your elected leader, then your personal preferences clearly matter; if you have inalienable rights, then your personal preferences clearly matter. In a word, self-governance, individual human rights, and a larger identity with democracy beyond religion and family all came together to make personal preference a new factor in choosing a partner. It was still very far from the dominant factor. Playing one's role effectively, as provider and protector and homemaker, was still primary. But the first glimmer of the fire made its appearance, the fire that would ultimately explode into soul mate relationship.

However, for the full appearance of soul mate relationships, intimacy had to extend to equality between men and women. The equality wouldn't be fully realized until the emergence of the best of modern feminism in the 1960s—meaning equal rights, equal work, equal pay, and equal opportunity. As this becomes part of the new social consciousness, soul mate relationship becomes the new dominant relationship mode. Role mate does not disappear. Rather, people want their partners to be both role mates and soul mates. We talk about this in depth in the first volume.[391]

6. Global Governance. The final form of intimacy expresses itself again in a new structure of society and governance. This new stage of intimacy is just about to burst into the mainstream. It is a new form of global governance.[392] It will recognize that the new challenges we face are global, not local. It will not abolish local democracies and their power but will introduce a larger global and evolutionary context.

Living in an evolutionary context emerges from an evolution of consciousness, which births new qualities of intimacy that have never been seen before. This new level of consciousness will birth an entirely new level of relationship, characterized by an entirely new quality of personal intimacy and relationships. We have called this new level of intimacy and relationship *whole mate* or *evolutionary* relationships. Whole mates live not only to fulfill their socially imposed roles (as role mates) and not only for their personal fulfillment and love (as soul mates). Whole mates live in an evolutionary context. They feel connected to, and intimate with, the Whole of Reality.

They identify not only with their democracy or even with all human beings. They identify with the evolutionary impulse itself, which they feel awakening in them. Their love is not merely the expression of social and spiritual roles or the intensities of personal love between only two. Their

---

391 Gafni and Hubbard, Whole Mate, especially chapters 2 and 3.

392 Note that we are not talking about a global government here. Governance refers to the coordination of transnational actors, the facilitation of cooperation, the resolution of conflicts, and the alleviation of collective action problems, e.g., by making, monitoring, and enforcing rules; see, for example, Global Governance in a World of Change, by Michael N. Barnett (2021).

love is an expression of the Evolutionary Love that animates the entire process of evolution and drives it forward. It includes the sense of duty and honor of role mate relationships and the deepest love of soul mate relationships, but it transcends them by adding the new dimension of whole mates. Whole mates intend their love and service not merely for their own success but for the sake of the larger Whole.

They may be focused on their spiritual or psychological development, or on their family, but whole mates in evolutionary relationships do not stand only for their own integrity, their own fulfillment, or even their own transformation. Rather, they often see their own fulfillment, development, and transformation as being not only for themselves but also for the sake of the larger Whole. They have a felt sense of intimacy with the larger Whole. That is what it means to live in an evolutionary context and have an evolutionary relationship to life.

This new context of intimacy introduces a new form of passion and potency. This new possibility is enacted when the couple awakens as Love and in service of its evolution. The key dimensions of this evolution of consciousness, which fosters a momentous evolutionary leap in relationship, are explored in depth in the first volume.[393]

2. We've Got to Get Ourselves Back to the Garden

Every level of evolution brings in, and is birthed by, an evolutionary leap in relationships. What emerges is something undeniably new, greater than the sum of all the parts that preceded it. Between fifty and two hundred thousand years ago, the ladder of emergence, driven

---

393 Chapters 5–7.

by Outrageous Love, brought forth *Homo sapiens*. The bards Crosby, Stills, Nash & Young end their 1960s ballad "Woodstock," written by Joni Mitchell, with the words

We've got to get ourselves back to the garden.

They refer to the poetic image of the Garden of Eden, where there was one man and one woman. It was the first relationship on the human level. At least one thing was clear: They knew that they were meant for each other, because there was no one else. And at least for a time, they felt like they were in the Garden of Eden.

But they could not stay in the garden. For higher levels of love to evolve, the mythical Adam and Eve—lines and circles—needed to evolve up from Eden. Eden was all about harmony and closeness between lines and circles. However, as we have seen, the nature of relationships is not merely closeness and communion. It is also autonomy, creative tension, and polarity. It is in the space in between both forces that the Intimate Universe births relationships that are both passionate and stable.

In the great mystical traditions of the perennial philosophy, we were not thrown out of the Garden of Eden but left it in a moment of relationship rupture. God is the first marriage counselor. In the mythical story, Eve eats from the forbidden fruit, and Adam, rather than finding his part in creating the rupture, chooses to deploy a blame frame. He blames Eve, and Eve blames the snake. No one takes responsibility. The relationship goes through its first crisis.

But from this crisis comes transformation. This is the beginning of the journey up from Eden. The great journey of human relationships has begun. As we have already seen, there are three great stages in this journey: role mate, soul mate, whole mate. Each new stage of relationship holds a particular level of consciousness. The entire point of this book is that the evolution of relationship belongs to the inherent structure of Cosmos itself. Thus, the evolution of relationship from role mate to soul mate to whole mate is not merely a new random social construct but an expression of the essential movement of Cosmos—the evolution of relationship and intimacy.

As humanity, we have already experienced the first two stages. The second stage, rooted in the second level of consciousness, is ending now (at least in the Western democracies). However, when a new stage begins, the stages that came before it do not disappear. The new stage transcends and includes the best elements of the previous stages.

We've got to get ourselves back to the garden.

This will not happen by bemoaning the current state of relationships. It will not happen by harking back to the good old days, when men were men and women were women. It is true that, at this pivotal evolutionary moment, we want to be informed by the best memories of yesteryear—by the previous two stages of relationship. Recovering an accurate memory of the past is always essential to recovery of health. T. S. Eliot, another bard of relationship, wrote:

> *We shall not cease from exploration*
> *And the end of all our exploring*
> *Will be to arrive where we started*
> *And know the place for the first time.*[394]

We need to recover the highest memory of the best of our relationships in days of yore, but evolution is now birthing new possibilities for passion and intimacy. This is level three, evolutionary relationships. This is the vision of becoming a whole mate. This is not merely a memory of the past but a memory of the future, the promise that must be kept. It promises a level of potency, passion, and power for which we do not yet have adequate words. It is the pull of this great possibility that keeps us yearning.

We know that intimacy, relationships, and therefore life can be so much more. We have a glimmer in our hearts of a world so much better than anything we have dared to admit to ourselves. That glimmer is the invitation to whole mate relationship—beyond lines and circles. It is

---

394 T. S. Eliot, "Little Gidding," originally published in 1943. See, for example, Four Quartets, by T. S. Eliot (2023).

from the level of whole mate relationship that we will be able to live in relationship to the Whole and, in so doing, become whole ourselves.[395]

3. Conscious Evolution

Science's new discoveries revealed two major principles alive in Reality:

- Creativity is not external but inherent to Cosmos.

- All of the previous levels of Cosmos live in us—subatomic particles and atoms from the Big Bang, from stars, and from supernova explosions, molecules, complex molecules, cells, and multicellular organisms, all the way up the chain of matter and life. Not only are we at home in the Universe, but the Universe is also at home in us.

We begin to understand what it means that evolution awakens as us in person. Our creativity is not separate from the creativity of all the previous stages of evolution. Rather, evolutionary creativity is awakening in us.

The entire process of human evolution, through all its stages, is the same process that has been happening all along. The same principles are at play in cosmological evolution (atoms, stars, galaxies, planets), in biological evolution (cells, plants, animals, mammals), and in our own human evolution from prehistoric to modern man. The entire grand process is driven by the evolution of new and deeper forms of intimacy. The core expression of intimacy is relationship—between celestial bodies, chemical compounds, cells, plants, animals, and humans.

For the first time in history, our choices have the capacity to change the future of evolution, because the evolution of ever-deeper forms of relationships drives the evolution of all of Reality to ever-deeper, more complex, more aware, more full, and more passionate expressions of life.

---

395 See Essay Two.

But there is one more essential step. Our success has given us power that we never had before. In the mid-nineteenth century, there were half a billion of us on the planet; today, there are more than eight billion. Our creative capacities have produced forces of destruction that never existed before in the history of Reality. For the first time ever, not only our future but the future of humanity and many other species on Earth rests in our hands.

We have the power to destroy everything.

We have the power to create a world of goodness, truth, and beauty beyond what has ever been seen.

We begin to understand why our unique creativity is, for the first time, able to consciously participate in the next stages of evolution. We wake up to Conscious Evolution.[396] Conscious Evolution simply means that we realize that the evolutionary process is living in us. We are not separate from the Universe. We are a conscious expression of the Universe's power of self-organization.

At the human level, self-organization involves not just physical or biological structures. It involves structures of consciousness. For example, the evolution from papyrus to the printing press is the evolution of tools of communication that allow for an evolution of consciousness (both individual and collective). The parallel evolution of governance from monarchy to democracy, however, is based on that evolution of consciousness. The awareness that every human being has inalienable and irreducible rights lies at the core of democracy.

The evolution of consciousness is the evolution of identity. It opens up a space of intimacy with oneself that simply did not exist before. The evolution of identity opens the door to the evolution of relationships. Catalyzing, clarifying, deepening, and humbly participating in this evolution of identity, which fosters the evolution of relationship, which is the evolution of love, is the purpose of these volumes.

---

396 This doesn't mean that evolution is only becoming conscious in us, as implied by Barbara Marx Hubbard's well-known formula, from evolution by chance to evolution by choice. It only means that we are becoming conscious of evolution happening through us. This crucial distinction is explored in more depth in Whole Mate, especially in chapter 8 (entry 8).

4. The Time Is Now

King Solomon in ancient Jerusalem knew something about timing. He wrote:

> There is a time for everything,
> and a season for every activity under the heavens.
> A time to be born and a time to die,
> a time to plant and a time to uproot,
> a time to kill and a time to heal,
> a time to tear down and a time to build,
> a time to weep and a time to laugh,
> a time to mourn and a time to dance,
> a time to scatter stones and a time to gather them,
> a time to embrace and a time to refrain from embracing,
> a time to search and a time to give up,
> a time to keep and a time to throw away,
> a time to tear and a time to mend,
> a time to be silent and a time to speak,
> a time to love and a time to hate,
> a time for war and a time for peace.

Sensitivity to time and its deep rhythms is essential to the evolution of love.

This is true from the very beginning of time. Perfect timing manifested protons, atoms, and stars, which led to galaxies and eventually to the birth of higher forms of life. If the timing, or what is called the expansion rate or the rate of the spatial emergence, had been a trillionth of a second faster, the elements of the Universe would have been too widely spaced for our Reality to manifest. If it had been a trillionth of a second slower, Reality would have collapsed in on itself.[397]

---

397 Brian Swimme and Thomas Berry, The Universe Story (1992), 18.

In many ways, we have lost our connection to the depth quality of time's invitation. This might have increased efficiency and productivity, but it has also caused the loss of intimacy and of the deep sense of location in the natural rhythms of the Universe.

With the creation of the clock in the early modern period, society organized itself around the ticking hands. There was no longer any need to be aligned with the natural patterns of the Sun's rising and setting. The mechanical marking of time became the primary organizing principle of human life.

It allowed for the massive organization of people into work shifts that punched clocks according to artificially measured time. The whole human world is tied into this sense of time, cut up into little discrete units. What was lost was a deep sense of location in the invitations of time. The sense of alignment with time's rhythms was effaced in the race for production, which gratified the ego's need to achieve and thereby be rewarded. The natural location of a person in the rhythms of time and nature was overridden. Billions of human beings are plugged into this vast matrix of production that serves inchoate goals that are often at odds with our deepest needs.

Getting a sense of evolutionary time is essential to knowing when it is your moment in life to transform.

There are many names given to the two distinct forms of time. Some call them *Chronos* and *Kairos*. We will use the words *mechanical time* and *evolutionary time*. Mechanical time is efficient at measuring time in small units that serve productivity. Evolutionary time understands that time is an invitation. Indeed, in some of the ancient Semitic languages, the word for *time* also means *invitation*. Time is an invitation for emergence. Every moment of time and every epoch of time has a unique quality, which has the capacity to birth a new emergent. Feeling into the inner quality of time is a subtle exercise that requires practice.

One of our last vestigial memories of time's quality of invitation are birthdays, anniversaries, and holidays. In a world of mechanical time, they make no sense. Arguments frequently arise around them in relationships because we do not quite grasp them anymore, even as we intuit their potential significance.

When is the invitation ripe for you to go to the next level?

The core quality of evolutionary time is what science calls emergence. There is a moment when things can emerge. A moment that's too early or too late will not birth them. Had galaxies tried to emerge any earlier, the forces of the Universe at the time would have torn them apart instantly.

We also live at a very specific moment in time. Do we kill time or let it birth its emergents through us? Are we one day closer to the new possibility, or are we farther away from ourselves, struggling to meet a measurement that is alienated from our true measure? Two people reading one clock may have very different answers for what time it is. Is it late or early? Is time slipping away or catching up?

Two images of the clock give us positive and negative versions of how love thrives or falters. In William Faulkner's *The Sound and the Fury*, Quentin Compson, the protagonist, is soon to commit suicide. The most startling image of his last day is a clock that he hears incessantly chiming. The face of the clock is broken. The hands no longer measure time. But it keeps chiming, with maddening regularity, as time slips away. Faulkner borrowed the title for his book from Shakespeare's *Macbeth*. Toward the end of the play, Macbeth cries out,

Tomorrow and tomorrow and tomorrow
Creeps in this petty pace from day to day
To the last syllable of recorded time. . . .
Life's but a walking shadow, a poor player
That struts and frets his hour upon the stage
And then is heard no more. It is a tale
Told by an idiot, full of sound and fury,
Signifying nothing. [398]

Macbeth asserts that the hour of our lives is insignificant, merely marking time on our walk to oblivion.

Standing against Quentin Compson's clock and Macbeth's measure, is the clock of the Seer of Lublin.

---

398 Macbeth, act 5, scene 5, lines 22–24, 27–31.

The inn was silent but for the sound of the impatient clock, the clod of heavy boots, and the innkeeper's tossing and turning. One of the guests at the inn, Yissachar Ber of Radshitz, student of the Seer of Lublin, and himself a master, paced the floor of his room, unable to sleep, mysteriously animated further by every passing moment. The innkeeper, whose room was right below the master, was kept awake and unhappy the whole night by his apparently insomniac guest.

When morning finally dawned and Yissachar Ber came downstairs, the innkeeper could scarcely control himself.

Why did you dance around your room the whole night? he demanded.

Are you mad?

Yissachar answered the question with a question.

Tell me, where did you get the clock in that room?

Why does it matter! It obviously didn't work—or you would have realized how many hours you wasted pacing your floor and keeping me up!

Yissachar tried again: *Forgive me if I disturbed you. I do apologize, but I must know. Where did you get that clock? For it must be the clock of my teacher. I can tell by the way it chimes.*

The innkeeper's anger was turning to curiosity.

And who was this teacher? he asked.

My teacher was the Seer of Lublin.

The innkeeper was amazed, for indeed, the clock had originally belonged to the Seer. It had been inherited by the Seer's son and then given to the innkeeper in payment of a debt.

But how is it that your master's clock could chime differently than any other clock? the innkeeper had to ask.

Yissachar Ber answered him, *Most clocks chime saying, 'Another day gone, another day gone.' But my master's clock says, 'One day closer, one day closer . . . '*

Yissachar Ber was able to infuse the clock with time's invitation. Mechanical time became animated by evolutionary time. There is a new possibility waiting to emerge. There is something wanting to be born, a new possibility for relationship, and the time is now.

There is a time for everything.

There is a time for line and circle relationships, and a time for going beyond line and circle relationships. The time for going beyond line and circle is now.

There is a time for role mate relationship. There is a time for soul mate relationship. And there is a time for whole mate relationship. The time for whole mate relationship is now. This book is your invitation to participate in that evolution.

Let's begin!

BIBLIOGRAPHY

Adrian-Kalchhauser, Irene, Sonia E. Sultan, Lisa N. S. Shama, Helen Spence-Jones, Stefano Tiso, Claudia Isabelle Keller Valsecchi, and Franz J. Weissing (2020). "Understanding 'Non-Genetic' Inheritance: Insights from Molecular-Evolutionary Crosstalk." *Trends in Ecology & Evolution.* 35 (12), pp. 1078–1089 (DOI: 10.1016/j.tree.2020.08.011).

Aldaz, Silvia, and Luis M. Escudero (2010). "Imaginal Discs." *Current Biology,* 20 (10), pp. 429–431. (DOI: 10.1016/j.cub.2010.03.010).

Aristotle. *Metaphysics,* translated by W. D. Ross (2009). https://classics.mit.edu/Aristotle/metaphysics.html.

Arnett, Joe (2014). "Coevolution and pollination." *Washington Native Plant Society. Botanical Rambles.* (https://www.wnps.org/blog/coevolution-and-pollination/).

Baldwin, James Mark (2009). *Genetic Theory of Reality.* Transaction Publishers, New Brunswick, New Jersey.

Balzer, Ashley (2020). "NASA's Roman Space Telescope to Uncover Echoes of the Universe's Creation," on the NASA website (https://www.nasa.gov/missions/roman-space-telescope/nasas-roman-space-telescope-to-uncover-echoes-of-the-universes-creation/).

Barnett, Michael N., Jon C. Pevehouse, and Kal Raustiala, eds. (2021). *Global Governance in a World of Change.* Cambridge University Press, Cambridge.

Baum, Buzz, and David A. Baum (2020). "The Merger That Made Us." *BMC Biology,* 18 (72) (DOI: 10.1186/s12915-020-00806-3).

Berkowitz, Eliezer (2010). *Not in Heaven: The Nature and Function of Jewish Law.* Shalem Press, Jerusalem.

Berry, Thomas (2006). *Evening Thoughts: Reflecting on Earth as Sacred Community.* Sierra Club Books, San Francisco.

Bianconi, Eva, et al. (2013). "An Estimation of the Number of Cells in the Human Body." *Annals of Human Biology,* 40 (6), pp. 463–471.

Biernacki, Loriliai (2023). *The Matter of Wonder: Abhinavagupta's Panentheism and the New Materialism.* Oxford University Press, Oxford.

Bloom, Howard (2016). *The God Problem: How a Godless Cosmos Creates.* Prometheus, New York.

Bohm, David (2002). *Wholeness and the Implicate Order.* Routledge, London.

Buck, John, and Sharon Villines (2007). *We the People: Consenting to a Deeper Democracy.* Sociocracy.info, Washington, DC.

Capra, Fritjof (1975). *The Tao of Physics: An Exploration of the Parallels between Modern Physics and Eastern Mysticism.* Shambhala; Random House, Berkeley, California.

Capra, Fritjof (1996). *The Web of Life: A New Scientific Understanding of Living Systems.* Anchor Books, New York.

Capra, Fritjof (2004). *The Hidden Connections: Integrating the Biological, Cognitive, and Social Dimensions of Life into a Science of Sustainability.* Anchor Books, New York.

Capra, Fritjof, and Pier Luigi Luisi (2014). *The Systems View of Life: A Unifying Vision.* Cambridge University Press, Cambridge.

Casillo, Stephanie M., Diego D. Luy, and Ezequiel Goldschmidt (2020). "A History of the Lobes of the Brain." *World Neurosurgery,* 134, pp. 353–360 (DOI: 10.1016/j.wneu.2019.10.155).

Clayton, Phillip, and Paul Davies (2006). *The Re-Emergence of Emergence: The Emergentist Hypothesis from Science to Religion*. Oxford University Press, Oxford.

Cordovero, Mosh (2007). *Pardes Rimonim: Orchard of Pomegranates*. Translated by Elyakum Gets. Providence University, Monfalcone, Italy.

Cohen, S., and F. A. Popp (1997). "Biophoton Emission of the Human Body." *Journal of Photochemistry and Photobiology*, B 40 (2), pp. 187–189.

Cornish-Bowden, Athel (2017). "Lynn Margulis and the Origin of the Eukaryotes." *Journal of Theoretical Biology*. 434 (1).

Cory Jr., Gerald A. (1999). *The Reciprocal Modular Brain in Economics and Politics: Shaping the Rational and Moral Basis of Organization*. Kluwer Academic/ Plenum, New York.

Creegan, Robert F. (1954). *The Shock of Existence: A Philosophy of Freedom*. Sci-Art Publishers, Cambridge, Massachusetts.

Dalio, Ray (2021). *Principles for Dealing with the Changing World Order: Why Nations Succeed and Fail*. Avid Reader Press, New York.

Dawkins, Richard (1978). *The Selfish Gene*. Ziff-Davis, New York.

Dawkins, Richard (1986). *The Blind Watchmaker*. W. W. Norton & Company, New York.

Deacon, Terrence W. (1990). "Rethinking Mammalian Brain Evolution." *American Zoologist* 30.3, pp. 629–705.

Dick, Philip K. (1985). *I Hope I Shall Arrive Soon*. Doubleday, New York.

Dowd, Michael (2008). *Thank God for Evolution: How the Marriage of Science and Religion Will Transform Your Life and Our World*. Viking, New York.

Dunsworth, Holly, and Anne Buchanan (2017). "Sex Makes Babies." Aeon (https://aeon.co/essays/i-think-i-know-where-babies-come-from-therefore-i-am-human).

Dyson, Freeman (1979). *Disturbing the Universe*. Basic Books, New York.

Eisler, Riane (1988). *The Chalice and the Blade*. Harper, New York.

Eliot, T. S. (2023). *Four Quartets*. Kino Lorber, New York.

Gabora, Liane (2013). "An Evolutionary Framework for Cultural Change: Selectionism versus Communal Exchange." *Physics of Life Reviews*, 10 (2), pp. 117–145.

Gafni, Marc (2002). *Soul Prints: Your Path to Fulfilment*. 1st Fireside ed. New York: Simon & Schuster, New York.

Gafni, Marc (2003). *The Mystery of Love*. Atria, New York.

Gafni, Marc (2010) *Radical Kabbalah*, Books 1 and 2. Integral Publishers, Tucson, Arizona.

Gafni, Marc (2012). *Your Unique Self: The Radical Path to Personal Enlightenment*, with Introduction and Afterword by Ken Wilber, Integral Publishers, Tucson, Arizona.

Gafni, Marc (2014). *Self in Integral Evolutionary Mysticism: Two Models and Why They Matter*, Integral Publishers, Tucson, Arizona.

Gafni, Marc (2014). *Tears: Reclaiming Ritual, Integral Religion and Rosh Hashanah* [Beta Edition], Integral Publishers, Tucson, Arizona.

Gafni, Marc, and Kristina Kincaid (2017). *A Return to Eros: The Radical Experience of Being Fully Alive*. BenBella Books, Dallas.

Gafni, Marc, and Zachary Stein (2018). *Homo Amor and CosmoErotic Humanism: First Thoughts*.

Gafni, Marc, and Barbara Marx Hubbard (2025). *Whole Mate: The Future of Relationships*

Gamow, George (1970). *My World Line:*

An Informal Autobiography. Viking Press, New York.

Gebser, Jean (1985). The Ever-Present Origin (translated from German by Noel Bastard and Algis Mickunas). Ohio University Press, Athens, Ohio.

Gershteyn, Mikhail L., Lev I. Gershteyn, Arkady Gershteyn, and Oleg V. Karagioz (2002). "Experimental Evidence That the Gravitational Constant Varies with Orientation." arXiv preprint physics/0202058.

Gikatilla, Joseph ben Abraham (1998). Gates of Light = Sha'are Orah. AltaMira Press, Walnut Creek, California.

Gilbert, Scott F. (2006). "Ernst Haeckel and the Biogenetic Law," in Developmental Biology, by Michael J. F. Barresi and Scott F. Gilbert, 8th ed. Sinauer Associates, Sunderland, Massachusetts.

Giroldini, W. et al (2015). "EEG Correlates of Social Interaction at Distance." F1000Research, 4, 457. (doi. org/10.12688/f1000research.6755.3).

Goodsell, David (2000). "Molecule of the Month: Cytochrome c Oxidase—Cytochrome Oxidase Extracts Energy from Food Using Oxygen." PDB-101: Molecular Explorations through Biology and Medicine (https://pdb101.rcsb. org/motm/5).

Gould, S. J. (1981). The Mismeasure of Man. W. W. Norton, New York.

Graeber, David, and David Wengrow (2021). The Dawn of Everything: A New History of Humanity. Farrar, Straus and Giroux, New York.

Gray, John (1993). Men Are from Mars, Women Are from Venus: A Practical Guide for Improving Communication and Getting What You Want in Your Relationships. Thorsons, New York.

Green, Arthur (2015). "God's Need for Man: A Unitive Approach to the Writings of Abraham Joshua Heschel."

Modern Judaism. A Journal of Jewish Ideas and Experience, 35, 3, pp. 247–261 (DOI: 10.1093/mj/kjv016).

Griffin, David Ray (2000). Religion and Scientific Naturalism: Overcoming the Conflicts. State University of New York Press, Albany, New York.

Gulick, Sean, et al. (2019). "The First Day of the Cenozoic." Proceedings of the National Academy of Sciences 116 (39), pp. 19342–19351.

Fisher, Roger, William Ury, and Bruce Patton (1991). Getting to Yes: Negotiating Agreement without Giving In. Houghton Mifflin, Boston.

Habermas, Jürgen (1971). Knowledge and Human interests. Beacon Press, Boston.

Habermas, Jürgen (1979). "What Is Universal Pragmatics?" In: Communication and the Evolution of Society, by Jürgen Habermas. Beacon Press, Boston, pp. 2–4.

Habermas, Jürgen (1988). Legitimation Crisis. Polity Press, Cambridge, UK.

Habermas, Jürgen (1996). Between Facts and Norms: Contributions to a Discourse Theory of Law and Democracy. MIT Press, Cambridge, Massachusetts.

Hansen, Lena (1997). "The Color Force" https://webhome.phy.duke.edu/~kole-na/modern/hansen.html.

Harari, Yuval N. (2015). Sapiens: A Brief History of Humankind. Harper, New York.

Harari, Yuval N. (2017). Homo Deus: A Brief History of Tomorrow. Vintage, London.

Heyes, Cecilia (2010). "Where Do Mirror Neurons Come From?" Neuroscience and Biobehavioral Reviews, 34 (4), pp. 575–583 (DOI: 10.1016/j. neubiorev.2009.11.007).

Hickok, Gregory (2009). "Eight Problems for the Mirror Neuron Theory of Action Understanding in Monkeys and Humans." Journal of Cognitive

Neuroscience, 21 (7): pp. 1229–1243.

Hickok, Gregory (2014). *The Myth of Mirror Neurons: The Real Neuroscience of Communication and Cognition*. W. W. Norton & Company, New York.

Hopster, Jeroen (2019). "The Speciesism Debate: Intuition, Method, and Empirical Advances." *Animals* 9 (12) (DOI: 10.3390/ani9121054).

Hubbard, Barbara Marx (2015). *Conscious Evolution: Awakening the Power of Our Social Potential*. New World Library, Novato, California.

Iliadis, Christian (2007). *Nuclear Physics of Stars*. Wiley-VCH, Weinheim.

Ishfaq, Ahmad (1971). "The Proton Type-Nuclear Fission Reaction." *The Nucleus*, 1 (42), 59.

Jablonka, Eva, and Marion J. Lamb (2014). *Evolution in Four Dimensions: Genetic, Epigenetic, Behavioral, and Symbolic Variation in the History of Life* (revised edition). A Bradford Book. The MIT Press, Cambridge, Massachusetts.

James, William (1896). "The Will to Believe" first published in *The New World*, Volume 5, 327-347.

Jantsch, Erich (1980). *The Self-Organizing Universe: Scientific and Human Implications of the Emerging Paradigm of Evolution*. Pergamon, Oxford.

Jeans, James (2017). *The Mysterious Universe* (revised edition). Muriwai Books, Chicago. Originally published in 1932 under the same title.

Jenkins, Jere H., and Ephraim Fischbach. "Perturbation of Nuclear Decay Rates during the Solar Flare of 2006 December 13." *Astroparticle Physics* 31.6 (2009): 407–411.

Jiang, Linxing, Andrea Stocco, Darby M. Losey, Justin A. Abernethy, Chantel S. Prat, and Rajesh P. N. Rao (2019). "BrainNet: A Multi-Person Brain-to-Brain Interface for Direct Collaboration Between Brains." *Scientific Reports* 9, 6115

(DOI 10.1038/s41598-019-41895-7).

Jones, Lauren V. (2010) *Stars and Galaxies*. Greenwood Press, Santa Barbara, California.

Kauffman, Stuart A. "Breaking the Galilean Spell." https://www.edge.org/conversation/stuart_a_kauffman-breaking-the-galilean-spell.

Kauffman, Stuart A. (1993). *The Origins of Order: Self-Organization and Selection in Evolution*. Oxford University Press, Oxford.

Kauffman, Stuart A. (1995). *At Home in the Universe: The Search for the Laws of Self-Organization and Complexity*. Oxford University Press, New York.

Kegan, Robert (1982). *The Evolving Self: Problem and Process in Human Development*. Harvard University Press, Cambridge, Massachusetts.

Kegan, Robert (1994). *In Over Our Heads: The Mental Demands of Modern Life*. Harvard University Press, Cambridge, Massachusetts.

Kerskens, Christian M., and David L. Pérez (2022). "Experimental Indications of Non-classical Brain Functions." *Journal of Physics Communications*, 6 (10): 105001 (DOI: 10.1088/2399-6528/ac94be).

Kevles, Daniel J. (1985). *In the Name of Eugenics: Genetics and the Uses of Human Heredity*. Alfred A. Knopf, New York.

Keysers, Christian, Bruno Wicker, Valeria Gazzola, Jean-Luc Anton, Leonardo Fogassi, and Vittorio Gallese (2004). "A Touching Sight: SII/PV Activation During the Observation and Experience of Touch." *Neuron* 42 (2), pp. 335–346.

Koestler, Arthur (1964). *The Act of Creation*. Hutchinson, London.

Kook, Abraham (1937). *Orot HaKodesh* [*Lights of Holiness*], Jerusalem.

Kropotkin, Peter (2011). *Mutual Aid: A Factor of Evolution*. Neeland Media, Stilwell.

Ksemarāja. *Pratyabhijna Hrdayam: The Heart of the Doctrine of Recognition* (translated by Wallis). https://www.seanfeitoakes.com/resources/Pratyabhijnahrdayam-notes-2014.pdf.

Kurakin, Pavel V., George G. Malinetskii, and Howard Bloom (2011). "Conversational (Dialogue) Model of Quantum Transitions." https://www.academia.edu/33106632.

Laszlo, Ervin (2014). *The Self-Actualizing Cosmos: The Akasha Revolution in Science and Human Consciousness.* Inner Traditions, Rochester, Vermont.

Layzer, David (1990). *Cosmogenesis: The Growth of Order in the Universe.* Oxford University Press, Oxford.

Leibniz, Gottfried W. (2005). *Discourse on Metaphysics and the Monadology.* Dover Publications, Mineola, New York.

Liebes, Yehuda (1993). *Studies in the Zohar* (translated by A. Schwarz). State University of New York Press, Albany.

Liebes, Yehuda (1994). "Zohar and Eros." *Alpayim* 9, pp. 1–84.

Linden, David (2020). *Unique: The New Science of Human Individuality.* Basic Book, New York.

Leong, Victoria. Wass, Samuel. "Using 'Naturalistic Dual-EEG' to Measure Mother-Infant Brain-to-Brain (b2b) Synchrony in Socially-Mediated Learning," (https://gtr.ukri.org/projects?ref=ES%2FN006461%2F1).

Lipton, Bruce H. (2016). *The Biology of Belief: Unleashing the Power of Consciousness, Matter & Miracles,* 10th anniversary ed. Hay House, Carlsbad, California.

Lucas, Jim (2022). "What Is the Strong Force?" LiveScience (https://www.livescience.com/48575-strong-force.html).

Luria, Isaac (1964). *Sod Iggulim ve Yosher.* Jerusalem.

Mackey, John, and Raj Sisodia (2013). *Conscious Capitalism: Liberating the Heroic Spirit of Business.* Harvard Business Review Press, Boston, Massachusetts.

Mahler, Margaret S. Papers (MS 1138). Manuscripts and Archives, Yale University Library (https://archives.yale.edu/repositories/12/resources/4493, accessed May 29, 2023).

Margulis, Lynn, and Dorion Sagan (1986). *Microcosmos: Four Billion Years of Microbial Evolution.* Summit Books, New York.

Margulis, Lynn (1998). *Symbiotic Planet: A New Look at Evolution.* Basic Books, New York.

Marshall, Perry (2015). *Evolution 2.0: Breaking the Deadlock Between Darwin and Design.* BenBella Books, Dallas, Texas.

Matt, Daniel (1996). *God & the Big Bang: Discovering Harmony Between Science & Spirituality,* Jewish Lights Pub., Woodstock, Vermont.

Maynard Smith, J. (1978). *The Evolution of Sex.* Cambridge University Press, Cambridge.

Mayr, Ernst (2001). *What Evolution Is.* Basic Books, New York.

MacLean, Paul (1990). *The Triune Brain in Evolution: Role in Paleocerebral Function.* Plenum Press, New York.

McCraty, Rollin, Mike Atkinson, Dana Tomasino, and William A. Tiller (1998). "The Electricity of Touch: Detection and Measurement of Cardiac Energy Exchange between People: An Exploratory Study," in *Brains and Values: Is a Biological Science of Values Possible,* Karl H. Pribram, ed., Psychology Press, New York, pp. 359–379.

Miller, Geoffrey (2011). *The Mating Mind: How Sexual Choice Shaped the Evolution of Human Nature.* Anchor, New York.

Mitchell, John F. (2004). "Aging Well: Surprising Guideposts to a Happier Life from the Landmark Harvard Study of

Adult Development." *American Journal of Psychiatry* 161 (1).

Morowitz, H. J. (2004). *The Emergence of Everything: How the World Became Complex*, Oxford University Press, Oxford.

Morton, Timothy (2013). *Hyperobjects: Philosophy and Ecology after the End of the World.* University of Minnesota Press, Minneapolis.

Myers, Frederic W. H. (1907). *Human Personality and Its Survival of Bodily Death.* Longmans, Green, 1907.

Nahum (2021). *The Light of the Eyes: Homilies on the Torah* (translated by Arthur Green), Stanford University Press, Stanford. Originally published in Hebrew as *Me'or Eynayim* (1881).

National Human Genome Research Institute, "Deoxyribonucleic Acid (DNA) Fact Sheet" (2020), https://www.genome.gov/about-genomics/fact-sheets/Deoxyribonucleic-Acid-Fact-Sheet.

Noble, Denis (2006). *The Music of Life: Biology Beyond Genes.* Oxford University Press, Oxford.

Noble, Denis (2016). *Dance to the Tune of Life: Biological Relativity.* Cambridge University Press, Cambridge.

Oberbye, Dennis (2001). "In the New Physics, No Quark Is an Island." *The New York Times*, March 20, 2001.

O'Donohue, John (2004). *Beauty: The Invisible Embrace.* HarperCollins, New York.

Ord, Toby (2020). *The Precipice: Existential Risk and the Future of Humanity.* Bloomsbury, London.

Ornish, Dean (1998). *Love and Survival: The Scientific Basis for the Healing Power of Intimacy.* Harper, New York.

Ouspensky, Pyotr (1997). *A New Model of the Universe.* Dover Publications.

Oztop, Erhan, and Michael A. Arbib (2002). "Schema Design and Implementation of the Grasp-Related Mirror Neuron System." *Biological Cybernetics* 87 (2), pp. 116–40. DOI: 10.1007/s00422-002-0318-1. PMID: 12181587.

Parker, Kelly A. (1998). *The Continuity of Peirce's Thought.* Vanderbilt University Press, Nashville.

Peirce, Charles S. (1893). "Evolutionary Love." *The Monist*, 3 (2), pp. 176–200. (https://academic.oup.com/monist/issue/3/2).

Peirce, Charles S. (2000). "The Fixation of Belief," in *Chance, Love, and Logic: Philosophical Essays by Charles S. Peirce*, edited by Morris R. Cohen and John Dewey. Routledge, London, pp. 7–31.

Pérez, Alejandro, Manuel Carreiras, and Jon Duñabeitia (2017). "Brain-to-Brain Entrainment: EEG Interbrain Synchronization While Speaking and Listening." *Scientific Reports* 7 (1) (DOI: 10.1038/s41598-017-04464-4).

Pieper, Mauk (2014). *Humanity's Second Shock and Your Unique Self.* CreateSpace Independent Publishing Platform.

Pigden, Charles (1999). *Russell on Ethics.* Routledge, London.

Preston Stephanie D., and Frans B. M. de Waal (2002). "Empathy: Its Ultimate and Proximate Bases." *The Behavioral and Brain Sciences*, 25 (1), pp. 1–72. DOI: 10.1017/s0140525x02000018.

Prigogine, Ilya, and Isabelle Stengers (2014). *Order Out of Chaos: Man's New Dialogue with Nature.* Verso Books, London. (Originally published in 1984.)

Prigogine, Ilya (1971). *Thermodynamic Theory of Structure, Stability and Fluctuations.* Wiley-Interscience, London.

Povh, Bogdan, et al. (2008). *Particles and Nuclei: An Introduction to the Physical Concepts.* Springer, Berlin.

Quigg, Chris (2013). *Gauge Theories of the Strong, Weak, and Electromagnetic*

Interactions. Princeton University Press, Princeton, New Jersey.

Radin, Dean (2018). *Real Magic: Unlocking Your Natural Psychic Abilities to Create Everyday Miracles.* Potter/TenSpeed/Harmony.

Radin, Dean (2009). *The Conscious Universe: The Scientific Truth of Psychic Phenomena.* HarperCollins, New York.

Rao, Rajesh P. N., Andrea Stocco, Matthew Bryan, Devapratim Sarma, Tiffany M. Youngquist, Joseph Wu, and Chantel S. Prat (2014). "A Direct Brain-to-Brain Interface in Humans." *PLOS ONE* 9 (11): e111332. DOI: 10.1371/journal.pone.0111332.

Raymo, Chet (1984). *Biography of a Planet.* Prentice Hall, Englewood Cliffs, New Jersey.

Raza, Azra (2019). *The First Cell: And the Human Costs of Pursuing Cancer to the Last.* Basic Books, New York.

Rilke, Rainer Maria, Anita Barrows, and Joanna Macy (2009). *A Year with Rilke: Daily Readings from the Best of Rainer Maria Rilke.* HarperCollins Publishers.

Rizzolatti, Giacomo, and Laila Craighero (2004). "The Mirror-Neuron System." *Annual Review of Neuroscience,* 27, pp. 169–192.

Rolston III, Holmes (2010). *Three Big Bangs: Matter-Energy, Life, Mind.* Columbia University Press, New York.

Ross, Tamar (2014). "Overcoming the Epistemological Challenge." In *Jewish Philosophy for the 21st Century: Personal Reflections,* edited by Aaron Hughes and Hava Tirosh Samuelson. Brill, Leiden, pp. 372–390.

Russell, David J. (2010). "Modeling Biological Structures via Abstract Grammars to Solve Common Problems in Computational Biology." Thesis for PhD in Electrical Engineering (https://www.researchgate.net/publication/228392049_Modeling_ Biological_Structures_via_Abstract_ Grammars_to_Solve_Common_ Problems_in_Computational_Biology).

Russell, Bertrand (1919). "A Free Man's Logic." In *Mysticism and Logic and Other Essays,* by Bertrand Russell. Longmans, New York.

Russell, Bertrand (1986). *Mysticism and Logic, Including a Free Man's Worship.* Unwin Paperbacks, London.

Schirrmeister, Bettina E., Jurriaan M. de Vos, Alexandre Antonelli, and Homayoun C. Bagheri (2013) "Evolution of Multicellularity Coincided with Increased Diversification of Cyanobacteria and the Great Oxidation Event." *Proceedings of the National Academy of Sciences* 110.5, pp. 1791–1796.

Schneider, Sarah (2001). *Kabbalistic Writings on the Nature of the Masculine and Feminine.* Jason Aronson, Northvale, New Jersey.

Schore, Allan (2021). "The Interpersonal Neurobiology of Intersubjectivity." *Frontiers in Psychology,* 12. DOI: 10.3389/fpsyg.2021.648616.

Schore, Allan (2022). "Right-Brain-to-Right-Brain Psychotherapy: Recent Scientific and Clinical Advances." *Annals of General Psychiatry,* 21. DOI: 10.1186/s12991-022-00420-3.

Schroeder, Gerald (1997). *The Science of God: The Convergence of Scientific and Biblical Wisdom.* Free Press, New York.

Shapiro, James A. (2011). *Evolution: A View from the 21st Century.* Fortified. Cognition Press. Chicago.

Shapiro, Robert (1986). *Origins: A Skeptic's Guide to the Creation of Life on Earth.* Bantam Books, Toronto.

Singer, Peter (1990). *Animal Liberation.* Random House, New York. Originally published in 1975.

Smith, Chris (2010). "The Triune Brain in Antiquity: Plato, Aristotle, Erasistratus." *Journal of the History of the Neurosciences*

19.1, pp. 1–14.

Smolin, Lee (1999). *The Life of the Cosmos.* Oxford University Press, Oxford.

Smolin, Lee (2012). "Precedence and Freedom in Quantum Physics." arXiv preprint arXiv:1205.3707.

Spencer, Herbert (1880). *First Principle.* A. L. Burt, New York.

Standish, Leanna J., Leila Kozak, L. Clark Johnson, and Todd Richards (2004). "Electroencephalographic Evidence of Correlated Event-Related Signals between the Brains of Spatially and Sensory Isolated Human Subjects." *The Journal of Alternative and Complementary Evidence*, 10 (2), pp. 307–14. DOI: 10.1089/107555304323062293. PMID: 15165411.

Stein, Zachary (2019). *Education in a Time Between Worlds: Essays on the Future of Schools, Technology, and Society.* Bright Alliance, Occidental, California.

Stein, Zachary (2014). "On the Use of the Term Integral." *Journal of Integral Theory and Practice*, 9(2), pp. 103–113.

Stone, Douglas, Bruce Patton, and Sheila Heen (1999). *Difficult Conversations: How to Discuss What Matters Most.* Viking, New York.

Swimme, Brian, and Mary E. Tucker (2011). *Journey of the Universe.* Yale University Press, New Haven.

Swimme, Brian, and Thomas Berry (1992). *The Universe Story: From the Primordial Flaring Forth to the Ecozoic Era—a Celebration of the Unfolding of the Cosmos.* Harper, San Francisco.

Taylor, Charles (1989). *Sources of the Self: The Making of the Modern Identity.* Cambridge University Press, Cambridge.

Taylor, Edwin F., and John A. Wheeler (2000). *Exploring Black Holes: Introduction to General Relativity.* Addison Wesley Longman, San Francisco.

Teilhard de Chardin, Pierre (1959). *The Phenomenon of Man.* Harper, New York. (Originally published 1955 in French as *Le Phenomene Humain.*)

Temple, David J. (2024). *First Principles and First Values: Forty-Two Propositions on CosmoErotic Humanism, the Meta-Crisis, and the World to Come.* Dandy Lion Publishing Group, Austin, Texas.

Thacker, T. (1995). "The Four Forces." https://webhome.phy.duke.edu/~kolena/modern/forces.html#005.

Tikunei Zohar (1865). Zhitomir edition by R. Chanina Lipa and R. Yehoshua Heshel Shapira, grandsons of the Rabbi of Slavita. English translation: *The Zohar. Pritzker edition. The Complete Set.* Translated by Daniel C. Matt. Stanford University Press, Stanford (2018).

Tillich, Paul (1954). *Love, Power, and Justice: Ontological Analyses and Ethical Applications*, given as Firth lectures in Nottingham, England, and as Sprunt lectures in Richmond, Virginia. Oxford University Press, New York.

Turing, Alan Mathison (1990/1952). "The Chemical Basis of Morphogenesis." *Bulletin of Mathematical Biology* 52.1 (1990): 153–197. Originally published in *Philosophical Transactions of the Royal Society of London. Series B, Biological Sciences*, Vol. 237, No. 641. (Aug. 14, 1952), pp. 37–72 (https://www.jstor.org/stable/92463).

Vayenas, Constantinos G., and Stamatios N.-A. Souentie (2012). *Gravity, Special Relativity, and the Strong Force: A Bohr-Einstein-de Broglie Model for the Formation of Hadrons.* Springer, New York.

Wallerstein, Immanuel (2004). *World-Systems Analysis: An Introduction.* Duke University Press, Durham, North Carolina.

Wan, Bin, Şeyma Bayrak, Ting Xu, H. Lina Schaare, Richard AI Bethlehem, Boris C. Bernhardt, and Sofie L. Valk

(2022). "Heritability and Cross-Species Comparisons of Human Cortical Functional Organization Symmetry." *eLife* 11:e77215 (DOI: 10.7554/eLife.77215).

Ward, Peter, and Donald Brownlee (2003). *Rare Earth: Why Complex Life Is Uncommon in the Universe.* Springer, New York.

Whitehead, Alfred North (1978). *Process and Reality: An Essay in Cosmology.* Based on the Gifford Lectures delivered in the University of Edinburgh in 1927–28. Edited by David Ray Griffin and Donald W. Sherburne. Free Press, New York.

Wilber, Ken (1995). *Sex, Ecology and Spirituality: The Spirit of Evolution.* Shambhala. Random House, Boston.

Wilber, Ken (1999). *The Marriage of Sense and Soul: Integrating Science and Religion.* Broadway Books, New York.

Wilber, Ken (2000). *Integral Psychology: Consciousness, Spirit, Psychology, Therapy.* Shambhala, Boston.

Wilber, Ken (2001). *Eye to Eye: The Quest for the New Paradigm.* Shambhala. Random House, Boston.

Wilber, Ken (2007). *Integral Spirituality: A Startling New Role for Religion in the Modern and Postmodern World.* Integral Books, Boston, Massachusetts.

Wilczek, Frank, and Betsy Devine (1989). *Longing for the Harmonies: Themes and Variations from Modern Physics.* Norton, New York.

Wilczek, Frank (2021). *Fundamentals: Ten Keys to Reality.* Penguin Press, New York.

Wilson, David S. (2016). "The Tragedy of the Commons: How Elinor Ostrom Solved One of Life's Greatest Dilemmas." https://evonomics.com/tragedy-of-the-commons-elinor-ostrom/.

Yalom, Irvin (1980). *Existential Psychotherapy.* Basic Books, New York.

Yamatomo, Mikio, Hideyuki Kokubo, Tomoko Kokado, Suzue Haraguchi, Tong Zhang, Masataka Tanaka, Dmitri V. Parkhomtschouk, Takao Soma, and Kimiko Kawano (1996). "An Experiment on Remote Action Against Man in Sensory-Shielding Conditions." *Journal of International Society of Life Information Sciences,* 14, 1 (pp. 97–101) and 2 (pp. 228–248).

Yeagle, Philip L. (2016). *The Membranes of Cells.* Elsevier, London.

Zeihan, Peter (2022). *The End of the World Is Just the Beginning: Mapping the Collapse of Globalization.* HarperCollins, New York.

Zimmerman, Michael (2001). "Ken Wilber's Critique of Ecological Spirituality." In: *Deep Ecology and World Religions: New Essays on Sacred Grounds,* edited by D. L. Barnhill and R. S. Gottlieb, pp. 243–269. State University of New York Press, Albany.

ABOUT THE AUTHOR

Dr. Marc Gafni is a visionary world philosopher and futurist, one of the leading formulators of world spirituality and religion of our time, and a beloved teacher and public intellectual.

He holds his doctorate in philosophy from Oxford University, as well as Orthodox rabbinic ordination. He co-founded the activist think tank now called the Center for World Philosophy and Religion, where he serves as the co-president with Dr. Zachary Stein. He also served with Barbara Marx Hubbard as co-president of the Foundation for Conscious Evolution, which he consented to lead at Barbara's request after her passing.

He is known for his "source code teachings"—including Unique Self theory and the Five Selves, the Amorous Cosmos, a Politics of Evolutionary Love, a Return to Eros, and Digital Intimacy—and has more than twenty books to his name, including the award-winning *Your Unique Self*, *A Return to Eros*, and three volumes of *Radical Kabbalah*.

He teaches on the cutting edge of philosophy in the West, helping to evolve a new "dharma" or meta-theory of Integral meaning that is helping to re-shape key pivoting points in global consciousness and culture, with the aim of participating in the articulation of what Dr. Gafni together with Dr. Stein and colleagues are calling CosmoErotic Humanism.

At the core of CosmoErotic Humanism is what Dr. Gafni and Dr. Stein are calling First Principles and First Values, Anthro-Ontology, and a Universal Grammar of Value. This is the ground of a new shared universe story and a new narrative of identity for the new human and the new humanity. This is what they are calling the emergence from *Homo sapiens* to *Homo Amor*. This shared story rooted in First Principles and First Values can then serve as the matrix for a global ethos for a global civilization.

Together with Dr. Stein and Ken Wilber, Dr. Gafni is writing a series of seminal books under the collective pseudonym of David J. Temple, which intends to evolve the source code of consciousness and culture in response to the meta-crisis. The first of those books is *First Principles and First Values: Forty-Two Propositions on Cosmo-Erotic Humanism, the Meta-Crisis, and the World to Come.*

INDEX

Note: Page numbers in *italic* refer to figures, and references following "n" refer notes.

of not counting, 13
of nothingness, 12
of pain of body, 12
fear of death, 15, 18, 20–21, 38
    existential, 12
    natural, 13
    tastes of, 12–14
The Fellowship of the Ring (movie), 226
    Anti-Eros, 228
    Eros, 227
    evolutionary relationship, 233
    Reality is relationship, 229
    Unique Self, 231
Fichte, Johann Gottlieb, 109, 178
Ficino, Marsílio, 22
Field:
    of Allurement, 197, 256, 257
    of Consciousness, 27, 43, 57, 83–84,
        148
    of Desire, 45, 194, 279
    of Devotion, 103
    of Meaning, 104–5, 110
    of Pure Potentiality, 179
    of Reality, 196, 279
    of shared intrinsic Value, 26, 30, 49
    of Wholeness, 84, 88, 109–10
Field of Eros, 55, 71, 84, 102, 107, 165
    evolutionary, 44
    as Field of Wholeness, 88–89
Field of Value, 2, 37, 49, 54, 72–73,
        100–102, 106, 204
    intrinsic, 101
    realization, 108
    shared, 105
First Big Bang, 120–21, 127
First Principles, 19, 22, 26, 32, 35, 37,
        62–63, 175, 214, 217, 341
First Principles (Spencer), 26, 213
first shock of existence, 11. *See also* sec-
        ond shock of existence
    inner gnosis, 14–16
    tastes of fear of death, 12–14
First Values, 19, 22, 62–63, 311
    of Cosmos, 37
    of Reality, 32
Four Big Bangs, 113
    emergence of life from lifeless matter,
        122–23

Great Flaring Forth, 120–21, 127, 130,
        173
    story of, 118–23
    Third Big Bang, 123
Fourth Big Bang, 4, 48, 139–40, 142
    first glimpse at elements of, 119–20
    shadows of early evolutionary narra-
        tives, 143–45
    unconscious to conscious evolution,
        145–46
    Unique Selves and Unique Self Sym-
        phonies, 146–50
fragile systems, 19, 25–26, 30, 49, 55, 138
freedom, 79, 81, 164, 227, 242, 313
    asymptotic, 197–98n200
    dialectic of, 126–29
    radical, 131
    surrender of, 275
Fuck, 168n147, 187, 269, 338, 339
Fuhs, Clint, 66n52
The Future of Love (Hamilton and Kemp-
        ton), 66n52

G
Gabbai, Meir Ibn, 41, 238
Gafni, Marc, 155n130
Gebser, Jean, 133
gender queer movement, 90. *See also*
        Unique Gender
genome/gene, 315–16, 318
global coherence, 26, 31
global coordination, 26, 31
global intimacy, 25–26, 31, 137
    disorder, 25, 27–28, 30, 49, 63, 139,
        160
global resonance, 26
global solutions, 26
God, 36, 111, 193, 204, 308, 310
    Eros, 187
    evolution of, 237–40
    infinite field referred as, 276
    as infinite intimate, 254
    Name of, 83, 88, 109, 128–29, 235
good life, 68, 78, 165, 349
Goodsell, David, 302
the Good, 23, 46, 99, 129
gospel, 335n379
Gould, S. J., 143, 167, 276

It'aruta De'Le'tata—Arousal from below, 129
It'aruta De'Leyla—Arousal from above, 128
It is only death that makes life a genuine option (James), 20

J

Jagger, Mick, 67
James, William, 20
Jeans, James, 178
Jenkins, Jere H., 338n383
joining genius, 76, 187
Jones, Lauren V., 250n266
joy, 40, 45, 58, 66, 71, 80, 95–96, 98, 189, 223, 229, 272
Jung, Carl, 255n277, 308
Jurassic Park (movie series), 334

K

Kashmir Shaivism, 154, 157
Kauffman, Stuart, 130, 164
Kegan, Robert, 219
Kempton, Sally, 66n52
Kenosis, 109, 275
Kevles, Daniel J., 143
Keysers, Christian, 224
Koestler, Arthur, 201, 235
Kook, Abraham, 125–26, 238, 288
Kropotkin, Peter, 168

L

Lamb, Marion J., 316n355
Lamb shift experiment, 179n171
Lamb, Willis, 179
Laszlo, Ervin, 267n286
Lawrence, D. H., 272
Lawrence, Jennifer, 91
Layzer, David, 173n160
learning algorithms of Cosmos, 217
Legitimation Crisis (Habermas), 44n39
Liebes, Yehuda, 251n267
life, 253n271
  on Earth, 321, 322
  emergence from lifeless matter, 122–23
  evolution from atoms to, 262–68
  good, 68, 78, 165, 349
  intimacy evolution from atoms to,

262–68
  microbial, 327
  post-tragic experience of, 98
Lifton, Robert J., 33
Linden, David, 78n58
lines and circles. *See also* Big Bang(s)
  harmony and closeness between, 352
  integration of, 91, 93
  making Outrageous Love, 286
  primary forces of Cosmos, 128
  principles of Cosmos, 241–43, 255
  qualities, 78–79, 90
Lloyd, William Forster, 18n19
loneliness, 190
love. *See also* evolution of love; planetary awakening in love
  and attraction, 256
  Cosmic Force of Eros as, 262
  eternal and evolving, 287–90
  falling in, 66, 74
  in Field of Eros and Value, 165
  ontological qualities of, 288
  Ordinary and Outrageous Love, 284, 285–86
  primary value for, 70
  stations of, 66n52
  Tillich's reading of, 285n314
  types of, 286
LoveBeauty, 37, 40, 333
LoveDesire, 37, 40, 333
LoveIntelligence, 37, 39, 40, 241, 333
Love Story, 13
LoveValue, 40, 333
Loye, David, 167
lumination, 182
Luria, Isaac, 243n257

M

Macbeth (Shakespeare), 358
Mackey, John P., 158
MacLean, Paul, 304
macromolecules, 27, 195, 203, 265
macroscopic objects, 181n173
Magisteria, 164n140
many-fathers theory, 278n304
Margulis, Lynn, 325, 327, 330
Marshall, Perry, 317, 318n358
materialism, 207–8n215

www.ingramcontent.com/pod-product-compliance
Lightning Source LLC
Chambersburg PA
CBHW020332270326
41926CB00007B/144